About the Author

Richard Butler is a lecturer in website design and management and Internet applications at Sallynoggin College of Further Education, Dublin, where he set up the first Post Leaving Certificate course in web design. Since its inception in 1997, this course has received International Certification from the Internet Certification Institute International.

After receiving his International Arts Degree from University College Dublin, Richard studied Teacher Training in Information Technology at Dun Laoghaire Senior College and received an honours Diploma from the Joint Examining Board. He has worked extensively in the private sector with such diverse groups as CPI and REHAB and as a Department of Education Tutor on ECDL courses. He has delivered courses at the Blackrock Education Centre and Froebel College of Education.

Richard Butler runs a number of websites: www.tintecsystems.com, his web design training company; www.howsitgoing.com, an online Irish community; www.2hostu.com, a virtual hosting company; and now www.internetdemystified.com, the website launched to accompany this book.

THE INTERNET DEMYSTIFIED

An Introductory Guide to the World Wide Web, Internet, E-mail and Electronic Commerce

Richard Butler

Oak Tree Press

Dublin

Oak Tree Press
Merrion Building
Lower Merrion Street
Dublin 2, Ireland
http://www.oaktreepress.com
http://www.internetdemystified.com

A catalogue record of this book is
available from the British Library.

ISBN 1 86076 171 2

Trademarks
Trademarked names appear throughout this book. Rather than list the names
and entities that own the trademarks or insert a trademark symbol with
each mention of the trademarked name, the publisher states that it is
using the names only for editorial purposes and to the benefit of the
trademark owner, with no intention of infringing upon that trademark.

Printed in the Republic of Ireland by Colour Books Ltd.

Contents

Acknowledgements .... *xi*

Introduction 1

PART ONE: BACKGROUND AND STRUCTURE

Chapter 1: History of the Internet and World Wide Web 7

Prehistory of the Web 7

The 1950s 11

The 1960s 12

The 1970s 19

The 1980s 22

The 1990s 24

Chapter 2: Structure of the Internet 31

Net and Web 31

The Infrastructure of the Internet 32

Making it Real 40

Websites and Web Pages 42

Types of Websites 43

PART TWO: BASIC APPLICATIONS

Chapter 3: What You Need to Get Started 47

Connecting to the Internet 47

Computers 47

Modems 49

Types of Connections 49

Bandwidth 52

Internet Service Providers (ISPs)..53

Choosing a Browser 58

Business Users 62

Other Ways to Connect 64

Chapter 4: Introduction to E-mail **69**

What is E-mail? 69

E-mail and Privacy 73

Basic E-mail Functions...77

Using Microsoft Outlook Express 78

Checking for New Mail 79

Creating a New Message 80

Replying to an E-mail Message 87

Forwarding a Message..89

Message Management 90

Web-based E-mail 93

Chapter 5: Advanced E-mail Techniques **97**

Getting More from E-mail 97

Attaching Documents to E-mail 98

Using Address Books 102

Using Distribution Lists 104

Creating Filters 108

Changing Priority Settings of Messages...................................111

Customising Outlook Express 111

Identities 119

E-mail Discussion Lists and Mailing Lists.................................120

Can E-mail be Faked? 121

**Chapter 6: Introducing the Web I: Web Addresses and Browser
   Basics** **123**

What's Your Address?...123

Navigating the Web using Internet Explorer 5 128

Opening Other Websites 136

Saving and Printing Web Pages 140

Recording Internet Addresses: Favorites 144

Chapter 7: Introducing the Web II: Effective Searching **149**

The World Wide Waste 149

The Good Search Guide 149

Finding Information on the Web 157

Directories: Using Yahoo for Searching 157

Search Engines 160

How Do Search Engines Work? 161

Search Techniques 163

Different Search Engines and their Merits....................167

Using Meta Search Engines 173

Why Use a Search Engine when I have a Search Button?.............174

Specialised Search Engines 175

The Future of Searching 176

PART THREE: GETTING MORE FROM THE INTERNET

Chapter 8: Building a Website **181**

Why Do You Want a Website?......................................181

Preliminaries..185

Planning your Site Layout..187

Creating your Site 189

HTML 189

HTML Packages..192

Graphics 193

Website Interaction..195

Creative Thought 200

Choosing a Domain Name..200

Going Live: Hosting Your Website 202

Uploading to Your Server..208

Marketing a Website..210

Measuring Your Website's Success................................216

The Next Step 217

Chapter 9: E-commerce **219**

What is E-commerce? 219

E-commerce Strategy: Doing Business on the Web..................220

Dotcoms..232

Shopping on the Internet..236

Safe Shopping on the Internet 240

Chapter 10: Interactivity and the Internet **243**

    The Social Web 243

    Both Sides Now 244

    Guestbooks...246

    Web-based E-mail Links 247

    Discussion Boards 247

    Chat Rooms..250

    Non-web-based Interaction 259

    Internet Relay Chat 259

    Pager Software 261

    Internet Telephone/Voice Chat..................................264

    Newsgroups..266

    Online Communities 272

    Portal Sites 274

    Online Gaming..275

Chapter 11: Downloading **277**

    Get Down..277

    Free for All! 278

    Distribution Methods..279

    Software 282

    Patches and Add-ons..284

    Drivers...284

    Plug-ins 285

    MP3 and the Music Revolution 288

PART FOUR: BURNING ISSUES

Chapter 12: Dangers of the Internet I: Security Issues **295**

    Viruses...296

    Hacking and Cyber Warfare 300

    Dangers of E-mail 310

    Spyware 312

    Copyright 313

    Security Measures..316

    Internet Rules for Business 324

Chapter 13: Dangers of the Internet II: Privacy, Pornography and Censorship 327

Pornography, Censorship and Freedom of Speech.....................327
Dangers of Newsgroups..334
Dangers of Chat Rooms..334
Internet Addiction 336
Cyberchondria 344
Cyberstalking 345
Personal Privacy 346
Protecting Yourself and Your Children 349
General Surfing Rules 354

Chapter 14: The Future.. 357

Future Computers and Computing Powers 357
Speed of Access..360
Bluetooth..360
Smart Houses 362
Digital TV...362
Web Design 363
Electronic Payments, Digital Cash and Smart Cards 364
M-commerce and W-commerce...366
Online Banking 367
Smart Applications...368
Publishing: E-books and Print on Demand 369
The Music Industry..371
Future Society 371

Glossary 373

Index 395

Acknowledgements

When writing a book, there are so many people to thank:

First and foremost, my parents for putting up with the "paperless" environment a book creates, and for always believing in me.

All at Oak Tree Press, especially Brian Langan for his help and useful tips.

Fred Meaney, for realising that an Internet course would be worthwhile!

Damien Dolan, for all his hints, tips and knowledge over the last couple of years, both computer- and teaching-related.

All the staff and students in Sallynoggin College of Further Education, who in their own ways contributed to the book.

Sister Darina in Froebel College of Education for all the support and help over the last few years.

The office staff in Froebel for the home baking, sarcastic remarks and always being nice!

And last but by no means least, to Sinéad who helped and supported me throughout the whole process of writing this book. Thanks for all the pep talks and words of encouragement; now life can get back to normal.

Dedicated to Sinéad
You've made a lot of things possible.

Introduction

You can't get away from the Internet these days. Everywhere you go, you see references to web sites, e-mail addresses, e-commerce. When you meet old friends, they won't ask for your address or phone number, they'll ask you for your e-mail address. Everybody, whether or not they've actually used it, has a different opinion of the Internet, what it is and what it means to them.

The Internet has become what television was to western society in the 1950s and 1960s — a cultural symbol of the age we live in. But, because of its global nature, its potential for changing that society is far greater than television's was. We have reached a point, in the early years of the twenty-first century, when the Internet has the potential to completely change the way we think about ourselves, about society, and about the world.

So what exactly is it? Some have claimed it is the greatest research tool available; others condemn it for its pornographic content. Some people flinch every time they go near a keyboard; others find they could not live or work without it. The Internet has taken hold of the modern world and has changed, and will continue to change, the way we work and play.

Technically, the Internet is a network of computer-based networks and nothing else. The Internet is the infrastructure that connects various computers around the world. The Internet itself only allows information to be passed from one computer to another. What makes the Internet interesting and useful is the programs or applications which use it and exploit it.

> **Myth**: *There is a common misconception that the Internet and the World Wide Web are the same thing. They are connected, but not the same.*

The World Wide Web is simply a means of viewing multimedia rich "pages" by using an application called a browser. The pages can only be viewed using these browsers. The Internet serves as the transport mechanism that allows you to connect to these pages.

Another widely used application is e-mail. The Internet provides the means by which messages are passed from one computer to another until they reach their final destination. Just because you can access e-mail does not mean you can access the web, and vice versa. But if you can access either, it does imply that you are "on the Internet".

The Internet is thus the mechanism, the cables and the computers, while e-mail, the World Wide Web, and a number of other elements, are the applications.

Another common myth is that the Internet is a "new thing". In fact, as you will see in Chapter 1, the origins of the Internet stretch back over 40 years! The reasons for the "sudden" explosion in Internet use over the last ten years are the huge strides that have been made in computer technology, including computers themselves, modems, browsers and software programs that allow access to the Internet. Largely as a result of this, and working in parallel with it, is the fact that the price of Internet access, the ease of use of the Internet and more on line content have increased usage dramatically.

In recent years, more and more people have been buying computers for entertainment and education purposes; it is now standard that, as part of the package, they will also get free Internet access and a modem included on their computer. A few years ago, the buzzword was to have a "multimedia-ready computer"; now, it is "Internet-ready computer".

To summarise, the World Wide Web has reached many users largely because of the following contributing factors:

❖ Ease of use

❖ Hardware already in place — modems, computers, telephone lines

❖ Greater awareness of the web.

About this Book

This book is aimed at anyone — students, teachers, business people, parents — who want to get a solid understanding of what the Internet is and how it works.

Each chapter is a self-contained piece, and as such can be read in a non-linear fashion. The book is divided into four parts: Part One outlines the history and structure of the Internet; Part Two provides a hands-on introduction to the key elements of the Internet, specifically e-mail and the World Wide Web, with two chapters devoted to each of these topics; Part Three delves deeper into the Internet for those who feel comfortable with the basics, looking at such subjects as interactivity, downloading, e-commerce and building a website; Part Four looks at some of the "burning issues" surrounding the Internet, in particular privacy and security, pornography and censorship, concluding with a tentative look at some of the developing technologies that will decide the future of the Internet and society in general.

As you read, you may find it helpful to have Internet access close at hand, as many of the points made, the programs and websites explored are best seen at first hand.

There is an extensive glossary explaining the most commonly used terms relating to the Internet, as well as a number of terms which the reader may be less familiar with. Where these terms are used for the first time in the book, they are underlined to indicate that there is a corresponding entry in the glossary.

It is, unfortunately, not possible, in a book of this size, to cover all the different versions of the various software packages discussed in this book, never mind trying to deal with variations such as different operating systems. For the most part, therefore, I am assuming that the reader is working on a Windows-based PC system, while the software referred to is usually Internet Explorer 5 and Outlook Express 5.

Writing a book about the Internet is no easy task, as the technology moves so fast that new innovations are being developed as we speak. In order to future-proof the book, we have designed a complementary website, located at *www.internetdemystified.com*. This site will give you extra information from many chapters, including tutorials and links to various sites of interest. Also contained on this site is a discussion board where you can leave questions and get them answered by myself and others. Feel free to read the book, visit the site and have your say; remember, this book, like the Internet, is all about interaction.

Richard Butler
August 2000

Part One

BACKGROUND AND STRUCTURE

Chapter 1

History of the Internet and World Wide Web

The World Wide Web is relatively new, having been developed in the late 1980s, but the origins of the Internet lie in the 1950s and 1960s. (See Chapter 2 for an explanation of the difference between the Internet and the web.)

Compared to other media forms, the Internet, and particularly the World Wide Web, appears to have developed into a mainstream media far more quickly than any other comparable invention. Consider the length of time it took for the following forms of media to reach 50 million users:

❖ Radio   37 years

❖ TV   15 years

❖ World Wide Web   3 years

Astounding figures, you may think, but let's just see how astounding. As you will see in this chapter, the Internet is in fact 30 years old.

While the World Wide Web *is* more recent in development than the Internet, the concepts that would eventually lead to the web's invention were in fact first being proposed in the mid-1940s. It is here we begin our story, before we get to the history of the Internet proper.

Prehistory of the Web

Associated Documents

The original idea for the World Wide Web can be traced back to about 20 years before ARPAnet, the precursor of the Internet, existed!

The web is made up of many electronic "pages" linked together for various reasons, often because they follow a common theme. One of the beauties of the web is that anybody can create a simple web page that will link to other pages. When a user creates a web page, they can enter a simple code that allows them to link to another page. Each click on a link, also known as a <u>hyperlink</u>, brings them to a new page. This idea of linking documents together because they contain an associated theme is far from new.

The first notable work about linking associated documents appeared in the *Atlantic Monthly* in 1945. The work was entitled "As We May Think" and was written by Vannevar Bush. Bush was concerned with the problem of storing and retrieving information. So much information was being created, he felt there had to be a way that machines could help store this information and allow speedy retrieval of it.

The problem was that information is catalogued by a rule — usually alphabetically. If someone wanted to find this information, they would have to search for it alphabetically and read the information; if they then wanted to cross-reference the information, they would have to go back and dig out the document. This was time-consuming and difficult.

Bush wanted to find a way in which any item that was connected to another item could easily be cross-referenced. After all, the brain works on association — one thought leads to another; surely a machine could be built that would do this as well?

He proposed a device, which he named Memex. Memex would be a machine that would take information from an individual and record it. The user would place a document on the machine and the machine would take a photograph of the information that was to be recorded. It had a scanner-type device that would record the information (similar to <u>document management systems</u> that many companies have in operation today). All the information would then be stored on microfilm.

All information could be interlinked using <u>trails</u>, which would connect one piece of information to another. Each piece of information could thus be accessed and cross-referenced. Speed was the key to his system; by pressing a lever, the pages of information could be "turned" through either one page at a time or, by pressing the lever a bit more, by ten pages, and so on.

Bush also believed that encyclopaedias would appear that could be inserted into the Memex; these encyclopaedias would already have trails in them, making life a lot easier. This is how encyclopaedias are now produced on CD-ROMs; articles can be cross-referenced very easily.

Non-linear thought

Twenty years later, Ted Nelson had ideas similar to Bush. He believed that works should be non-linear in format. You do not necessarily have to constrain works to one book or page. Many pages can and should be interconnected. For example, if I refer to another book here, you must go out and buy or borrow that book. In Nelson's world, you could reference that book much easier, as it would be linked to the text that I am writing now.

In 1965, he coined a phrase known as <u>hypertext</u>.

 **Hypertext** *is a way of creating and linking documents together in an easy-to-use fashion.*

Hypertext is text that is not constrained by linear formats, but instead is linked by association with other text. By using some sort of linking process, related documents could be called up at will. Nelson went on to coin the phrase <u>hypermedia</u>, which was any collection of documents that are not constrained to text only. Hypermedia could contain links to sound files, and later on video and animation.

Bush had the Memex and Nelson had Xanadu — a system that would publish all the works available in a global hypertext. Any work you wanted could be created or accessed at will. Xanadu did not propose a way of deleting documents. Therefore when a document was created, it remained "alive" forever.

Nelson hoped that all documents would be available on a pay-per-view basis — you would pay to retrieve certain information. This was quite a visionary view, as many specialised search engines are now charging for industry-related news.

Putting Theory into Practice

Nelson's work never became a finished product. It has been in development for the past 30 years. During the 1970s and 1980s, many programmers came and went, trying to build this amazing new system that would revolutionise the world. Unfortunately, it was more conceptual than concrete. It became something of a running joke through the decades — the longest development time for one piece of software.

In the 1980s, Nelson extended the idea, to include a universe of documents or a "docuverse" — ultimately, this would resemble the World Wide Web as we know it today. One company that put a lot of backing behind the idea was Autodesk. They put the first real commercial face to Xanadu. A few new ideas were added to the system. Documents had to be easy to edit. Documents could be connected easily to any part of any other document. Only one original of any document would exist; no document would be copied. If you wanted to quote from a document, you would create a shortcut to it.

You may already be familiar with <u>shortcuts</u>. When you use any Windows interface, you see icons. When you click on the icon, say on your desktop, the program launches. The program is not located on your desktop, but the icon points to the executable file that is located somewhere on your hard disk. The shortcut allows you to access a file that is somewhere else, without having to copy all the program files to your desktop.

This idea was called <u>transclusion</u> — where one document could be "included" in another document by association. Copying and copyright infringement would not take place in Xanadu; instead, the viewer of the document would pay a fee to view the document. This idea caused many problems for the programmers of Xanadu, as they could not have any <u>redundancy</u>; only one file could be created and everyone had to have access to it at the same time.

Xanadu nearly made it as a system, but its one shortcoming was the fact that is was a proprietary pay system. People had grown up with the notion of information sharing; along came a product that would be proprietary and cost the user money. The other problem was that it was a very ambitious product, which would require computers with vast memory and very fast processors, were it to work correctly.

Another such system that came out in the mid-1980s was Apple's HyperCard. HyperCard resembled Bush's ideas in many ways. It was a way of storing different types of information and allowing it to be displayed easily. HyperCards could contain anything, but each of them had a link or hotspot that, when accessed, would go to another card.

A stack was a collection of HyperCards. The main card in a stack was known as the home card (very similar to the expression <u>homepage</u>). A language was developed called Hypertalk (very similar to hypertext!)

that would allow people to program cards and stacks. Again, the main shortcoming of HyperCard was that is was a proprietary system (i.e. not platform-independent), requiring the use of the Mac operating system.

Before we look at the development of the World Wide Web itself, let's go back in time again.

The 1950s

Our journey through the history of the Internet begins in the 1950s, a time of Cold War, space races and computers that took up entire buildings and whose main function was for mathematical problem-solving. The early pioneers had no easy-to-use point-and-click operating system like we have today!

During this era, computers were delicate monsters, attended to by scientists, taking up entire buildings. They had as much memory as very low-end electronic personal organisers, the types that now cost a few pounds! Computing power like this would have cost you a few hundred thousand dollars!

Myth: *There is a common myth that the Internet began because the Americans wanted to build a network that would survive a nuclear attack from the Russians. This is not true.*

In 1955, President Eisenhower announced that the Americans hoped to launch a satellite into orbit. This would be the US's first foray into satellite technology. But on 4 October 1957 the Russians launched the Sputnik satellite into orbit.

This came as a shock to the Americans and made them think about their research and development efforts. Eisenhower wanted to make sure that their rivals would never get the upper hand over them again. He set about creating an agency, a sort of think tank, that would research and develop military projects.

This agency became known as the Advanced Research Projects Agency (ARPA). Its prime function was to spend time (and money) researching military projects — specifically, communications and space programmes. It was based in the Pentagon. When ARPA was set up, its budget was half a billion dollars, which even now is quite an amount. The Americans were taking their research and development very seriously.

Then the most extraordinary thing happened. In 1958, the government decided to set up NASA. ARPA had been told it was meant to spearhead development of the space programme and suddenly another agency had been appointed for that very purpose! However, ARPA continued its research, mainly into missile testing, nuclear test monitoring and, most significantly for our story, computer technology development.

While all this was going on, a man named Leonard Kleinrock was undertaking a PhD in the relatively unknown field of data networks. It was his research and thoughts that would help ARPA shape out a new network.

The 1960s

Early stirrings

The 1960s were a crucial period in the development of modern computing and networks. There were a number of major developments, the first being IBM's introduction, in 1961, of time-shared computers.

Up to this point, all computers worked in batch mode. This meant that when they were in operation, they were doing one job and one job only. Time-sharing would allow users to run separate programs on the same computer from different terminals. In essence, the CPU power of the computer was divided up and used by a number of users. The user sat at what was known as a dumb terminal. This was made up of a keyboard and monitor. Any commands entered on the keyboard were echoed or sent to the time-shared computer. The time-shared computer would then process the commands and send the results back to the user's terminal.

The significance of this was:

❖ One computer resource could be used by many researchers;

❖ No processing was done locally; all processing was done on the main time-shared computer.

Time-sharing was revolutionary and began the idea of sharing resources. Very basic e-mail became available at this time. Users of the *same* system could leave messages for each other. There was no way of sending e-mail out to a *different* system yet.

Sharing of resources like this meant that institutions could use the power of a large computer without having to pay huge sums of money for a number of separate computers. Not only this, but sharing resources also led to sharing ideas and eventually allowed remote users to communicate with each other.

Remember that typical users at this time would have been researchers, academics and research students. Not every Tom, Dick and Harriet had access to these computers. Even if they did, they could do very little of interest, in terms of today's computers.

Up to this point, computers were seen as powerful arithmetic machines, but they had yet to develop any other use. Many of the computer manufacturers of the time, most of whom are still in business in some form or other, saw no future for computers on a personal level! Luckily, their perspectives changed!

October of 1962 saw J.R. Licklider arrive at ARPA to take control of the Command and Control Division. Licklider, or Lick as his friends knew him, believed that the future of computing lay in interactive computers. He believed that if computers and humans could work together, they could solve problems more efficiently. He had detailed some of his theories in a paper called "Man–Computer Symbiosis", which was published in 1960. He believed that computers should become powerful so that they could:

* Answer questions

* Create simulations of problems

* Display graphical results

* Extrapolate solutions to new problems based on past experience.

Computers would be more than an adding tool; they would become a learning tool for humans. Licklider believed they could also be used as a community-building tool, allowing people to communicate with each other. In 1962, Lick and a colleague, Welden Clark, published a paper entitled "Online Man–Computer Communication". Indeed, this idea has definitely been fulfilled in today's Internet. As we will see later, communities are very important in cyberspace, as is communication.

Although Lick spent only two years in ARPA, he made many changes. He was very interested in time-sharing rather than batch mode processing and channelled funding into finding some of the best researchers in the field of time-sharing to work in ARPA. He changed the title of his office from Command and Control Research to Information Processing Techniques Office. Because of Lick, ARPA became a more research-oriented organisation, rather than a completely military organisation.

Military Research

RAND, which was based in California, specialised in researching information regarding nuclear warfare and its consequences. RAND dealt with the "what if" scenarios. Although a pessimistic job, in 1962 Paul Baran was in charge of investigating what would happen to the communications system "if" there were a nuclear attack. Baran concluded that the communications systems of the time were not very reliable in the event of a nuclear attack and could not survive such an attack. Baran's research was focused on finding a more reliable, durable and lasting system of communications for military command and control.

Baran believed that information could be broken up into packets and then sent along a distributed network, where they would be reassembled at their destination. Coincidentally, two other researchers were working on similar projects: Donald Davies in the UK; and Leonard Kleinrock, who had just finished his PhD on networking and had come up with a similar idea.

In 1964, Baran wrote a paper entitled "On Distributed Communications Networks". His paper discussed how the US military communications system at the time was vulnerable to attack. He had the idea of using voice transmission over a secure packet network (what we know now as Internet telephony). According to Lawrence Roberts, it is this one paper that "confused" everyone into thinking that the Internet was set up for military purposes.[1] Although Baran's ideas were used as the basis for the ARPAnet, they were used only because they made sense technically and not because the developers of the ARPAnet were worried about a nuclear attack. While the work that was being done at RAND was focused on nuclear contingency plans, ARPA's work focused on developing a system that would enable the sharing of resources. It was this misconception that led to the belief that ARPAnet and the Internet emerged from military research!

---

[1] From Internet Chronology (http://www.ziplink.net/~lroberts/InternetChronology.html) by Lawrence G. Roberts.

However, Baran concluded there were a number of problems associated with building such a network.

Building a Network — the Problems

One notable obstacle to building a communications network was that the telephone system at the time was very vulnerable. In those days, the telephone system was not very robust, because all calls from certain regions were routed through central switches. When one made a call, it was sent via a central switch or exchange. All it took was for that one switch to be destroyed and the whole system in that area would be destroyed. This is known as a <u>centralised network</u>.

This system would certainly collapse or be the target of enemy destruction. If the centre were removed, the whole network would collapse. If you remove the hub from a wheel, the wheel collapses.

A slightly better approach was to have a <u>decentralised network</u> where there were no main nerve centres but many smaller ones. Of course, the problem with this system was that if one section were destroyed, all communications connecting into that particular switch would be without communications. But at least the whole communications system would not go down.

Building a Network — the Solution

Baran's idea was to create a network that could pass traffic from one point to another. There would be no central core to this network. What was proposed was the idea of a <u>distributed network</u>, which had no points of control. Instead of being centralised like the telephone system, it would be distributed — there would be no central core. All computers would be more or less equal on the network. They could pass information from one computer to another. The modern Internet is built on a distributed network, and the concept is described in more detail in Chapter 2.

Connection Problems — Analogue vs. Digital

The fact that the telephone system was not set up as a distributed system was one problem. The second problem concerned the quality of the signal. One of the main drawbacks of using the existing telephone infrastructure was that any signal that was analogue in nature could not be transmitted an infinite amount of times due to signal degradation.

Think of videotape. If you were to copy a videotape and lend it to someone and they copied it and lent the copy to someone else, when it eventually gets to the fifth or sixth person, the picture and sound quality would become unwatchable.

One solution Baran contemplated was the possibility of using digital signals that would not suffer from degradation as they travelled around the network. Digital data transmission would also be quicker. This would later become one of the most important aspects of the new network.

Circuit Switching vs. Packet Switching

Another problem with traditional phone networks was that once a call was placed, the user had a complete monopoly on that section of the network. If I place a call between my house and my place of work, no one else can use that chunk of the telephone network until I have hung up. If I am on hold for two minutes, I still retain control of that portion of the telephone network. Often when you are on the phone, you remain silent while the other party talks. During this time, although you are not communicating, you still have a dedicated connection between your phone and the other person's phone. No other person can use that part of the telephone system. This is circuit switching — a circuit is dedicated to your call.

With packet switching, this problem is overcome.

United we Fall, Divided we Stand!

Baran came up with the idea of dividing up all communications into smaller chunks of information, or what Donald Davies, a researcher working for the National Physical Laboratory in the UK, called "packets". Baran's original term was "message blocks".

> *A **packet** is a chunk of information that when combined with other packets makes up a whole message. If a whole large message was sent out over the network, it would cause congestion; if everything were made smaller, no one user could monopolise the network.*

In 1964, Leonard Kleinrock had published a book called "Communication Nets" which described and detailed packet networking. Up to this point, many still thought that packet-switching would not work; this work proved that it could work as a reliable system.

This idea of Baran's, coupled with Davies' work, would later be known as <u>packet switching</u>: each packet is switched or sent from one point on the network to the next. Packets are stored and forwarded as quickly as possible — like in the old game of pass-the-parcel, the aim of which was to get rid of the parcel as quickly as possible, passing it on to the next person. Again, as this technology still forms an essential element of the modern Internet, it is described in more detail in Chapter 2.

Making the Connections . . .

Now the question was how to build the network. The solution was to connect up all the time-shared computers on a network.

In 1965, Bob Taylor became director of the Information Processing Techniques Office. He was struck by one thing when he entered his office — the fact that he had a number of terminals to access different time-shared computers. He wondered if a network could be set up that would allow his staff to use any of these computers. The major problem was that the computers were not compatible with each other. Overcoming this obstacle was to lead to the modern Internet as we know it, but at this stage, the solution was buried deep in the minds of researchers and academics.

There were a number of terminals in the office, each one connecting up to different time-shared computers. If one computer could access all other computers, this would be more efficient and would save money. It would seem that this is the main reason that research was started on a network that could eventually connect different computers, and this was to be one of the many ideas that brought the Internet to life.

More problems . . .

There was another problem, as is usual in the case of computers!

If information was being passed from one computer to another, somewhere along the line each computer would have to do a certain amount of processing of information, i.e. find where the information was meant to go, pass it on to the next computer, etc. Since computers were a scarce resource, no one wanted to put any extra work on their computer

puter system. Everyone was in favour of the network, as long as his or her resources were not used!

IMPs

In October 1967, a paper was published describing the use of <u>IMPs</u> or Interface Message Processors. These IMPs would make up the network.

IMPs were mini-computers (remember, "mini" in those days were not exactly mini by our standards!) whose job was to route or pass all information to the relative computers on the network. Each of the four sites would have an IMP that would deal with all their messages. IMPs could be seen as a PA or secretary — the Boss has no time to deal with passing messages! This meant that no valuable resources were wasted on the time-shared computers, all message processing was done by the IMPs.

Lawrence Roberts conducted an "ARPAnet Design Session" where such important elements as user authentication and transmission of characters were developed and designed. ARPA then sent out a Request for Quotations for the building of this sub-network of IMPs to 140 possible suppliers, out of which 12 proposals were received. Believe it or not, IBM were not interested in the idea! In 1968, a company based in Massachusetts — Bolt, Beranek and Newman — was awarded the contract. It was their job to build the network.

BBN decided to use Honeywell DDP-516 mini-computers to act as IMPs or switching nodes for the four sites that would be on the network. The Honeywell DDP-516 was one of the most powerful mini-computers of its time. It had all of 12k of memory. These days, a very cheap personal organiser would have more memory than this!

An agreed set of rules had to be implemented so the computers could talk to each other. In 1969, the Network Working Group was set up to look at and deal with these issues. On 7 April of that year, another new three-letter acronym — one of many — was born: <u>RFC</u> or Request For Comments. Any ideas or suggestions would be outlined in a paper along with a Request For Comments. These RFCs are still in use today. The very first one dealt with "handshakes" — literally, the way two computers initiate a conversation with each other! RFCs also led to the idea of sharing knowledge and ideas rather than trying to keep all the glory for oneself; this philosophy lives on in today's Internet, as there is a sense of community and sharing amongst many Internet pioneers. This was the beginning of what is now known as the <u>Open Source Movement</u>, whose main ideal is the sharing of information and source code of programs so that everyone and anyone can modify and improve the program.

In August 1969, the University of California, Los Angeles (UCLA) became the first site on the network, with the arrival of the first IMP. One month later, Stanford Research Institute got its IMP, followed by University of California at Santa Barbara, and then finally the University of Utah. These four centres were the first four sites on the network. The first two centres above were the first two computers to communicate over the network. The first attempt to connect up the two computers resulted in a system crash! ARPAnet was born with a bang!

One node (or computer on the network) was established at each of the four universities. These four points were connected via lines that could transfer information at a speed of 50kbps. Standard modems can now transfer at a slightly higher speed than this! This connection for all the nodes was known as the <u>backbone</u>. So ARPAnet was said to have a backbone that ran at a speed of 50kbps.

> **Backbone** *is a term used to describe the main cabling or structure of a network.*

For many years, ARPAnet was the backbone of the Internet. Much like a human backbone, it was where every other point would connect to the network. It provided much of the support that was needed for points or nodes to connect to each other.

The 1970s

A Protocol is Born!

ARPAnet now had to try to deal with the issues of sharing resources between research facilities. BNN soon realised that the network would not always be reliable and that some packets could get lost in transit, so some sort of error-checking was needed. Error-checking would ensure that all packets arrived; if they did not, the sending computer would have to re-send the missing packets.

In 1970, the Network Control Protocol was developed. This <u>protocol</u> or set of rules was essential to ensure that all computers on the network could communicate with each other. Internet protocols are similar to diplomatic protocols — sets of rules that are used for communicating with other diplomats. Computers would all use the same set of rules or protocol to communicate.

However, the Network Control Protocol had a number of flaws, as we will see shortly.

Where are You @?

By the early 1970s, the network was used primarily by the military and academics. It was meant to be only an experimental network, but since everyone found it useful, it continued to exist.

In 1971, the network was demonstrated to the general public for the first time. The year 1972 can be seen as a turning point for this new network, as the first e-mail message was sent by Ray Tomlinson of BNN, though it was not called e-mail then.

E-mail was as such not an entirely new thing. For years, people had been exchanging electronic messages with each other on the *same* time-shared system. This new application allowed users of the network to send messages to each other via the ARPAnet. No longer was e-mail only usable on the same computer, one could now contact anyone who was on the ARPAnet. It was quick and efficient.

One could think of the e-mail up to this point as internal mail in a company; what Ray Tomlinson did was to allow two different machines, miles apart, to exchange mail messages. This was revolutionary!

He also needed to find a way of distinguishing:

❖ Internet e-mail and internal e-mail

❖ Different users at different host computers on the ARPAnet.

He decided to use the @ symbol for two reasons. Firstly, he wanted to use a symbol that could not under any circumstances appear in anyone's name. He looked at the keyboard on his terminal and found the @ symbol. Secondly, it made sense to use the @ symbol, since mail was being sent to a user who was "at" or using a certain computer system. Therefore, if Richard was a user at the computer in UCLA, his "address" might be *richard@ucla*, for example.

Tomlinson's e-mail program was called CYPNET, which in essence was a program to transfer *files* between computers. With some modification he found that *messages* could also be transferred from one computer to another. His modification, in those days, would have been referred to as a <u>hack</u> — a simple but clever modification to something that made it work slightly differently. The term hacking has changed quite a lot since then!

File Transfer Protocol

Before e-mail could be properly used, another protocol was needed. If the Network Control Protocol established how two computers could initiate and maintain contact, a new protocol was needed to define a set of rules on how programs would be sent from one computer to another. During 1972, File Transfer Protocol or <u>FTP</u> was in the final stages of development — its aim being to allow any program to be retrieved or sent over the ARPAnet easily. E-mail was officially born!

There was one thing missing from this scheme: you had to use one program to send mail and another to receive it. The breakthrough came in 1975 with the inclusion of an "answer" (reply to) command in a program called MSG, written by John Vittal. From this point on, only one program was needed to send and receive e-mail. Things were looking brighter!

The first international connections of the ARPAnet occurred in 1973, with points in England and Norway. In this year, it was also found that over three-quarters of all traffic on the ARPAnet was made up of electronic mail — which was not quite the original purpose of the network! It was apparent that people liked to communicate; being able to share resources was great, but the ability to communicate and build communities were important issues as well.

There were still a few major problems with ARPAnet. For one thing, machines on *other* networks could not connect to it. Also, one assumption of the Network Control Protocol was that the network was reliable and there would be no error in any packets sent. In order words, the network always worked! Today, anyone who uses computers for any length of time knows that nothing is reliable or dependable! An alternative protocol had to be found.

A Protocol for the Masses

The year 1972 is often cited as the most crucial year in laying the foundations for the modern Internet. That year, Vinton Cerf and Bob Kahn began to investigate the possibilities of a more reliable and common protocol that all computers could work with. They wanted to develop an "open architecture" system in which any computer system could be used and the code could be modified to suit any type of computer.

They published a paper entitled "A Protocol for Packet Network Interconnection". In beginning the development of such a protocol, they had a number of premises:

❖ There would be no need to make internal changes to any network in order for it to connect to the ARPAnet. As long as the network could run the protocol, they could connect to the Internet.

❖ If packets were lost, they would be re-transmitted. It was assumed that such losses could and would happen; therefore this type of assumption had to be built into the protocol, as did the ability to re-send any missing packets.

❖ Instead of using IMPs, what would later be called <u>routers</u> would be used, which would ensure that traffic was directed or routed to the correct destination. <u>Gateways</u> would also be used. Gateways would ensure that traffic from different networks was formatted in such a way that the receiving network could understand it.

❖ There would be no one controlling body in charge of the protocol.

Cerf and Kahn came up with Transmission Control Protocol/Internet Protocol (<u>TCP/IP</u>). This protocol would not only allow computers on the same network to communicate, but also those on other networks! TCP/IP forms another major element of the infrastructure of the Internet, and as such it is described in Chapter 2.

The 1980s

Development of TCP/IP progressed and it was decided that in order to use the network, all users would have to run TCP/IP, which was thus adopted as the standard in 1983. A user would not be able to connect to the ARPAnet unless their computer was running this new protocol.

This was a major decision that led to the growth and acceptability of the network. Up to this point, computers had been using the Network Control Protocol to connect to the network; this, as discussed, was a flawed protocol, as it assumed reliability of the network. TCP/IP did not make this assumption.

Just before TCP/IP took hold, the National Science Foundation in the US created a backbone called CSNET (Computer Science Network).This was to allow universities and colleges to have their own networks, as they were not connected to ARPAnet. It was seen that CSNET would need to be able to communicate with ARPAnet; therefore TCP/IP was an ideal protocol. This backbone ran at a speed of 56kbps — the same speed at which the most up-to-date modem can transfer information. This was an important step, because it created a network that was accessible to ordinary academic users. Up to this time, users only had access to ARPAnet if they were academic or military researchers.

Also in 1983, ARPAnet was divided into two networks: MILNET for all military networks and associated institutions; while ARPAnet would continue to be used for research purposes.

By 1984, telecom providers MCI had won a contract to upgrade the original CSNET, which they did — from 56k to T1 lines, which transferred 1.5 megabits of information per second (in and around 25 times faster than a 56k modem!).

The National Science Foundation established the National Science Foundation Network (NSFnet) in 1986. This linked a number of supercomputers together using a 56kbps backbone. The idea was that smaller colleges and universities would link into bigger regional colleges, which in turn would link into one of the main supercomputers. This would allow the smaller colleges to access the supercomputers without having to link to them directly. All they had to do was to link to the next university in the line.

The National Science Foundation took over the running of the network for academic use — it became the national backbone. By 1990, the original ARPAnet was out of commission. Much of the backbone of the network was by then running at T3 capacity.

The establishment of the NSFnet brought the Internet to the student masses. However, it must be remembered that, in the mid-1980s, the Internet was still very awkward and difficult to use. At this point, there were no "commercial" uses of the Internet; it was all academic-based. It is possible that this was a conscious decision in order to get the network up and running, and making sure that no company could create proprietary software and gain control of the network.

Domain Name Servers

In the mid-1970s, while the network was small, it was easy to remember each IP number, but as the number of servers on the network grew, this became increasingly difficult. Obviously, it would be easier to remember words — such as names or addresses — rather than IP numbers. The main problem here is that every computer on the network already had an IP number, which was a system that worked, as computers talk or communicate in numbers. The only reason for using words would be to make life easier for humans. If only there was a way to create words or letters to correspond with IP numbers of computers . . .

The solution came in 1984 in the form of the Domain Name System or DNS. DNS would translate IP numbers into alphabetic addresses or <u>domain names</u> and vice versa. Certain computers on the network would become DNS servers, whose only function was to accept queries from other computers looking for the IP numbers of other servers (see Chapters 2 and 3 for more on IP numbers and domain names).

One thing that was taken into account was the fact that different types of networks that were funded by different agencies should be identified. This led to the creation of what are now known as top level domains. These top-level domains are still in use to this day. There are seven top level domains that now identify what a site on the Internet is about:

- ❖ .edu   for educational establishments
- ❖ .com   for commercial organisations
- ❖ .net   for organisations involved in networks/networking
- ❖ .org   for non profit organisations
- ❖ .mil   for military establishments
- ❖ .int   for international organisations
- ❖ .gov   for government departments

The 1990s

The 1990s was, of course, to be the decade when the Internet exploded. From a useful, if somewhat awkward, academic tool, within three or four years, it was to become a global media phenomenon.

The Internet had, by this stage, accumulated its major elements. It was the exponential development of one of these elements — the World

Wide Web — that was to capture the imagination of the world. For the rest of this chapter, we will be looking briefly at the main developments in the Internet and the web throughout the 1990s; but as most of the innovations are still current and important elements of the web, most of this discussion is in fact left to later chapters.

The Spinning of the Web

From America, we travel back to Europe. The year: 1989. This is the year that the idea for a true World Wide Web was spun.

It happened in Switzerland, in a research institution called CERN, which was a laboratory for particle physics research. One of the researchers there, a man called Tim Berners-Lee, was to invent what is now the World Wide Web.

He realised that there was so much research going on in CERN and so much information being processed that it would make sense if all this information could be accessed quickly and with ease. Instead of having to go to another room or building, if the information was stored on computers it would make it easier for every researcher to find; it would also lead to less duplication. Once again, we find that researchers were at the heart of the development of the web!

Berners-Lee's idea was to link documents together, much like Vannevar Bush's idea of trails. "Documents" as such were flat pieces of work, such as other research papers. He wanted to extend the document, allowing people to easily call up other documents that were referred to. If I insert a footnote or reference in any chapter of this book, you must physically go out and find the book, find the page and read it — this takes time and effort. But if this book was available in hypertext format, all you would have to do is click on a link and the information would be brought to your screen instantly.

This idea made a lot of sense. Researchers may spend hours finding old works that they wish to refer to; linking them together would make it easier and more efficient to work.

Another problem was that, even if documents were in an electronic format, different users might be using different programs and different computers. Therefore if one person was using a certain type of word processor, and another person was using a different type of word processor, there would be compatibility problems.

Berners-Lee suggested that the new system would have a common user interface, so that everyone accessing the document would use the same common application or program to view the documents. There were a number of key elements that Berners-Lee wanted for his new system:

- ❖ Easy to use;
- ❖ Platform independent;
- ❖ Application independent;
- ❖ Accessible to all.

That is how the web started off. (Unfortunately, some of these ideals of the web have been lost. More and more sites are being branded with graphics saying "best viewed in Internet Explorer" or "best viewed in 800x600"; other websites are using proprietary technology such as Macromedia's Flash. All of these things lead us away from the idea of a uniform website that everyone can enjoy. We will look at this in more detail in a later chapter.)

The solution was to provide this common user interface and to use a common language to create these documents. The language that was developed was called HTML or HyperText Markup Language.

The web exploded in the early 1990s because it was easy to use. It used, for the most part, a point-and-click method of navigation. Users of computers were becoming increasingly familiar with point-and-click interfaces from operating systems such as Mac OS and Windows. The web brought the Internet to the masses through an easy-to-use system that computer users were familiar with.

Berners-Lee considered many names for the interlinked document universe he was creating, including:

- ❖ **MESH**: Sounded too much like "mess"!
- ❖ **MOI**: Stood for "Mine of Information", but also meant "me" in French and may have seemed too egotistical!
- ❖ **TIM**: Acronym for "The Information Mine" — again, may have been misconstrued as egotistical!

He finally settled on the name World Wide Web. The name was appropriate; in previous years, he had developed a similar application called "Tangle"!

Berners-Lee was a true pioneer and a selfless person. If he had made the web a proprietary system, he could have become very very rich. Instead, he realised that a free system would propagate faster and serve humankind better. The year 1994 saw the development of the World Wide Web Consortium (W3C), a body set up by Berners-Lee to ensure the continued development of the WWW. Its function now includes creating recommendations for languages and technologies on the web.

The browser looms . . .

The first browser was developed within CERN in beta form in 1990. In May of 1991, the browser was released to other users in CERN; announcements were made in various newsgroups about the browser. Newsgroups are a very important part of the Internet, and have played a major role in helping to shape the Internet and the web; they will be discussed later on.

At this time, the browser was only text-based; it was still necessary to remember commands to view the available documents.

Berners-Lee also gave us the URL or Universal Resource Locator, as well as the HTTP protocol. We have already discussed one the most important protocols, TCP/IP; this is the most essential protocol for using the net. Your computer must be able to run this protocol in order to communicate on the Internet. In order to access the World Wide Web, however, you use a program called a browser, but also a protocol called HyperText Transfer Protocol or HTTP.

 *HTTP or HyperText Transfer Protocol tells computers how to receive and view web pages. This allows computers of different types to see web pages.*

Mosaic — the First Real Browser

If Tim Berners-Lee is the inventor and godfather of the web, Marc Andreessen was the person who made it available to the world.

While still at college, Andreessen worked in the National Centre for Supercomputing Applications (NCSA). The Centre made its computing resources available to other researchers via the Internet (we talked about time-sharing earlier — this was a site that provided such services).

Andreessen created an application that would allow people to view web pages; his program used <u>point-and-click</u> technology, i.e. using a mouse to select items or icons on the screen. Up to this point, the web relied on text-based browsers, which required specific commands to read the pages.

 ***Point and Click*** *is a method whereby users move a cursor on their screen by manipulating their computer's mouse. Objects such as icons, folders or file names are selected by pointing the cursor at them and clicking the mouse.*

In 1993, Andreessen brought out a beta version of <u>Mosaic</u>. Mosaic has been heralded as the "Killer App of the 1990s". He announced to the <u>Usenet</u> world that his browser was available in beta format to download using the File Transfer Protocol (the protocol used for downloading and uploading files on the network). Within hours hundreds of people had the browser downloaded and working on their computers.

This was an important moment in Internet history. This was the first browser that allowed pictures to be displayed online alongside text in the same browser window (some earlier browsers had allowed pictures to be displayed but only in separate windows). More important was how it was distributed: for free and available to anyone to download. Andreessen could have chosen to package and market the browser; instead, he used the Internet to propagate the software. Many companies use this method to distribute their software over the Internet today.

Allowing pictures to be displayed in web browsers caused, to say the least, a bit of controversy. Berners-Lee envisioned the web as a way of sharing research information. Now this research tool was being used to display pictures. This was not on! This single development made a huge impact on the shift in the use of the Internet from research tool only to something that could actually be fun!

The Dawn of Netscape

Soon after Andreessen left NCSA, he was approached by Jim Clark of Silicon Graphics. Clark wanted to build a browser commercially. In 1994, Netscape Communications was born.

One problem they faced was that if they used the original code from Mosaic, although Andreessen had written it, they could be in for tough legal action from NCSA, who "owned" Mosaic. Andreessen decided to re-write the code from the bottom up. The new browser was released in December 1994. Netscape Navigator was an immediate hit, as it was free for educational and academic use (businesses had to pay for it) and it was easy to use. Microsoft at this time knew little of the Internet and had no interest in the passing fad! There was little or no competition, and Navigator soon became the dominant browser in the market.

Netscape concentrated on selling their other products to make money, knowing that if people liked the free product, they would stick with them and purchase some of their server products. So Netscape began to take hold of the server market as well, making their profits not from the Internet market, but from the Intranet market. Many businesses found that Intranets were the way to go and started developing them using Netscape's server software and their browser.

The giant enters the market

Netscape had a very accurate view of the future, where everyone's computer would have an operating system that would be integrated with a browser. Netscape would be integrated into the whole operating system, which in turn would be integrated in the web.

Unfortunately, Netscape had no operating system, but one Bill Gates had! It was easier to integrate a browser into an operating system that you were launching in 1995; thus, Microsoft's Internet Explorer was born. Internet Explorer was not originally coded by Microsoft but was a re-badged browser from a company called Spyglass, who had bought the licence to use the Mosaic code from NCSA. Suddenly the dominant market position that Netscape had enjoyed had vanished.

Windows 95 was revolutionary for many reasons:

❖ It was easier to use;

❖ It came with its own browser;

❖ Many of Microsoft's applications were to become "web-enabled". Thus, for instance, one could create HTML web pages directly from a Microsoft Word document.

Netscape's browser at this time was still considered better than early versions of Internet Explorer. For one thing, Navigator would allow access to web sites, but also had a built-in e-mail program and newsreader for newsgroups — everything you wanted in one package. Later versions of Explorer would resolve this situation, and Netscape saw their market share drastically reduced by the late 1990s.

Microsoft and Monopoly

Internet Explorer was now an integral part of the Windows operating system. Microsoft knew that if a user received a browser with the computer they bought, they would have no reason to install another one. Think of what this meant: 80 per cent of personal computers, if not more, come with Windows preinstalled; put your browser in with this bundle and you capture the Internet browser market.

This led to a long drawn-out legal battle between Microsoft and the US Department of Justice, with Microsoft being accused of monopolising the browser market. In May 2000, the court found that Microsoft had indeed abused their market position, and ordered that the company be broken up into two separate companies, one to produce the operating system, and one to produce other software, including Explorer. Microsoft have vowed to appeal this decision.

As we settle into the twenty-first century, we have seen many changes in the World Wide Web. Between 1996 and 1999, web usage expanded exponentially. The technologies in use have changed. One of the main changes has been speed of access for web users. Also, streaming audio and video now make overseas radio and television stations available at the click of a mouse. As you will see in later chapters, there are now many ways of using the Internet, and many ways of accessing it through different devices. The emergence of e-commerce is changing how we shop and saving us money. Alongside these great strides have emerged some fresh problems, including privacy and security issues, pornography and criminal users on the Internet. Also, some of Tim Berners-Lee's original vision has been diluted by the fierce competition and innovation that has emerged. These and other issues are discussed later in the book, but first, we will look at the structure of the Internet, followed by an extensive guide to how you can launch yourself online and get the most from the Internet.

Chapter 2

Structure of the Internet

Net and Web

Many people talk about the Internet and the web as though they are the same thing. It is important to understand that the Internet and the World Wide Web are not in fact the same.

The Internet consists of a number of elements, including the World Wide Web, electronic mail (e-mail), newsgroups and file transfer. Each of these is discussed in detail in later chapters. This chapter is chiefly concerned with looking at the different *technical* components that make up the Internet — the physiology, as it were, that makes the Internet live and breathe.

The Internet provides the structure and infrastructure of the overall network all computers, cables and routers that pass information from one network to another. The World Wide Web is an application that uses the Internet as a means of transport. Therefore the Internet is the transport mechanism, while the web is just an application. Similarly, e-mail uses the Internet as a way of transporting messages from one computer to another.

Tim Berners-Lee explains this difference: "The Internet . . . is made from computers and cables. . . . The web exists because of programs which communicate between computers on the Net."[1]

---

[1] Quoted from http://www.w3.org/People/Berners-Lee/ShortHistory

The Infrastructure of the Internet

Many of the components of the Internet were introduced in Chapter 1, as they were developed over the course of 40 years; other components are of more recent vintage. This section looks at the major elements in more detail.

A Network of Networks

The Internet is a global network of computer networks that are attached to each other. A network, in its simplest form, is any two computers that are connected to each other and can share resources or communicate. Many offices have simple networks that allow many users to print to one printer. They are all sharing the resources of one printer.

At the heart of any network are a number of elements:

❖ Computers that access information;

❖ Computers that provide or serve information;

❖ Network cable or infrastructure;

❖ Protocols.

Clients and Servers

The basis for all modern computer networks is the client/server architecture. In this type of system, there are two types of computers.

Some computers on a network are dedicated to doing one job only. They are not used by any user on the network. The job of this computer may be to store files or look after the printing of documents. These computers are simply known as servers.

Webopedia (*www.webopedia.com*), an online dictionary of computer terms, defines a server as:

> *A computer or device on a network that manages network resources. For example, a file server is a computer and storage device dedicated to storing files. Any user on the network can store files on the server. A print server is a computer that manages one or more printers and a network server is a computer that manages network traffic. A database server is a computer system that processes database queries.*

So servers share resources between other computers on the network. Computers that connect up to these computers are known as clients.

> *Clients are PCs or workstations on which users run applications. Clients rely on servers for resources, such as files, devices, and even processing power.*

Again, the clients can run their own applications but rely on the server for resources. Note the last part of the definition — adding to processing power was very important in the early days of computing, when computers were huge machines attended by men in white coats. Users (mainly academics and scientists) would connect to these computers with <u>dumb terminals</u>. All the processing was done on the main computer rather than on the terminal users were using.

Under the client/server architecture, however, most of the processing is done on the local machine. All applications are stored on the local hard drive and only certain operations, like printing, are handled by the server. So, for example, every time a document or file needs to be printed the client makes a request to the server and the server processes that request and either proceeds with the request or rejects the request.

Most client/server technology uses a decentralised system.

Centralised, Decentralised and Distributed

As we saw in Chapter 1, the early pioneers struggled with the problem of what type of network the Internet should be built on. There were three alternatives.

In a <u>centralised</u> system, all the processing power and information is held on one central computer, usually called a <u>mainframe</u>. Many companies still use mainframes that their staff can connect to. When commands are issued on the client computer, they are processed on the mainframe and the results are shown on the client computer's screen. The important thing to note here is that there is no processing of the commands on the client computer; all processing is done on the mainframe. When computers were big and expensive, this was the most cost-effective way of using computers. Client computers were in fact dumb terminals.

In the last two years, there has been a renewed interest in this type of computing. Organisations have found that equipment becomes outdated very quickly. By installing a high-powered server, running an operating system called Windows NT Terminal Server and software called Citrix Meta Frame, it is now possible, in theory, to use Windows NT on a 386 machine. Citrix systems rely on the server, rather than the client machine, to do all the processing.

Such a system is very useful when a company has old computers. However, in the centralised model, if the mainframe crashes, the local computers are absolutely useless.

On a <u>decentralised network</u>, the client computers are more powerful and more than likely do most of the processing locally and store more information locally as well. The server is used only for certain tasks, such as printing or storing vast databases.

The advantage of decentralised computing is that if the server is knocked out, the local computers can still function to a certain extent, but they may not be able to print or access the database.

A third type of network is possible: in a <u>distributed network</u>, there are no central computers. All computing tasks are divided equally among all computers.

The Internet is a <u>distributed network</u>: there is no central core to the network, and each computer is connected to a number of other computers. Any communication passed from one point to another can follow a number of different routes. This means that if one particular route is disabled, the communication can still reach its destination by choosing a different route. This makes the network virtually disaster-proof.

Think of the rail system. If there is a crash or a fault on the line, no other train can use the track until that fault is rectified. If we were to rely entirely on such a system, there would be chaos.

Now visualise the road system. Since there are many ways to get to any place in the country or in a town, if there are road works, the traffic on the road can be re-routed or diverted. Road users do not depend on one direct route, therefore the road system can be seen as a distributed network.

An important element of the network is the idea of <u>redundancy</u>. Some points on the network would not be used all the time to connect to that server on the network; therefore part of the time they would be redundant. However, it was another option if traffic had to be re-routed.

Again, visualising a road, there are a number or redundant connections between different roads. The more ways there are of getting somewhere, the better. But not all those other roads will be used all the time; they may only be used every two months when there are road works.

When the Internet was being developed, it was decided that a redundancy level of three or four was substantial — this meant that every point on the network would be connected to three or four other points. As you can imagine, it would be very difficult to cause major damage to such a network. If one line of communication to a particular computer goes down, there are at least another two ways of getting to it from the same node.

So, we now have a number of computers which we want to connect. But how are all the computers physically connected?

Network Cards, Cables and Topology

There are other physical connections that need to be put in place so that a client and server can communicate. These may include:

❖ Network cards

❖ Cables

❖ Topology.

In an office environment, every computer on a network must have a network card. This is inserted into the back of the computer and allows the computer to connect to the physical cables of the network. Without a network card, the computer would not be able to connect to the network.

Once the network card is installed, cables must connect computers to the network in some way. The two main types of cabling are co-axial and RJ45 cabling. Co-axial cables are similar to those used for TV aerials. They used to be very popular and were used for bus-type networks (see below). RJ45 cables, which look similar to telephone cables, are now a more popular choice and are used with star-type networks.

Topology refers to how a network is laid out. There are two common types of topology.

In the bus topology, every computer is connected to the next computer beside it. There is one line of cable running from the first computer to the last computer. At the end of each end of cable, there is a terminator device.

> *A **terminator** is a device used to ensure that information on the network knows where the end of the network is. Without a terminator, the information will literally fall off the end of the cable — the message will think there is another computer connected to the last computer and try to send information to it. Without a terminator, the network will not be able to function.*

This type of network uses co-axial cable. It is not an ideal network topology, because if one computer becomes disconnected from the network, the whole network goes down, since there is no termination. You then have to try to locate the break in the cable to get the network back up and running.

In a star network, all computers are connected to a central hub. The advantage of this type of network is that if one computer gets disconnected from the network, it does not affect every other computer on the network. Since all computers are not connected to each other and only the hub, there is no disruption. Of course, the danger is that if the hub goes, the network will not function.

Connecting to the Internet: Modems and Telephone Lines

When the network is not based in one office — as is the case for the Internet — the computers must be able to link to the "outside world" through modems and telephone lines. The choices available to the Internet user are discussed in greater detail in the next chapter. For now, I will briefly mention how these important pieces of hardware fit into the overall infrastructure of the Internet.

Modem stands for MOdulator/DEModulator. Computer data is sent as a digital signal, but at present domestic telephone lines can only accept analogue signals, unless they are updated to ISDN. The modem modulates the digital signal into an analogue signal when the data is being sent down the telephone line and then demodulates it (converts it back into a digital signal) when it arrives at the destination computer. It is like an interpreter.

Once the modem has converted the signal, it sends it through the telephone system to your Internet Service Provider (ISP). Your ISP is connected into a larger Internet connection (much like the system used by universities on the early NSFnet). All information that is requested, no matter what country it comes from, is received by you, but you are only charged a local call rate.

Your request for information travels across many networks and then the reply is transmitted back over networks to your computer. You never have to make a "dedicated" connection to any server on the web. The only true dedicated connection is between you and your ISP, which is charged at local rates.

As you can begin to picture, the Internet is made up of many different types of networks, all interconnected via cables, telephone dial-ups, leased lines and ISDN lines.

Some networks do not use physical cables to connect together; they use infrared signals to communicate, in much the same way as remote control works. These types of networks are quite expensive to set up and require a lot of technical skills, but can make offices safer places as cabling is kept to a minimum. Many mobile phones now have infrared ports that can communicate with infrared ports on laptop computers.

Transmitting Messages: Packet Switching

In Chapter 1, I described how researchers such as Paul Baran and Donald Davies developed the concept of <u>packet switching</u> for sending messages over the network. Packet switching involves breaking up computer data into manageable chunks or "packets" for transmission.

The advantage of breaking up messages into packets is that each packet can take a different route to the destination and they are all reassembled in order when they arrive; thus no segment of the network is monopolised. If many people are sending data across the network, those sending large amounts of data would not clog the system.

Let's bring back the analogy of the road system. Roads, for the majority of the time, see spurts of activity; most roads are not busy all the time. Now think of a bus lane. Again, it is not being used all the time, but cars cannot use it for certain periods of the day, even when there are no buses around. It is a dedicated circuit; sure, the bus gets there quicker, but imagine building many of these dedicated circuits to every point in the country! This would not be a good scenario for Baran's network; it would have to be a network of equality, which no one user could monopolise.

Look at another "real world" scenario: it is cheaper and easier to disassemble furniture before we move it than to try moving it as a whole entity. If one buys a fitted kitchen, it is delivered bit by bit, possibly by different firms, and then assembled at its destination.

Each point on the network has a routing table — a map that tells the point on the network how many links or hops it is to every other point on the network, and which is the quickest route. Since each point on the network has its own routing table, there again is no central nerve centre containing all the information; each point on the network would learn from all other points when there is new information. Thus, computers can automatically update their routing tables from other computers; again, the idea of a distributed network comes into play — no one computer controls the routing table!

Protocols and IP Numbers

Protocols are the mechanisms and rules that allow computer networks to communicate. The principal protocol that is essential to the functioning of the Internet is TCP/IP.

In order for computers to be able to communicate with each other, they must first of all be capable of understanding each other. If all computers are running a certain operating system, such as Windows 98, then there is no problem in communication. Since all computers on the network are using the same operating system, they all know how to operate and talk to each other (although they must still run a common protocol).

The problem occurs when different computers want to talk to each other. An Apple Mac will not understand what a PC is saying and vice versa. Each computer system comes with its own distinct set of protocols. In order to communicate with other computers, all computers must communicate using a common protocol. This is where TCP/IP comes in. Once all computers are running this protocol, each computer can communicate with every other computer. All computers on the Internet use the TCP/IP protocol to communicate. If TCP/IP was not the standard, the Internet could not function. This protocol was made the standard protocol in 1983.

TCP/IP is a vendor-neutral, platform-independent protocol. This means that no one company, organisation, or computer type "owns" the protocol. If the protocol was, say, Microsoft-specific, then only computers running a Microsoft operating system could communicate. If the protocol was only available on PCs, then Apple Mac users could not connect to the network. This would lead to many problems for companies trying to connect different types of computers to the network.

TCP/IP is in fact a suite of protocols. Transmission Control Protocol or TCP looks after the transmission and control of information passing from one computer to another. The TCP part therefore ensures that the information is transmitted correctly. If a packet got lost, it would be resent.

Computers on the network each get a unique <u>IP number</u>. The Internet Protocol ensures that each packet is numbered and told which address it should go to. Internet or IP numbers consist of four sets of up to three numbers separated by a full stop (for example 123.134.51.1). Every computer connected to the network has its own unique IP number; no two computers could have the same number.

The original ARPAnet could only handle a limited number of hosts. TCP/IP was built in such a way that it could support up to 256 networks. Each network could have 16,777,216 computers each. That's almost 4.3 billion computers! The amount of networks and computers available may sound like a lot, but the world is actually running out of IP numbers currently. Think about how the Internet is growing exponentially. Every user who connects to the net and every computer on the network must have an IP number. Every ISP has to ensure that it has enough IP numbers for all its present and future customers. If you think about this on a worldwide level, you can see why so many numbers are needed.

IPV6, the latest upgrade to the protocol, hopes to expand the number of networks and computers that can be connected. IPV6 will allow for 340 undecillion (340 x 10^{36}) connected computers — unless we learn how to clone the world's population exponentially, we should never run out of IP numbers again! IPV6 also has more technical advances; remember, the IP protocol is over 20 years old.

Since the network can only work efficiently if each message is broken into packets, and each packet takes a different route, it is essential that:

❖ Packets be numbered;

❖ They be reassembled in the right order;

❖ Any packets that may have got lost or discarded be resent.

This is exactly what TCP/IP does.

Domain Names

As outlined in Chapter 1, IP numbers are very difficult to remember, so a system was established to translate these numbers into alphanumeric addresses — the <u>Domain Name System</u> (DNS). Thus, each IP number can correspond to an Internet address or Universal Resource Locator (<u>URL</u>). Instead of having to remember 194.125.61.1, all you have to remember is *www.scs.dife.ie*. Without DNS, web surfers would have to remember long strings of numbers rather than easy to remember URLs.

Every Internet Service Provider (ISP) has a DNS server, which is a dedicated computer that converts URLs into IP numbers and vice versa. When a user requests a website, such as *www.loadza.com*, their ISP's DNS server is queried to see what IP number that website corresponds to. The DNS server searches its database, responds with the IP number and the user is taken to the site.

If the ISP's DNS server does not know the IP number, it will query another DNS server until it finds the right IP number. This is one reason why connections to servers can take a few seconds (sometimes minutes!). If you type in a web address such as *www.doesnotexist.com*, it may take a few minutes before an error message is displayed.

ISPs, domain names and IP numbers are discussed further in the next chapter.

Making it Real

So, the major components needed to set up and run the Internet are in place. That means anyone can now simply surf the web, right? Wrong! While the infrastructure described above is essential to the functioning of the Internet, the World Wide Web would be unusable without one final essential element: <u>HTML</u>. Before we discuss HTML, let's look again at what makes the web a unique resource.

Hypertext and Hyperlinks

Why, you may ask, is a web page better than a book? The reason lies in <u>hypertext</u>. Remember the discussion on associated documents in Chapter 1? The concept of hypertext is over 30 years old, but it is still the basis for navigating the World Wide Web.

Hypertext is a way of linking documents together electronically. Instead of plain text on paper, hypertext is "live" text, allowing the user to move around the web in a non-linear fashion. This is done through

<u>hyperlinks</u>. A hyperlink is a piece of hypertext that is directly linked with another piece of hypertext. When you click on this piece of hypertext you will be brought to a new page or place within a page. Textual hyperlinks are usually distinguished from surrounding text in some way, e.g. using a different colour, underlining and/or bold.

Every web page contains, or should contain, links to other resources. If you read a book, it may make reference to another book. If you want to read that reference, you must go to the library and borrow the book if you can find it. Not so with hypertext. If a document is referred to in hypertext, you can simply click on the link to it and instantly read the information. This allows for extensive use of cross-referencing, which means the web is an ideal medium for research.

Web pages and sites differ from traditional media in another important way. Web pages and web sites are non-linear in structure. You do not have to enter a site at the beginning and progress through it until the last page, as you would probably do with a book. With a newspaper, you may start in the middle and work your way out, but you are not going to hop from one paper to another to another. You are still reading in some sort of linear fashion.

Due to the nature of hyperlinks and the web, you may read one page of one site and then choose a link that brings you to another related site. You will probably never read or view every single page in a site. Therefore the web is a non-linear medium.

Web pages are not solely limited to pages of text; they can also contain pictures, sound files, even animation and video clips. Therefore hypertext has evolved into <u>hypermedia</u>. Hypermedia is the term used to describe what web pages have now become. Web pages can contain various types of media on a page or they can link to other pages or other media sources.

But how are these hyperlinks created?

What is HTML?

HTML is the language used to create websites. As such, it is not a programming language; all it does is dictate what should appear on the screen and how it should be displayed. It provides a user interface that allows for point-and-click navigation. HTML allows rudimentary formatting. The original purpose of HTML would have been to display text-only documents, mainly for academics, so graphics and fancy layouts were not so important! HTML allows a web author to link their page to any other resource on the Internet, be it a picture, sound, video or e-mail address.

Lack of layout facilities has been a problem for web designers, as HTML was never intended to make things "look nice". In Chapter 8, we will see how advances in web design are changing this; there is also a basic introduction to HTML.

Websites and Web Pages

What is the difference between a website and a web page? A web page is simply one page of information or resources. A website is a collection of web pages connected by hyperlinks.

In the good old days, web pages simply contained text and, sometimes, pictures. One problem with HTML was that it did not take into account different page layout techniques. Therefore companies began to develop proprietary technology that extended the functionality of a web page. Web pages can now contain much more than simple text and pictures. Many web pages contain what is known as active content. Active content allows the user to see moving pictures and hear sounds when they open a web page.

Some examples of active content include:

❖ Video clips

❖ Audio

❖ Flash (from Macromedia — allows compact animated user interfaces to be created)

❖ Java (Java can take many forms but may be used to animate parts of your page or even to run full programs on a web page).

As an example, live video and audio broadcasts can now be obtained over the Internet. The one problem with any of these technologies is that if the user does not have a plug-in installed on their computer, they may not see the web page as it should be displayed.

Chapter 6 looks more closely at the basic elements of a web page, while active content and some of the more advanced uses of the web are discussed in later chapters.

Types of Websites

When is a website not a website? There are many answers to this, as there are many different types of website, reflecting the diversity of uses of the World Wide Web and the unregulated way in which it has developed. Examples of different types of websites include:

❖ **Company/Organisation's Website**: Most companies are now on-line with their own websites, usually with a URL such as *www.mycompany.com*. These types of sites will be informational and/or trying to sell a product or service.

❖ **Personal Websites**: A website set up to promote a person's ideas, views or interests. Some individuals set up sites on their own servers; others are hosted by other companies. The URL of the latter type is usually in the form *www.asite.com/~richard*.

❖ **Online Communities**: These are individual sites that have come together because of mutual interests or a common philosophy.

❖ **Search Engines/Directories**: These are the sites that try to make sense of the rest of the web by trawling through it for whatever information the user requires, using keywords to link to sites.

❖ **Portals**: These are "gateway" sites that provide information and access to parts of the web dedicated to a particular subject or theme, e.g. *www.ireland.com*.

❖ **Vortals**: These are even more specialised than a portal site, e.g. restaurants in Ireland.

Each of these types of website is discussed in detail later in the book.

Part Two

BASIC APPLICATIONS

Chapter 3

What You Need to Get Started

Connecting to the Internet

Now that you know how the Internet came about and how it works, you have to learn how to connect.

There are two categories of users who will want to connect to the Internet: home users and business users. While the business user will generally need the same basic equipment to set up their Internet account, there are some extra pieces of hardware and software which are essential for many business users, but which have little relevance to most home users. What follows is therefore relevant to both home and business users, but business users can refer to the last section of the chapter for information on the "extras" they may need.

To connect to the Internet, the average user must have the following items:

- ❖ Computer
- ❖ Modem
- ❖ Phone Line
- ❖ Service Provider
- ❖ Software.

Computers

You may think a computer is an obvious and essential piece of equipment to possess before you can access the Internet. However, today this is not strictly true: with the advent of Internet kiosks, cyber cafés, web TV and WAP mobile phones, it is often not necessary to own a computer to gain access to the web. Chances are, however, that you have bought or are about to buy a computer, so these newer forms of access are discussed at the end of this chapter.

If you do buy a computer, the minimum requirements are a 486 with about 32MB of RAM, and 100MB of free hard disk space. Nowadays, you would not find such a low-spec machine on sale generally. If you are using Microsoft Internet Explorer, you will need a more powerful system. (In fact, an older computer could be used with a browser called Opera.) Inevitably, the more high-powered and state-of-the-art your computer, the better will be its ability to access certain aspects of the Internet/web and function efficiently. At the time of going to press, a mid-priced PC has an Intel Pentium Processor with a speed of about 600MHz, 64MB of RAM, a 7.5GB hard drive, and a 56K modem. However, you can only browse as fast as your modem and telephone line allow (see later). So, there is no point in owning a top-of-the-range PC if your modem can only run at a minimal speed.

Internet access is now available on most laptops via built-in modems, but these tend to be considerably more expensive. More recent Apple Macs, such as the iMac, also allow access to the Internet. iMac is the Internet Mac. It is a computer without a built-in floppy disk drive, although these are available as an optional extra. The reasoning behind this is that if you need to share information/documents, you will e-mail them.

This brings up an important question: is there a difference in accessing the Internet using a Mac or a PC? Firstly, all web pages will appear the same; remember, the whole idea of the web was that it would be platform-independent. One problem you may have is finding an Internet Service Provider (ISP — explained later) that is skilled in Mac connectivity. If you have a Mac or are thinking of getting one, be sure to contact your local ISPs to see if they support Mac connectivity — then there shouldn't be any problem.

Most modern computers are also fully multimedia-ready; i.e. they have a sound card and speakers and allow the user to view video images, etc. This is essential if you want to gain the most from the various media available on the World Wide Web.

Of course, you should always bear in mind that, for most people, the Internet will be just one of the applications they use their computers for, so look at the whole package (including any in-built software) in terms of your needs.

Modems

A <u>modem</u> is a very important piece of hardware. As described in Chapter 2, a modem translates digital signals into analogue for transmission over the telephone system, and vice versa for receiving.

Types of Modems

❖ **Internal Modems**: These are normally pre-installed inside your computer. They are handy if you not going to be moving the modem around and take up no extra space on your desk.

❖ **External Modems**: These are like little boxes connected to your computer via one of the serial or parallel ports at the back of the computer. They are a little bit more expensive than an internal modem. The advantage of an external modem is that you can take it from one computer to another, without having to dismantle your computer. There is also no need to open up the computer if something goes wrong.

Different Modem Speeds

When buying a modem, you will see that they are categorised as 28.8K, 33.6K, 56K, etc. These numbers (kilobytes per second) represent the *potential* speed at which information can be sent and received by the modem. I say "potential" because this also depends on other factors which are discussed later. The rule of thumb is to buy the fastest modem possible. The current standard speed is 56K.

*A **bit** is either a 1 or a 0 in digital or binary terminology. Eight bits make one **byte**, which is equal to one character or letter. Therefore a 56K modem is capable of transferring 56,000 bits per second.*

Types of Connections

The next thing you will need is a telephone connection (although WAP phones allow for limited Internet access over a mobile phone). There are a number of options available here:

❖ Ordinary Telephone Line

❖ ISDN

❖ Cable Access

❖ DSL

❖ Dedicated Leased Line

❖ GSM mobile phones available for laptop users.

We will discuss each of these in turn shortly. ISDN and leased lines are, in general, more relevant to the business user. However, ISDN is becoming cheaper and more readily available to the home user, so it is discussed below, while leased lines are discussed later in this chapter, under "Business Users".

Telephone Line

For most home and many business users, a simple telephone line is enough to gain access to the Internet. You can simply plug your modem into your current connection. If you plan to be online for long periods of time, however, it might be worth investing in a second line, or even to consider one of the other options such as ISDN.

The main advantage of using an ordinary telephone line is that it is already there, so it won't cost you any more for the connection. The main disadvantage is that the speed of the connection is limited, and the connection is not as reliable as, say, an ISDN line.

ISDN

ISDN stands for Integrated Services Digital Network. An ISDN line is a digital telephone line. There is no need for a traditional modem, as the signals do not need to be modulated or demodulated, although a device called a terminal adapter must be purchased to connect your ISDN line to your computer. This allows for faster simultaneous access. ISDN lines come in speeds capable of sending and receiving data at 64,000 bits per second.

ISDN also allows you to use the phone at the same time that data is being sent; therefore having an ISDN line serves two purposes — faster access to the Internet and voice calls at the same time! ISDN is also useful if you want to integrate your data (Internet access) and telephone system.

How is this possible? When you get an ISDN line, you get what are called B-channels — in effect, two lines. If you decide to use both lines at once for Internet access, you get a maximum speed of 128K. The trouble is, you are charged for two calls, so use this option with care. ISDN is also quick as it does not need to convert the signal from digital to analogue and back again.

One problem with an ISDN line is that it is charged under the same pricing structure as a normal phone line. Therefore, if used during peak hours, it provides faster access to the net but costs the same as a traditional phone line. Check with your local telecom provider to see if ISDN access is more expensive than normal calls.

It is not recommended to get an ISDN line if you are using it for more than three hours a day. This is particularly relevant to businesses. Let's assume that one hour's peak local rate is 15 pence per three-minute period. It would cost £9 per day for three hours of peak access. Over a five-day week, that would be £45, or over £2,000 per year. If a company needed to have, say, seven hours a day access, the cost would rise to over £5,000 per annum. By investing in a leased line (see below), they could get 24/7 access for a fixed rate.

Cable Access

Cable access has only recently become a possibility in Europe. This type of access is provided via your cable TV connection. Using a cable modem, this type of access provides a permanent connection, thereby eliminating the need to "dial up" to your Internet access provider.

Cable access can provide access speeds of up to 10Mbps, which is very fast; the only problem is that everyone on your street would be accessing the Internet through the same cable, so access speeds may decrease. It would still provide faster access than a conventional modem.

DSL

Another up-and-coming option is Digital Subscriber Line (DSL). This type of access will allow you to browse at speeds up to 6Mbps or more, but only allow you to upload files at up to 640Kps. For the average user, the download time is more important than the upload time, as downloading in essence means browsing the web.

The beauty of DSL is that you already have it! It uses the same wire as your standard telephone line to send and receive data; not only that, but it will not interfere with your voice calls, so you can chat and surf at the same time.

Such technologies are already available in America but as yet remain new in Europe. If people can access and navigate the Internet at such speed, web designers will be able to create truly interactive multimedia-rich websites.

Of course, it could be argued that everything will eventually slow down due to the amount of data passing along the wire and we will have more attractive websites but access will still be slow.

Bandwidth

You may hear people talk about how slow the Internet is and that they are in fact crawling on the World Wide Wait instead of surfing the World Wide Web!

It is true — sometimes the web can be very slow. But suppose you have a modem that can transfer information at 56kb per second — surely this means that you can send and receive information at top speed. Theoretically, your modem can transfer at 56kb per second. Note the word *theoretically*. In reality, this will not happen because of bandwidth considerations.

So what is bandwidth? Bandwidth is the amount of space information can travel along. The more bandwidth you have, the faster the information can transfer. Actually, this is not quite true! Bandwidth is like a three-lane motorway. All things being equal, you will get to places faster on the motorway. But have you ever seen the motorway at 8 a.m.? Not exactly a pleasant place to be! If you have a fast car (the same as a fast modem) you may be able to get a top speed of 110mph out of it (*Honestly, officer, I was trying to understand this bandwidth lark!*); but if the road is congested at rush hour, you will have to share the road with everyone else and everyone's speed is reduced to 2mph.

The same goes for the Internet. You may have a fast modem, and access to a huge amount of bandwidth, but if there is a lot of traffic on the Internet, then everyone's access will slow down. Remember we said the Internet was a network of equality, that no user can monopolise the network, the same as the road system. Since everyone shares the same road, no one gets there any quicker. Since everyone shares the same bandwidth, no matter how fast your modem is, you will not get the information any quicker.

Another consideration is that, although you may have a fast modem and a huge amount of bandwidth, you still may find that accessing a site is slow! Why is this? Again, the more people who are accessing a site, the slower the server delivers the information. If a server is not powerful enough, it will not be able to deal with all the requests which clients are sending it.

Think again of the analogy of a car on a motorway. Although you may fly along the motorway, if the entrance to the hotel you are going to only allows two cars to enter at any one time, you will have to wait your turn. If the entrance to the hotel is too small or inadequate (not a powerful server), everyone's access slows down!

So when you find that your Internet access has slowed down, don't worry, there is nothing wrong with your computer or your modem. It just means that lots of people are either accessing the site or using the Internet.

Internet Service Providers (ISPs)

Even when you get all of this equipment, you cannot directly access the Internet — you must use an Internet Service Provider (ISP).

*An **Internet Service Provider** is a company that is directly connected to the Internet. It provides the user with a username and password that allows the user to log onto their network, which in turn allows them to log on to the Internet.*

Most countries now have a choice of ISPs to which you can subscribe, all of them based locally. Typically, you purchase a CD-ROM (some ISPs provide these CD-ROMs for free), which sets up your account for you; you simply have to follow the instructions on the screen. Most set-ups are fairly easy, but each ISP will have slightly different methods.

You will probably, at this stage, have to familiarise yourself with some of the basic functions of a web browser in order to complete your set-up. The different browsers are described briefly below, while Chapter 6 details their functions. Most CDs from ISPs provide a "connection wizard" to make it easy to connect to their service. Once you have set up your account with your ISP and installed your browser, you will be provided with an e-mail address, username and password. Your computer is now directly linked to the Internet. You can now connect to any computer in the world that is on the Internet and it will only cost you the price of a local call! You can send and receive e-mail, surf the web, or even set up your own website (ISPs usually allow subscribers a limited amount of space on their servers to host a website — see Chapter 8).

Local Call Prices

When you connect to the Internet, you do so through an ISP. When you connect to your ISP, you become part of their network; your request for information is routed through different servers, but all you pay for is your connection to your locally based ISP! All communication on the Internet, no matter where the information is coming from, is charged at local rates.

It is the same with e-mail: if you send ten e-mails within a single dial-up, you are only charged for one local call; it does not matter how many e-mails you send, or how many web sites you visit.

Remember that accessing the Internet during the day can be expensive; if you can, it is best to wait for an off-peak period before connecting.

Free Internet Access versus Paid Internet Access

In the late 1990s, as a result of competition, many ISPs unveiled free Internet access packages. The idea was simple: do not charge the consumer any annual subscription or registration charges. The consumer would save over £100 a year on these subscription charges. However, although *subscribing* to the Internet was now free, users still had to pay phone costs. Some people have been stung by this, not realising that the ISP will not pay your phone bill! It is more important, therefore, to monitor the amount of time you spend on the Internet when you have one of these free accounts.

As an example, one of the first ISPs to offer subscription-free access in the UK was Freeserve, which is now one of the most successful free Internet providers. They make their money by getting a percentage of the cost of each call. For example, if the call charge per unit is 3p, BT get 2p of the call charge while Freeserve get the remaining 1p. Many free ISPs have claimed they make little or no profit on their service. Much of their income comes from selling value-added services to companies; that is, they try to sell bigger and better products to business users, such as faster, dedicated access, web hosting, etc.

More and more companies are co-branding their products with ISPs and offering free Internet access. Don't be surprised if you go into a clothes shop and are handed a free disk for their new ISP service!

With all of these services, all you pay is the price of the local call, but there are a few conditions to take into account:

1. Free Internet access means you do not pay a monthly or yearly charge for your account. It does not mean that the company pays for your phone calls!

2. The majority of ISPs who provide fee-paying accounts have low-call numbers that allow cheaper Internet access during peak hours. The same charges apply off-peak.

3. Calls to the support lines of a "free" ISP may have to be made to a premium number. You should very rarely need to call the technical support line, as the software sets itself up automatically. In my experience, the technical staff are well trained and good at sorting out problems as quickly as possible.

4. Since these are free services, they attract a large number of users. Since so many people are trying to use the service it could in fact become quite slow. Therefore you may find a paid service faster and more reliable; after all, fewer people will be using it.

For these reasons, many users are reluctant to change over to these "free" services. Also, some ISPs offer incentives to those who choose the "paid" service.

Another new service that is emerging is flat rate pricing for Internet phone calls. The user will pay a flat rate of, say, £20 per month, and then get unlimited weekend and off-peak Internet access. The more you use it, the better value you get. This service is ideal for those who spend quite a lot of time on the Internet at the weekends. If you access the Internet during the day under this service, you pay the local call charges as per your telephone company.

In some countries, it is also possible to pay a once-off local call rate each time you log on to the Internet, after which the user can stay online for as long as they want, either during peak or off-peak hours, without paying any extra.

These are obviously the best ways to go for Internet access from the consumers' point of view, but it may take some time for these systems to spread to Western Europe. This is one of the main reasons that the Internet took off and is more widespread in the US.

AOL and CompuServe

You may well have heard of or seen CD-ROMs for services such as AOL and CompuServe. These are American services known as on-line services, and are somewhat different from ordinary ISPs. They are very popular in the US but have never caught on to the same extent in Europe.

Back in the dark ages of the Internet, only geeks, academics and scientists could understand and remember all the necessary commands to find information. Since there was less organisation of the Internet then as there is now, it was a very difficult and awkward system to use.

AOL and CompuServe had a network that provided organised content and information for people. They were not directly connected to the Internet but were more of an <u>Intranet</u>-type network that only subscribers could use.

They charged users on a per-hour usage system. As you used their system, you were charged for the price of the call and then by AOL/CompuServe for the amount of time you used their system. They had sections in their network that were premium areas for which you had to pay more to access. This would be useful and interesting information, maybe about sports, financial information, etc. This worked much like a pay-per-view system. If you wanted the more interesting information, you paid for it! They also had partnerships with many firms and organisation that provided useful and timely information that was not available anywhere else.

Since the Internet was so difficult to use, these on-line services were more user-friendly and contained all the information one needed in one site. But they were popular for another reason and that was because the service could be accessed by dialling a local number from anywhere in the States. Therefore, if I had an AOL account in New York and went on business to San Francisco, I could log onto AOL in San Francisco by dialling a local number. Other smaller services at the time did not have this facility. If you wished to access the smaller services from other areas apart from where they are based, you could only call the one number, which would mean you would incur a long-distance phone call.

AOL/CompuServe provide what is known as local call access or local **Points of Presence**.

 ***Point of Presence*** *is a term used to describe a local number that a user can dial in order to connect to their ISP. This saves you dialling a non-local number.*

Not only did they offer POP in the US, but in all major cities in the world. Therefore, if a businessperson was away in Paris, they could log onto AOL by called the local POP in Paris and not have to dial an international number.

As the Internet became more user-friendly with the invention of the web, people began to realise that the information that was available on CompuServe/AOL was good, but it was possible with a bit of effort to find the same information and more on the Internet. People thus began to sign up with local ISPs. Realising that they could lose business, AOL and CompuServe began allowing access to the Internet through their systems.

There were, however, problems. Internet access was restricted to 9.6Kbps, which was very slow. The AOL browser could be used to access websites but it rendered pages differently to Netscape's browser. Some sites would not work with the AOL browser. In fact, AOL has suffered so many problems that, in the US, some users have renamed it AO-Hell!

In the UK, AOL is seeing an increase in popularity, as they have many value-added features, such as allowing parents to set up different usage settings for children and special homework help areas for schoolchildren.

AOL have recently acquired Netscape; subsequently, Time Warner and AOL merged; then Time Warner merged with EMI. This is an interesting situation and time will tell how this will affect music and entertainment on the web.

IP Numbers

Chapter 2 described how every computer and user of the Internet must have an IP number to access the Internet. In fact, it is your ISP that assigns this number, which is yours to keep and treasure for the duration of your current surfing session. You simply borrow it for the time you spend online. When you are finished surfing, the IP number returns to a pool of IP numbers. Every ISP has a huge pool of IP numbers that it lends out to web surfers. Every time you connect up to the Internet, you get a different IP number.

Why, you might ask, can you not have one IP number forever? It seems a lot of hassle to have to automatically assign these numbers every time you connect up to the Internet. Can you imagine if this was the case with your mobile phone number? Every time you connected to the network, you were given a new number! How could people contact you?

However, when you are connected to the Internet, people contact you through your e-mail address, which doesn't change. Your friends and colleagues do not need to know your IP number; all they need is your e-mail address. So one reason that you are not given a permanent IP number is because you simply don't need it.

But there is another reason. Suppose a typical ISP has 50,000 subscribers in any one year; out of that 50,000, maybe 10,000 use the Internet at least once a week. At any one time, maybe only 3,000 people are online. It would be a waste to give each person a permanent IP number when 47,000 of them will not be using them during this time! This would mean that the ISP would have to have 50,000 IP numbers.

The ISP estimates how many people will be online at any one time and then provide enough IP numbers to cover this amount — say, 10,000, which would leave plenty of "redundant" IPs in case of a surge in use. Every time you log on you are automatically assigned an address for the duration of your surfing from a pool of IP numbers, using a protocol called Dynamic Host Configuration Protocol (DHCP). When you finish, the IP number returns to the pool.

Choosing a Browser

We have looked at the hardware end of the Internet, but one essential part of connecting is the software you use. In particular, you will require a browser to use the Internet properly. A browser is a piece of software that allows you to view web pages. The development of web browsers in the early 1990s was described in Chapter 1; here, we will focus on how they function and what you need to do to set up a browser on your computer. Chapter 6 will look at how to make the best use of your browser.

The basic functions of a browser are to:

* ❖ **Display text of pages**: All web pages are primarily pages of textual information, so it is essential that your browser can display text.

* ❖ **Show pictures**: Many websites contain pictures to enhance their appearance. If you have an old browser that does not display pictures, you should consider getting one that does. Pictures were supported since the early versions of Netscape Navigator. (There are still some browsers that are only text-based. These may be used by people who only want to see text and not images; they may have a slow connection to the net and not want to have to wait for images to appear.)

* ❖ **Indicate when one page is linked to another**: Links are at the heart of the web. They allow one page to be connected to another page. Most browsers show links as blue underlined words. Your cursor changes from a pointer to a hand when rested over a link.

* ❖ **Display a symbol to indicate when a picture is not available for viewing** — if for some reason the picture is unavailable, the browser should display a symbol to indicate this.

These are the basic functions of your browser. All browsers have more advanced functions than this, but in order to experience the web your browser must at least be able to do the above. Don't worry — unless you have a prehistoric computer, your browser will do all the above and much more! The more advanced functions of the browser are described in Chapter 6.

Netscape versus Microsoft

What is the difference between one browser and another? The two best-known browsers are Microsoft's Internet Explorer and Netscape's Navigator. The rivalry between Microsoft and Netscape, which culminated in the antitrust action taken against Microsoft, was described in Chapter 1. Here, we will concentrate on how the two browsers function.

From the point of view of a user's functionality, there is not a whole lot of difference between them. Both of them have the same fundamental functions under different names. It is essentially a personal preference as to which browser you use.

One problem is that some pages may look slightly different in either browser, or perhaps may not display correctly. If this happens, it is a programming problem. When a web author designs a website, they should ensure that the web pages display correctly in each browser. Some web authors don't do this and as a result the page may display incorrectly. Most professional websites are designed and tested to ensure that everyone can view them, so you should not worry about this too much! If you are interested in web design, see Chapter 8.

Microsoft's Internet Explorer is an easy to use browser, and has certainly become very popular. The latest version of Internet Explorer, released in 1999, is IE5. IE4 had added some interesting features to Windows 95 and had become standard in Windows 98. For example, from a Windows Explorer window, you can directly type in web addresses. Other interesting features include the Active Desktop, which allows you to set up your desktop like a web page. You can underline embed links onto the desktop to your favourite sites. You can open folders by single-clicking them rather than double-clicking (on the web, you single-click links to activate them). The web was fully integrated into the operating system and became even more integrated with the release of Windows 98; in fact, this was the main reason behind the antitrust case.

Internet Explorer also comes with Outlook Express, a dedicated e-mail client that is easy to use and also has news-reading capabilities. Outlook Express is discussed in greater detail in Chapters 4 and 5.

Netscape Navigator is perhaps declining in popularity. Remember, Navigator was the original browser, and it was the first to have a built-in e-mail client. However, IE feels and acts more integrated with the Windows OS. Mac users may not find this to be the same, as IE would not be integrated into their OS. It is really a matter of personal preference, but since IE5 comes as standard with Windows 98, users tend to stick with it.

How often do you upgrade?

An interesting report from browserwatch.com indicates that in the early years of the Internet, users upgraded their browsers as soon as newer versions came out. Now the jump between upgrading from one version of a browser to the next has declined. The reason is simple; users have in Internet Explorer 4 or Navigator 4 a good reliable browser. Any updates and changes in the new browsers are, for the most part, cosmetic.

The other problem is size: as each new version of a browser is released, the more features it has, the amount of hard disk space it requires gets bigger and bigger.

If you want to get the latest version of a browser, you have two options:

❖ Download it from the Internet (takes time and costs money)

❖ CD-ROMs containing the browsers are often given away by ISPs or on the front of computer magazines.

At this stage, most people are happy with the browsers they have and are unlikely to update them on a regular basis.

Other Browsers

Internet Explorer is one of the most popular browsers on the market. It is an easy-to-use browser with many advanced functions, which will be explained in later chapters.

Although most people have only heard of the two most popular browsers — Internet Explorer and Netscape Navigator — there are many more available. A number of browsers are included on the website accompanying this book, including Opera, a very small but efficient browser. If you want more information about browsers, refer to *www.browserwatch.com*

It is possible to have any number of browsers installed on your system, but one browser should always be the default (main) browser.

So, now your computer has everything you need to start exploring the mysteries of the Internet! If you are a home user, you can skip the next few pages, as they describe some of the extra bits and pieces that most businesses need. Over the following chapters, you will learn how to use the two most important applications of the Internet. Chapters 4 and 5 look at e-mail, the most popular use of the Internet, while Chapters 6 and 7 look more closely at web browsers and how to search the web. You can therefore continue your journey in either Chapter 4 or 6.

Tip! *If you do not wish to spend the money getting all the necessary equipment together in order to connect to the Internet, it is still possible to sample the delights of the web! You can visit a cyber café or an Internet kiosk, which are springing up all over the place.*

Business Users

When a business decides to get connected to the Internet, there are a number of issues that they must consider:

1. What type of access is needed?

2. What type of dedicated equipment is needed?

3. Do you want your own domain name?

4. How much are you prepared to spend?

What Type of Access is Needed?

The most essential element of the Internet that every company should have is e-mail. If a company simply wants to get an e-mail address, all they need to do is sign up for an account with any major ISP. If a company want to develop a website, they will usually have to sign up for a business account. Most ISPs will not allow commercial websites to be developed using a free or home user account; they must have a business account. Building a website is dealt with in Chapter 8.

This type of access is fine for a very small company, as no special equipment other than the standard equipment discussed above is needed. But it does come with a few problems: it is basically the same type of access that a personal user has; it does not allow for a number of people to use the Internet at any one time.

Multi User versus Single User

If a company wishes to have e-mail access for everyone, they need to invest in more specialised software and hardware. Many of the ISPs can provide you with company-wide e-mail via special hardware solutions. ISPs also usually provide "Internet in a box" equipment, which allows for company wide e-mail, full browsing capabilities for all, as well as enhanced security features. These "Internet in a box" systems are cheaper than buying dedicated equipment and are much easier to use.

It is possible to get a number of e-mail addresses tied to the one ISP account. The problem is, all e-mail is then collected on one computer. Your ISP may be able to set up a "catch-all" e-mail account. This means that any e-mail addressed to your company is received to one account. When the e-mail is collected, a program on your network can distribute the e-mail to the correct users.

What type of Dedicated Equipment is Needed?

If your business does go down the route of buying dedicated equipment, you would be looking at computers equipped with Windows NT (for a Windows-based network), special e-mail software, a <u>firewall</u> (this is a combination of hardware and software that will protect your network from intruders or hackers once you go online), and software that would allow many users to surf using the same ISDN line. To set this up could cost you a few thousand pounds and would require maintenance and knowledge of the NT operating system, as well as other software. Chapter 8 looks at the issue of dedicated equipment in the context of building a website.

Dedicated Leased Lines

This equipment can only be connected over digital lines such as ISDN (discussed earlier) or <u>leased lines</u>. Leased lines provide a dedicated connection to the Internet, 24 hours a day, seven days a week. Leased lines are available in fractions of 64K. If you bought a "full" dedicated leased line, you would get access speeds of 1.54 Mbps; this is known as a T1 connection.

Leased lines are fast, reliable and relatively cheap forms of communication. If a company needs permanent connectivity, this is the best option to choose. Again, connecting an "Internet in a box" solution to your leased line will allow you to administer and set up e-mail and web browsing accounts easily, and to have your own website up and running in minutes rather than hours.

Leased lines are ideal for medium to large companies, colleges and universities that need continuous and simultaneous Internet access. For large companies, standard dial-up or ISDN connections are not fast enough or cost-effective enough.

Leased lines allow companies to budget how much their Internet usage will cost. Regardless of the number of users or the amount of time spent online, the company will pay the same amount, as the costs are fixed. The initial costs of a leased line may be enormous, but then you pay a fixed rental cost to the telephone company and a service cost to your ISP per year. Whether you use the leased line for 1 hour a day or 24 hours a day, you pay no more. With ISDN, you pay on a per-usage basis; therefore if your Internet usage increases, you may be faced with huge bills down the road.

Of course, you can go for the cheaper option of getting a free Internet account and paying for your phone calls as you go, but this will not be efficient if you want simultaneous access amongst all your staff.

Do you want your own domain name?

If a company wants to have personalised e-mail that reflects their company name, they need to buy a domain name. Purchasing a domain name is dealt with in Chapter 8. Having your own domain name means your e-mail will reflect your brand name. For example, my company name is Tintec Systems; it is more professional to have an e-mail address that reflects my company name, such as *richard@tintecsystems.com* rather than *tintecsystems@hotmail.com*.

Security

One consideration that every business needs to take into consideration when connecting to the Internet is security.

Remember we said that the Internet is a network of networks? Well, when you connect to the Internet, your business's network becomes part of that network. Even though only one computer is connected to the modem and the Internet, any computer that is connected to your computer through an office network will now also be connected. We will see what the security risks are in Chapter 12.

Other Ways to Connect

At the beginning of this chapter, we mentioned that there were a number of ways of connecting to the Internet without having a computer. The main technologies are web TV, Internet Kiosks and Cyber Cafés, and WAP mobile phones.

Web TV

Web TV is essentially a box that sits on top of your television and allows you to surf the net; it comes with a built-in modem.

There are a number difficulties in using a web TV unit. First and foremost, TVs and computer monitor displays are different, therefore the colours on some pages may not be as bright or clear as on a monitor. Computer displays can be set to display different numbers of <u>pixels</u> on the screen.

 **Pixel** *is the term used to describe the smallest unit that can be displayed on a computer screen.*

Common pixel sizes or resolutions for computers are 640x480 (this means that the screen is made up of 640 pixels by 480 pixels); most computers now run at a resolution of 800x600. TV screens cannot display this number of pixels, thus leaving some pages looking fuzzy. Web pages where the text is quite small may not display clearly.

There is no facility that allows you to use any browser other than that installed on the web TV unit; therefore there could be a compatibility issue with pages that use the latest active technologies.

One of the great things that you will later learn to do is to download and install programs from the web; unfortunately, this function is not available on web TV boxes.

For all these reasons, it may be more advisable to buy a cheap computer if you want to surf the web rather than a web TV unit.

Recently, in Ireland, a company called Internet Ireland launched a new web TV system called Unison. This box sits on your TV and plugs into your telephone line. You use a remote control unit and infrared keyboard to surf the web.

Web TV is still a relatively recent development, so it is likely that improvements will be made, which may make it a more worthwhile investment. Web TV should not be confused with digital television, which is discussed in Chapter 14.

Sampling the Internet: Cyber Cafés and Internet Kiosks

Over the last couple of years, many cyber cafés have opened up across the world. These are cafés that have computer terminals and high-speed Internet connections. You can have a mocha or cappuccino and surf and check e-mail at the same time! Prices in cyber cafés typically range from about £4–£6 per hour of surfing — quite expensive if you wish to use them all the time. They are very useful if you wish to see what all the hype is about before you decide to spend money buying a computer and getting connected to the Internet.

Another option is the new Internet kiosks that are appearing in many shopping centres. These kiosks look similar to arcade machines, they have a screen and also a keyboard and some sort of mouse attached.

The user can pay as they surf; once their credit is getting low, they are prompted to enter more money.

These kiosks are great if you want to quickly check your e-mail or find information while on the move! Most of these kiosks have their own web-based e-mail systems, so you can even set up an e-mail account with them.

As you can imagine, in the long run it is easier to get your own connection set up rather than relying on using cyber cafes/Internet kiosks on a regular basis.

WAP Mobile Phones

The first few months of 2000 saw the emergence of WAP telephones. Nokia was the first company to put a WAP-enabled phone on the market. This provided access to the Internet, but only to specially prepared WAP pages. The WAP phone comes with a special WAP-enabled browser that allows you to surf.

In theory, you could buy one of these phones, connect up with your telecom provider and surf the web. In reality, what is provided is access to an "intranet" style area, where users can access servers from chosen suppliers. For example, provider A might form partnerships with a newspaper, bank and music website and would allow people access to their specially created WAP sites. Provider B might form partnerships with other businesses and websites. If you happened to be using provider B but provider A had a partnership with your bank, you would not be able to use their WAP banking service. This is quite similar to the early days of the web, when people using providers such as AOL and CompuServe could only access their resources. So with WAP, we are back where the web was in the early 1990s. At present, WAP pages are very simple text-based pages, with only limited black and white graphics.

The next problem is that many of the pages will look different, depending on the phone you are using. This is because of different screen sizes on WAP phones. So a page that displays well on a Nokia phone may not display so well on a Motorola phone.

Mobile phones can only access data services at 9.6kps, which is very slow, so if you were to "surf" using your WAP-enabled phone, everything is going to be very slow. Another criticism is that many of the services were initially unreliable and kept disconnecting from the service.

Another problem is that mobile phones were not designed for typing with. In order to type in a WAP address (similar to a web address, except that instead of files having a .htm extension they have a .wml extension) can take forever, as you try to punch in the correct letters via the numeric pad on your phone.

People seem to be taking a "wait and see" approach to WAP. Perhaps as the phones get more intelligent, we may see better use and wider acceptance of these phones. Companies that provide WAP-enabled services will find that in order to surf, they will need to ensure that their pages are as up-to-date as possible. If information is mission critical, they will have to have people on hand to update at a minute's notice. One example I came across was when I tried to access the lottery results via my WAP phone — I got the result for two weeks previously! Obviously this is a good idea but if not implemented probably, users will see it as a waste of time!

Chapter 4

Introduction to E-mail

What is E-mail?

Electronic mail, or e-mail for short, is a way of sending messages across a network (such as the Internet) at a fraction of the cost of sending a letter. It is the most widely used application of the Internet.

In Chapter 1, we traced the first e-mail ever sent back to 1972, when Ray Tomlinson succeeded in "hacking" or modifying an FTP program that allowed him to send a message from one server to another. As the ARPAnet grew, people realised that not only could they share files and information across the network; they could also send each other text messages. This became known as electronic mail or e-mail.

Remember that e-mail is only an application that uses the Internet to receive and deliver messages. Therefore, just because you have e-mail may not mean that you also have web access.

E-mail is extremely popular, and is available to most people in the developed world, either at home, in work or through a cyber café. The reason it is popular is because it is:

❖ Quick

❖ Cheap

❖ Efficient.

For the home user, e-mail is an ideal way for individuals to keep in touch with friends and family. It is quicker than the postal system, which is often referred to these days as "snail mail"! It is also cheaper than a phone call or fax and allows you to send messages when you wish. For the business user, it is now an essential tool.

Proper use of e-mail is one skill that everyone who uses the Internet should master, although not everyone will reach the highest levels of competence. In this chapter, you will become familiar with Microsoft's e-mail package <u>Outlook Express</u> and will learn how to use it to carry out basic e-mail tasks. Many of the specific tasks referred to in this chapter are based on functions of Outlook Express, but they are generally adaptable to other e-mail packages.

What makes up an E-mail Address?

In order to send or receive e-mail, you must have an e-mail address. E-mail addresses are in the form of *name@domainname.extension*. For example, my e-mail address is *richard@tintecsystems.com*. This means that my name is Richard and my mailbox is at (@) a company called Tintec Systems; we know it is a company/business because of the **.com** extension.

How cheap is e-mail?

The only cost incurred in sending an e-mail is the price of the phone call to your Internet Service Provider.

When you connect up to your Internet Service Provider, the telephone company will see this as a telephone call; they do not usually distinguish between data calls and voice calls. Therefore the more time you spend on the Internet, either surfing or sending e-mails, the more it will cost you. As outlined in Chapter 3, it is often cheaper to use the Internet at night or at the weekends, when local call charges are cheaper.

Some ISPs are now introducing a flat-rate pricing where you pay them £20 per month and you get unlimited access to the Internet at off-peak times and at the weekend. Other ISPs offer sign-up charges so that you can access the Internet via a free 1800 number. Always check with these services that there are no hidden catches, like only being allowed to surf in three-hour blocks before being disconnected.

If you send a lot of e-mail, you should consider reading and replying to e-mails <u>offline</u>. This means that you type up all your e-mails, including replies, while you are not connected to the Internet.

 **Offline** *refers to any activity that you do while not connected to the Internet. It is possible to use your e-mail package while being offline.*

This means that you are not paying phone charges while writing e-mail. When you use this method, you write all your e-mails and save them into your <u>Outbox</u>. When you connect up to the Internet, you can then send all your e-mail in one go — thus saving you even more money! This will be explained later in this chapter.

Will I miss my e-mails if I'm not online?

What happens if you are not connected to the Internet and an e-mail is sent to you? Will you miss the e-mail? Does it simply not arrive or is there some way that you can receive e-mails while you are not connected to the Internet?

Once you have set up an account with an ISP, all your incoming e-mail is stored on their server until you log on to the Internet. When you log on, your e-mail program checks their server to see if you have any new e-mail stored on it. This type of facility is known as <u>store and forward</u>. All your e-mail is stored on their server and then forwarded to you when you connect up to the Internet. Remember that a <u>server</u> is any computer that provides a service to another computer. In this case, their e-mail server provides the facility to receive and store your e-mail and can also act as a way of sending your e-mail out to its required destination on the Internet.

Think of a house with a mailbox at the entrance to the driveway. The owners' new mail is left in the box until they collect it. If they are away for a few days, all new mail stays in their mailbox until they retrieve it. This is what happens on the Internet, except you have a virtual mailbox housed on the ISP's computers. This ensures that you never miss an e-mail message.

How does e-mail really work?

We noted above that e-mail uses a Store and Forward technique. Your e-mail is stored and forwarded from one computer or server to another. Your e-mail server has no direct connection with any other e-mail server. When it wishes to send e-mail, it passes your e-mail onto another server, then that server determines how to route or send that e-mail to the nearest server, and so on until your e-mail is received at the correct mailbox.

Think again along the lines of the postal system. When you post a letter, it is sent with everyone else's letters; the postal service does not lay on a special plane just for your one letter. The post office in your hometown looks at the address of your mail — say it is to a town in California. It is not concerned with trying to find the best way to send your mail to California; it is only concerned with sending it on to the main post office to get sorted.

When the main post office receives the e-mail, again they are not concerned about getting it to California; they are concerned only with putting it on the right plane to the US. Once in the US, the postal system there ensures it gets to California. When in California, the post office makes sure it goes to the right town . . . this continues on until the postman delivers the letter into the correct mailbox. Along the way, each post office is only concerned with completing the next stage of the journey.

The same applies to e-mail; it is stored and forwarded from one mail server to the next until it arrives at its destination. Remember, a fundamental concept described in Chapter 2 was that the network uses packet switching. This can lead to problems, as your e-mail could be intercepted at any point in its journey across the network.

In order to send and receive e-mail, there are two <u>protocols</u> used. It is worthwhile knowing about these protocols so that you can set up your e-mail package correctly. Ninety-nine per cent of the time, everything is set up for you by your provider, but with the advent of free Internet providers, this may not be the case.

When you are sending out e-mail from your computer, you use a protocol called Simple Mail Transfer Protocol (<u>SMTP</u>). This sends your e-mail from your computer to the ISP's server and then to the other person's ISP's server. Every ISP has an SMTP server that allows e-mail to be sent out. If your e-mail package does not have the correct information regarding the SMTP server, your e-mail will not be sent. This, along with POP3 (see below), is usually automatically configured at registration.

When you wish to receive the e-mails that are stored on your ISP's computers, you use a protocol called <u>POP3</u> (sometimes referred to simply as POP — not to be confused with points of presence, discussed in

Chapter 3), which stands for Post Office Protocol 3. This is the protocol that allows you to receive e-mails from your ISP's computer to your e-mail package. Again, if you enter the wrong POP3 server, your e-mails will not arrive in your mailbox.

Your service provider will give you all this information. Sometimes the POP3 and SMTP servers will be the same, but more than likely they will be different.

Sometimes you may need to alter the settings on your e-mail account. If you change service provider, you will need to set up your e-mail account again. This is not very difficult and is worth knowing how to do. Changing settings is discussed in the next chapter.

E-mail and Privacy

E-mail is *not* a secure way of communicating. In Chapter 1, we described how when any form of communication is sent via the Internet, be it requests for web pages or e-mail, it is broken up into <u>packets</u>; each packet takes a different route to reach its destination.

This can lead to an obvious security problem, your e-mail could be intercepted at any point as it travels across the Internet (remember it is a public network), and the contents of it could be read or examined. In mid-2000, the British government announced that they were planning to implement a system whereby all e-mail entering or leaving Britain would go through a set of servers that could check every e-mail for certain content. They realised that many criminals may be communicating through e-mail and this is their "reason" for setting up such a system. It would seem unlikely that this would work unless all Internet Service Providers were forced to adhere to it, which is what is being suggested.

Therefore, if you need to send a confidential document, it is best to either post it or send it as an attachment with password protection. You can also encrypt your messages, which will be dealt with in a later chapter.

Can my employer read my e-mail?

In business, more and more companies are allowing their employees to have access to e-mail as they begin to realise the benefits of speedier communications.

Believe it or not, even if you think you have not used e-mail before, you could be using it everyday! Many companies have internal e-mail systems based on their local area networks (LANs). This means that the e-mail never leaves the internal network of the company. This type of e-mail can differ in some respects from standard Internet e-mail. For example:

❖ Different addressing system: an Internet e-mail has the following form: *richard@tintecsystems.com*; an internal e-mail address might look like: *richard/IT:blackrock*.

❖ Some internal systems will allow the user to recall e-mails after they have sent them in case they want to make changes to them or delete them before the user reads them. This is *not* true of Internet e-mail.

Many companies reserve the right to read their employees' e-mail. There are many reasons for this:

❖ Most employees are given e-mail for business use only. If you are using it for business purposes, you have nothing to worry about.

❖ They also feel that you are using company property — their computers, network and Internet connection — therefore it should be reserved for company use. You would not use your company's photocopier to copy 20 CVs or for other personal use; therefore, the same applies to e-mail.

❖ Many companies employ programs that check the contents of every e-mail before it is sent out. If certain words, such as *job application, CV* or *recruitment*, are contained in an e-mail message, it will send an alert to the head of IT or to a certain person in the company. Again, companies do not want people using their resources to find jobs.

❖ Finally, there is a threat to companies from attachments; this is where a file is attached to an e-mail message. This file can be anything from a document to a program. Firstly, an employee will find it easier to send confidential information out from the company via e-mail rather than photocopying it and walking out with it. Secondly, attachments can include programs or files that contain viruses. In a networked situation, if the virus infects one computer, it can spread throughout the company. We will discuss attachments in greater detail in the next chapter, including different views that companies may have on the subject, and viruses are discussed in more detail in Chapter 12.

Can anyone else read my e-mail?

If you share a computer with someone, say at home or in a small office, it is possible to open Outlook Express or your e-mail client and read all your old e-mail. They should not be able to read any new e-mail because they will not know your e-mail password. You will learn later on how you can avoid this problem. Another problem that can occur is the possibility of someone finding out your e-mail password and then intercepting your e-mails before you get them. If the person gets to know your password and knows the POP3 setting of your service provider, they can access any incoming e-mail sent to you. This is why it is essential that you never divulge your password to anyone.

Are there any rules on using e-mail?

There are no "rules" as such, but there are some guidelines that should be followed. These guidelines are known as netiquette!

❖ **Case:** Never type in all capitals. This is important for two reasons: first, it is harder to read, AS YOU CAN SEE; second, it is referred to as "shouting" — it indicates that you are annoyed.

❖ **Length:** E-mails are usually short and to the point, don't write an essay if three lines will suffice.

❖ **Formality:** E-mails tend to use less formal language, particularly when e-mailing friends and colleagues. One of the original joys of e-mail was the ability to talk to supervisors in a less formal way than normal!

❖ **Subject:** Always include a descriptive subject line; this helps people categorise your e-mail and get an idea of what it is about. The subject line should be no more than five words long.

❖ **Retrieval:** Once an e-mail is sent, it cannot be retrieved. Some internal mail systems in companies will allow you to retrieve their mailings, but this is not the case for Internet e-mail; once you hit that "send" button, it's gone. This can cause problems for people who are used to internal systems, and don't understand why they cannot retrieve their Internet e-mails once sent!

❖ **Politeness:** Never say anything in an e-mail that you would not normally say to someone, since e-mail is a statement and may be stored permanently on someone's computer. Re-read your e-mail in case it seems too abrupt or if the point you are making could be interpreted incorrectly. Remember, you would not write an offensive message on company notepaper; therefore don't do it on company-based e-mail!

❖ **Attachments:** Don't attach large files, such as documents or photos, without telling the recipient first. These files can take a long time to download and will serve to frustrate the user at the other end. Anything over 60–100k is deemed as large.

❖ **Links:** If you wish to include a web address, always ensure you type in the address in the form of *http://www.domain.com* — this will ensure that the link becomes clickable, i.e. the person can click on the link in the e-mail, which will then open their browser.

❖ **Promotion:** If you run a business, don't blatantly advertise it everywhere you can on your e-mail; this is not deemed polite!

❖ **Replying:** When replying to an e-mail message, the original message will be quoted. You may wish to turn off this function in your e-mail package; otherwise it can make your e-mail much longer (this will be explained later).

❖ **Forwarding:** when you forward a message, do put a comment in your message at the top so the receiver will know what the message relates to.

❖ **Emoticons:** Since e-mail does not convey your tone of voice, you may wish to use "emoticons" to express emotion. Emoticons are little symbols used to represent emotions, such as :(for sadness (tilt your head sideways to get the full effect). A full list of emoticons is provided on the website (*www.internetdemystified.com*).

❖ **Abbreviations:** Net enthusiasts often use acronyms or abbreviations as shorthand for commonly used phrases, mostly to save time and space; for example, BTW means By The Way. Use appropriate abbreviations, but be careful because some people many not understand them. This harks back to the olden days — the more a message could be shortened, the less congestion it would cause on the network; therefore abbreviations became commonplace. A full list is provided on the website (*www.internetdemystified.com*)..

❖ **Pause:** Before you send an e-mail, pause for a second, read through it again, ensure that it makes sense, that the tone is correct, etc. It is too easy to write an e-mail hastily and then regret it; remember, once it is sent it is gone and you can do nothing to retrieve it, apart from apologise or resign!

Now that we have that out of the way, we can begin learning how to send and receive e-mails!

Basic E-mail Functions

E-mail is a very simple application to use. There are also some more advanced functions, which you can live without, although you might find them extremely useful. These are discussed in the next chapter.

The most basic functions include:

❖ Receiving e-mail

❖ Composing and sending new e-mail

❖ Replying to e-mail

❖ Forwarding e-mail

❖ Message management.

If you master these basic functions, you will be able to use e-mail more efficiently.

In order to access your e-mail, you need to know a number of specifics:

❖ The computer that receives your incoming e-mail (known as a POP3 server);

❖ The computer that sends out your outgoing e-mail (known as a Simple Mail Transfer Protocol or SMTP server);

❖ Your user name (the part before the @ symbol);

❖ Your password.

These will be supplied to you by your ISP (it is possible to choose your own username and password). Once you know this information, you can set up your e-mail package to receive e-mails from your account. This is very handy, because if you travel abroad, you could use anyone's computer, set up all these details and send and receive e-mail as if you were at home. It is even easier if you use web-based e-mail.

Using Microsoft Outlook Express

There are many e-mail packages available, but the most popular one is Outlook Express. If your computer is relatively new, it is quite likely that you have Outlook Express on your system, either because it came on the disk of software from your ISP or because it was preinstalled as part of Internet Explorer within your Windows operating system. As stated earlier, I focus in this book on Internet Explorer and Outlook Express because of their popularity and ease of use, but many of their functions are adaptable to other packages.

So, let's begin! Double-click on the Outlook Express icon on the <u>desktop</u>. Depending on how your Internet connection is configured, you may see a dialog box that will dial up your Internet connection at this stage. You don't need to connect, especially if you have a number of e-mails to write. However, let's assume you want to connect now. This is known as <u>working online</u>. We will discuss working offline shortly.

Enter your username and password here, and ensure before proceeding that you are connected to the Internet. The following appears:

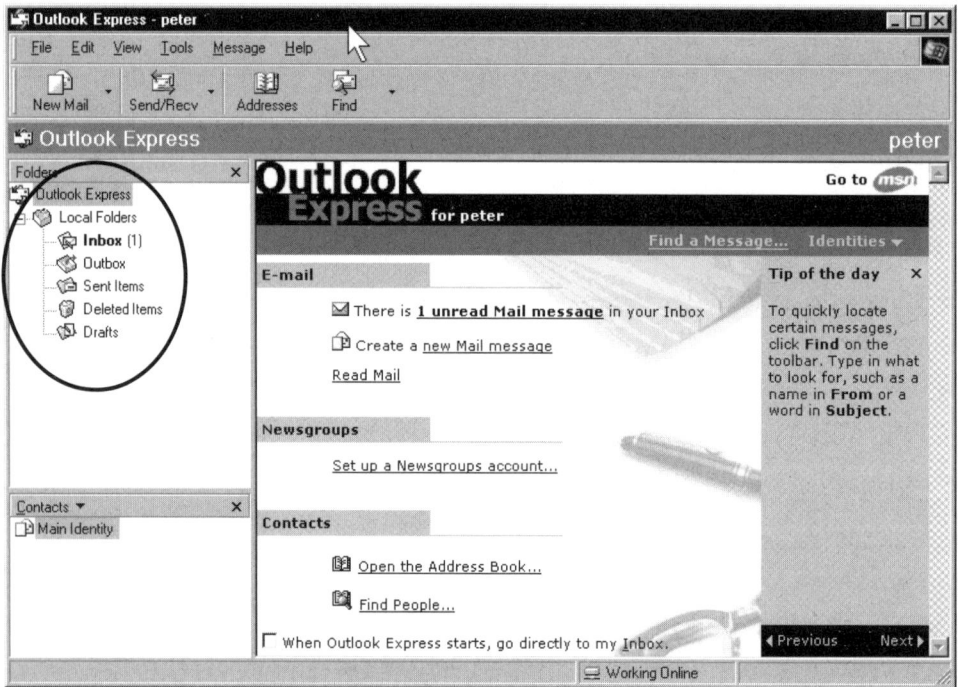

This is the main Outlook Express screen. You will see on the right-hand side of the screen that it tells you how many unread e-mails you have (in this case there is one message). It is important to understand what each

<u>folder</u> (the five items under the heading **Local Folders** on the left-hand side) mean:

❖ **Inbox** is the area where all e-mails that you receive are kept;

❖ **Outbox** is the area where all e-mails waiting to be sent are stored;

❖ **Sent Items** stores copies of all e-mails sent out — this is useful when you want to see if you actually sent an e-mail to someone or if you want to remind yourself what you said;

❖ **Deleted Items**: when you delete a message it is placed here, although to remove it completely from Outlook Express, you must also delete it from here;

❖ **Drafts**: if you are called away while writing an e-mail, you can save your message to finish it later; it is stored in this folder.

Checking for New Mail

To check if you have any new messages, click on the **Send and Receive** icon to retrieve new e-mail and to send any messages you have queued. By default, Outlook Express should automatically do a Send and Receive at start-up. It is also possible to go to the **Tools** menu and choose **Send All** or **Receive All**; this is useful if, for example, you want to send a message and are expecting an e-mail with a large attachment, but don't have the time to collect it at present. I tend to hit the **Send and Receive** button as it is just that bit quicker!

> *Tip!* *Outlook Express will automatically check for new messages when you connect to the Internet for the first time. Every time you wish to check for messages after this, you must click the **Send and Receive** button. By default, Outlook Express will try to check for new e-mail every 30 minutes.*

When you click on **Send and Receive**, a dialog box will pop up showing the progress of your new messages being received. When you receive new mail, it appears in your Inbox as illustrated below:

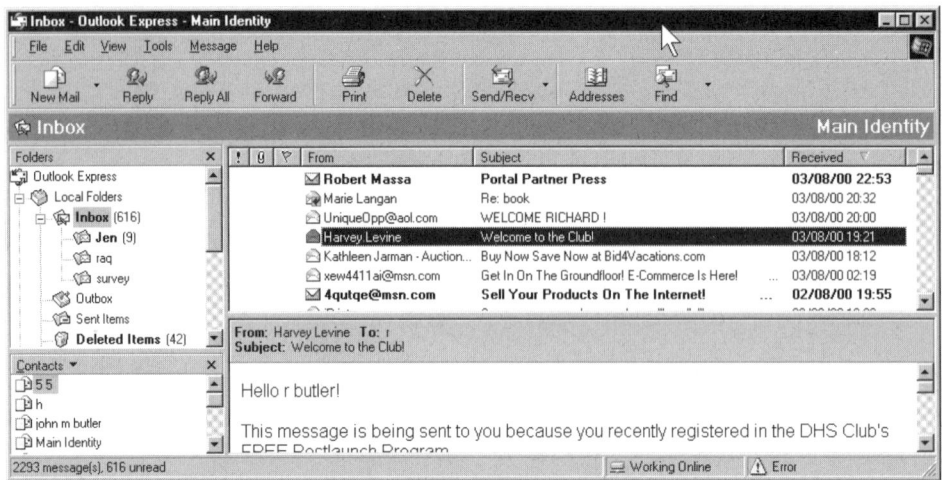

As you can see, I am told whom the e-mail is from and what the subject of the e-mail is. The message appears in the lower right-hand pane of the window. You can read the e-mail by clicking once on it and viewing it in this preview section, or you can double-click on it to open it in a new window. You will also see that the "inbox" heading is in bold and has a number beside it. This is the number of unread messages. If you look at the very bottom right-hand corner of the screen, in the section of your taskbar containing the clock, you will see that an envelope appears as illustrated below:

This indicates that you have a new message.

How often will Outlook Express check for new e-mail?

Outlook Express is configured by default (the standard settings) to check for new e-mail every 30 minutes, assuming you are online. Therefore if you e-mail someone and it appears they have taken half an hour to reply but you know they are online, this is because Outlook Express is only checking for e-mail every 30 minutes. You will find out later on how to change this setting. I usually have Outlook Express set up to check for e-mail every minute!

Creating a New Message

Before you receive any e-mails, chances are you may wish to send a message or messages, perhaps letting people know you are now connected to the Internet and giving them your e-mail address. Later, as you build up your correspondence, the simplest way to compose a new message is to click on **Reply to** (see later). However, for now, let's assume nobody has written to you yet. Sometimes you may find an e-mail address in an ad, or someone may give you his or her e-mail address. In this instance, you will have to create a new message.

> ***Warning!*** *It is extremely important to type in the e-mail address exactly as you were given it. E-mail addresses can **never** contain spaces. So* richard butler@tintecsystems.com *is not a valid e-mail address, but* richard.butler@tintecsystems.com *is, as is* richard_butler@tintecsystems.com. *Also, be careful of hyphens on e-mail and web addresses.*

Click on the **New Mail** icon in the toolbar (this is sometimes called **Compose Message** in some versions of Outlook Express). The following now appears:

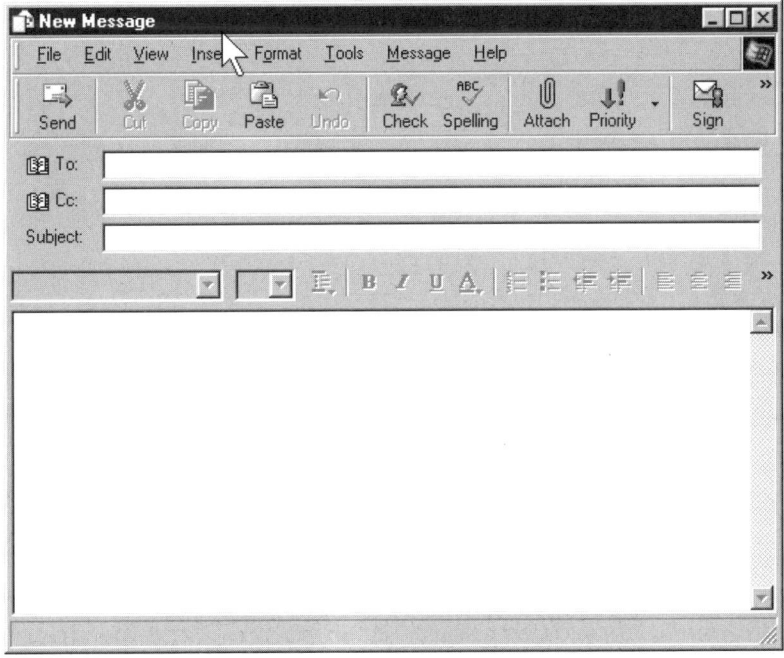

There are a number of areas in this window that we need to explain:

❖ **To**: this is where you type the e-mail address of the person who is to receive the e-mail. You must always ensure you type out their full e-mail address — e.g. *richard@tintecsystems.com* — and not just Richard. Later, we will see how you can create a shortcut by using <u>nicknames</u> and your address book, but for now, let's assume you must enter the full address. If you wanted to send the message to a number of people, you could keep entering e-mail addresses separated by a semicolon (;).

❖ **CC** allows you to send a copy of the message to another person. When you **CC** a message to someone, it means they are not the main recipients of the message, but that the message may be of interest to them. For example, a sales manager might send an e-mail to the marketing manager and copy it to the sales team — the main recipient of the message is the marketing manager, but the message may also be of interest to the sales team.

❖ **Subject**: this is where you type in the subject of the message. The subject is very important. It makes it easier for the receiver of the e-mail to see what your message is about rather than having to read the whole message; e-mail can then be divided into categories according to their importance. If you do not include a subject, you will get an error message before you can send it. If this happens you can click on **OK** to continue sending without a subject or **Cancel** to allow you to enter a subject.

Type in the body of your message in the space provided in the lower half of the window.

If you wish to spell-check your message, go to the **Tools** menu and choose the **Spelling** option (or press F7 on your keyboard).

Click **Send** to send the message. Note that, by default, Outlook Express sends out your message immediately, if you are connected to the Internet. You can, however, change the settings so that e-mail is only sent when you click on **Send and Receive**. If you want to make sure your message was sent, you can do one of two things:

❖ Click on the **Outbox** folder; if your message appears here, it means that you must click on the **Send and Receive** button in order to send it out.

❖ If you find your message is not in the **Outbox**, go to the **Sent Items** folder, click on it and check to see if it is here; if it was not in the **Outbox**, it is more than likely here.

Of course, if you are not working online, you will have to click on **Send and Receive**; this will pull up the **Dial-Up Connection** dialog box mentioned earlier.

What if your message is not in the Outbox or Sent Items? Where has it gone? What can often happen is that new users get confused between the **Send** command and the **Send and Receive** command. Users compose a message and, without saving it (clicking on **Send**), then click on **Send and Receive**; what has now happened is that the message has been minimised on the taskbar. So new users may think they have got the hang of sending e-mail but may soon discover that they have not! Always ensure that you first click the **Send** button on the window where you typed the e-mail.

Saving Money: Working Offline

If you read and reply to all your messages while connected to the Internet, you will be wasting money. Think about it: if it takes ten minutes to reply to an e-mail message and you have ten e-mail messages to reply to, it will take 1 hour and 40 minutes to reply to all messages. So, if possible, read and reply to all e-mail during off-peak hours.

Perhaps more significantly, there is an even better way to save money. You can compose all your e-mail replies while not connected to the Internet! Remember when we were starting Outlook Express earlier, by double-clicking on the Outlook Express icon. By default, you will probably see something similar to the following dialog box:

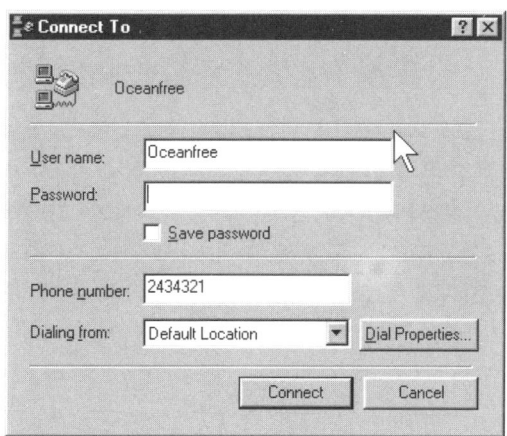

This is simply asking you to connect up to the Internet. Click on **Cancel,** as you do not wish to connect up to the Internet now. After a short time, you may receive an error message (depending on how your Internet connection is set up). If you see such a message, don't worry, you have done nothing wrong; simply click on Hide or on the X in the top right-hand corner of the dialog box. You are now working <u>offline</u>.

Compose a message as usual. Instead of clicking on **Send**, go to **File** and choose **Send Later**. (Again, if your e-mail is configured differently, clicking on **Send** will have essentially the same effect; your e-mails will only be sent when you click on **Send and Receive**.)

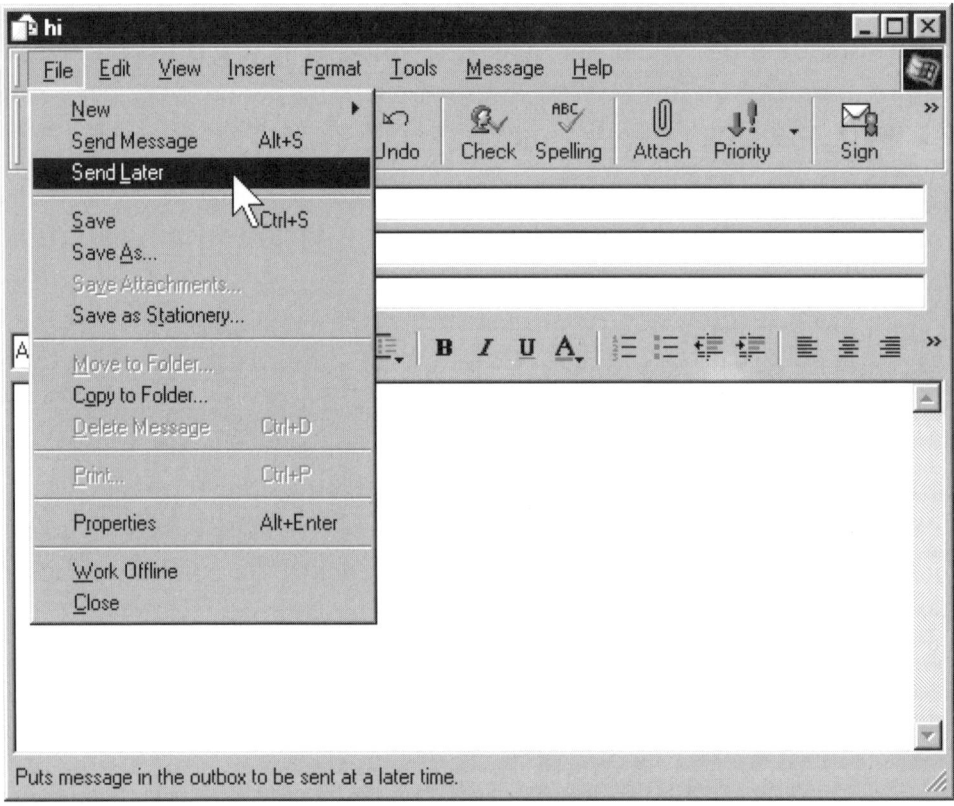

You will then see a dialog box saying that your message has been saved in your Outbox and will be sent the next time you choose the **Send and Receive** command. Remember that your Outbox allows you to store as many e-mails as you want until you are ready to send all of them in one go. You can now exit the application if you wish (click on the X in the top right-hand corner). The following will appear:

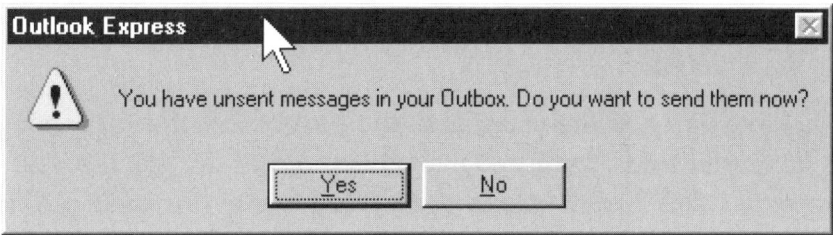

If you choose no, your e-mails will still be stored until the next time you choose the **Send and Receive** command.

The Save Command

Save allows you to save a draft message so that you can work on it later (the same way that you would save a word-processing document). This is ideal if you are typing out a really long e-mail and get called away. You can save it and continue later, without losing all your work. Save a message by going to **File** and choosing **Save**. A dialog box appears telling you the message has been saved in the **Drafts** folder. Click on **OK**, and on the X in the top right-hand corner of your message to close it. Notice how the **Drafts** folder is now in bold with a number beside it:

When you wish to open the message again to continue working on it, simply click on the **Drafts** folder. Double-click on the message. Your message reappears, ready for editing. You can then continue to type your message and send it as usual.

It is also possible, if your message has been sent to your Outbox, to recover it and change it as though it were a draft. You simply open your Outbox, double-click on your message, and when you have made your changes, click on **Send** again.

How do I know if my e-mail message has arrived?

There is no way of knowing as such if your e-mail has been *read*, but it is usually safe to assume that it has been *received*. If for some reason your e-mail has not being delivered, you will receive notification to tell you this next time you click on **Send and Receive**. The usual reason that the message cannot be delivered is if the address has been keyed in incorrectly. For example:

1. You have typed in the username (the part before the @) incorrectly. In this instance, you will receive a message to say that the user does not exist. This problem can occur very easily; for example, if you type *ricard@tintecsystems.com*, your message will be returned to you, as the user does not exist, or else you will receive an immediate error message.

2. You have typed in the domain (the part after the @) incorrectly. In this case, you will get a message to say the host (another name for the domain) does not exist. This can happen if you add or miss out a letter when typing the e-mail address; *richard@tintesystems.com* will return this error message. Sometimes if your e-mail cannot be sent it may stay in your outbox and you will see this error message forever! The secret is to go into your outbox and delete the offending message.

3. Case sensitivity: e-mail addresses should be regarded as case-sensitive; if you send e-mails to *RICHARD@tintecsystems.com*, *Richard@tintecsystems.com* or *richard@tintecsystems.com*, some of the e-mails may be returned, because the server will only recognise the third (correct) e-mail address. Anything before the @ symbol is case-sensitive, the domain name part (that part after the @ symbol) is not case-sensitive. Depending on the operating system your ISP uses, their e-mail server may be case-sensitive. Unix, an OS which is very popular with ISPs, is case-sensitive, therefore *Richard* and *richard* would be seen as two different users. The rule of thumb is to always type e-mail addresses exactly as given to you.

4. Underscores, hyphens, full stops: some addresses may contain any of the aforementioned characters; for example: *richard_butler*, *richard.butler* or *richard-butler*; always be careful of putting in the right character, as the difference between "_" and "-" can be vital! No Internet e-mail addresses will contain spaces, slashes, question marks, etc.

Warning! *Ensure that you always enter the person's username exactly as given. Look at the following e-mail addresses:*

Jon@tintecsystems.com

John@tintecsystems.com

Both of these are valid e-mail addresses, but if you misspell the username, your message will go to the wrong person. If somebody is giving you their e-mail address by telephone, ensure that they spell it out accurately; better still, ask them to e-mail it instead!

The majority of failed deliveries are a result of such incorrect addresses. It is also possible that the e-mail address you contact is no longer in operation (for example, your correspondent has changed ISP or, if their e-mail is work-based, they have moved to a different job). There are also other more technical reasons why your message is undeliverable. Depending on how busy the Internet is, you may receive a notification of failed delivery within minutes.

By default, if the receiver's ISP server is down, an attempt to deliver will be made for up to seven days. After this, your e-mail will be lost in cyberspace.

Replying to an E-mail Message

If someone has e-mailed you, you may wish to reply to them. To do this, you simply click on the **Reply** icon. The following appears:

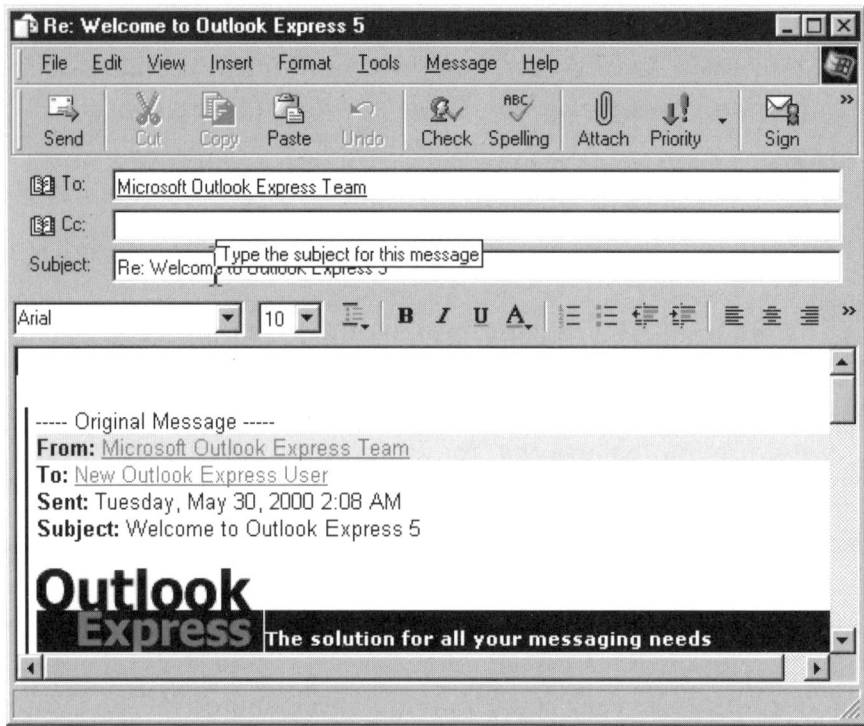

As you can see, the person's e-mail address is already filled in, as is the subject line, which you can change if you wish.

Your e-mail package will automatically quote the original message, unless you change the settings to hide the original (see Chapter 5 on changing settings).

You will notice that sometimes Outlook Express will simply display the person's name instead of their e-mail address, such as Richard Butler rather than *richard@tintecsystems.com*. Since you have hit the Reply button, it knows who to send the message back to. Whether it displays the name or e-mail address of the person will depend on how the other user set up their e-mail package.

Type your message out in the bottom half of the window as usual. When you are ready to send your message, simply click on the **Send** button, followed by **Send and Receive**, if your settings require it. Your message will be sent to the person, assuming you are connected to the Internet at this time.

Reply to All

Clicking on **Reply** only replies to the main recipient of the message; **Reply to All** will send your message to all recipients of the original message. Be very careful of using this; you don't want to send a reply to a friend, criticising somebody else, only to find that your message has also been sent to that other individual!

Forwarding a Message

Sometimes you will receive a message that you would like to send on to a third party. There are three ways of doing this:

1. Retype the whole message;

2. Highlight the whole message and copy-and-paste it into a new document;

3. Simply click on the **Forward** icon.

Option three is the easiest. By clicking on the Forward icon, the message is automatically copied into a new message. The following appears:

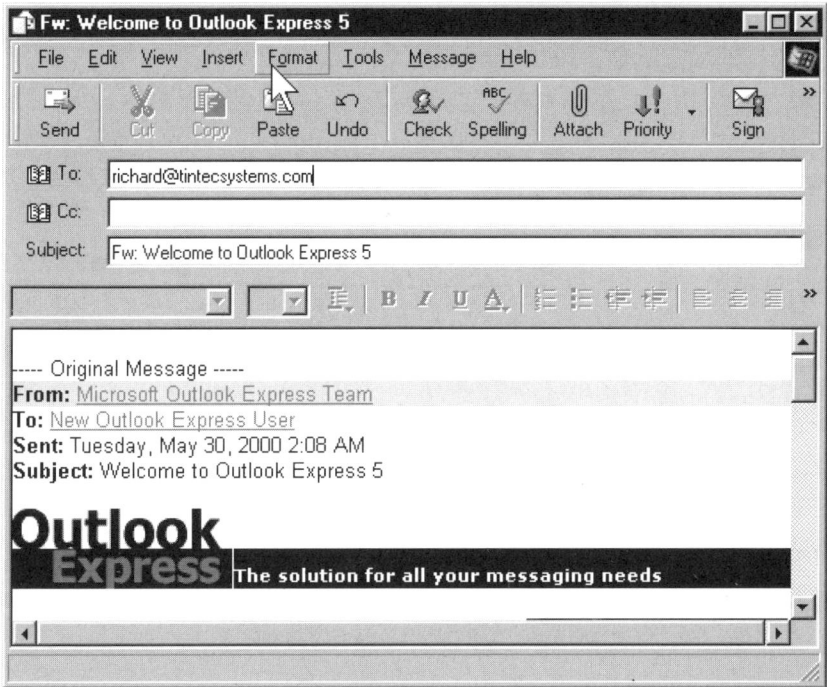

Type in the person's e-mail address and continue as usual. Notice that the subject is automatically filled in with: "Fw: Funny story" ("Funny story" is the subject of the original message). This indicates that the message is a forwarded message. You can change this subject heading if you wish.

Message Management

This section outlines the important feature of Outlook Express that allows you to categorise and file away your messages correctly by creating <u>folders</u> and allowing you to move messages from one folder to another. A folder is an area that is used to store related items, in this case related e-mails.

Another important aspect of message management is deleting messages that are no longer needed. Messages will take up space on your hard drive and it is best if you delete unwanted messages on a regular basis.

Viewing Criteria

By default, e-mails are sorted by the date they were received (newest first, oldest last), but you may wish to sort them by name of who sent them, subject, whether they have attachments, etc. Look again at the right-hand pane of the Inbox:

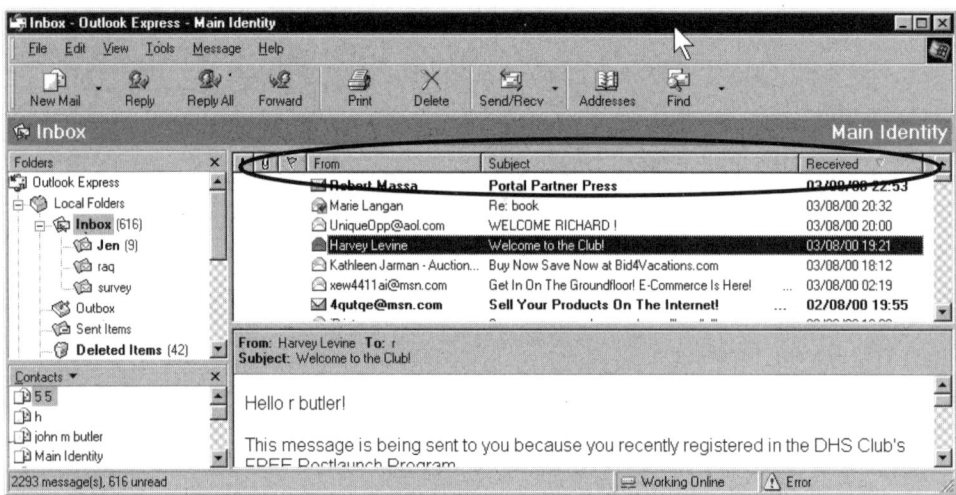

By clicking on any of the headings above (e.g. **From, Subject, Received**), you can sort your messages according to that criterion. An example of how this can be useful will be seen shortly.

Creating New Folders

Folders are an easy way of storing your e-mails and putting all related e-mails into one area. Click on the **Local Folders** icon. Go to the **File** menu. Choose **New**. From the sub-menu, choose **Folder**. The following appears:

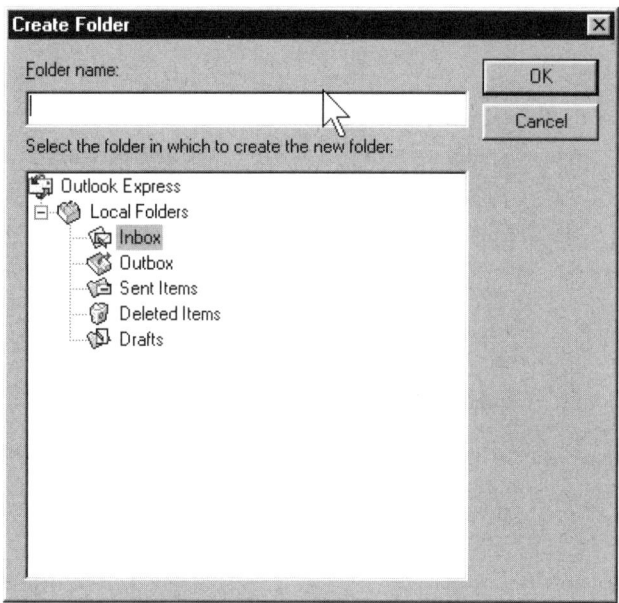

Type in a name for this new folder, e.g. "important". When you click on OK, you will see the following:

Notice that the folder "important" has been created as a <u>sub-folder</u> of the Inbox. Sometimes it might be better to create your folder as a sub-folder of the Local Folders. This makes it easier to see all of your folders. To do this, create your folder as usual by going to **File**, **New**, **Folder**. When the initial screen appears, click on **Local Folders** and continue as usual. Your new folder will appear as a sub-folder of the Local Folders rather than the Inbox.

To delete a folder, simply click on it and press **Delete**. You will be asked to confirm the deletion; click yes to delete the folder. Of course, you must make sure you have no important messages in this folder before you delete it!

Transferring Messages into a Folder

Right-click on the folder. From the menu that appears, choose the **Move to Folder** option. The following appears:

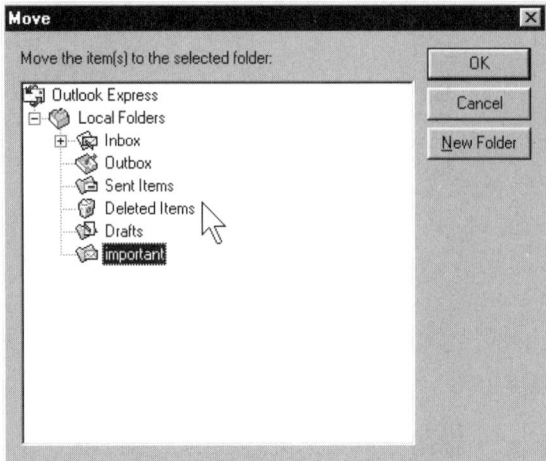

Click on the folder you wish to move the message to. Click on **OK**. The message is now moved. You can also move messages by <u>dragging and dropping</u> them into the new folder. You can also make a copy of a message in your new folder without deleting it from the old one; simply follow the above instructions, but instead of clicking on Move to Folder, click on **Copy to Folder**.

Also, you can select a number of messages and move them to a different folder. Suppose, for example, that you wanted to move all messages from a particular person to a different folder. In your Inbox, click on the **From** tab in the top right-hand window. All of your e-mails are now listed alphabetically according to who sent them to you. Find the person whose messages you want to move, and select them using your mouse and **Shift** key. Then you can move them in any of the ways described above.

Deleting a Message

As you use e-mail more and more, you will receive messages from new people or replies from your <u>contacts</u>. Your Inbox will become full of messages, so it is a good idea to ensure that you delete messages you no longer want from your Inbox. To delete a message, simply click on the message and press **Delete**; it is moved to a folder called **Deleted Items**. As you will notice, the number of items in each folder is displayed beside the folder's name.

You should also remember that every time you send out a message, a copy of it is placed in the **Sent Items** folder. Ensure that you also delete what is in this folder on a regular basis; most people forget that there are a lot of messages stored there, taking up space.

> 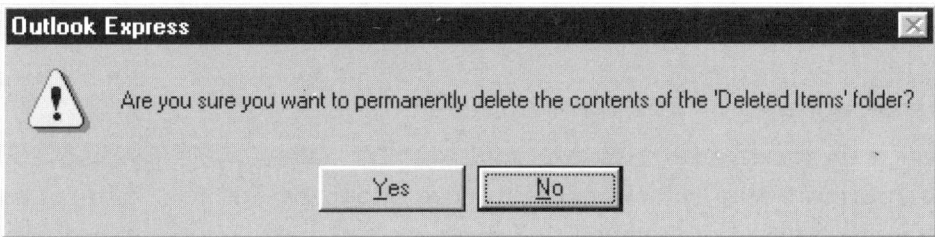 ***Warning!*** *Although you have moved the message to Deleted Items, it is still readable; therefore if you accidentally deleted it, it is still recoverable. If you want to ensure that nobody can access your deleted messages, you must delete them completely.*

In order to delete the entire contents of the Deleted Items folder, simply right click on it and choose the **Empty "Deleted Items" Folder** option. The following appears:

Outlook Express

⚠ Are you sure you want to permanently delete the contents of the 'Deleted Items' folder?

[Yes] [No]

Choose Yes.

Web-based E-mail

If you travel a lot, you may be interested in getting a web-based e-mail account. Web-based e-mail allows you to set up an e-mail account with a company, usually for free, that can be accessed via their website.

Web-based e-mail works on exactly the same principles as normal e-mail, except that all messages are stored and accessed via the web rather than through a standard e-mail package. When you wish to read, reply to and compose e-mails, you log on to their website and then enter your username and password. You can then receive and send e-mail via this service. You don't need a separate e-mail package to do this; everything is stored and processed from the website.

Advantages of Web-based E-mail

Web-based e-mail is very handy because, no matter what computer you sit at, in any country in the world, you can access it without having to change any settings or worry about such technical matters. Simply go into a cyber café and you are away! Actually, it is now very common to see people in shopping centres checking their e-mail from the Internet kiosks that are popping up all over the place.

Web-based e-mail accounts allow you to do everything that a normal e-mail package allows, including most of the features described above. Web-based e-mail is just as private as an ordinary e-mail account, if not more so; you do not have to worry about someone reading your e-mail, since none of your e-mail is stored on the local computer. It is stored on servers in another country. People can only access your account if they have your username and password. Of course, there is always the possibility of hackers gaining access to your account (see Chapter 12).

Another advantage of these accounts is that they are free; of course, since they are accessed via the web, you will be paying phone charges while reading and replying to e-mails!

Disadvantages of Web-based E-mail

The main disadvantage is that you must be online while reading and composing e-mail, which makes it more expensive for you. There is no offline facility as such with these accounts, although you could type out the text of your messages beforehand in your word-processing package, and copy-and-paste it into the area where you would write out the main body of your message. This can be time-consuming and tedious, though!

Many companies will deny their employees access to these web-based e-mail accounts. With normal e-mail, the company can scan every message that leaves through the e-mail server, but they cannot do this when you are using web-based e-mail. Therefore, you could in theory send out confidential information. For this reason, they will deny access to any site offering web-based e-mail.

How do these services make money?

These services make money purely through advertising. Every time you log on, an ad will be displayed. Some services have rotating ads that change every couple of seconds. The hope is that an ad will capture your attention and you will click on it. Every time a message is sent out from the service, a marketing ad is placed at the bottom, simply informing others that they can receive a free e-mail account from this service.

Hotmail

Hotmail is probably the best-known web-based e-mail service. It has been around for at least four or five years. It became so popular that Microsoft bought it over and now run it. Microsoft thus gained a fully recognised brand name, and also a huge customer base about which they had a lot of information.

When you set up one of these accounts, you are asked certain demographic and lifestyle questions. Microsoft now has access to all this information. Although many of the companies say that they respect your privacy, there have been incidents where information was sold on to other companies (one example is a company called Geocities). In recent times, companies have become more aware that users are more conscious of online privacy, so most companies have a privacy statement.

Unfortunately so many websites are now either under the control of or part of huge companies that when they say your information will only be used by their company or subsidiaries, this means a lot of other companies! The other problem is: under what country's law is your data protected? What if the company is incorporated in a foreign country with lax data protection laws?

Hotmail recently hit the news when the service was "hacked", or broken into. Hackers managed to find a backdoor into the system, which allowed them access to anyone's e-mail account. This problem was soon sorted out but was quite embarrassing for Hotmail/Microsoft. These privacy and security issues are discussed in Chapter 12.

There are a few other problems with Hotmail. Firstly, it can be quite slow when you are trying to access it (remember, the longer it takes, the more money it costs you). Secondly, Hotmail is the target of junk e-mailers who have programs that will send out unsolicited e-mails to numerous Hotmail accounts. This means that when you log onto your account, you may have ten new messages, nine of which may be junk e-mail! Essentially, all of the following web-based e-mail services offer the same features:

❖ *www.howsitgoing.com*

❖ *mail.yahoo.com*

❖ *mail.lycos.com*

❖ *www.btinternet.com*

❖ *www.ireland.com*

These are some of the more popular web-based e-mail services, but there are numerous others.

Why should you get a web-based e-mail account?

The main reason is for privacy. When you sign up for a free service on the Internet, or download some software, you will often be asked for your e-mail address. The company may then begin to send you unwanted e-mails, or even worse they may sell your address to other companies who will then send you unwanted e-mails.

When you have a free web-based e-mail account, all these unwanted e-mails will be collected by the web-based account, thus keeping your home or business account free of such junk mail.

When using any of these free services, e-mails are not stored on your local computer; thus, no one can read your received or sent e-mails. If you share a computer, it is more private to use a web-based e-mail account. However, as mentioned above, if hackers can get into the main server, they have access to a huge database of e-mail accounts!

You may wish to use chat rooms and not want to give out your real e-mail to strangers; after all, you do not know who you may meet in chat rooms, mainly because they could begin "cyberstalking" you. At least if you have given them a Hotmail e-mail address, you can simply stop using that account and set up a new account under a different name at no extra cost. Remember, people can find out a lot about you by reading your e-mail address. An address such as *richard@indigo.ie* immediately tells people my name and what country my e-mail address is held in. Immediately, people can tell I am based in Ireland; however, if they see *richard@hotmail.com*, they have no idea where I am from.

Warning! *One problem is that you cannot identify the source of e-mails, unless they are from a known contact. This is a worry for parents and educators especially; it is advisable to monitor all e-mails, both incoming and outgoing, to ensure that there is no undesirable information being passed.*

Chapter 5

Advanced E-mail Techniques

Getting More from E-mail

The last chapter introduced the basic concepts of e-mail. At this point you should be able to:

- ❖ Receive e-mail
- ❖ Compose e-mail
- ❖ Reply to and Forward e-mail
- ❖ Manage your e-mail.

You should also be familiar with the following:

- ❖ Inbox
- ❖ Outbox
- ❖ Deleted Items
- ❖ Drafts Folder.

This chapter will help you gain a more advanced understanding of e-mail that will allow you work more efficiently. By the end of this chapter, you should be familiar with the following functions of e-mail:

- ❖ Attachments
- ❖ Address books
- ❖ Distribution lists
- ❖ Filters
- ❖ Changing priority settings

❖ Setting signatures

❖ Setting up and managing identities

❖ E-mail discussion lists and mailing lists.

Attaching Documents to E-mail

All modern e-mail packages on the market allow you to attach documents from different applications or programs to your e-mail. Instead of having to send a floppy disk to someone, you can send a whole file, formatting and all, to the person via e-mail. This saves time and money. There are a number of important considerations when using these attachments:

❖ Recently, the most notable comment about attachments that has been made is: don't open them! This is largely because there are many computer viruses that can be spread via attachments. Some of these viruses can be extremely dangerous for your computer system; viruses are discussed in more detail in Chapter 12, but this chapter looks briefly at what you can do to avoid downloading viruses with attachments.

❖ You should ensure that the person receiving the attachment has the same version of the application that you are using. For example, if you are using Word 97 and the receiver of the e-mail is using Word 6, they will not be able to open the attachment. Many programs have converters that can covert from one version, or even from one program, to another, but be warned: some or all of the formatting of the document may be lost.

❖ If your attachments are spreadsheets, Word documents, etc., they will usually not be too large; however, if you are sending pictures, animations or, say, a large training manual via e-mail, be warned that it may take a very long time to send. Anything over about 500KB should not be sent via e-mail. The reasons for this are:

1. If you are sending e-mail from work it can slow down the network;

2. If you are sending from work and you have a dedicated connection to the Internet, it does not cost you anything if it takes ten minutes to send. However, if the receiver of the e-mail does not

have a dedicated connection, ten minutes can be quite a long time to remain connected during business hours. Also, if they have to wait ten minutes to receive an e-mail of your holiday snaps, they may not be impressed!! What may be slightly inconvenient for you may be highly aggravating for the person you are sending it to — especially if they are not expecting it!

With these factors in mind, let's look at how to attach a file to an e-mail message. Once again, I will be looking at Outlook Express here, but other packages follow similar rules.

1. Compose a new message as usual (see Chapter 4). Notice the icon on the second toolbar that looks like a paper clip. This is the icon for adding attachments. Click on this icon. The following appears:

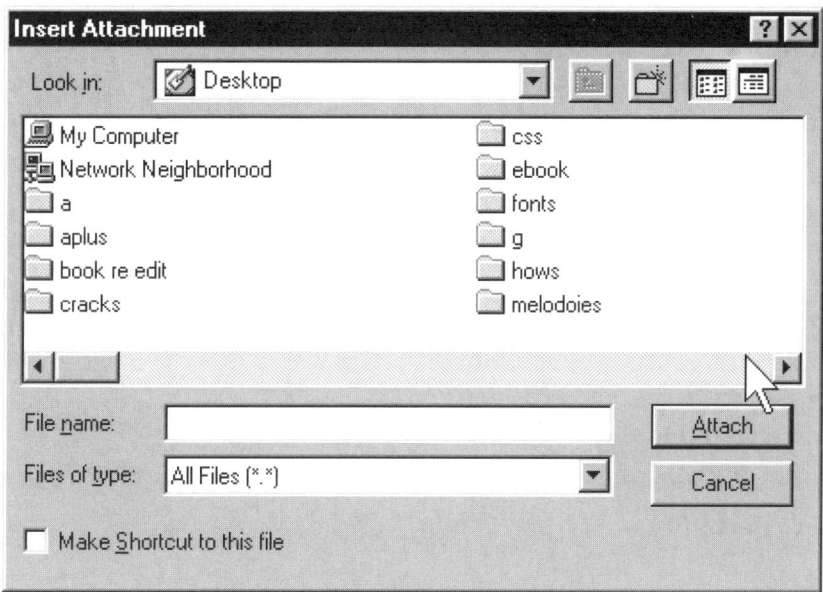

2. Locate the file that you wish to attach. Click on it and press **Attach**.

3. Now when you return to your e-mail message, you will see the following:

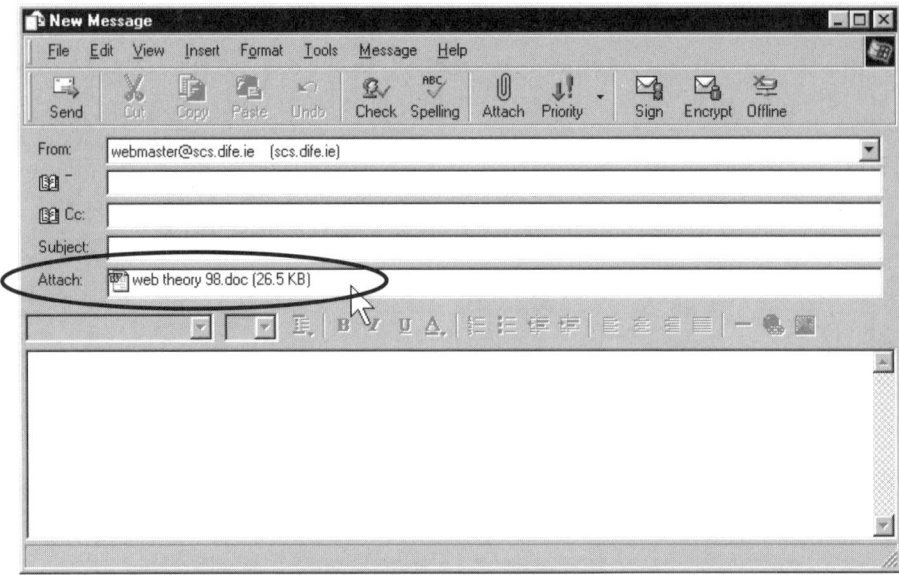

4. As you can see, a new item has appeared beneath the **Subject** area, showing there is an attachment. Send your e-mail in the normal way.

It is also possible to attach a file to an e-mail by dragging-and-dropping the file from, say, Windows Explorer into the body of the text. When sending a file with an attachment you may find that the e-mail takes longer to send — this is normal. Consider sending attachments during off-peak hours or at weekends when call charges are slightly cheaper.

How do I know when I receive an attachment?

When you receive an attachment, the message will have a paper clip beside it in your Inbox.

How do I access an attachment when I receive one?

Simple! Double-click on the message in the top right-hand pane, and you will see the attachment or attachments appear as icons in the lower pane of your message's window.

Problems with Attachments

Before we continue, let's look more closely at some of the problems that can occur with attachments — particularly the scourge of viruses.

Viruses can be spread simply by opening the program or file where they are "hidden". Before you panic, let's see how this happens. When someone sends you an attachment, it is usually one of three things:

❖ A picture

❖ A file, such as a word processing or spreadsheet file

❖ A program.

The last two are the ones that can cause problems. Microsoft Word and other programs have the facility to create <u>macros</u>, a (usually harmless) way of simplifying tasks in a document. Some of these macros can, however, be malicious. Simply be opening an infected Word document, you can infect your system with this macro virus.

The effects of these macro viruses are varied; some of them are relatively harmless, more a nuisance than anything else. However, the more vicious viruses can do anything from replicating themselves by e-mailing themselves to your entire address book, to deleting your entire hard drive!

In general, most of the attachments you will have to deal with will be files. Some people send programs via attachments; these are usually small funny programs that, when run, do something silly. One such program which was distributed by e-mail, caused a flock of "sheep" to walk around on your desktop until you closed it off — fun but completely useless!

The problem is that some of these programs may be accidentally or purposely infected with a virus. As soon as you run the program, the virus will infect your computer.

The bottom line with attachments is: Never open them unless you are sure of what they are. Even then, run a virus check on them before opening them. We will deal in greater detail with viruses and virus checkers in Chapter 12.

Myth: By opening an e-mail, your computer can become infected with a virus. At the time of writing, viruses can only infect your computer when you open the attachment. Currently (mid-2000), there are no known viruses that can infect simply by opening an e-mail.

The other problem with attachments, mentioned above, is that you may not have the right program or version to open them; it may be possible, if it is a small program, to download it from the Internet, but generally, the best thing to do is, if possible, to get the sender to re-send it to you in a different program or version.

So, assuming you are now happy that your attachment is not infected and that you have the appropriate program to open it, let's continue. When you double-click on the attachment, you will be given the choice to either open the attachment or save it to disk. Under no circumstances should you open an attachment directly! Always save it to disk. Save it in the appropriate folder on your hard disk. You can then open it as you would any file, after running a virus checker on it.

Using Address Books

Your address book allows you to store frequently used e-mail addresses. It also simplifies the process of sending an e-mail. There are two ways of inserting someone's address into your address book from within Outlook Express.

When Replying to E-mail

1. Click on the **Reply to Author** button as usual.

2. Right-click in the **To** area. Under the menu that appears, click on the **Add to Address Book** option. The following appears:

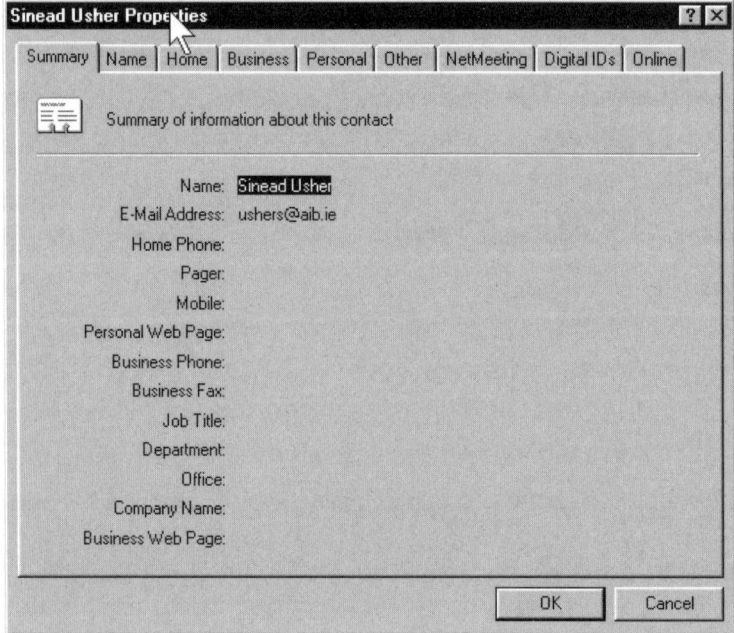

3. Click on the **Name** tab. The following will appear:

4. As you can see, the person's first and last name will automatically be entered. Add a <u>nickname</u>.

> *When you set up an entry in your address book, you can assign each person a **nickname**, which makes addressing easier. The next time you wish to send me an e-mail, instead of typing richard@tintecsytems.com, you can assign the nickname "Trainer" and type this into the **To:** area of the e-mail. This; from now on, if you want to e-mail me, simply type in my nickname.*

5. Add any other relevant details, such as company name, phone number, etc., at this point. Click on **OK**.

Setting up a New Entry

To set up a new entry (use this option if you have not received an e-mail from this person):

1. Go to the **Tools** menu and choose the **Address Book** option (or click on the word **Addresses** on the toolbar). The following appears:

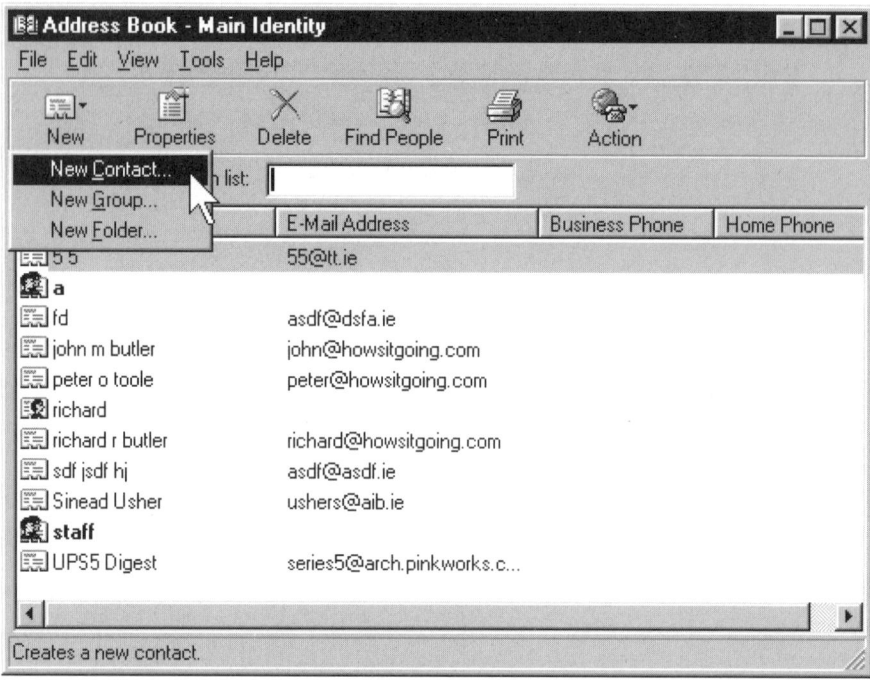

2. Click on **New** and select **New Contact**.

3. The same dialog box as before appears. Fill in all the relevant fields.

Using Distribution Lists

A <u>distribution list</u> is a special group in your address book that contains a group of related e-mail addresses. For example, if you want to send the same e-mail to 15 people, instead of retyping or copying and pasting the e-mail into 15 new e-mails, you can set up a distribution list — you send one e-mail and everyone receives it!

What is Spamming?

<u>Spamming</u> is a term used on the Internet to describe the activities of some direct marketers and individuals who send unsolicited bulk e-mail to people. I categorise the two types of unsolicited e-mail as follows:

❖ **Commercial Unsolicited E-mail** (CUE) is where a company sends you an e-mail trying to sell their product. The e-mail is sent to thousands of people in a matter of minutes using programs called bulk e-mailers.

❖ **Personal Unsolicited E-mail** (PUE) is where a person sends an unsolicited personal e-mail such as a chain letter and asks you to pass it on to a certain number of people. Usually you are promised love, money or happiness, or else you are told of a person who is dying that wishes to be remembered on the Internet through e-mail; most of these are hoaxes!

Why is Spamming Bad?

First of all it is junk e-mail; like junk mail that you receive in the post, it is a nuisance to have to filter through it. Secondly, if a company or organisation has 500 employees and each employee receives two junk e-mails a day, this leads to excessive waste of resources of the company's server/network.

How Can I Stop Spammers?

There are two ways to stop spammers:

1. Report them to your ISP;

2. Set up filters, which are dealt with in a later section.

Is a Distribution List Spam E-mail?

Although a distribution list is used for sending the same e-mail to a number of people, if it is used within context it is not considered bulk e-mail or spam. If a company sends out e-mail to everyone on its distribution list (such as a list of employees), this is fine; but if you have numerous distribution lists for sending out junk e-mail, this would be spamming!

Creating the Distribution List

In order to create a distribution list, you should already have a list of contacts in your address book; if you don't, you can create them as you go.

1. Go to the **Tools** menu. Choose the **Address Book** option as before.

2. Clicking on the **New Group** option under the **New** icon brings up the following dialog box:

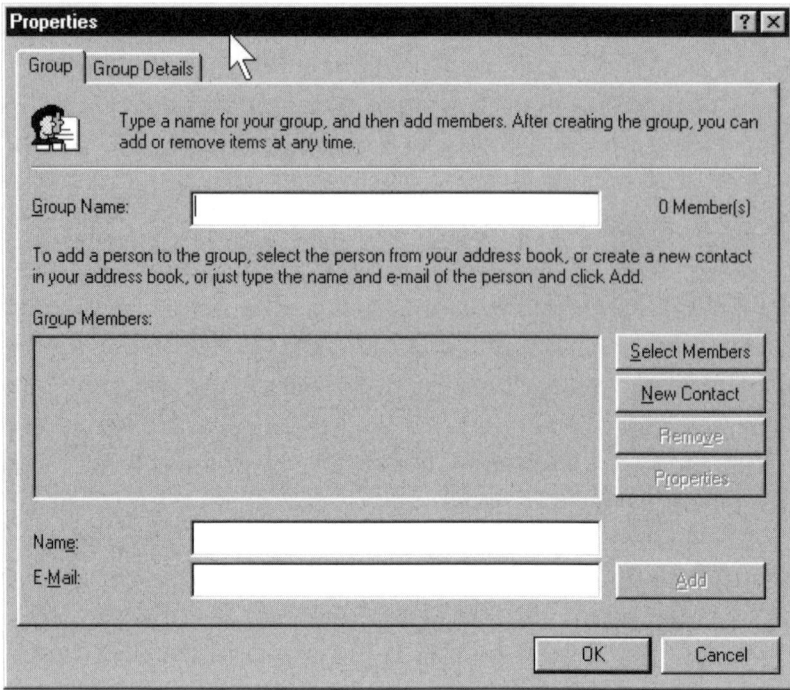

3. Type a name for the new group. In this case we will call it **Staff**.

4. If you already have the people's e-mail addresses in your address book, click on **Select Members**. The following now appears:

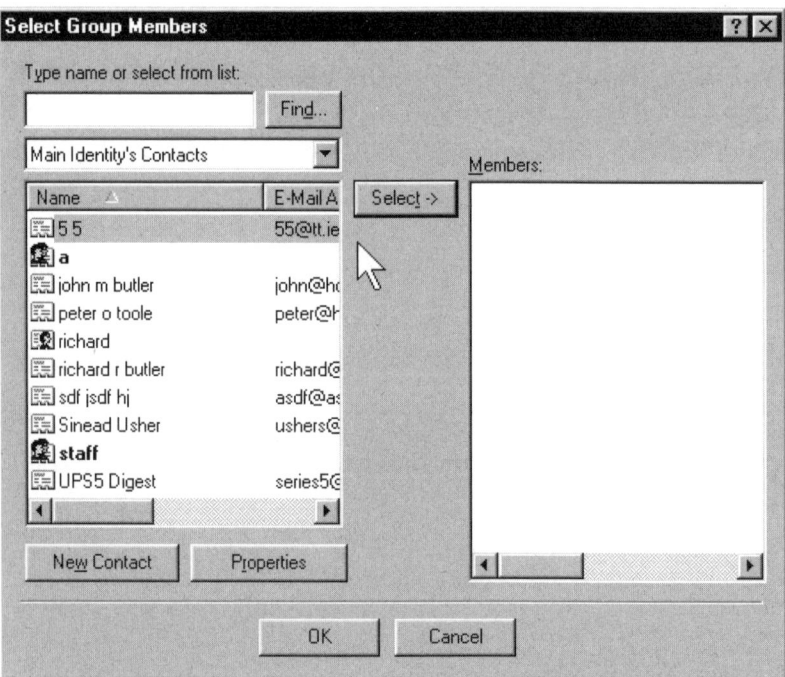

5. As you can see, I have a number of contacts in my address book. Click on each contact on the left-hand side and click on **Select**. Their names will appear on the right-hand side of the window.

>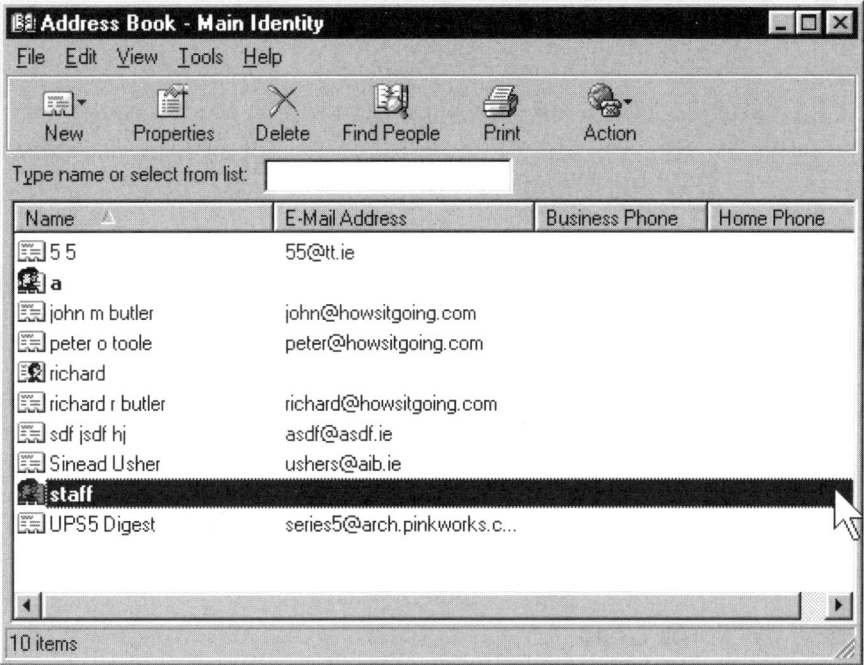
> *Tip!* To select a number of contacts in one go, do one of the following. If they are sequential on the list, hold down the Shift key and click each contact with the mouse. If you want to select the first, fifth and tenth contact, click on the first contact, then hold down the Control key (Ctrl) and click on the fifth and tenth contact.

6. Click on **OK** when finished. You will see a list of all the members of your new distribution list or group called "Staff". Click **OK** and your Address Book reappears as below:

7. You will notice that the group you created is in bold type to indicate it is a group and also it has a picture of two people beside it instead of the normal icon. Close your address book by clicking on the **X** on the top right-hand side of the screen or by going to **File** and **Close**.

Using your Distribution List

Having created the distribution list, you will now want to use it.

1. Create a new message in the normal way.

2. Now instead of typing in an e-mail address, simply type in the distribution list name, such as "Staff". The program will recognise this as a distribution list and enter all the correct e-mail addresses. You then send the e-mail in the normal way.

If you type in the wrong name, it will tell you that the contact is not a valid name and is not entered in your address book.

Creating Filters

Filters allow you to automatically disregard certain messages, such as spam or CUE, as described in the previous section. Filters work by checking each message for criteria or rules that you specify and then taking an action that you have specified.

You can set up a filter that will check the subject line of each message; for example, if the subject line contains the word "diet", you can tell Outlook Express to send it to a folder of your choice for checking at a later date. Alternatively, you could get it sent automatically to the **Deleted Items** folder.

 ***Warning!*** *Be careful when setting filters, as Outlook Express will always act upon the rules you set; you may accidentally delete important e-mail!*

Setting up a Filter

1. Go to the **Tools** menu.

2. Choose **Message Rules**; from the sub-menu that appears, choose **Mail**. The following appears:

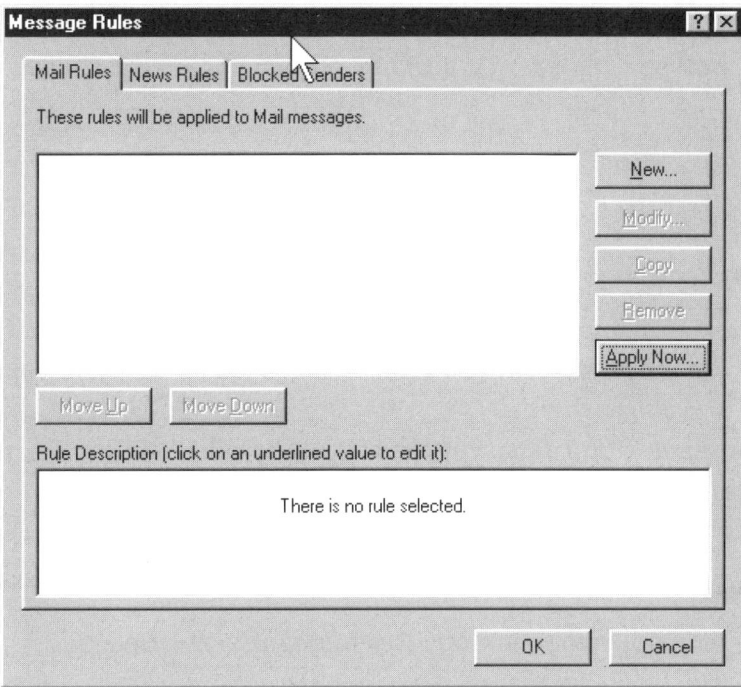

3. If you have any filters set up, this screen will show them; your screen will show no filters set up. Click on the **New** button. The next screen allows you to define your filter:

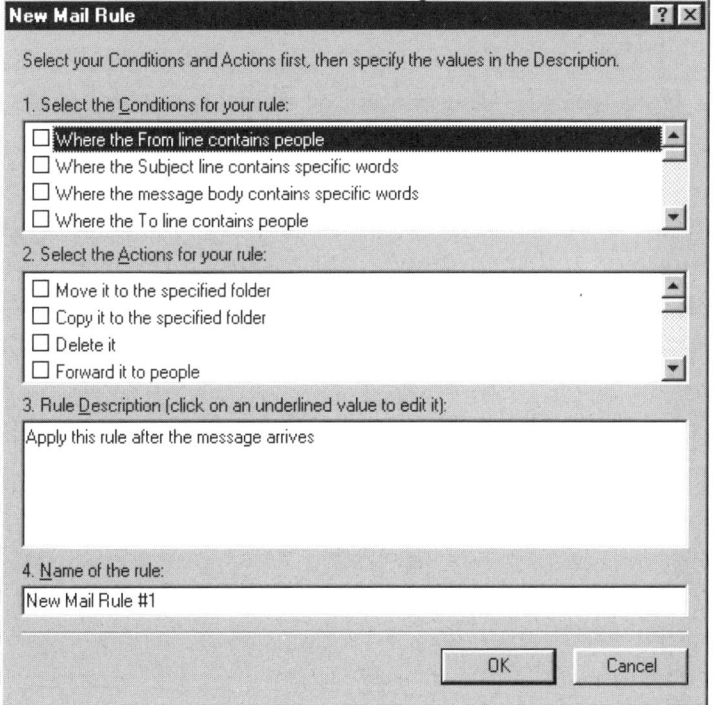

The first thing to decide is how you want to filter the message. You can filter the message based on a number of criteria, the most important being:

❖ **To**:   who the message is to;

❖ **CC**:   who the message is carbon copied to;

❖ **From**:   who the message is from;

❖ **Subject**:   what the subject of the message is; here you can type in a keyword that you wish to use, such as the word "spam".

Once you have done this, you must specify what action the program takes when it receives such a message. The second part of the screen above allows you to do this. You can:

❖ **Move to**: Moves the message to a folder you decide.

❖ **Copy to**: Copies the message to a folder you decide.

❖ **Forward to**: Forwards the message on to another e-mail address.

❖ **Reply with**: Allows you to send a specific message back to the person.

❖ **Do not download from the server**: Leaves the message on your ISP's computer.

❖ **Delete from server**: Automatically deletes the message from the server.

The last two options may only work with certain ISPs. Decide the criteria for each message and then decide the action to be taken. Experiment with each of the options to see exactly how they work, but be careful not to apply the rule unless you want it to be saved on your computer

Changing Priority Settings of Messages

When you send out a message in Outlook Express, it has no <u>priority</u>, i.e. it is treated as a routine message, but it is possible to increase the priority of a message to urgent — much like you would write "Urgent" on a fax or letter.

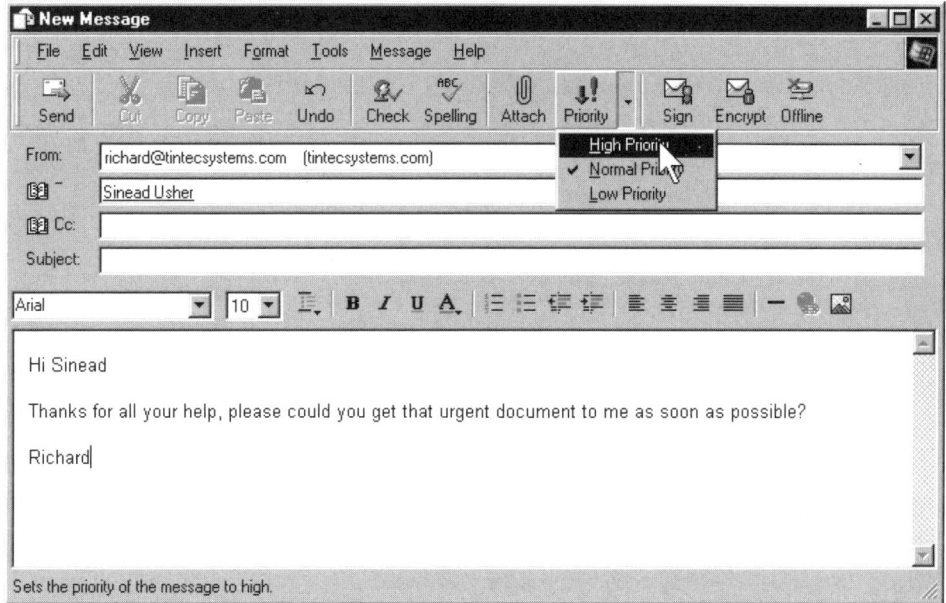

As you can see the priority of the message has now been set to **High**. When the user receives this message they will see a little exclamation mark beside the message. This can be useful if you need to make sure that the person sees your message; sometimes the subject line is not enough to catch their attention. Don't use a high priority for every message or the usefulness of this tool will be lost!

Customising Outlook Express

General Options

Now that you are feeling more confident with Outlook Express, let's take a look at customising it so that it works the way you want. Go to the **Tools** menu. Choose **Options**. The following dialog box appears:

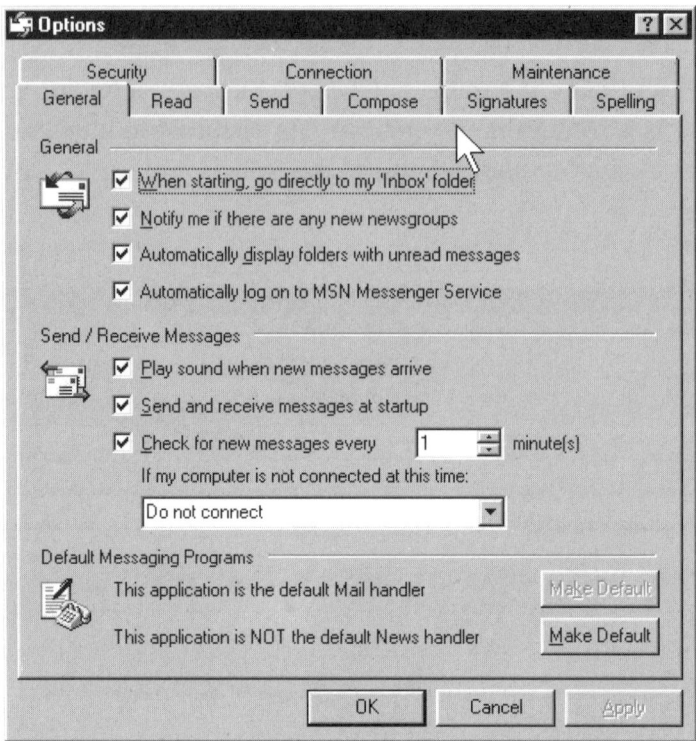

There are a number of interesting options here. The first option will automatically display your Inbox when you start up Outlook Express, rather than the screen you would have seen.

For now, we will ignore the second option, as we have yet to discuss Newsgroups. The third option will notify you when you receive new messages, which can be very handy if you are going to be connected to the Internet for a while, as you will gain instant notification when a message arrives in your Inbox. The last option from that set deals with an application called MSN Messenger, which we will deal with in a later chapter.

The next section on this tab concerns **Sending and Receiving**. If you have a sound card, you will hear a little sound every time a new message is received. Remember, you also see a little envelope on the system tray, so this gives you an aural indication as well!

When you start up Outlook Express, it will automatically **Send and Receive** any new e-mail. By default Outlook Express only checks for new messages every 30 minutes; if you are going to be online for a while, it may be a good idea to reduce this time, so that when you get a new message it is instantly delivered to you. When it checks every 30 minutes, this means that if you send an e-mail and get a reply within 5 minutes, you will not see it for another 25 minutes because Outlook Express will not be checking the server. As you can see, I have my time set to 1 minute — this ensures that I can get my new messages almost as soon as they are sent!

The next option allows you to define if your computer is not connected when the computer wishes to do a send or receive. The options are as follows:

❖ **Do not connect**: this will not try to dial up the Internet.

❖ **Connect only when not working offline**: if you are working online, then it will attempt to connect to your mail server.

❖ **Connect even when working offline**: even if you are offline, it should try to connect.

This can cause problems; for example, I have my e-mail set to check every 1 minute. If I choose the last option and I am working offline, Outlook Express will attempt to dial up the Internet every minute, which will get very frustrating; you may decide therefore to choose the second option as the best.

The next tab, **Read**, holds little of interest for us at the moment. Click on the **Send** tab:

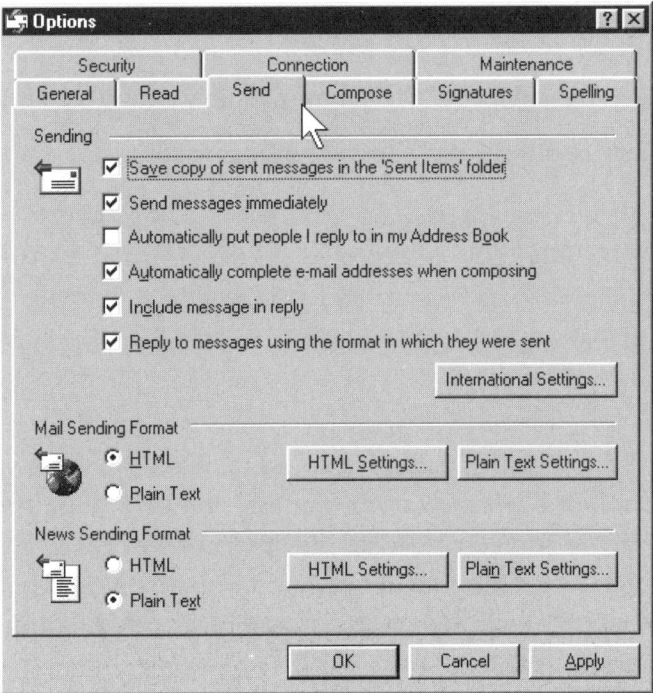

This screen is of particular interest. As you can see, every time you send an e-mail message, it is copied to your Sent Items. One problem with this is that if you send out a lot of messages per day, the Sent Items folder can get very large. But it is a good idea to keep this option selected, as you can always make sure that you sent a message; if someone says they did not receive it, you have a copy saved!

The next option, **Send message immediately**, is good to have ticked if you are working online a lot of the time, as your messages go out as soon as you choose **Send and Receive**. If you expect to work offline a lot of the time, uncheck this option; your messages will automatically be placed in your Outbox waiting until you connect to the net — this is like choosing **File**, **Send Later**.

If you have the third option ticked, anyone you reply to will automatically be placed in your e-mail address book; this can be a good time-saving option. The next option can be either annoying or helpful, depending on your preferences; if this option is checked, Outlook Express will automatically fill in the user's address as you type it. This function is similar to a function you will learn about in Internet Explorer called auto-complete. The second last option will allow you to specify whether you want the original e-mail message to be quoted or not. It most cases it is good to have the original message quoted, because it allows the sender and receiver to follow the conversation. Since e-mail is informal and may be quite short, the following can happen:

❖ John sends an e-mail to Mary asking if she is available for a meeting;

❖ Before Mary replies, John sends another e-mail asking if the report is ready;

❖ Mary in the meantime replies to Johns first e-mail with a simple "yes";

❖ John does not know whether Mary is replying about the meeting or the report!

If you have the original message quoted, it is easy to see what people are replying to! One problem with quoting the original message is that as people reply to the same e-mail, the previous reply and all other replies are quoted; after ten replies, although the main content of the message may be short, included in the message are the original message and the subsequent replies!

E-mail Formatting

The last option here, Reply to messages using the format in which they were sent, deserves a careful look. Originally, e-mail packages could only send text messages, with no formatting whatsoever. If one wanted to send a formatted e-mail, it would have to be attached to the e-mail. As e-mail packages became more sophisticated, it was possible to increase font sizes, use different fonts, font colours, etc. This all came about because of MIME. Multipurpose Internet Mail Extension or MIME allows for e-mails to be more decorative; you may find that if someone sends you a picture, instead of it coming as an attachment, it will appear in the body of the e-mail.

However, when you send a formatted message to someone who does not have a MIME-compatible e-mail package, they may see a whole message filled with hieroglyphics. This is because their e-mail package is trying to make sense of what you sent. Outlook Express overcomes this by automatically sending your message back in the exact format that the sender sent the message. Therefore, if the message came from an e-mail package purely as text, your message is sent back as text. This is a very handy feature and should always be checked. The last sections of the **Send** tab deal with this issue as well.

The **Compose** tab, as illustrated below, deals with how messages are written and what fonts are used:

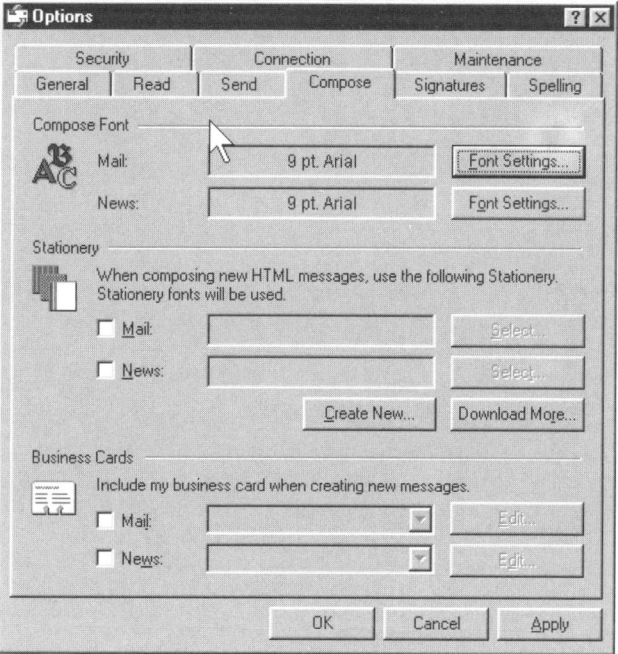

As you can see, it is possible to create your own stationery for each e-mail message sent out. This can be useful, as you can automatically put the company logo on each e-mail. Using personalised stationery is a very good idea for companies as it will implant your brand into the minds of your clients! But remember, if your client does not have a MIME-compatible e-mail program, they may find that your e-mail will be scrambled in parts (their e-mail package is trying to decipher the graphics that make up your stationery). Experiment with creating your own stationery, or else visit the website (*www.internetdemystified.com*) for a brief tutorial on setting up your own stationery.

Signatures

The next tab is called **Signatures**. Signatures are small pieces of text (usually in the form of a marketing message) that are automatically attached to the end of every e-mail you send — another great way to implant your company information firmly into the minds of your clients! Creating a signature is very easy! Just follow the steps below:

1. On the **Signatures** tab, choose the **New** option. Enter your signature as illustrated below:

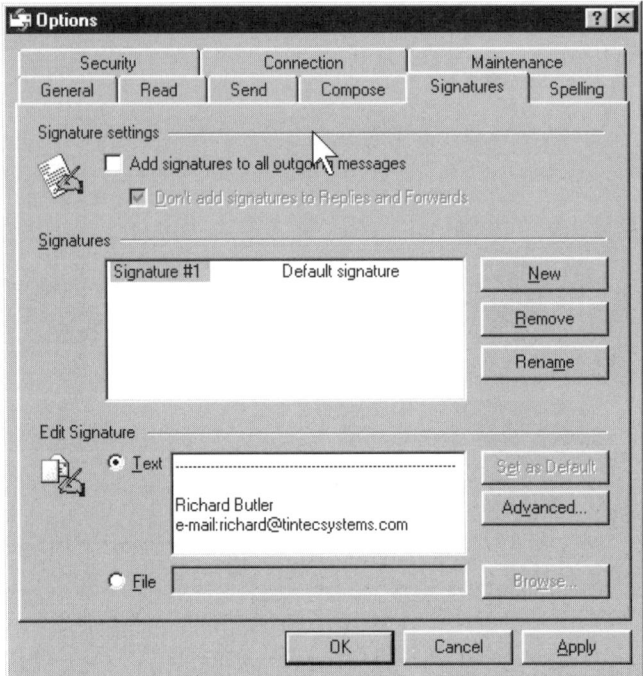

2. Make sure you click on the box to the left of the text: **Add signatures to all outgoing messages**.

After you click on **OK**, every new e-mail you compose will have the signature automatically attached to the end of the document.

> ***Tip!*** *Don't overdo signatures either in length or in blatant advertising; the usual length for a signature is 4–5 lines long.*

The signature and stationery I set up is illustrated below:

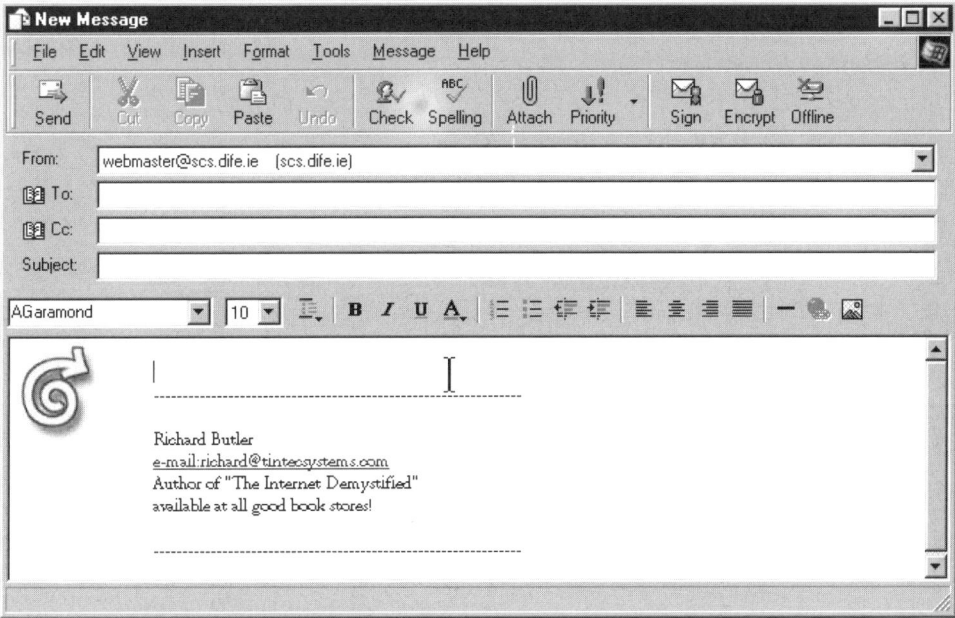

Other Options

The next tab concerns **Spelling**. The first option, **Always check spelling before sending**, can be handy. A message will not be sent until the spellchecker has been run. This is a great option to have checked if you sometimes rush things and forget to take time with your spelling!

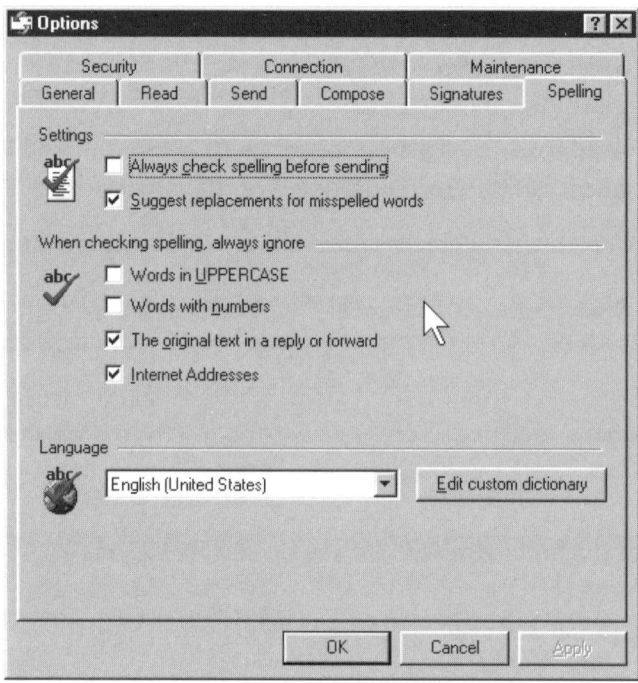

Maintenance is a very handy tab, as it contains some useful functions to ensure trouble-free e-mailing!

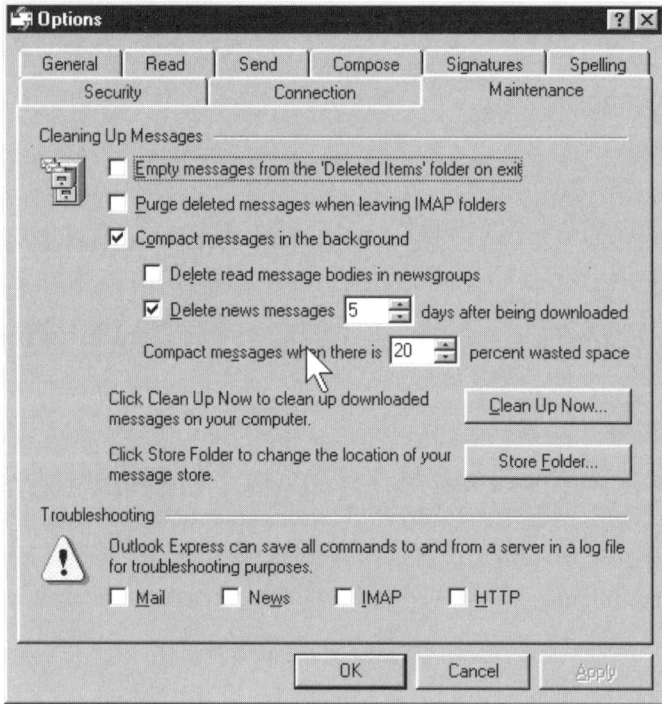

The most useful option in this window is **Empty messages from the "Deleted Items" folder on exit**; this means that as soon as you close down Outlook Express, everything in the Deleted Items folder will be deleted for you!

As you can see, Outlook Express is configured to compact messages and make more space when there is 20 per cent wasted space. Wasted space can occur from not deleting old messages or having too many messages in your Sent Items folder. Outlook Express will automatically warn you when you are wasting space!

We will ignore the **Connection** tab, as there is no need to change anything here. The final tab is the **Security** tab. This tab allows you to encrypt your message so that no one, other than the intended recipient, can read it.

The message will also contain a digital signature, a unique ID that verifies your identity to other parties — the electronic version of a normal signature. In order to use this facility, you must have a digital certificate. This digital certificate is issued by a trusted third party such as Verisign and indicates that you are who you say you are.

Let's assume I want to send a message to Peter. I would encode the message using his public key — so-called because it is given out to people so that they can encode messages that can only be read by Peter. When Peter reads the message, he will decrypt it using his private key; if anyone else tries to decrypt the message, it will not work. When Peter wishes to reply to me, he encodes his message with my public key so that only I can read it. It is essential that no one ever knows what your private key is! It is beyond the scope of this book to go into detail on obtaining a digital certificate, but *www.verisign.com* is one website that deals with this.

Identities

If the whole family have different e-mail accounts and are using the same computer, it may be difficult to maintain privacy of your e-mail account. There is a solution in the form of Identities.

Suppose there are two members of the family using the same computer for e-mail. You would set up two identities, one for each. An identity allows you to password-protect access to Outlook Express. When you have identities in place you will see the following when Windows loads:

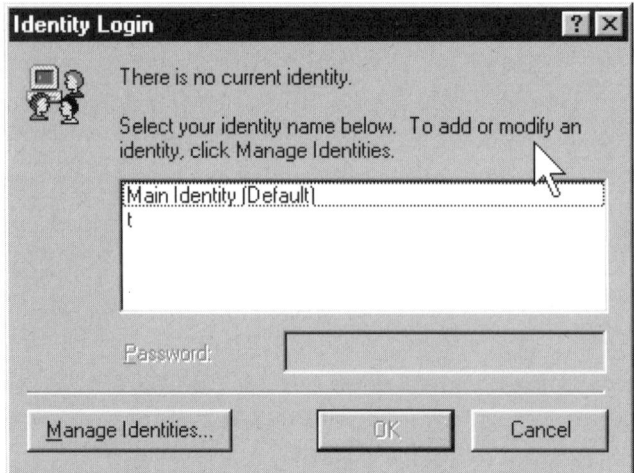

If you click on **Main Identity**, you will be asked for a password; if you supply an incorrect password, you will not be allowed to start Outlook Express. An identity will guard all your new, read and sent e-mails. To find out how to create an identity, visit the website at *www.internetdemystified.com*. It is a great idea to create an identity for each family member so that you can ensure privacy for everybody.

Note that if you close down Outlook Express and then re-open it, you will be back into your identity, so it is essential that you log off your identity when you are finished your e-mail session. This will ensure that the next person who uses the computer (assuming the computer has not been shut down) will be asked to log in.

E-mail Discussion Lists and Mailing Lists

There is more to e-mail than the applications we have been describing over the last two chapters; it is beyond the scope of a book of this size to describe every single tool and technique. However, there is one more important application worth mentioning: adding your name to a mailing list. By submitting your e-mail address to a mailing list, you can receive updates from companies and websites.

A mailing list is a list of opt-in subscribers (someone who decides to join the list) who receive e-mail on a regular basis from a particular source. This list may be an e-mail newsletter (also known as an e-zine), information sent out when a site is updated, a product update newsletter, and so on. Whatever it is, they are very useful because you can receive up-to-date information and then decide to visit the website or act on the information.

Be warned that when you sign up for a service on a website or download software, they will provide an option for you to join their mailing list. Nine times out of ten, the checkbox that says you want to receive their e-mail is already ticked; most people don't bother to "untick" the box. Therefore you may unwittingly join their e-mail list. From the company's point of view, they say they have provided you with an option to join or not join, and since you did not remove the tick from the checkbox, they say that you opted to be part of it. It is, of course, possible to ask the company to remove your name from their list.

A mailing list is useful for the site owner, as they get a list of subscribers (and their e-mail addresses) who have willingly signed up for the service. The e-mail newsletters are often sponsored by advertisers. As they get more subscribers, the company can then seek more sponsorship. The chances of people reading or clicking on a link from an advertiser are usually fairly slim, but some mailing lists attract large enough numbers to give advertisers good reason for sponsoring them.

One such mailing list is that of Nua, a Dublin-based web design company. Nua's mailing list provides an excellent insight into the Internet written by their chief executive, Gerry McGovern. They have found that, over time, the list has grown and grown. This means that their message reaches a wide market, people respect their opinions and will recommend them as a professional, knowledgeable web design and management company.

E-mail discussion lists are slightly different. A mailing list is usually a one-way communication; the e-mail is sent to you, you read it and either take action or ignore it. An e-mail discussion list allows subscribers to respond and see their response on the list. This can be a great source of interaction and information, providing very useful hints and tips, as people send in questions and others answer them.

One problem with discussion lists is that they can sometimes be quite large and, in some cases, they may be sent out as often as twice a day. If you subscribe to a number of lists, you may end up receiving a huge amount of e-mail per day!

Can E-mail be Faked?

The simple answer is, yes it can. Remember when you were setting up a new e-mail account? One of the first questions you were asked was to enter the name that people would see the e-mail is from. If you wanted to, you could change this name to Bill Clinton, Bill Gates or anyone you wanted. When the e-mail arrives, the person will see it is from Bill Clinton, as illustrated below:

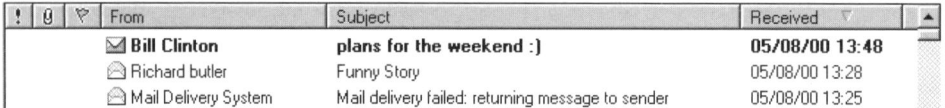

There is a way of finding out where an e-mail message came from. This is done by looking at the <u>header information</u> of the e-mail. When a message is sent from one computer to another, a lot of additional material is included in the message; this material is not normally seen by the user. To view the header information of an e-mail:

1. In the right-hand pane of the **Inbox**, right-click on the person's name in the **From** column. Click on **Properties**. The following screen appears:

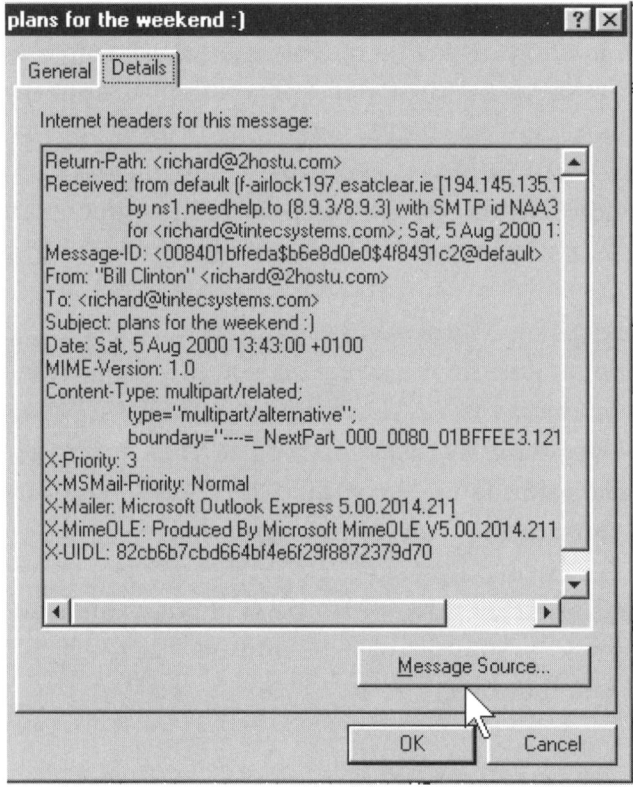

2. By clicking on the **Details** tab you see exactly where the e-mail originated.

Chapter 6

Introducing the Web I:
Web Addresses and Browser Basics

The World Wide Web is at the very heart of the Internet. It is a vast, diverse resource that contains information on almost every subject imaginable, a multimedia experience that offers everything from education to entertainment, from news to shopping.

However, largely because of this size and diversity, searching the World Wide Web can be one of the most frustrating aspects of using the Internet. If done correctly, though, it can also be one of the most rewarding, linking you with exactly what you need, or opening up a multimedia world you hadn't even imagined. But to do it correctly requires a lot of skill and determination. There are two essential techniques that will make your job a great deal easier:

❖ Using your browser, which is an essential skill even if you never actually do a search;

❖ Using search engines and directories.

Because the web is such a huge resource, I will be discussing each of these in separate chapters. In this chapter, I concentrate on the basic mechanics of navigation: web addresses, links and browsers. In Chapter 7, we will be entering the often confusing world of search engines and directories to show you how to search the web easily and efficiently.

What's Your Address?

Every website on the Internet has a unique address or URL. Much like a telephone number, no two addresses on the Internet can be the same. As was discussed in Chapter 2, each computer on the Internet has a unique

IP number assigned to it, which is converted into alphanumeric addresses or Universal Resource Locators (URLs) by DNS servers. Perhaps now would be a good time to refresh your memory on IP numbers and DNS servers from Chapter 2.

Back already? Great!

What makes up a URL?

Most URLs follow a certain format, but some are different. Let us examine a URL that adheres to the common format — *www.2hostu.com* has three parts:

❖ **www** stands for **W**orld **W**ide **W**eb, telling you that the address is on the World Wide Web. This is also known as the host name.

❖ **2hostu** is the name of the company or organisation. This part of the address is very important, as it tells you something about the site that you are visiting. This is called the domain name.

❖ **com** is the extension at the end of the address, which tells you even more about the type of company or organisation, or possibly where it is located.

Each part of the address is separated by a dot (.). Be very careful, as if you type *www2hostu.com* with no ".", you may go to a different site. There are many different types of extensions, but the most commonly used ones are:

❖ **.com**   signifies a commercial organisation or company.

❖ **.org**   signifies a non-profit organisation such as greenpeace.org.

❖ **.net**   signifies a company dealing with networks, such as an ISP.

❖ **.edu**   signifies an American educational institution.

❖ **.gov**   signifies a site that belongs to the American government. For example *www.whitehouse.gov* is the address for the White House.

❖ **.mil**   signifies a US military site.

Other sites use the two-letter country code as the extension; for example:

❖ **.ie**   Irish website;

❖ **.de**   German website;

❖ **.au**   Australian website.

Some countries, such as the UK, use two two-letter extensions such as:

❖ **.co.uk** signifying a UK company;

❖ **.ac.uk** signifying an academic institution in the UK.

Most American sites use either .com, .net or .org.

Is there a difference between a .com and a .net name?

Yes! .com addresses signify a commercial organisation. A .net address signifies a company involved in networking, perhaps not for commercial purposes; for example, *www.oceanfree.net*, *www.eircom.net* or *www.buyandsell.net* (*Buy and Sell* also have an address for their commercial transactions, *www.buyandsell.com*).

Whether you put .com, .gov, .net, etc. can make a huge difference. Some "enterprising" individuals try to register domain names with similar spelling to other domain names, or are spelt correctly but have different extensions; for example, there is a site called *amazom.com*!

What's in a Name?

Believe it or not, names or domain names on the Internet are very important and companies have paid some very substantial sums for the exclusive rights to use the name. Consider the following:

❖ *www.richardbutler.com*

❖ *www.bmw.com*

❖ *www.cityguides.com*

❖ *www.tcd.ie*

The domain names above, apart from the first one, immediately tell you what the site is about and may also indicate what country the information is coming from. If you saw richardbutler.com, you would have no idea what the site was about. The other sites listed are more self-explanatory.

Domain names that are easy to remember will stay in people's heads. One example is the Irish Times website. The simplest way to get to it is by typing *www.ireland.com* — easy to remember, it is a one-stop shop (also known as a <u>portal</u> site) to everything about Ireland. This is much easier to remember than *www.irish-times.ie*; you might, for instance, forget the hyphen or type an underscore (_) or a dash (–) by mistake.

As the web has expanded, some wily individuals have been engaging in domain name speculation. They buy a domain name at a regular fee and hope that they can sell it for more than its face value at a later date. One recent domain name sale was that of *www.linux.com*. Many years ago, a hobbyist bought this name to promote his interest in the then new operating system. The operating system has now proved very popular and many companies are producing software for it. One company in particular wanted to brand their software as the software to use with Linux; therefore, linux.com would be the ideal domain name. They proceeded to buy the domain from its owner — for a couple of million dollars! The original owner of it had great foresight; he saw that it was an easy-to-remember name, short and to the point and realised at the time of sale how valuable a name it was.

Other recent sales include *business.com*, which was sold for $7.5 million, and *loans.com*, bought by Bank of America for $3 million. When you consider that domains cost $35 per year to register, you can see that these speculators made a handsome profit. There are now companies that evaluate the potential worth of domain names, while other companies auction such names. Domain name speculation has also led to many legal problems, with people buying up such names as pepsicola.com and then trying to sell them back to the registered trademark owners. In recent times, it has been found that if you do not have a valid right to ownership over a trademarked name, the registered trademark owners can acquire it from you.

The ease of registering .com addresses, which are by far the most common domain names, have caused some of these problems. This is not always the case with other extensions; in Ireland, for example, it is quite difficult to register a .ie domain name. You cannot register domain names that do not belong to you. For example, you can't register *mcdonalds.ie*, as you have no legal claim to that name — you are not trading as McDonalds. If you had a registered company name or could prove that you had some legal entitlement to the name, you could put a case forward; for example, "McDonald's House Painters" could, if they were trading as McDonald's, have a legal claim to that name. Domain name speculation in the Irish market has thus been kept to a minimum, if indeed there is any activity at all.

Why are some URLs different?

Along your Internet travels, you will probably see URLs that look something like this:

❖ *www.howsitgoing.com/entertainment/mysite*

or

❖ *members.tripod.com/~mysite*

The first — howsitgoing.com — is a site (my own!) that allows you to set up your own free website; however, you do not get your own unique domain, you must use theirs. Your page is set up in a <u>subdirectory</u> of the main site, similar to the way you would have directories and subdirectories on your hard disk. The forward slash (/) indicates that it is a subdirectory.

The second site is a website created on the free space that a company provides for its users. Notice that there is no *www* at the beginning; you will see this occasionally on the web. This signifies that you are going to a certain part of the website; the first or primary part is always called the host name. You may see:

❖ *sales.tripod.com*

❖ *subscriptions.tripod.com*

This tells you that you are visiting a certain section of the site and not the main site, which is indicated as usual by *www*. It is also easier to remember than *www.tripod.com/subscriptions*.

Are URLs Case Sensitive?

The answer to this is yes and no. The main site — *www.domain.com* — is not case sensitive but what follows it is. Try, for example, the following:

❖ *www.tintecsystems.com/mypage.htm*

and

❖ *www.tintecsystems.com/Mypage.htm*

You will see two completely different pages!

To recap: a web address or Universal Resource Locator (URL) is made up of *hostname.domainname.extension/path_to_file*.

What's the difference between an e-mail address and a URL?

While a web address (URL) takes the form *www.domainname.extension*, an e-mail address takes the form *username@domainname.extension*.

There are some similarities, as you can see below:

❖ *www.tintecsystems.com*

❖ *richard@tintecsystems.com*

As you can see, the *tintecsystems.com* part is shared both by the web address and the e-mail address. *tintecsystems.com*, the domain name, refers to the name of the server. The main difference is what is to the left of the domain name. In the first address above, we see *www*, which immediately tells us that we are dealing with a World Wide Web address — a URL. The second address has an @ symbol — this always indicates an e-mail address. The above address tells me that my account (*richard*) is at (@) *tintecsystems.com*.

Navigating the Web using Internet Explorer 5

Now that you understand the basics of how the Internet works and how to connect, let's see how to actually navigate the web. First, let's recap briefly on what the web consists of.

The web is a multi-sensory experience. On a web page, a user may experience any of the following:

❖ Text

❖ Pictures

❖ Videos

❖ Sound recordings

❖ Interactivity

❖ Three-dimensional worlds.

As discussed in Chapter 2, the web is a collection of interlinked <u>web pages</u> that make up larger <u>websites</u>.

❖ **Web page**: This is a page of information that one accesses using a browser such as Internet Explorer. A web page can contain text, sound, images, and video.

❖ **Website**: This is a collection of web pages, usually following a common theme. For example, the *Irish Times* website is made up of all the pages that make up *The Irish Times*.

Basic Features of Internet Explorer 5

You can only view web pages when you use a web **browser**. For the purpose of this book, we will concentrate on the browser from Microsoft called Internet Explorer. Internet Explorer is now one of the most popular browsers for a number of reasons:

❖ It comes pre-installed on every new computer bought that comes with the Windows operating system.

❖ It also probably comes on the installation disk that you receive from your ISP.

❖ It is easy to use!

Once you become experienced, you may wish to compare Internet Explorer and Netscape Navigator to see which you prefer.

In order to make your surfing easier, all browsers come with some buttons on the toolbar to help you navigate. If you open up Internet Explorer, you will see something like the following screen:

Look closely at the main toolbar near the top of the screen. Below is an explanation of the main icons on the Internet Explorer 5 toolbar:

❖ **Back**   Allows you to move back any number of pages that you have visited.

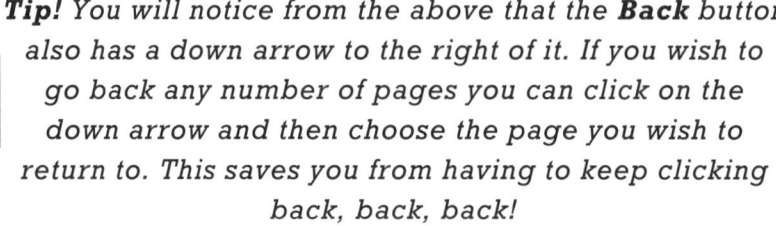

*Tip! You will notice from the above that the **Back** button also has a down arrow to the right of it. If you wish to go back any number of pages you can click on the down arrow and then choose the page you wish to return to. This saves you from having to keep clicking back, back, back!*

❖ **Forward**   When you have gone **back**, to a page you can go **forward** to another page.

❖ **Stop**   Sometimes pages take a long time to appear or <u>download</u> (retrieving a page from the web); you can stop the page downloading by hitting the clicking on **Stop**.

❖ **Refresh**   Reloads the current page.

❖ **Home**   Brings you back to the first page you see when the browser starts up.

❖ **Search**   Allows you to search for topics on the Internet.

❖ **Favorites**   Sometimes you will see a page that you really like. Instead of trying to remember the address, you can <u>bookmark</u> or add it to your list of favourite pages.

❖ **History**   History shows you all the pages you have visited to date.

❖ **Mail**   Allows you to access your e-mail.

❖ **Print**   Allows you to print a page from the Internet.

❖ **Edit**   Allows you to create and edit web pages locally.

Most of these features are explained in detail later in this chapter, while the Search function is discussed in Chapter 7. There are also additional functions which can be accessed through the menus in the main toolbar of Internet Explorer.

Connecting to the Web

A few assumptions are made at this point:

❖ You have installed a disk provided for you by your ISP;

❖ You have your modem/phone line connected;

❖ You are a home user.

(If you are not properly set up yet, go back to Chapter 3 before continuing.) So let's begin!

1. Double-click on the Internet Explorer icon on your desktop. Depending on how you have set up Internet Explorer, you should at this stage see the following dialog box:

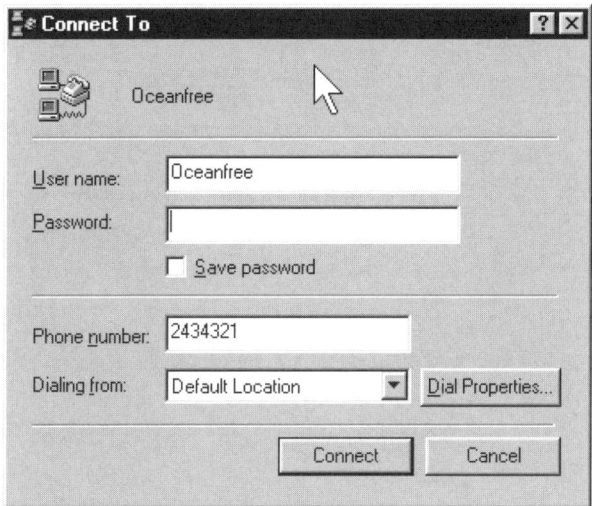

2. If necessary, key in your <u>username</u> and <u>password</u> and click on **Connect**. (Usually, your username and password will appear automatically.)

3. After a couple of seconds and a lot of noise you should be connected to the Internet. If not, refer to the Troubleshooting section on the website accompanying this book (*www.internetdemystified.com*).

Homepages

Once you are connected, the first page that you should see is the home-page of your ISP. This page will be different, depending on what ISP you use to connect to the Internet. "Homepage" has two meanings. Firstly, it is the first page that appears when you start up your browser, this is more than likely the website of your ISP. Whenever you click on the **Home** icon in the IE standard toolbar, you will return to this page. The other meaning of homepage is the very first page of any website, a bit like the front cover of a book.

Notice that the page — as with any web page — is made up of graphics (pictures), text and links. Links are the nerve-endings of the web, moving you from page to page and site to site. By and large, links are shown as underlined words, often in a different colour to the main body of the text. Sometimes pictures are links. When you are in a website, try moving your mouse pointer over pictures; if the pointer changes to a hand, you have found a link! Some websites may have no text-oriented links; all their links may be pictures. Remember to explore everything on the page that looks like it might be of interest!

Tip! *Most pages contain more than one screen of information; make sure you use the scroll bar on the right-hand side of the screen to view all the information on the screen.*

From the page you are looking at on your computer, you can click on any link to go to a new page.

Explore the links on your Internet Service Provider's homepage. Use the Back and Forward buttons to navigate between the sites.

Anatomy of a Web Page

Let's look at a typical web page and see what makes it up:

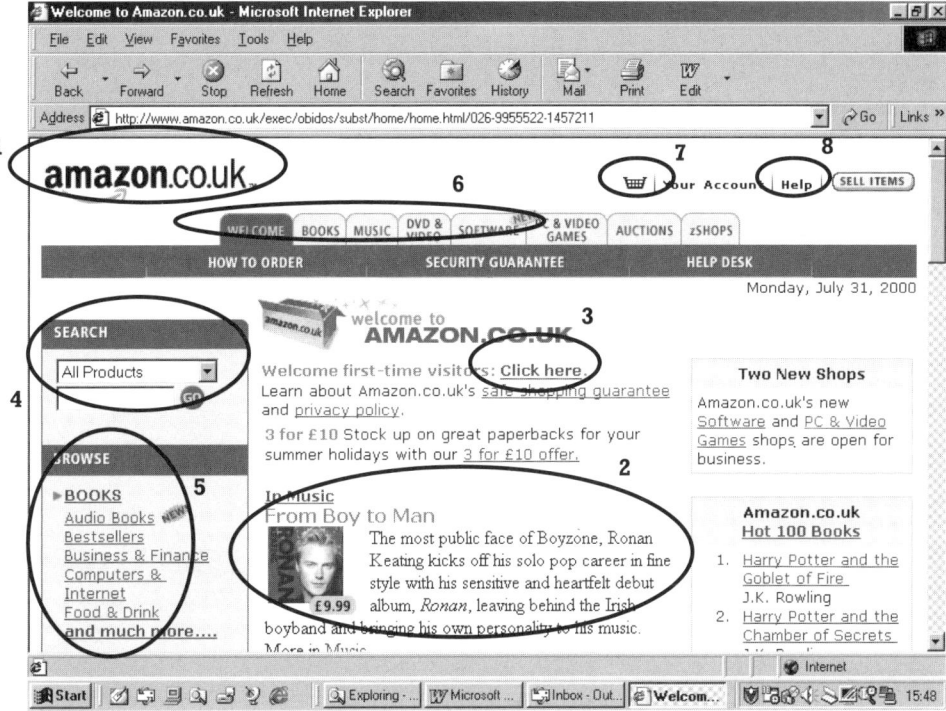

1. **Company Logo/Heading**: Obviously, most websites will want to present a professional image, and will head up each page with their logo.

2. **Graphics, Text and Images**: These are the basic content of a web page. They should be clear, uncluttered, providing just the right information in the limited space available. Headlines should direct you to places of interest, while pictures and graphics should be used sparingly, working best by improving the look of the page.

3. **Links**: No website worth its salt will be without a number of links. They are the basic navigational aid of a web page and of the Internet itself.

4. **Search Facility**: Many websites contain search boxes, which allow the user to search the entire website for a specific page or keyword.

5. **Contents List/Index**: Many websites include links to different sections and sub-sections of their site, arranged in an easy-to-follow bar to the side of the screen.

6. **Tabs**: Tabs are another way of displaying links to different sections of a website.

7. **Shopping Basket**: Most e-commerce sites now have the facility to add items to a "shopping basket", which makes it easier to move around without having to remember what you wanted to buy.

8. **Help**: A lot of sites will give you guidelines on how to use their facilities if you are visiting the site for the first time.

These are just some of the basic parts of a web page. The "page" above also continues further down the screen; you would read on by moving the scroll bar on the right-hand side. Other types of content that you might encounter include:

❖ **Active Content**: You may find links to active content such as streaming video or audio.

❖ **Interactive Form**: Some web pages have these forms, which allow the user to fill in certain details in order to gain access to free products or information, to register with a site, to complete an order, and so on.

❖ **FAQs**: Frequently Asked Questions are pages specially designed to provide the sort of information that is commonly requested by other users.

❖ **E-mail Links**: There is usually some way of contacting the company through an e-mail link.

❖ **Site Map**: Some sites contain a "map" outlining the contents of the entire site and how each page is interlinked.

What actually happens

When you request a page from a web server, your browser connects to the web server, which sends you the page. Remember how, in Chapter 2, I said that when you place a telephone call, you have a dedicated circuit from one phone to another, and nobody else can use that circuit while you are on it? The Internet was set up in such a way that this does not happen. When you access a website, you retrieve the page and then are disconnected from the web server, so that others can access the site as well. This means that the information that appears on your screen does not normally change or update. The information is completely static when it is displayed on your screen.

Your connection to the web server is one-off — it remembers no information about nor does it recognise that you have already accessed a page on the website the next time you visit. Even though you are disconnected from the server, you are still connected to the Internet (<u>online</u>); you are simply not requesting any information at the moment. As soon as you click on a link, a request will be sent out to the server asking for that page to be displayed.

But what if you just want to stay with the same page? Let's assume that you are looking at share prices on the Internet. If you were to leave the page on your screen for 12 hours, the share price would remain the same; the page is being displayed on your computer and the connection between you and the web server has been terminated. (Of course, if you're still online, you are paying for watching the same screen for 12 hours! Usually your computer will automatically disconnect if there is no activity between your computer and the Internet for a set amount of time.) In order to get the most up-to-date content, you have to click on the **Refresh** icon. This will cause the browser to contact the web server and request the most up-to-date copy of the page, if there is one available.

If there are moving pictures on my screen, does this mean I am getting updates from the web server?

Some pictures that you see on a website are constantly moving; these are known as animations. They are a series of pictures put together in a special program that makes them move in sequence. This does not mean that you are still connected to the web server.

If the image does not display properly, it is often a fault on the part of the web designer; they may have made a mistake when creating the web page. You can read more about this in Chapter 8, "Building Your Own Website".

A 404 error is displayed when a page you requested is not found on the server. This may be because the page has been deleted from the server or you typed in the address wrong. Always ensure that you enter the address exactly as given, and remember that uppercase and lowercase do matter!

Working Offline

Any time you perform a task on your computer when you are not connected to the Internet, you are working <u>offline</u>. For example, if you write a series of e-mails without being connected, you are working offline. It is only when you dial up to your ISP to send them that you go online. Remember when you first opened Internet Explorer and a dialog box appeared asking you to dial up? You may have noticed that, if you didn't connect immediately, you had the option of working offline, either by clicking on the button for "offline" or just by clicking on cancel.

You might wonder how it is possible to use the web when you are offline. How come you can still see web pages and click on links?

When using Internet Explorer, many pages are stored in your <u>cache</u>.

 **Cache** *refers to an area where web pages are temporarily stored on your hard drive.*

When you are online and you press **Back** or **Forward** on your web browser, the page appears, on most occasions, almost instantaneously. This is because the page and a lot of its graphics are coming direct from your hard drive. Depending on your settings, Internet Explorer can cache hundreds of pages on your hard disk. These pages will usually be deleted from your cache after a certain length of time, or overwritten with an updated version the next time you visit the page online.

Opening Other Websites

Typing in Web Addresses

As you can imagine, you will soon get bored if all you can do is visit the links that your ISP has on its website. Therefore it is essential that you have the ability to type in addresses that you are given or have seen on ads, flyers, etc.

In Internet Explorer, look at the toolbar just below the Back button; you will see the word **Address**. To the right of it is an area containing the URL of the current page.

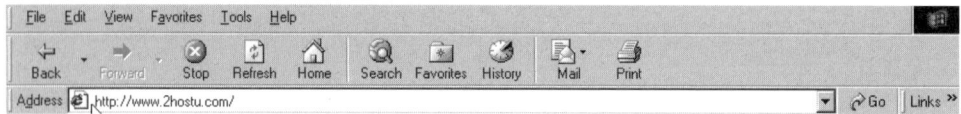

1. Click on the URL in this address area. The text should be highlighted in white text on a blue background.

2. Press the **backspace key** or the **delete key** (if the cursor is flashing but the text is not highlighted, press the backspace/delete key until all the text is deleted), or simply type over the address.

3. Now you can type in any address you wish (for example, *www.internetdemystified.com*).

4. Press **Enter** or click on **Go** and the page should now load up.

 ***Important!*** *After entering a web address in the address bar, ensure you press* ***Enter****; otherwise nothing will happen.*

Sometimes web pages can take a while to load because there may be a lot of graphics on them or there may be a large number of people trying to access the site at once. You will know when a web page is loaded because the globe in the top right-hand corner will stop spinning and show the Microsoft logo:

If you type in the address incorrectly, you may receive an error message. Don't worry; it could mean that the server you are trying to connect to is busy, doesn't exist, or you misspelt the address.

You can also enter web addresses another way:

1. Go to the **File** menu

2. Choose **Open**

3. You can now type in the web address.

Must I always type in HTTP?

HTTP stands for HyperText Transfer Protocol — the agreed set of rules for the transfer and viewing of web pages. With modern browsers, it is not necessary to type in *http://* before the www part of a domain name. In fact, the new browsers will automatically put this in for you.

Autocomplete Function

A new feature in Internet Explorer 4 was the introduction of the autocomplete function. If you have already read the e-mail chapters, you will be familiar with this. This function means that Internet Explorer will automatically finish the address you are typing into the address bar. After you have visited a couple of sites, Internet Explorer will remember these sites, and as you type them, the following will appear:

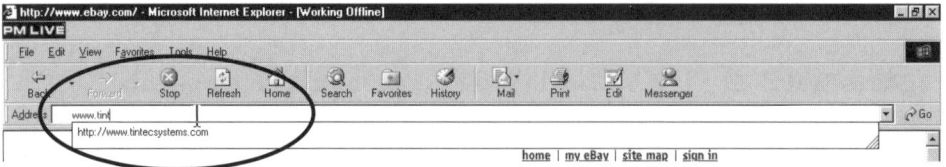

You can now simply click on the site name to go to that site.

If you have visited many pages within that site, you will see a list of all the web pages visited within that site.

Can I view more than one page at a time?

Yes, it is possible to open two or three windows at the same time. This allows you to look at one page while another page is loading. To open a new window, simply go to the **File** menu; choose **New**; from the submenu, choose **Window**. A new window will open. You can now type in another web address and flick between one window and another by selecting it from the taskbar.

Tip! *If you press **CTRL + N**, you can open a
new window quickly!*

I clicked on a link and a new window appeared; why?

Some websites are created in such away that if you click on a link, the content of that link will open and display in a new browser window. This can be quite annoying, as you could end up with a large number of windows open.

Tip! *Always check the taskbar to see how many
windows are open. You can close any window
by right-clicking on it and choosing **Close**.*

I saw a flashing image that said "click here"; what should I do?

You have just had your first exposure to the world of Internet advertising and <u>banner ads</u>! Banner ads are usually rectangular ads that are placed at the top of web pages, with a hyperlink to the advertiser's website. The advertisers hope that people will click on the ad and visit their site. These ads bring in substantial revenues for the websites that display them. Banner ads are what keep the majority of websites free. The consumer gets free information and the website owner gets advertising revenue. The better the site, the more people that visit, the more the owner can charge for advertising — essentially, it is a win-win situation.

Banner ads can be quite annoying, but you soon get used to distinguishing what is an ad and what is not. Many website advertisers now use Fake User Interfaces (<u>FUIs</u>). This should not be confused with a <u>GUI</u> — Graphical User Interface — which is what most modern operating systems, including Windows, use as their interface with the user. Anybody who uses Windows will be familiar with the GUI's use of windows, icons and menus; you interact with the computer by pointing and clicking, rather than having to type in long technical commands. Now what advertisers have done is to create Fake User Interfaces in their ads. These ads reproduce the look of a Windows dialog box or menu asking you to select an option from a list, or what appears to be a list. However, it is actually all just one big graphic which acts as a hyperlink. When you click on the down arrow beside the list, you end up in another website — very sneaky!

Some of the other FUIs that advertisers use include messages such as "Warning — Your system is not optimised" or "Click here for faster downloading". Be warned that as a new user to the Internet, you may be fooled into clicking on these ads; always take your time and examine the ad before you click on it.

The latest types of ads are now fully interactive; for example one for a lottery website allows you to use an on-screen coin to "scratch" a scratch card. Other ads involve punching a monkey running across the screen; if you click on it at the right time you win a prize. The prize is usually a free piece of software to download! Other types of banner ads encourage you to click on them by promising prizes, special offers, love and happiness, etc. You will, no doubt, witness many other types of ads and see how innovative the advertisers on the web can be.

 ***Tip!*** *If you click on a banner ad by accident, simply click on* ***Back*** *to get back to the page you were at.*

Saving and Printing Web Pages

Saving Web Pages

When you come across a web page or site that you like, you may wish to save it so you can view it later.

1. To save a web page, go to the **File** menu; choose **Save As**. The following appears:

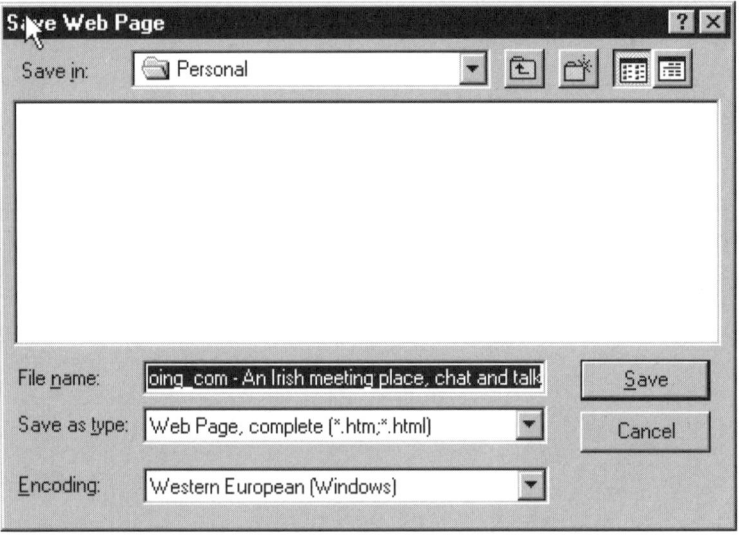

2. Choose where you wish to save the web page; you can also give it a different file name at this stage. Click on **Save**. You will notice the following dialog appearing:

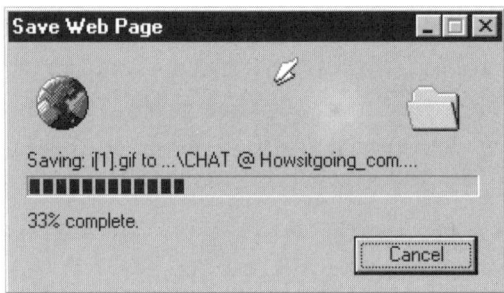

What is happening is that Internet Explorer is saving the page and all the graphics that are associated with it. This means that when you wish to view the page when you are offline, you will see the page exactly as it was on the web. This is different from the web page being stored in your cache; you are instead permanently saving it as a file in a directory of your choice on your hard drive.

Note that if you now go to the directory where you have saved the web page, you will see it listed under the file name you assigned it. If you now open the page from here, you will see the page exactly as it appeared when you opened it online — with one difference. Look at the web address: where before it was listed as its standard URL, now it shows up as the location, or path, where you saved it on your hard drive. For example, suppose you saved amazon.com's homepage in the folder "My Documents" on your C-drive, and gave it the file name "Amazon home". While the actual web page online will show the address as *http://www.amazon.com*, your saved version of the page will have its address as *C:\My Documents\Amazon home.htm*.

Before Microsoft introduced this facility, users had to save the web page and then save all the associated graphics — a time-consuming process! If you just want to save the text of a page, do exactly as above, but before hitting **Save**, click on the down arrow beside **Save as type**; choose **Text** from the list that appears. Now click on **Save**, and only the text is saved!

Saving Individual Images from a Web Page

It is not only possible to save the page you are viewing; you can also save any image you want from a page.

1. Right-click over the image. The following menu will appear:

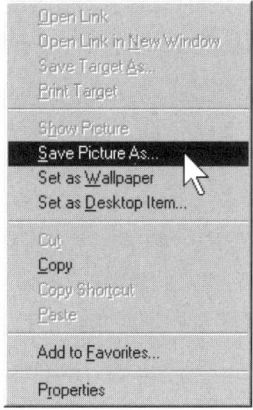

2. Choose the **Save Picture As** option.

3. Find a folder to save the image in and then click on **Save**.

Is this illegal copying of other people's copyrighted images? Anything on a web page is copyright and deemed as intellectual property. This includes text, images, sounds and videos that may be contained on a page. The question of copyright is discussed in Chapter 12.

Printing out Web Pages

As you come across web pages, you may wish to print them out. Most people do not like reading from a computer screen; in fact, people read 25 per cent more slowly on computer screens. As a result, many people like to print out web pages.

If you wish to print out a web page, simply click on the **Print** icon on the toolbar; this will print out the entire page. Unfortunately, it is very hard to know how pages will come out, as screen sizes are not the same as standard paper sizes. Another problem is that some web pages may not print out full sentences correctly, due to differing line lengths between the screen size and A4.

Screen sizes and paper sizes are not the same! If a web designer has created a web page using a table (a method used to arrange text and graphics on a web page) and the table is set to a fixed width, this can cause problems. If you see a horizontal scrollbar, your page will not print all of the text on the right-hand side. If in doubt, copy and paste text, as described below.

Many websites now give the user an option to view a web page in a "print-friendly" format. Always look around the web page to see if there is a link to a print-friendly page. An example of a website that does this is *www.wired.com* (a very good site dealing with technological and computer news). When you print out a web page, everything is printed including all graphics and text; the only thing that will not print out is the background image on the page and, of course, any active content.

Tip! When printing web pages, change your printer settings so it only prints out in black and white. This will save your colour cartridge. Some pages are designed with the body text in colour; printing 20 pages in colour will take a while and also use up a lot of ink.

I tried to print a web page but the text came out blank!

Some websites have a coloured background with white text. Of course, your printer cannot print white text on white paper! If you do come across a page with white text, the best thing to do is:

1. Select the text by clicking and dragging with your mouse

2. Go to the **Edit** menu and choose the **Copy** command

3. Start up a word-processing program such as Word

4. Go to the **Edit** menu and choose the **Paste** command; the text will now appear on the page. If it is still coming out white-on-white, you can change the text colour in your word-processing program.

Remember, your web browser is still open and can be brought up by clicking on it on the taskbar.

Printing a Section of Text

More often than not, you will find that only a section of a web page is of interest to you; the rest of the information is of no use. You have two options here:

1. **Copy and Paste** the text as detailed above; *or*

2. Highlight the section of the text you want to print out:

   a) Go to **File**

   b) Choose the **Print** option. You should see an option that allows you to print only the highlighted **Selection**, as illustrated below:

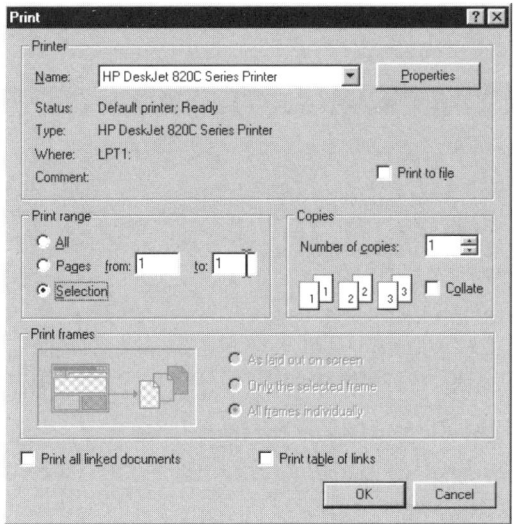

The above screen will look different, depending on the printer you have.

Note that there are a couple of other options at the end of this dialog box. **Print table of links** will print out a list of links that are connected with the current page. Every link from the page you print out will be listed. **Print all linked documents** will do just that — every document linked to the current page will be printed. This could run to hundreds of pages! This is, however, useful if you are looking at a report that is on the web and you need to print it all out. Simply go to the contents page and click on **Print all linked documents**. This saves you the time and hassle of visiting each individual page and printing it!

Recording Internet Addresses: Favorites

As you travel around the Internet you will see and visit many sites. Some will be of interest, others will not. One of the problems is trying to remember every site you visit. Luckily, one of the key features of all browsers is the ability to "remember" addresses of websites; this is a lot easier than trying to write down the addresses.

The ability to do this is known as adding a site to your <u>Favorites</u> within Internet Explorer 5, or to the <u>Bookmarks</u> section in Netscape Navigator. (Note the spelling of Favorites; this is of course because Microsoft is a US company.)

Adding sites to your list of Favorites

1. When you find a site that you like and wish to record, go to the **Favorites** menu.

2. Choose **Add to Favorites**. The following appears:

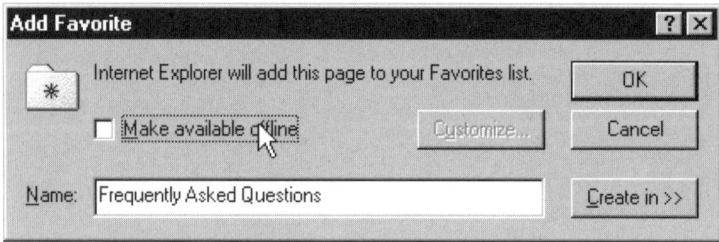

3. If you click on **OK**, the site is added to an existing list of sites.

4. If you select **Make available offline**, this will save the page in your cache. You will then be able to view this page while you are not connected to the Internet.

Creating Folders for your Favorites

It is fine to simply click on OK, but the list will eventually become huge and you will not be able to locate the site you want from the rather large list of sites.

Instead, you can create <u>folders</u> that will help categorise your sites for you. A folder is a storage space on your computer that stores all related files. Within Internet Explorer's Favorites, a folder is a section that you can designate for related websites. For example, you might create a folder for education sites, business sites, games sites, etc. Internet Explorer contains a number of preinstalled folders, with some favorites already added, which you may or may not find useful.

1. Go to the **Favorites** menu.

2. Click on **Create in**. You can now click on one of the folders displayed, or if you wish you can click on the **New Folder** option to create a new folder to store related sites.

3. If you have clicked on **New Folder**, the following appears:

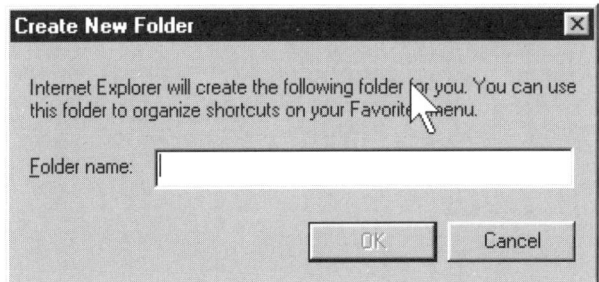

4. Enter a new name for the folder.

5. You can now either click on **OK** or you can divide your newly created folder into a number of sub-folders. To do this click on the newly created folder and repeat the instructions above.

When you wish to add a favorite to one of these folders, simply click on **Favorites, Add to Favorites, Create in** and choose the desired folder.

The eagle-eyed amongst you will also have spotted an icon on the toolbar called **Favorites**. When you click on this icon, your screen will be split in two and the list of your favorites will appear on the left-hand side of the screen. This makes it somewhat quicker to access your favorites, but you may wish to close the panel on the left-hand side to ensure that the web page is displayed fully, once you have found it. By and large it is easier to access your favorites by using the Favorites menu option.

Organising your Favorites

Let's assume that you have surfed a bit, added sites to your Favorites and now realise that you have a huge list of Favorites in no particular order. You have created all your folders, now you must try to organise your sites into these folders.

1. Go to the **Organize Favorites** option on the **Favorites** menu.

2. You can now choose to **Move, Rename or Delete** any of your favorites. If you choose to **Move** a favorite, you will be shown a list of folders.

3. Choose the folder you wish to move your favorite to:

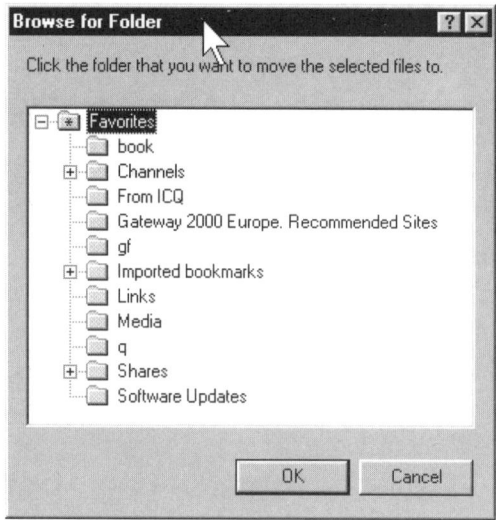

4. Click on **OK**.

For more detailed information on Favorites, visit the website at *www.internetdemystified.com.*

History versus Favorites?

You can also revisit sites by going to <u>History</u>, but this is quite different from <u>Favorites</u>. History remembers every site you went to and what pages you saw; this is meant to help you go back to certain pages of sites at a later date. History files are deleted after a certain number of days. Favorites, on the other hand, are sites you specifically want to record and remember, and they remain on your hard drive unless you delete them.

The History function can be very useful, because it often happens that you visit a site, but don't add it to your Favorites; if you then want to return to the site, you may not remember the address or how you found it. Remember, since the Internet is made up of links, you may have started on one page, and then moved from one link to the next without even noticing that you were moving from one website to another.

In this case, you can click on the History button, choose a date and see what sites you visited. Not only that, but if you click on any site address, it will reveal a list of all individual pages you visited at that site!

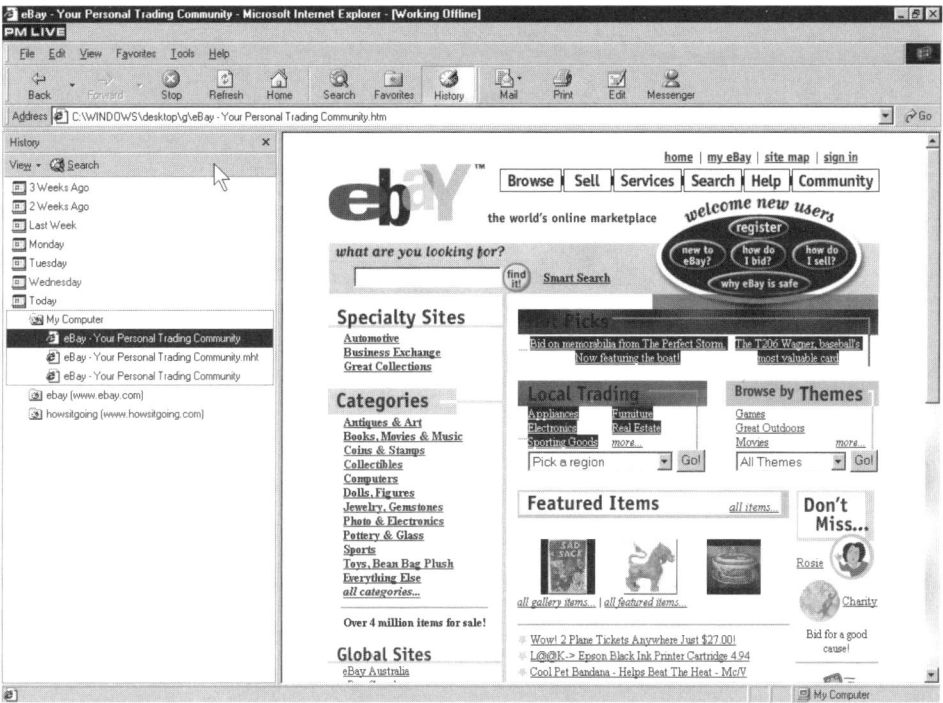

You should now be confident enough to use a browser, enter web addresses, use links and favorites, and so on. However, this is only the start of navigating the web — you're not even on the open seas yet! What if you want to research a topic or find specific information? What if you know what you want to find out, but don't have any addresses or links to relevant sites? Read the next chapter to become a master at exploiting the World Wide Web's search engines.

Chapter 7

Introducing the Web II: Effective Searching

The World Wide Waste

The hype merchants will sell you the Internet as the world's largest library, the best and richest encyclopaedia, a goldmine of information. However, one criticism of the web that is constantly raised is that there is so much information on it, apparently without any proper organisation, that it is extremely difficult to find what you are looking for. Imagine a vast library without a classification system! This leads many to believe that there is little of interest on the web.

One essential skill that any web user must have is the ability to search and locate information efficiently and also to be able to authenticate the sources of such information. This is important due to the large volume of information available and the vast number of sources that the information may come from.

The Good Search Guide

One of the most obvious (or perhaps not so obvious) problems that new users have is that they actually approach searching on the Internet in the wrong manner; they don't know where to start. Therefore, the first thing you must do is ask yourself the following question:

"What am I looking for?"

This may seem obvious but many people overlook it. They go to a search engine and type in a word, see that there are over one million sites containing that word, get fed up and then complain about the Internet. Thus, the secret to good searching is first to know what you want to find, what topic you are concerned about. It may help to think in specific terms; for example, rather than saying to yourself, "I am looking for a holiday", be more specific and say "I am looking for a budget holiday in the south of Spain". This will help narrow your search and provide you with more targeted results.

When thinking about what you are looking for, consider the following:

❖ **Facts**: Are you looking for factual information? For example, "Where can I find the current temperature and exchange rate of Spain?"

❖ **Opinions**: Do you want to find the opinions of other holiday-makers who have been to this particular region?

❖ **Arguments**: Is there a site that will give a fair case for and against this type of holiday or destination?

❖ **Statistics**: Perhaps you may want to find out how many people holiday in this particular resort.

❖ **Action**: Are you looking for a website that will allow you to book a hotel and flight?

Some or all of the above will be important, depending on what you are looking for. The above list allows you to determine what type of page or site you are looking for on the Internet to answer your questions. There are four types of websites on the Internet:

❖ **Informational pages**: These pages usually give factual information about a topic, such as a government or organisational homepage.

❖ **News sources**: News pages offer views on current affairs or related to a particular topic.

❖ **Advocacy pages**: This type of page has a particular viewpoint it wishes to push.

❖ **Personal homepages**: Pages set up by users who may have their own personal opinions or areas of interest they want to share.

If you want to find facts, the best type of page to visit is an information page; this could include a page from a motor society, the motor company itself — they will certainly have technical details. Opinions can be found in news sources, advocacy pages and personal pages, as can arguments. Statistics will be found in informational pages such as government pages or non-profit pages (usually with extensions such as .gov or .org).

So, now you know the type of information you are looking for. The next problem is ensuring that the information you find passes the CARS[1] test. There are four distinct elements to the CARS test:

❖ Credibility

❖ Accuracy and Timelessness

❖ Reasonableness

❖ Sources.

Credibility

The first test you must perform is to ask yourself whether you believe the information you have found. This test in other areas of the media or research is much simpler: if you see a story in a national newspaper, you can be almost assured that it is real, but if you see it in a supermarket tabloid, it is probably more sensationalist than "true".

But a website makes it more difficult. Anybody can write and post a story on the website; there is no quality control; nobody can say, "You can't write this; it isn't true!" So how do you judge what is a credible website? There are a number of clues:

❖ Who is the author? A website author should not fear giving out information about him/herself, background, qualifications, how they actually came to know the information themselves (do they cite other authorities?). If you find a website with opinions or facts on it and cannot trace the author of the work, ask yourself why they are hiding their identity.

❖ Does he/she represent an organisation? If they do, any information on an organisation's website must usually be vetted before it is published. For example, if you visit the website of a newspaper, any pages published by its journals would first be vetted by the editorial team; therefore information from this type of site may be more reliable than information from a personal homepage.

---

[1] A system of testing information gained from the Internet as described by Robert Harris of the Vanguard University of Southern California.

❖ What are their qualifications in that particular field? If they are talk-ing about medical issues, are they actually qualified or experienced in the particular medical area they are talking about? It may be very easy for a person to set up a site about an illness and give their per-sonal thoughts on it; this does not make it a medical point of view. Again, the author should make it clear that it is their personal view. Is there any way you can check the person's credentials if they claim to be a doctor, lawyer, etc.?

❖ Is there a contact address/phone number if you wish to get in touch with them? Again, if their page is an isolated piece of work with no information about the author or how to contact him/her, you must ask yourself why this information is not forthcoming.

❖ How well written is the piece of work; are there grammatical or spell-ing mistakes? Examine the overall tone of the work as well: is it hu-morous, cynical, sarcastic? Perhaps it is intended as a joke.

❖ Does the work present new ideas, based on solid foundations, or is it a re-hash of other information found on other websites? There are so many websites on the Internet that many users are now "publishing" what are seemingly their own thoughts on particular subjects on which they have become "experts"; but on close examination, you may see that they are re-hashing other people's work.

Another important test is to look at the URL. If the URL ends in .com, you are dealing with a commercial organisation; therefore their views and opinions may be biased towards their products or services. Beware of "facts" that are merely trying to persuade you to buy a product!

If their domain ends in .org, this shows they are a non-profit organisa-tion. They may be a non-political society or organisation; perhaps they are an advocacy site, in which case their views may be biased. Domains ending in *.edu* and *.gov* represent educational and government web-sites. These sites usually contain factual, academic information.

Visit the websites of newspapers or organisations that you know from the world outside the web, such as *The New York Times*, *The Examiner*, *Time*. These are all "brands" that we trust in the real world, so informa-tion on their websites is likely to be reliable and informative.

If you find a site with a URL such as *members.tripod.com/~joesmoe*, this indicates that the page is more than likely a personal homepage, which may therefore not be a reliable source of unbiased information.

Many companies on the web offer users free space where they can can publish their websites. Since they have so many people creating pages, it is hard for them to police all the websites that their server contains. Many people set up all types of weird and wonderful pages, some of which add a great deal of fun, dynamism and colour to the web, but some of which are just plain strange! The key point to remember about these sites is that they are personal pages and their content may not be vetted by the host company.

Some of the these free services include:

❖ *www.tripod.com*

❖ *www.geocities.com*

❖ *www.fortunecity.com*

> ***Tip!*** *If you come across a web page with an address such as* members.tripod.com/~joesmoke, *try deleting everything after the first / so that you are left with* members.tripod.com. *This will be the main page of the site that will indicate what the site is about, i.e. it will tell you that it is a free homepages provider.*

Which of the following is most likely to be the official Nokia website?

1. *www.nokiaphones.com*

2. *www.nokia.com*

3. *pages.freesite.com/~nokia*

4. *www.nokia.edu*

As you will soon realise, the second site is the official site; if you arrive at the first site, make sure you find contact information that proves its identity as a website that is endorsed by or part of the Nokia group.

Accuracy and Timelessness

The second test to be taken is the accuracy of the text. Is the information you are looking for timeless? For example, if you are looking for information regarding Spanish painters from the sixteenth century, you should see if any new theories regarding their work have been put forward. More than likely any information you find may be relevant, no matter when it was written.

If you are looking for information about current Internet trends, however, any information that is more than three months old may not be valid. A survey on Internet usage would need to be very up-to-date; there is no point in giving out information that is two years old.

Try to find out who the information is intended for. Is it for a specialist audience, such as a trade organisation, or for consumption by the general public? Why and where was it produced? Was it sponsored by a company or organisation? Information geared towards a professional association or trade body may be very technical and too advanced.

Is the information intended as a general introduction to a topic or does it focus in on a particular aspect of a larger topic? If you are investigating a topic such as Internet security and your intended audience is a group of beginners, you will not want information that is too technical. If you are writing a training manual for a computer-literate audience, you will not want to use sites that offer only basic information.

When researching information on a site, look out for the following warning signs that may indicate problematic information:

❖ No indication of a date of creation/revision on the document;

❖ Vague information with few specifics;

❖ No update history — many sites will contain an update list telling you when and what was updated on the site.

This may be difficult to establish, as many sites would not automatically include a creation/revision date. Some search engines may give the date when the page was indexed; this may give you some indication of how old the information is.

Reasonableness

When researching information, you should try to make sure, to the best of your ability, that the information you are reading gives a fair and accurate overview of the topic.

Informational sites should be objective in nature; government sites, for instance, usually do not express an opinion but give you facts and figures as required. Other sites, such as personal homepages, may offer one-sided views, while advocacy sites will only present their view as being correct.

Ask yourself if the information you are reading is likely and probable; compare it to other websites or other facts you know to be true. If you visit a website that says shopping on the Internet is perfectly safe, find out if the site is an authority on e-commerce or Internet issues in general. Visit other sites or find a book on the topic; see what they say before making a judgement. Do they link to other sites that back up this information? If every other site you have visited says that shopping can be dangerous and this is the only site that says shopping is safe on the Internet, perhaps you should take the opinion of the majority rather than the opinion of one website. Never take the first opinion that you read as the truth.

Is the argument or information presented consistently throughout the document? If the person is unsure of what they are saying, they may contradict themselves in different sections of the document.

Tone can play an important part in assessing the reasonableness of a document. Assess the tone of the document: is it racist, bigoted, ranting, cynical, serious, humorous? People sometimes create websites as skits and not until you read down the page do you begin to realise this!

E-mails are especially prone to this type of "humour". E-mails have circulated talking about a virus that will infect your computer, destroy all your data, open your fridge and eat your food, drive your car . . . as you read on through the e-mail, you realise that it is not a real virus warning!

Indications of lack of reasonableness include.

❖ Improper tone or language

❖ Exaggerated claims

❖ Sweeping statements

❖ Conflict of interest.

Sources

The final test is to find out what, if any, links or sources the author refers to. Many sites will quote other sites/publications to back up their ideas; they may also provide links to sites that are related. If a website appears to be an isolated piece of work, with no links, sources, etc., you should be wary of it.

The nature of the web is links; therefore it is easier for an author to link to a website that will back up and verify what they are saying. With books, it takes time and a bit of effort to find the sources quoted. With the web, this is eliminated; therefore, if the author of a website has not linked to other resources, you should ask yourself why this is so.

Does the site proclaim to be the best there is? Find out who made this claim; was it an industry standard organisation? Does the site link to a recognised authority or umbrella organisation? If they make claims, can they back them up? Any website is only one click away from the site that you are reading; therefore why has the author not included a link to a site to back up his/her information?

The CAFE Method

Robert Harris has one final piece of advice that you should bear in mind when searching, a method he calls the CAFE:

❖ **Challenge**: Always challenge every piece of work that you find on the Internet, or indeed in the "real" world. Ask yourself: Why should you believe it? Who wrote it? Why did they want to write it? Is their view a valid, reasonable view? Never take anything for granted; work on the premise that the work may be invalid until proven otherwise.

❖ **Adapt**: Always be adaptive and open to new information. Perhaps it is a new field of thought, but you should still question every source. See if the "new" idea contained in the work could be true. Again, find out if it is backed up by credible sources. Fields such as technology and medicine are constantly developing new methods and technologies that are being tested before they are accepted.

❖ **File**: Record everything you have found, but make no judgements. It is not until you have read many works that you can then decide which sources are reliable and which are not. If you go looking for information on a certain topic, don't take the first site that you visit as the authority. Record its address, file it away until you have visited many sites and then begin to form judgements.

❖ **Evaluate**: Understand that some information will be in a constant flux or state of change. Learn to effectively evaluate the information you find on the Internet. Be aware of the changes that are talking place. Critically analyse each source as you discover it.

Using the guidelines above, you are now ready to begin searching on the Internet for information on a desired topic. Perhaps now is a good time to write down a checklist of what type of information you are looking for and what you expect to find.

Finding Information on the Web

The value of the web is in the vast amount of information that can be accessed. If you don't know the URL of the document, however, it is very hard to find the material. A number of companies have tried to address this problem by setting up <u>search engines</u> or <u>search directories</u>.

*A **search engine** compiles its database of pages in a different way to a search directory. Your searching is based solely on <u>keywords</u> (a word that appears in the contents of the page). A **directory** is more organised and allows you to search under different headings.*

Because of the organic nature of the growth of the Internet, it took a while for these search tools to develop, and to refine the way they searched and categorised the web. But, without them, the Internet could not have developed to the extent that it has.

A search directory lists categories that, when clicked, display further sub-categories, gradually refining the search; the user can then click on a website listed in one of those sub-categories. It makes searching much easier, particularly for the less experienced. It also means that it is easier to locate information.

A search engine primarily works on the use of keywords (explained below). What this means is that you must first have a very specific idea of what you are looking for. Search engines take a bit more practice to get used to but can often yield better results and are more suited to complex searches. We will look at each in turn, starting with directories.

Directories: Using Yahoo for Searching

As the Internet changes constantly, it can be very hard to find up-to-date information. A good directory is often the best way of finding quality information, as the (human) editors weed out the mass of useless sites.

One of the best search directories for beginners is **Yahoo** (*www.yahoo.com*). Yahoo began as an exercise to help two students from Stanford University organise the websites they had visited; from an initial couple of links in the early 1990s it soon grew into a multimillion dollar corporation and an extensive website that offers not only searching, but also chat, classified ads and auctions. Yahoo, like other directories, has a number of advantages:

❖ It's easy for beginners to search for websites;

❖ Information is categorised and displayed clearly;

❖ Before being entered in Yahoo's database, each new submission is checked by a human — this means that better quality sites may be available to users of Yahoo.

However, there are some disadvantages

❖ More complex searches are not suited to Yahoo;

❖ Having to click through so many pages to find the information you want can be time-consuming;

❖ Since pages are checked by humans prior to submission, censorship may or may not occur.

Illustrated below is the opening screen of *www.yahoo.com*. It might be a good idea to go online while you are reading this and open up this page.

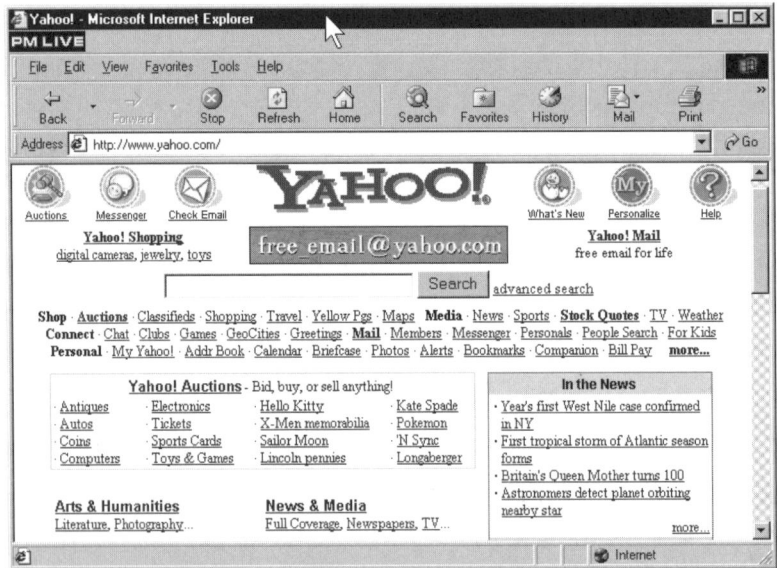

As you can see, there is an area where you can type in a search term. There are also headings and links — categories — that you can click on. You can choose to search in a certain category (e.g. Arts, Education, Computers, Business), or you can search through all categories and then narrow down your search.

Searching by Category

Say for example you wished to find information on drinking in Ireland. You could begin your search by clicking on **Countries**, which is under the **Regional** heading on the homepage. When in the Countries section, you would select **Ireland**. Click on the link to Ireland, then choose the **Entertainment** option. If you then click on **Food and Drink**, you will get more information about places to eat in Ireland.

At the top of the screen, you will be shown how you got to the particular page. You went from the **Home** page to **Regional**, then to **Countries**, **Ireland**, etc.

Searching by Keyword

What if you want to find a specific topic but are not sure of the category? Yahoo also allows you to conduct <u>keyword</u> searches, which are very useful, for example, when you think that there may be a number of categories into which your information could fall.

 *A **keyword** is a specific word typed into a search engine or directory in order to locate information.*

If you wish to conduct a keyword search, simply type in the keyword; for example, *property*. You will be presented with a number of categories and quite a number of web pages; these are known as **hits**.

The more specific your keyword is, the better the results. Instead of using the keyword *property*, specify *apartment*. Always think carefully about what keywords you enter, as they can make a huge difference. When you search Yahoo, it will display your results in one of three ways, depending on what you searched for:

1. Sites created by Yahoo about the chosen topic;

2. Sites that belong in Yahoo categories;

3.   All websites that contain the keywords.

Simply click on a link to see the information. This makes finding information much easier for the beginner. You can also submit your search to
another search engine by clicking on a link at the bottom of the page of
results. Don't forget, you can press **Back** in order to return to the list of
search results.

So far we have seen two methods for searching in Yahoo — clicking
on a category and "drilling down" (i.e. clicking on sub-categories) until
you find the desired information. The second method was to use keywords. But there is a third method, which is actually a combination of the
first and second. This method allows you to do a search, but you can decide whether to search **All of Yahoo** or **Just this Category**. By clicking
on the **Just this Category** option before you search, your keywords
would only be searched for in the chosen category. This means you
should get more accurate results for your search, i.e. a much smaller list
of website matches.

Yahoo also gives you a list of what it considers to be related searches
of interest. You can also try the exact search you performed in any of the
other listed search engines, simply by clicking on a link.

An even better way to search Yahoo for local content is to use the local version of the website. Thus, you can search for information about
Ireland at the Irish Yahoo site, located at *http://www.yahoo.ie*. While this
site looks the same, there is one difference. Below the area where you
enter your keywords, it says **You are searching**, with a choice of "All of
Yahoo" "UK Only" or "Ireland Only". To use this search engine just to
search for Irish sites, you must first click on **Ireland only**, then type in
your search term, then click **Search**.

Search Engines

When you want to find more information, you must use a search engine.
The key to search engines is knowing exactly what you are looking for,
also known as "devising good keywords".

Let's say you go into a bookstore and want a book on cooking. You
know this is too general a category, so you might ask the assistant for
any books on Italian cooking, including pasta. You have chosen your
keywords and the assistant can provide you with more detailed informa-

tion. The same goes for search engines; before conducting your search, think of what keywords you are going to use.

The major global search engines are:

❖ **Altavista**　　　*www.altavista.com*

❖ **Infoseek**　　　*www.infoseek.com*

❖ **Excite**　　　*www.excite.com*

❖ **Lycos**　　　*www.lycos.com*

❖ **Webcrawler**　　*www.webcrawler.com*

Each search engine has its own advantages and disadvantages. Which one you use will depend on your own particular preference and you can only find this out with practice. Later, we will look at each of the above, as well as a number of others, and examine which one is best for different types of search. Before we look at the individual engines, however, we will look briefly at how search engines do their job and how you can conduct a simple search.

How Do Search Engines Work?

When web authors submit their site to a search engine, an automatic program, known as a spider or robot, indexes the page and finds out what the page is about by recording the words on the page of the website. When a user types in a keyword, the search engine will search its database to find the most relevant matches.

How does the search engine rate or rank a page? This depends on each individual search engine, but there are certain criteria it looks for:

❖ How many times the keyword is repeated in the body of the text;

❖ How many other pages link to the particular page (the more pages that link to this page, the more popular it is).

These are the two main criteria but each search engine has different methods of categorising pages. An author of a web page can try to increase their ranking in a search engine by the use of meta tags — special pieces of code that only interests search engines and web authors.

When the spider visits a page, it remembers all the keywords on that page. If the page has a lot of the keywords that you are searching for, it ranks that page highly. It also looks at the title of the page, where the keywords are positioned in the text of the document, etc. Most of the time, you can expect that a page with a high ranking is relevant.

Ranking simply lists the pages in order of keywords and relevance; while the first result should be better than the second, there is no way of knowing *how much better*.

Excite (*www.excite.com*) and Lycos (*www.lycos.com*) both have a rating system. They give a percentile rating of each match returned based on your keyword. Therefore if a search returned a page that had a 90 per cent rating, it should be more relevant than a page with a 26 per cent rating.

 ***Tip!*** *Always read the help pages that are available with search engines, as they can provide some very useful information regarding how the search engine works.*

Why do different search engines return different results?

If you try your search on two or three different engines, you will find that each engine will produce a different set of results. There are two principal reasons for this. Firstly, not all search engines contain the same sites, as site authors must submit their pages to each search engine. Secondly each search engine indexes pages differently, so what is relevant on one search engine may not be relevant on another.

Some search engines like Infoseek have a facility on them that allows you to search within the results shown. This can be very handy for narrowing down your search results.

Spamming the Index

Sometimes you will find that, after you enter a search term, the first page on the list of hits has absolutely nothing to do with what you were looking for! There could be two main reasons why this might happen. Firstly, the search terms you used may have been too general (see below). Secondly, the authors of the web page may have succeeded in "spamming the index". This means that the authors have used deceitful methods to fool the search engine's spider into ranking their page higher.

It is possible to purchase a program that resides on your server and waits for a search engine's spider to contact the server. As soon as the spider contacts the server, the server will deliver a highly optimised page, full of keywords, to the spider. Thus the spider indexes this page. Once the spider has indexed the page, the original (not optimised) page is reinstalled. Web authors use this method for two reasons:

❖ To increase their ranking in a search engine;

❖ To ensure that other authors don't find out how they optimised their page.

> *Tip!* *If you run a website, it is very important that your page be indexed by many search engines; after all, most people find the information they require through a search engine, therefore if your website appears at the top of a list of hits, you will get more visits. See Chapter 8 for more on building and running a website.*

Search Techniques

Searching is an art and there are many techniques that can be used to get the best from the search engines you use.

To use any search engine, simply type in the keyword you wish to look for in the space provided on their main homepage. Sometimes you may have to reword or think of another keyword.

When you enter your keyword into the search engine, you will be given a list of results, also known as hits. The problem is, you may get millions of hits. If you are a beginner, chances are you will look through the first three or four screens of hits. As you look through the hits, you may find that some, or even most, are not at all relevant. At this stage, you may be tempted to give up. But don't — there are a number of options open to you to improve the quality of your results. These are described below.

Refining your Search

Firstly, you can refine your search. One way of doing this is to think of a more specific word to search for. Rather than search for "cars", search for a particular manufacturer or model of car. This is relatively easy if, for example, you are looking for a Renault, a BMW, or a Toyota. These names are specific to the car manufacturers. But what if you want to do a search for a Ford? Ford is a relatively common surname, so you will need to think again.

Think very carefully about the words you specify. For example, anything to do with computers will probably return millions of results: "computer", "network", "Internet", "PC", "web" will all yield too many results. Suppose you were looking for a window cleaner. Do you think it would be a good idea to search for "Windows"?!

Remember also that cultural differences may restrict your search; if you can't find what you are looking for under "car", for instance, try "automobile", etc.

> *Tip!* Remember, if the web page that you visit after a
> search is not what you require, use the **Back** icon to
> get back to the listing of search engine results.

Keyword Grouping

It is possible to group keywords together. Try entering two words to be more specific; for example, *Ford Focus*. The problem now is that pages with the word *Ford* **or** *Focus* (an even more common word than Ford!) appear in your results; this may lead to thousands more web pages being displayed, very few of them relevant to your search.

As another example, to search for property in Ireland, simply type in *Property Ireland*. There is one problem with this. The search engine returns matches for any page that contains either of the keywords. This type of search tells the search engine to display any pages that contain either word. Depending on the search engine, you could get anything from 100,000 to two million hits, because every time the word *Property* or *Ireland* is encountered in the database of the search engine, it returns that page.

The search engine does not know that you want to search for the word as a phrase. There are ways around this; in order to limit your search to a particular phrase, enter it into the search engine in quotation marks, such as *"Property in Ireland"*; this now tells the search engine to look specifically for the phrase *Property in Ireland* so only pages that may contain this phrase will appear.

> **Tip!** *You should always assume that the search engine you are using is case sensitive. If you search with initial capitals (*Irish Hotels*), you may very well get fewer results (which can be better), than if you searched for* irish hotels*. You should try both initial capitals and lowercase and compare the results. You can also check the help pages of the search engine for more information.*

Specifying Words that Must Appear

You can specify certain words that have to appear in your search results, though not necessarily in a specific phrase. Nearly all search engines let you decide which keywords must be included in the results of your search. To ensure that certain words are contained in the hits that are returned, you can use the **plus sign** (**+**) before each keyword that *must* appear in the results.

Therefore, if you type in *"Property in Ireland" +Wicklow*, this will find all pages with the word *Wicklow* in them but not necessarily the phrase *Property in Ireland*. The reason for this is simple: all you specified as a required word was the word *Wicklow* (as you only put a plus before that word and not before the phrase). By leaving out the + before *"Property in Ireland"*, you told the search engine that the most important word to search for was *Wicklow*. If the page contained the other phrase, well and good; if not, it did not matter.

> **Note:** *there is no space between the + sign and the keyword. Therefore +* Wicklow *is wrong; +*Wicklow *is correct.*

In order to search for all pages that contain the phrase *Property in Ireland* **and** the word *Wicklow* try the following search terms:

+"Property in Ireland" +Wicklow

This will now find all pages with both the phrase and the word Wicklow. You can add more words that must be included simply by putting a + in front of them; each keyword should be separated by a space.

By the way, when you are formulating your keywords, it is worth thinking about regional differences — e.g. try *real estate* rather than *property*.

Excluding Words

You can also exclude certain words from your search query; this is done, naturally enough, by using the minus sign on your keyboard (–).

Let's assume that you want to find accommodation in Dublin, but do not want an apartment; you could type +*"accommodation in Ireland"* +*Dublin* –*apartment*. This tells the search engine that it must return results that include the phrase *"accommodation in Ireland"*, located in Dublin, but excluding apartment accommodation.

Only by practice can you begin to find what keywords work well; remember, keywords that worked in one search engine may not work in another. You will also then begin to construct bigger, better and more complex searches.

Boolean Searches

The type of searches described above are known as Boolean searches.

> ***Boolean*** *is a mathematical term used to describe a situation when there are only two choices, either "true" or "false". In general computing, for example, digital information is represented by choosing between 0 and 1. In search terminology, using Boolean terms means that the phrase will be included or excluded.*

Boolean terms are like mathematical functions using words such as *AND* or *AND NOT*, which we represent as + and –. When you do not include a Boolean term in front of a word, it takes it as an "or" expression.

To look again at our previous example, if you search for +*Wicklow* +*property* –*Ireland*, you are saying you want to include the words *Wicklow* and *property* (true) and exclude (false) the word *Ireland*. You can also use the *OR* expression, which means you want to search for one phrase *OR* the other; if one phrase is not available, you will accept the other phrase.

phrase *OR* the other; if one phrase is not available, you will accept the other phrase.

> *Tip!* Not all search engines accept AND, AND NOT; they may simply require + or – instead of using the specific words. Most large search engines recognise + and –, but with some of them you can spell out the words. However, you will probably find it easier to use + and –.

Different Search Engines and their Merits

Now that you can construct your queries, we will look at the major search engines that are available and describe each one in turn. This section lists some of the major search engines and their relative merits, special features and disadvantages, if any, of each.

What to Look for in a Search Engine

Before we look at each individual search engine, there are a number of facilities that may make your searching easier, and you should check to see if the search engine you are using has any of these facilities:

❖ **Language**: Can you search in a specific language? This will thereby exclude or include results that may or may not be relevant. Perhaps you want to search for a German poet; the best pages may all be in German, so can you specify this.

❖ **Translation**: If you do find a page in German, does the search engine allow you to translate it? Currently only Altavista and Infoseek have this very useful facility. Translations are usually passable in order to gain an understanding of the topic, but they can throw up a number of inaccuracies.

❖ **Type of Search**: Can you choose only to search web pages, newsgroups, etc.? Some search engines allow you specifically to search in newsgroups only or to search only for images, which can be useful.

❖ **Related Searches**: Many search engines will give you a suggestion of topics that may be of interest to you, either from a directory or in order to refine your search.

❖ **Date**: See if the search engine will give you any information about when the page was added to the search engine. For some types of research, knowing the date of publication will either render the information useful or useless.

❖ **Address**: Does the search engine display the web address before you click on the link? Again, this can be useful, as you can judge by the address whether the information is coming from a personal website, organisation or commercial company.

Altavista

Altavista is one of the largest search engines on the web and has been in existence since 1995. Its many advantages include "natural language searching", where the user can simply type in a question and the answer to it will be returned. For example, if you type in "Where can I find information about Ireland?" you will receive a list of sites about Ireland. This facility can be very useful for searchers who are new to search engine technology. Of course, not all types of questions will be understood, so try a few different ways of phrasing your question if you don't succeed first time.

Altavista also allows you to search for pages in specific **languages**. This is very useful if you want to find a topic that pertains to a certain language. Coupled with this is Altavista's ability to **translate** documents. If you enter a search phrase and there are matches that are in a foreign language, you will be able to translate them.

You can also find a listing of **related pages**, i.e. pages that are related or similar to the page that is listed. You can also get facts about the website that is supplying the information by clicking on the **Facts about** link. Altavista will also suggest **related searches** that you may wish to conduct to find more useful, perhaps more focused, information. Altavista has already helped us assess the value of the information by providing all those other links for us. Being able to search for related pages is extremely handy.

Excite

When search results are returned, Excite breaks them up into **Resources**. For example, if you search for "Ireland", you will see a map of Ireland plus links to "Travel and tourism", "Where to stay", etc. When you click on any of these resources, you will be given directory listings and then finally a ranked display of results. Excite will evaluate each website it presents and then give it a percentile ranking based on your keyword. The higher the percentile ranking, the more relevant the content may be:

You get very limited information about the site, the reason being that the default view is set so that only the titles of the document are displayed. Click on **Summaries** to see summary information or click on **Web site** to view all pages from a particular website.

Lycos

Lycos is quite a clever search engine; depending on where you are in the world, you may be directed to the "national" version of the search engine. If you ensure that the **UK & Ireland** box is checked, it will mean that your results will pertain to these two countries.

Lycos works in a similar manner to other search engines, but its results are quite interesting. For example, you can click on:

❖ Web pages about Ireland

❖ Pictures of Ireland

❖ Sounds of Ireland

❖ Books about Ireland.

When given all these choices, you must decide what type of information you are looking for. Again, I must emphasise the need to think before you search!

It is also interesting to note that the results that Lycos gives you initially may be sorted by domain names. Therefore any sites that mention the word "Ireland" will be show first. Take note of this point if you are considering buying a domain and setting up a website!

You could also sort the results by relevance, which may be better for research purposes.

Webcrawler

Webcrawler is owned by the same company as Excite, but offers fewer indexed pages than any of the other search engines; this may be a good thing, as fewer results will be returned, which means you will not be overwhelmed by useless information.

The default option is to view a minimal amount of information about the web page. Sometimes this tells us nothing about the site; therefore it is best to click on **Summaries** to get more detailed information about each website.

Fast Search/All The Web

Fast Search is a relatively new search engine. It has indexed over 300 million web pages. It is a very simple and fast search engine, which displays basic results; you do not have the sort of options available in Altavista to search similar sites, etc.

Using the advanced search, you can refine your search, search for information in over 30 languages and include or exclude words and certain domains. I have found Fast Search to be a very good engine that delivers well-targeted results.

Direct Hit

Direct Hit is not a standard search engine as such; what it does is analyse the results of queries that people have entered in other search engines and displays which results they clicked on, ranked according to those sites with the highest click-rate. Therefore the results that you see have been acknowledged as being relevant by millions of other searchers. Many other websites use the Direct Hit technology to power their own search engines.

Direct Hit does not have any other "advanced features" above the ordinary Boolean searching, but one nice feature is the related searches options it gives.

GoTo

GoTo is an unusual search engine in the way it operates. It knows that most users find results through search engines; therefore it has decided to let the companies who want to be at the top of the search engine pay for the privilege. When you search in GoTo, the results shown include a note of the "cost to advertiser"; when you click on the link, the advertiser will be charged this amount, say $0.59. Advertisers bid for each keyword; if I want my site to be at the top of the list, then I would bid $0.60 for the keyword. This would ensure me a number one ranking on the GoTo search engine — until somebody outbids me!

This should mean that websites that provide valid, timely information will pay to have the top spot on the search engine. It could also mean that quality sites that cannot afford big advertising budgets may not get a ranking in this search engine.

From a business point of view, there is a danger that either your competitors or the search engine itself may keep clicking on your link, which would cost you a lot of money!

Google

Google is another search engine that operates slightly differently than an ordinary search engine. When ranking pages, it uses a technology called PageRank. Google decides how relevant a site is by analysing what other sites link to it and who it links to. If 100 websites link to the particular website in question, PageRank considers that each website is giving the site a vote. If more sites link to a resource, it would seem that the site is more popular; therefore, it probably contains more relevant information.

On top of this, Google rates the linking sites, which it divides into categories. If the linking sites are popular sites, then their vote is given greater weight. For example, if 10 sites link to my site but one of these is Microsoft, this may be the equivalent of 20 votes. Smaller, less well-known sites may fair badly in this system, but Google does return good results.

In the search results, the word <u>cached</u> is included beside the URL. This means that Google has stored a copy of the page on their server so that if the page is removed from the original location, Google will still be able to display it.

A rather novel feature of the search engine is their **I'm Feeling Lucky** option — clicking on this will automatically take you to the first listing that is returned. Google feel confident that their results will match what you are looking for. Therefore, when you click on this, rather than being given a results listing, you will be brought straight to the website that they feel is most relevant to the topic you searched for!

Another link called Google Scout will find pages that are similar to the hit returned; this feature is similar to the Related Pages option in many search engines.

HotBot

HotBot is owned by the Lycos network but operates independently of their results. This is one of the many search engines that use the results collected by Direct Hit. The technology behind HotBot, and used by many search engines, is powered by Inktomi, a company that has a huge index of pages. Each search engine can then become an Inktomi partner and use their results. Each search engine can also pay Inktomi so their results are filtered in various ways.

One interesting feature allows you to **Read and Write Reviews**; if you want to see someone's view on Ireland or want to write a review about it, you can! You will see that directly beneath this is a list of related categories and then a list of websites that matched your query.

Another good feature of this search engine, which is also seen in some other search engines, is the ability to search within your results by checking a box. This means you can check the box and only search within the results shown; this can help to narrow down your search.

LookSmart

Although it is listed here as a search engine, LookSmart is more of a directory service. All its listings are compiled by people rather than machines; this usually means that the information in this directory is more concise and focused than the information presented by a search engine.

LookSmart provides content categories for many other search engines. When you search in LookSmart, you get links to Sponsors' websites. Sometimes you will be given links to other websites that offer you additional information on Ireland; for example, Amazon.

Northern Lights

This search engine is a good place to start for serious search results. Northern Lights not only allows you to search the web; it also has its own listings that it has built up on its own website. It has also partnered with companies, periodicals and journals to bring specific content. This comes at a price, however! When you search through Northern Lights, you will come across some articles that you have to pay for!

I believe more and more search engines will offer this facility in the future. If you wish to read an article from a periodical or a business-related website, you will be charged a nominal fee for doing so. This fee can range from $3 to $20; while this may seem steep, think of how much time you could spend searching the web for inferior information. Certainly many serious researchers will decide that it is worthwhile paying for quality articles rather than wasting time looking for irrelevant information.

Northern Lights are so confident that you will like the information that you receive that they offer a money back offer; if you have downloaded an article and don't feel it is worth what you paid for it, they will refund you the money. Obviously, this system is open to abuse, but they feel it is necessary to reassure fee-paying customers that they are getting value for money.

An interesting feature of this search engine is the use of custom folders. When you search for information, the result will appear but you will also see a list of custom folders that allow you to view other topics that may be of interest to you. This is essentially similar to a related topics/ search items option but presented in a more elegant manner.

Northern Lights is definitely worth a good look when you need to find specific articles or conduct an in-depth search.

Snap

Like LookSmart, this site provides human-compiled directories of websites; if information is not found in one of its directories, it will display information from Inktomi. You get a list of related searches, which are quite in-depth compared to other search engines; below them is a list of interesting sites taken from their directory.

Perhaps over time both Looksmart and Snap will provide much competition for Yahoo.

As you can see from our brief look at some of the major search engines, each one has its merits and demerits; experiment with a few search engines until you find one that you like and then stick to it. Always look out for new features as well.

As you begin to use search engines, you may find one that you prefer. It is possible to customise the search engine that you wish to use. Check with your favourite search engine to see if they offer this option.

At this stage you must be asking yourself if there is a way of searching a number of these engines at once; after all, typing in the same query into search engine after search engine would be a laborious process . . .

Using Meta Search Engines

As we said earlier, each search engine will contain different results, simply because people submit their pages to one search engine and not to another. In order to find the best information, you really need to try your search on a number of search engines. This can be a long and laborious process; thankfully, there is a solution in the form of <u>Meta Search Engines</u>.

A Meta Search Engine is itself not a search engine! What it does is submit your search to a number of search engines simultaneously. Instead of you typing in the same keywords into five different search engines, you type it into the meta search engine and it will display the results from the five search engines for you (how many search engines the meta search engine displays can vary). These sites do all the hard work for you!

One very easy-to-use and popular meta search engine is *askjeeves.com*. AskJeeves uses real language queries, like Altavista; in fact, AskJeeves provide this service for Altavista. For example, if you type in *"Where can I find property in Ireland?"*, it will know that you are looking for property in Ireland and return a list of hits from different search engines. Sometimes you need to rephrase the question, but it is a very effective way of searching quickly and efficiently. This type of searching can save you valuable time and expense.

Other meta search engines include:

❖ Dogpile (*www.dogpile.com*)

❖ Metasearch (*www.metasearch.com*)

❖ Mamma (*www.mamma.com*)

Meta search engines can be extremely useful and allow you to search numerous search engines quickly and efficiently. Remember, the Meta search engine is not as such a search engine itself; it acts as an interface that allows you to search multiple search engine at once. I have found that for serious searching, it is best to go to a search engine.

Why Use a Search Engine when I have a Search Button?

The eagle-eyed among you will have noticed that the main Internet Explorer toolbar actually has a button called **Search** on it, as illustrated below:

This also allows you to search using various search engines. By clicking on the **Search** button, your screen splits into two panels, as it also does when you click on Favorites or History in this toolbar. When you search using this Internet Explorer Search button, your result will be displayed in the left-hand pane of the window. When you click on a link, it will appear in the right-hand pane, as follows:

So what is the advantage? The main advantage is you do not have to press the **Back** button if a page you visit from a search is not one that you like.

If you wish to conduct the same search in another search engine, click on the down arrow beside the word **Next**. You will be given a choice of search engines. Click on whichever search engine you wish to submit your query to and it will be submitted.

So why not use the search button all the time?

The search button is a very useful tool, but as you can see from the above illustration, the screen can become cluttered in the process. If you can stand clutter, by all means use it!

Specialised Search Engines

More specialised search engines exist for specific topics, such as medical research, etc. There are also regional and geographical search engines available.

As a sample, some specialised search engines include:

❖ *www.webmd.com*: A search engine specifically for medical information

❖ *www.companysleuth.com*: a search engine used for finding information on companies

❖ *www.jobfinder.ie*: a site that allows you to search for job vacancies in Ireland.

The Future of Searching

It would appear that more sites will appear that offer valuable, useful and timely information to the user — for a fee.

"Pay-per-view" sites are on the increase, and as more and more companies realise the potential of e-commerce, they look likely to be with us for some time. Search engines are leading the way. For example, if you were to search for information on Cervantes, a site would give you a list of documents and articles that you could download for a small price, perhaps 10 cents per document. To draw you in, a short extract or highlights might be available for free.

There are a number of sites that already do this. The *northernlights.com* search engine searches websites but also contains information from over 5,000 premium sources, ranging from business directories to medical directories.

When you search for an item, you will get a list of matches. Some will be web pages as per normal on a search engine, but some will be from their special collection of reports, etc., which you have to purchase.

The company realised that there was so much information on the web that people would appreciate this type of service. Reports can cost anything from $1 upwards. They also have a guarantee that if you are not happy with the report, you can get your money back. This type of guarantee will help make people feel they are getting legitimate information.

You have to be careful, as some of the information may be publicly available if you searched long and hard for it, but many don't have the time and would therefore prefer to pay for it than have to go through endless searches.

Another such service is *elibrary.com*. You pay a yearly subscription to their service (currently $59.95) and you get access to their vast library of information. Their information is proprietary information that they have gathered, rather than information from other search engines.

Again, for those who want up-to-date information that they can find easily, these services will be the way forward for searching. You may be able to find the information elsewhere for free, but the key phrase is *may be*. It could take hours, days or months to find the information that is already available on these sites for a small fee.

These sites operate on the principle that you would have an account with the website. When you find information that you like, the amount is deducted from your account.

There are already numerous sites in the financial marketplace that provide information to individuals and companies for a yearly or monthly subscription. It is only fair when you think about it: if you are a consultant, you do not give out your information for free; you expect to be paid for it. You could find out the information yourself by trial and error but the consultant makes the information available to you more quickly. The same goes for these websites. They have spent time gathering and filtering the information, so they expect some payment for it.

The possibilities for websites are endless. What about a site that gave you wine tips, or receipts for special meals? Surely they would be worth subscribing to?

What some search engines have begun to do is to sell keywords to site owners. We have already seen how this is in operation with the GoTo search engine. If I want my site to appear at the top of a list of results, I agree to pay the search engine, say, one cent every time someone clicks on the link to my page from the search engine. Since anyone can buy the search term, some search terms can be quite expensive.

This has the effect of increasing the value to the searcher of the search term. You should now find more valuable links. But you — the consumer — are not the one who pays for this!

The only problem is that sites with commercial interest or sites that sell products may very well be up at the top of the listings. More often than not, some of the smaller, less well-known sites are the ones with more interesting or valuable views and information on a particular topic.

Later, we will explore many of the possibilities that the web has opened up, and list some of the most interesting sites to explore. For now, use the techniques described in this chapter to search. Below we list the search engines mentioned in this chapter:

❖ *www.altavista.com*

- ❖ *www.askjeeves.com*   meta search engine
- ❖ *www.dogpile.com*meta search engine
- ❖ *www.google.com*
- ❖ *www.goto.com*
- ❖ *www.hotbot.com*
- ❖ *www.infoseek.com*
- ❖ *www.looksmart.com*
- ❖ www.lycos.com
- ❖ *www.mamma.com*   meta search engine
- ❖ *www.webcrawler.com*
- ❖ *www.yahoo.com*   search directory

Part Three

Getting More from the Internet

Chapter 8

Building a Website

Why Do You Want a Website?

If you are considering setting up a website — whether you are an individual, a business, a school, or whatever — you should think long and hard before doing it. The gurus of e-commerce have created the illusion that by setting up your own website, your company can reach a potential audience of over 50 million users. The key word here is *potential*. Certainly there are 50 million users on the Internet, but you may set up your site and find that out of 50 million users you only get ten visitors!

There is more to a website than just creating it. A website will not run by itself. Most successful websites have dedicated teams to look after the site. They invest time and money in it, which rewards the owners with visitors. Not only do they ensure that the site looks good, but also that it contains relevant, up-to-date material. They also ensure that it is marketed correctly.

Too many people think they *must* have a website since everyone else has one. It is true that a website is essential for many companies and organisations, but you must ask yourself why you need it, how it will help you and your clients/colleagues. The best way to answer this question is illustrated below. Before deciding to set up a site, you should take time to read and understand the following points.

Statement of Purpose

Every website must have a Statement of Purpose. Ask yourself exactly what the purpose of your site will be. Why have it there, what will it do, how will it benefit your organisation? If you can find no purpose for your website, then surfers will not be interested in it. Why would you go somewhere where there is nothing to see or do? A Statement of Purpose will help you decide on the direction of your website.

A simple Statement of Purpose could be as follows:

> *The aim of this website is to promote our company online as a*
> *key player in the training and web authoring market.*

Short, sweet and to the point. You now know that you are going to use the website to promote your company. From here you must develop what information you wish to convey to your visitors about your company. For this, we develop a Statement of Objectives.

Statement of Objectives

The Statement of Objectives will list out what you hope to achieve on your website. Once you know what you wish to achieve or accomplish through your website, you will have a better picture of how to develop it.

When thinking about your Statement of Objectives, you should consider what you would like the user to know or to have gained after having visited the site. How many times have you gone to a website that you think contains the exact information you are looking for, but after browsing it for 20 minutes you leave the site with very little information? The creators of these sorts of site obviously did not take the time to write out what they wanted to have achieved by the time you had left the site. Remember, the user or surfer is the main reason you construct a website. If you give them what they want, they will return.

When the user finds a site that gives them what they want, they will return to it. So it is extremely important that you list out your objectives for your website. Remember, your objectives should be based on what you want the surfer to know about you and your company/organisation/ school after they leave.

An example of a Statement of Objectives is detailed below:

> *The objectives of this website are:*
>
> ❖ *To ensure that the user of the site gains enough information about our products in order to make an informed purchase.*
>
> ❖ *To provide an understanding of the history and structure of our company.*
>
> ❖ *To create awareness of new products/services that we offer.*
>
> ❖ *To allow the user to interact and develop our website.*

The above are very general statements of objectives but serve to help you formulate your basic website structure.

Have you ever tried to open a web page and found a little animation with the message "This site is under construction"? Your website is *always* going to be under construction. Since the web is a dynamic, constantly changing medium, you must be prepared to change your objectives on a regular basis.

From the above list of objectives, you will see that you already have at least four web pages in the conception stage. You want to have a page about:

❖ Products

❖ History of company

❖ New products and services

❖ Interaction.

From this basis, you can now begin to think about the development of your site.

Audience Definition

One important factor we have left out so far is who your site is aimed at. After all, with any publication, you must know your audience. It is very important that you decide what type of audience your site is aimed at. Websites are often aimed at two different audiences (at least), and the site is then divided up accordingly.

As part of your website documentation, you must include an audience definition where you decide what type of person your site is aimed at. If you are unsure of who your site is aimed at, you will have problems trying to develop. Knowing your audience helps you decide on layout — if it is a young audience you are targeting, you need to make a site that is fun and interesting, perhaps utilising animation and vibrant colours. If your audience is businesspeople, there is no point in designing your site in a childish manner. Be aware that your audience definition will change over time.

Example

Let's work with an example of an imaginary training company called Tender Training.

TENDER TRAINING: WEBSITE STRATEGY

Statement of Purpose

To try to capture a larger market share of the training market and to promote our training manuals.

Statement of Objectives

Visitors to our site should come away with a thorough knowledge of the following:

- ❖ *Who we are*
- ❖ *Services we provide, both corporate and domestic*
- ❖ *Course schedule and prices*
- ❖ *Course outlines*
- ❖ *Qualifications and experience of staff*
- ❖ *Self-study training material available*
- ❖ *Surfers must be able to know about booking procedure*
- ❖ *Special area for discussion and question answering.*

From the above, we can see that we will have a website with the following pages:

- ❖ *About us*
- ❖ *Services*
- ❖ *Course information*
- ❖ *Training staff*
- ❖ *Other products we provide*
- ❖ *Booking information*
- ❖ *Help section.*

Audience Definition

We envisage that those who visit our site will be corporate users who are interested in planning an in-house training session. The site may also be of interest to some home users who wish to buy our training manuals.

> *From our audience definition, we can infer that the website must be clean and professional looking. We must provide timely and up to date information for our corporate clients. We must also make sure that we provide an interesting and intelligent discussion and help section on our site, so that corporate users will see that the service goes on even after training is completed.*

As you can see, by laying out and defining a few essential items, this company are now on their way to designing their first website. Designing a site should not be undertaken in a haphazard way. Users will find the site hard to understand and your message will not be conveyed properly. Therefore it is essential that you spend time preparing your website on paper before you think of building it.

Preliminaries

Now that you know what you want, you must consider the following:

How will you present your website?

At this point you should begin to sketch out on paper what you would like your site to look like visually on screen. Will you use mainly graphics or text? Will you use a menu along the left or right-hand side of the screen?

The presentation of a site is very important. It should be clear, attractive and (most importantly) load very quickly. The average web user will wait for about 20 seconds when they visit a site; if nothing has appeared in that time, they will move onto another site, unless they are really interested in your site. Graphics, while attractive, will slow down your site. Later in this chapter, when we look at the mechanics of building a site, and in particular at HTML, we will be able to find out how to calculate how long it will take to download a web page you are designing.

Graphics must be used on a site to make it more interesting and visually appealing to the user, but they should not be used unnecessarily. Again, think about why people are visiting your site; 70 per cent of people want information from a website; therefore if you were to take away all the graphics and fancy animations, would it still be interesting? If the answer is no, perhaps you need to think out what you are doing wrong.

How many times have you been to a movie and been blown away by the special effects? But when you come out of the cinema and think about the film, you realise there was not much of a plot. The special effects are only there to disguise the lame plot.

What sort of content will you have?

With the advent of more powerful computers, many game critics would say that the quality of gaming has decreased. Many games now have wonderful sound and brilliantly breathtaking graphics, but very little game play. Don't let your website fall into this trap.

You must ensure that the content of your site is interesting. Remember the phrase **content is king**; if you ever lose sight of this fact, your website will suffer. Without content, your site is nothing, people will not visit. You must build a website that has interesting and useful content. If you have a product to sell, you have to create compelling copy (or text) about it. You have to build a want and a need for the product.

For example, I recently bought an e-book on the basis of the compelling copy on the publisher's website. The site itself was not going to win any design awards, but that's not what I was after; I wanted to buy an e-book about product selling on the Internet. The content sold the book to me. And I was not disappointed by the e-book either.

You want to sell to the user as quickly as possible; if they read the first few lines of the text and it is boring, they will "click off"; if you can create the urge, capture their imagination, they will stay.

Don't be afraid to give out free information. The web is built on sites that make a fortune by giving out free information and then sell advertising space because their site is so popular.

I am a firm believer in this principle, and it is a valuable lesson that many websites need to learn. Many sites feel that all information should be paid for. This may be true to a certain extent, but entice your readers, give them a page of a report that will provide them with useful information; then if they wish to read more, they need to contact you to buy the rest of the report.

Give them free tips and hints about your products. If you are a mobile phone shop, give them hints on how to save money on their phone bills. If you are a car retailer, tell them how to keep their car running more smoothly. They will return for your updated tips, and, sooner or later, may well buy your products.

Who will build and maintain the site?

By now, you will also begin to realise that you may need a team of people to help you design your website. Of course, not every site will need a team of people, but if you have one you may get better results. In a school environment, you may find that the more artistic students could do the graphics, while teachers concentrate on the proofing end of things.

A few people who would be essential as part of a web development team would be:

* ❖ **HTML expert**: This person would be well versed in the HTML language. They may also be familiar with such packages as FrontPage or Dream Weaver (see later).

* ❖ **Graphic Designer**: This person should be able to design and create your graphics for you. They should also have a good background knowledge of traditional design techniques — not just computer graphics.

* ❖ **Editor/Writer**: If your site is going to be quite large, you should have a professional who is good at proofing and writing copy for the site. This person will ensure that your content is interesting and enjoyable to read.

* ❖ **Marketer**: you should ensure that you read up on current literature — available on the web — on marketing a website. Although some traditional marketing techniques can be used, you should be well aware of how websites are marketed. Getting the right person to market a site is essential; they should have knowledge of the techniques used on the Internet.

Planning your Site Layout

Before continuing, you should consider drawing out a sketch of your website on paper; this is known as storyboarding, a term borrowed from the movies. The first page of your website is always the homepage. This page should appear at the top of your page. You should then decide what pages are linked from the homepage, and what pages link to these secondary pages, etc. Looking at our example of Tender Training, their storyboard might look like this:

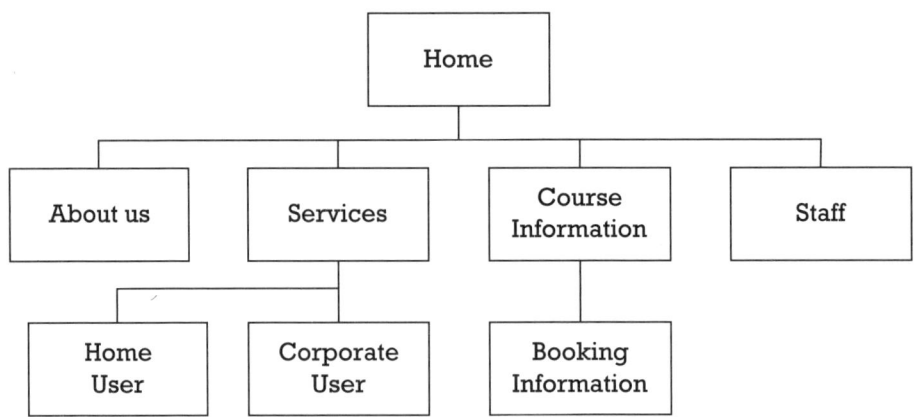

This helps you decide the site structure/map. Not every page will be linked to the homepage. If a site contained 100 pages, there would only be space on the homepage for links! But every individual page should be linked back to the homepage and the site map.

*A **site map** is a page on your website that shows users where every page is located. A site map is an essential part of a website.*

Some pages may only be visible as links when the user is on a certain page. Take, for example, course information: this may have sub-pages (or "children") such as booking information, detailed information about courses, etc.

***Tip!** The **3-click rule** states that users should be able to find the information they require within three clicks of their mouse.*

I have been to too many sites where you have to trawl through endless pages to find what you are looking for.

Coupled with this is the need to think about navigation. One complaint that people have about websites is that they are so difficult to navigate. This is one fault of many e-commerce sites. There are too many pages to navigate in order to buy their product. Amazon.com have a "one-click" system; it literally takes one click to buy a product, once you are a registered user.

In short, preparation is the key; spend time doing all your pre-planning for your website.

Creating your Site

Here you have two options: if you want to become a web author (i.e. someone who designs web pages for a living), it is essential that you learn and have a very good understanding of HTML and other technologies such as Flash, CGI and JavaScript. If you just want to create a website and not bother about learning HTML, there are plenty of packages to help you.

In order to create a website, you will probably need:

❖ A HTML authoring package for coding the site

❖ A paint package for creating graphics

❖ A scripting language for interactivity

❖ Web space

❖ A small FTP program

❖ A dash of creative thought

❖ A pinch of luck!

We will look at the different elements in turn, starting with HTML.

HTML

While it is beyond the scope of this book to go into the sort of detail on the HTML language that a professional web author would need, it is worth knowing the basic instructions that go into making up a simple web page. From the point of view of the user, a web page is an Internet document, made up of text, graphics, hyperlinks and active content. From a web author's point of view, however, a web page is a set of instructions that are saved as a text file with the extension .htm or .html. The instructions tell the browser how to display text.

HTML is the language in which web pages are encoded. HTML is a mark-up language, which means that it tells the browser how elements on a page should be displayed; the formatting of these elements is left up to the individual browser. If you look at a web page in Internet Explorer and then use Netscape Navigator, you may find that the page looks different: colours may be brighter, images may be positioned slightly differently. This can lead to problems for web designers, as the page looks perfect in Internet Explorer but appears completely different in Netscape!

Example

Web pages can be created in a simple text program such as Notepad, you can find notepad by going to **Start**, **Programs**, **Accessories**, and clicking on the **Notepad** icon.

A simple HTML page might look as follows:

```
<html>
<head>
<title>my web page</title>
</head>
<body>
This is some text
</body>
</html>
```

This page would display the text:

This is some text

As you can see, HTML is made up of <u>tags</u>, which are words enclosed in <>; most HTML tags have closing tags, as you can see in our example above.

A web page can be instructed to display an image by using the following command:

```
<img src=myimage.gif>
```

This tells the browser to look for an image called myimage.gif and display it on the page. Adding this to the previous code, we have:

```
<html>
<head>
<title>my web page</title>
</head>
<body>
This is some text <img src=myimage.gif>
</body>
</html>
```

This would display the text as above and also include a picture beside the text.

Try typing in the example above in Notepad; when you are saving the page, you must choose **All files** in the **Save as** area. Make sure you then save the page with a .htm extension; for example, call this page you have created "page1.htm".

You can now open Internet Explorer and view the page, by going to **File**, choosing **Open** and clicking on **Browse** until you find the place where you saved the page.

How do I determine the size of a web page?

So a web page is made up of a text file with commands in it, which tell the browser how to display information. This page of text is saved with an extension .htm to signify it is a web page.

Each character in that file takes up one <u>byte</u>; this includes spaces. If you wanted to display the word "hello" on pages using HTML, you would have to use the following code:

```
<html>
<head>
<title></title>
</head>
<body>
Hello
</body>
</html>
```

To display a word that takes up only 5 bytes, the actual file with all the coding takes up 73 bytes! (A few extra bytes are added by the program when saving!) The more commands that a .htm file has, the larger the file is, and the longer it takes to view on your screen.

Now imagine filling the page up with pictures, animations, etc. The more images a person includes on their web page, the longer it will take to display the page on your browser; the reason is the browser must fetch all the text and images from the server and then display them on your screen. The images themselves may be large in terms of disk space, so it will take longer for the browser to display them. Imagine how long it would take to show animation or video!

HTML Packages

There are numerous packages available that will help you create your own web page. The majority of these must be bought, although there are freeware ones available. Below we look at a number of packages, indicating which are free, which are available as trials or shareware.

One problem is that many of the packages will assume you have some HTML experience; as you get into more advanced features, you will have to know one or two things about HTML, so it is always good to get yourself a tutorial or two on HTML.

Many Microsoft products are now "web-enabled". This feature allows you to save Office documents as web pages! Go to **File**, **Save as**; in the **Save as type** area of the dialog box, choose **HTML**; your word document is now saved as a HTML page. This is not, however, a great method of creating pages as Word will add an enormous number of unnecessary tags to your page. Microsoft Publisher also allows you to create web pages, but the same problem occurs.

Dreamweaver

Dreamweaver is available from Macromedia (*www.macromedia.com*). Some would argue that this is the best web authoring package. It is easy enough for beginners to use, but has many advanced features. Many web designers use this package in conjunction with other Macromedia products in order to design sites.

FrontPage

From Microsoft, FrontPage is not available as a trial version. Quite a good package, it looks and feels much like any other Microsoft product. For HTML purists, it can be a pain, as it presumes to "know" what you intend to code, and tends to alter your coding to suit itself. One advantage of FrontPage is that when used in conjunction with a server that supports FrontPage extensions, saving and publishing complex websites becomes quite easy.

Before using FrontPage with your hosting service (see later), you must ensure that the company can enable FrontPage Extensions on their server. This means that your site can fully exploit some of the in-built functions within FrontPage. You can still use FrontPage to create your site, even if your hosting company does not have FrontPage Extensions installed on their web server, but you will not be able to take advantage of some of the added functionality of FrontPage, such as the WebBot.

A WebBot allows you to create web page items such as counters and forms very easily without you needing to know programming. You simply tell FrontPage where you want the WebBot element placed (often called a FrontPage component) and it simply inserts it.

Depending on your installation of Internet Explorer 5, you may have received FrontPage Express, which is a very cut-down version of FrontPage, but is still a useful tool.

Both Dreamweaver and FrontPage are known as website management tools, as they can do more than just create the site. They can also help manage it, check for links that don't work, etc.

Adobe Page Mill and Hot Dog

Adobe Page Mill (*www.adobe.com*) and Hot Dog (www.sausage.com) are two other well-known authoring tools. Both offer more or less the same options, each with its own distinctive style! They are simple-to-use WYSIWYGs (What You See Is What You Get); you can easily create web pages with them. Both come with built-in website up-loaders (easy-to-use FTP software).

Graphics

On the web there are two types of images. GIF (Graphics Interchange Format) is used for images that have 256 colours or less. These are usually for simple logos/icons. JPG or JPEG (Joint Photographic Experts Group) is used for high-quality images such as photographs. JPG images can display millions of colours. Both formats use compression to reduce file sizes. Remember, the bigger the image, the more web space it will take up and consequently the longer it will take to download.

For your paint package, you could try *www.jasc.com*. They are the makers of Paint Shop Pro, a very good package that would be more than enough for the average web designer. Paint Shop Pro is <u>shareware</u>, so you can use if for 30 days before deciding to buy it.

If you are artistically inclined, you can create your own graphics within this program; otherwise, you can import graphics you may have, such as scanned images or photos you may have taken with a digital camera, and then alter them. For a detailed explanation, use your knowledge of searching to search for Paint Shop Pro tutorials.

The industry standard for graphics packages is Adobe's PhotoShop, which will cost you a considerable amount. If you are seriously thinking of designing web pages for a living, you should consider buying this package.

I can't draw — Help!!!

If you are not artistically minded, don't worry, as there are many sites that will provide you with free <u>clipart</u> and other images for non-commercial projects.

Unfortunately, this is where you can run into problems. If you are designing web pages for a non-commercial organisation, there are hundreds of sites that will provide you with graphics for free. If you are designing professional, commercial pages, you will usually have to pay a licence or royalty charge. Be sure to check this out.

If I use someone else's graphics will I be caught?

Legally, you are breaching copyright if you use artwork created by someone else without their consent and do not acknowledge it. It is very difficult on some sites to ascertain the copyright owner of the images, as many sites have a disclaimer on them saying that, as far as they were aware, the images were in the public domain.

Public domain *refers to any program, code or graphics that are available to use for free with no charge or credit to the author.*

If in doubt, contact the owner of the site and seek their permission before "borrowing" their graphics. Copyright is discussed in more detail in Chapter 12.

Saving Graphics from Another Website

Assuming you have obtained copyright permission, if it is necessary to do so, it is very simple to save a graphic from a website. Simply place your cursor over the graphic and click with the right mouse button. A menu will appear from which you should choose **Save Picture As**. Save the graphic into your chosen folder. The graphic has now been saved onto your hard drive.

Source Codes

It is very easy to "steal" other people's images, as described above. Not only that, but you can also see how they designed the code of their web page by going to **View**, **Source** in Internet Explorer 5; as you can see, the source code is now available to read and change as you desire.

If you save the source code and change it, does this change it on their website? The answer is no! When you save the source code, you save it onto your local machine; any changes you make are only reflected on your computer and not on the owner's web server.

Since the user has spent time writing the code, it is like any other piece of work and it is copyright work. However, a lot of people "borrow" ideas from other people's code. As such, it is a murky area. As the web is developing, so are its legislative structures. If you directly copy it and it is evident, then you are breaching copyright. It can be assumed that anything on a website, be it graphics or text, or protected by copyright and are, as such, the intellectual property of the creator.

Website Interaction

Let's go back to Tender Training for a moment. They wanted to have an interactive area on their website where past course attendees could get help and discuss some of the finer points of the courses.

The solution Tender Training could go for is to set up a discussion board. A discussion board is a program on a web server that allows users to post comments (or in this case questions) to which other users can then post replies. Many discussion boards, including the one for Tender Training, would be moderated; that is, before any comment is posted on the board, it is checked by the person who runs the board to ensure it is suitable for inclusion.

There are two immediate problems here:

❖ How do you set up such a discussion board?

❖ The information contained in it is valuable and should only be available to those who have paid for and attended a course. How do you ensure they are the only ones with access to it?

In the first instance, you will need to find out how to set up a discussion board. You can either program one from scratch or buy a package off the shelf. Again, one of the great things about the Internet is choice. If you go looking for discussion board software, the program that allows you to set up and use the discussion board, it is easy enough to find hundreds of likely programs. In order to run a discussion board, you must have CGI access (see below).

The interactive nature of discussion boards is dealt with in Chapter 10. Here, we will concentrate on the technical side of setting one up. If you need help explaining some of the processes and terms described below, there are plenty of tutorials available on the web.

PERL and CGI

Most discussion boards are created using a programming language called PERL. PERL stands for Practical Extraction and Report Language. It is the language most commonly used to write server-side scripts for websites. Scripts are special programs which process information and react to it. PERL has a great ability to process text input and is therefore ideal for website programming.

You may also have heard of CGI, which you need to have access to in order to run these PERL scripts. CGI (Common Gateway Interface) is a way in which a web page can send information to the web server to be processed.

CGI is very popular and many service providers will allow you to use their own simple CGI scripts, free of charge. Most will not let you install your own CGI scripts for security reasons. If the script has not been installed properly, it can, in some circumstances, be possible for people to send commands to the PERL program that, when interpreted, will yield unexpected results. Service providers do not want their clients experimenting with scripts if they do not know what they are doing.

There are many sites that provide lists of scripts which you can use on your server. Examples of scripts which you could set up on your server include:

❖ The ability to provide free homepages

❖ A classified ads service

❖ Free e-mail

❖ Surveys.

One problem with CGI scripts is that they can be quite tricky to install on your web server. This is because a lot of web servers are Unix-based, which is a case-sensitive operating system. Therefore if you name a directory Myscript, and refer to it in a script as myscript, the CGI program will not work. It is essential when installing CGI scripts that you read the instructions completely before installing the script. You may need to seek assistance!

JavaScript

You may have heard of something called Java, and something else called JavaScript. As a matter of fact, Java and JavaScript are two completely different things! We will talk more about Java when we discuss chat rooms in Chapter 10.

The key thing to note is the word *Script* — JavaScript is a scripting language.

 *A **scripting language** is a type of programming language that is used in conjunction with another program.*

JavaScript can only be used in conjunction with HTML and a browser. As such, you cannot write a program in JavaScript and run it. It can only be run within a web browser. The reason for this is that JavaScript is an interpreted language. This means that when a browser encounters JavaScript within a web page, it interprets the code line by line and then responds to each line. This can sometimes be quite slow. With a fully-fledged programming language, the code is compiled before it is run.

This means that when you click on a program, like Microsoft Word, it does not have to read every line of code before it does something — it just runs! The average program might have millions of lines of code. Imagine having to wait for each line to be processed!

Client-side versus Server-side Scripting

JavaScript is used to create a more interactive website. The advantage of JavaScript is that it is what is known as client-side scripting. This means that the web page appears on your computer and then executes the JavaScript when it has arrived on your computer. The server does nothing.

CGI is a server-side scripting language, which means that the server does all the processing of the script. If you have ever tried to sign up for a free e-mail account from any of the free e-mail providers, you may well have run into problems filling up their application forms. You type everything out and submit the information only to be told your password is too short, or does not have a number in it, etc.

What has happened is that as soon as you hit the Submit button, the information is sent to the server, the server checks the information and then sends back an error message. This therefore requires the server to take up time and process each application, verify that everything is OK and then perform some task. The problem occurs when there are, say, 2,000 people doing exactly the same thing as you are and making the same mistake. This causes the server to slow down due to the load imposed on it!

It is important that you set up your website with a company that allows you the freedom to install your own CGI scripts.

In the example above, JavaScript could have been used on the client to check that the password was adequate, which would have saved resources on the server.

Scripting and Security

Website security is important; you do not want people who have not taken part in your training course to have access to valuable information which they did not pay for. In order to password-protect your website, you could use a CGI script or a small Java applet. Whichever one you use will serve the same function.

They will both maintain a list of users and their passwords. If the user is on the user list and enters their password correctly they will gain access to the secured part of your website. If they enter in the password incorrectly or are not on the user list they will be denied access. One problem that many sites are having is that some users will share their passwords with other users. Therefore one user pays for the subscription or course but multiple users get access to the site. You should consider looking for software that detects if multiple users are using the same username/password.

Other Types of Interaction

Flash from Macromedia is another application that is used widely on websites. Flash allows web authors to create highly interactive and colourful websites that are quite quick to download, compared to those designed using other technologies such as Java.

Flash allows you to create mini-movies that can be completely interactive. On the training site example used earlier, Flash could be useful for designing a tutorial so that users could learn more skills.

Another way that people create interaction on their sites is through chat rooms; if used correctly, they can greatly enhance a website. Chat rooms and other forms of interactivity are discussed in detail, from the user's point of view, in Chapter 10.

The one rule of thumb that must be adhered to is not to put Java, Flash or any other kind of interactivity on a web purely because you can or because it looks good. If it serves no purpose, then leave it out. Ask yourself if by adding this element you might be alienating certain users who cannot access the program required. Use any of the technologies available to you if they are going to enhance the user's experience.

Look at a site such as Yahoo — not a sign of Flash in sight! Why? Simply because it is not needed. Certain sites, such as entertainment sites, will find it useful and essential, but for many sites it may be a hindrance.

Initially small sites can survive without any or some of the above, but after a certain level of exposure you may find you need to re-design the site and will need to get specialists in.

The above and other points described below would come under the general heading of *web specifications*; this involves identifying the weaknesses and constraints of the website project.

Creative Thought

Unfortunately, it is beyond the scope of this book to help you with creative thought. If you are not creatively inclined, the best advice is to surf the web, look at what other people have created and then see if you could copy the designs or improve on them.

Remember the important points for web design:

❖ Statement of Purpose

❖ Statement of Objectives

❖ Audience

❖ Content

❖ Web Presentation

❖ Web Specifications.

When you have figured all of these points out, your site will be put together in a more professional manner.

Choosing a Domain Name

So far we have looked at the processes that go into putting together a website but have not mentioned how you go about getting a <u>domain name</u>. We discussed the mechanics of domain names in Chapter 2.

 *A **domain name** is a unique name that identifies your site on the Internet. It forms a part of your e-mail address and of your web address.*

Why choose a .com name?

A lot of companies decide to get a .com domain name, rather than, say, a .ie one if your company is Irish, simply because it is:

❖ More universal

❖ Easier to get

❖ Cheaper.

We will look at each of these points in turn.

❖ **Universal**: People now generally expect all companies to have websites; if they wish to find out if a company has a website, they may simply try adding .com to the end of the company name. If, for example, you were looking for a website for ABC Skip Hire, chances are you would try typing in *abcskiphire.com* rather than *abcskiphire.ie*.

❖ **Easier to Get**: Registering a .com domain name is a very simple procedure. You apply to the naming authority, which is Network Solutions (formally InterNic — *www.networksolutions.com*) and fill up some information about yourself and some technical details (outlined later on). You supply a credit card number and within about 72 hours or less you have your own domain name!

❖ **Cost**: At the time of going to press, to register a .com domain name costs an initial $70 for two years; after that you must pay $35 per year to retain your domain name. Compare the cost of a .ie domain name — £100 per year!

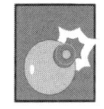 **Warning!** *If you forget to pay (you will be reminded by the naming authority) your name will be put back on the market.*

It is no harm to first get your website up and running with a .com domain name and then at a later stage get the version relevant to your country of business. The .com can be up and running within 72 hours or less.

Other Factors in Choosing a Name

When deciding what domain name to use, think long and hard about it. Too many people register long domain names that are not easy to remember. Short, easy-to-remember domain names are best.

It is always best to avoid domain names with hyphens; it makes it too easy for people to make mistakes. I recently heard an ad on the radio for an Irish website; the voiceover went something like this:

"Visit www.jobs *dash* ireland.com"

Now to many people, a "dash" means an em-dash; i.e. a longer line with a space before and after it (—); whereas a hyphen is a shorter line used to join two parts of a word, as in re-invent. If someone were to put in a dash in the web address, they would get an error message. This means that particular website could lose potential customers. Similarly, hyphens can cause confusion when addresses are being given out over the phone, especially with e-mail addresses.

One of the most confusing domain names I have seen was: *www.new-years-eve-dublin.com* — there are so many places you could make a mistake, and it is quite a mouthful to say!

Spend a lot of time thinking about a good domain name, but be aware that many easy-to-remember generic names are already gone. One example is a leading DIY store, which has the address *www.diy.com*! If you can find a generic name or a name that people will remember easily, go for that. You can register as many domain names as you like.

Can I use my business name?

Businesses often use their company name as their domain name; for example, the domain name of the Irish supermarket chain Superquinn is *www.superquinn.ie*.

However, if your business name is Richard Butler Computer Consultant Limited, try reducing it to *rbcc.com*; this is easier to remember and less prone to typos. Of course, if you could get a domain name like computerconsultants.com, this would be ideal!

The latest trend for website addresses is to drop the "www" part and simply say "Visit *sky.com*"; be careful and ask your web hosting company if people can access your site using either *www.mydomain.com* or *mydomain.com*. Some hosting companies may not provide this service.

Going Live: Hosting Your Website

When you have decided on a domain name, you need to find someone to host it. Hosting is where you or a company will set up a web server that will allow people to access your site using your URL, such as *www.mydomain.com*.

There are two options available to those who wish to set up a website with their own domain name:

❖ Host it yourself

❖ Virtually host it.

Hosting it Yourself

There are some advantages to hosting the site yourself:

❖ You have full control of the server. You can decide what goes up and what access people have to the website. You can have CGI access if you wish. You are the boss! If you need more space for your website, you don't have to pay any extra for it; you could put whatever multimedia content on you wish.

❖ If a problem occurs, you will know about it straight away and not have to wait for an outside company to deal with it.

However, for many smaller companies, the disadvantages can outweigh these advantages:

Cost

Hosting it yourself is a very expensive option and one that many companies will not be prepared to pay. In order to do this, you will need the following:

❖ **High specification server**	£1,500+
❖ **E-mail server software**	£2,000 (industry standard would be Isocor's Nplex)
❖ **Web server software**	Usually free; Apache for Unix or IIS for Windows NT
❖ **Firewall software**	£5,000 for industry recommended software
❖ **Dedicated connection**	£8,000+ annual rental (initial set-up cost about £16,000)
❖ **Dedicated technician**	£18,000–£20,000

This option may cost a company up to £20,000 to set up, excluding the cost of employing a dedicated technician — a huge figure for small to medium companies. If you are getting a dedicated line into your company, this may be an option that you should consider, as you will have all the hardware in place (see Chapter 3).

You may well need to employ a full-time administrator to ensure that everything is running smoothly. The other option is to have a maintenance contract.

Security

If you allow people to access your website, which is on your LAN, you are opening up your network to the web.

> **LAN** *(Local Area Network) is a term used to describe computers connected together in a small area, such as an office or office building.*

Remember, a web server is simply a computer running special software that allows people to access web pages on that computer. When you set up a web server, it designates a number of directories on your hard drive that are available to the public. This is where you place your website.

Let's assume you set up your web server. There will be a directory on your hard drive called wwwroot. This is where you place all your website documents. When someone accesses your website, they actually are accessing the information in the wwwroot directory. Suppose someone accidentally places a confidential report in the wwwroot directory; it is possible that anyone could access that report.

However, it is not enough just to guard against this sort of carelessness. The normal user should only be able to see the files available in the wwwroot directory. The danger is that an experienced hacker may be able to get access to the rest of the hard drive of the server if you do not have proper security in place. If people can access the computer's hard drive, they can completely change your website. In order to protect yourself, you will need to invest heavily in firewall software.

> *A **Firewall** is a combination of hardware and software that protects your internal network from the Internet and thus from unauthorised users coming in from the Internet.*

This software alone may set you back up to £5,000. Also, you may need to employ the services of a security consultant to ensure your site is un-hackable.

Internet-in-a-box

Many companies who have dedicated connections do not host their own websites because of some of the problems outlined above. They prefer to host with a hosting company, as this means that their website and LAN are separate from each other (see below).

However, in recent times, many companies have produced a product that provides "Internet in a box" solutions. Instead of having to buy a web server, e-mail server, proxy server and firewall, you get everything you need in a box. This type of solution is very good. It will, in its basic form, set you back around £2,500–£3,000 pounds. In this basic form, it comes with limited but adequate security features.

From an administrator's viewpoint, it is easy to use; you can set it up over the network from any computer. You have all the server software you need. Many come with full auditing, which means that you can view information about what each user has done during their surfing sessions. You can also see how many e-mails they have received, the size of them, etc. This allows you, as an employer or educator, to see who is accessing the Internet, for how long and how often.

Many small to medium-sized firms can set up their website, have company-wide e-mail and security features for £3,000 compared to dedicated servers, software, etc., which will set you back a minimum of £8,000.

The other option that many companies and individuals use is called virtual hosting.

Virtual Hosting

Virtual hosting means placing your website on a server owned by a separate company. You then get an e-mail server, web server, etc. — all of the above — for a fraction of the cost.

The reason it is called a virtual server is that it functions exactly like a real server, but there may be many websites running on the same master server. You get all the functionality of a real server. For example, I run a small virtual hosting company (*www.2hostu.com*) and have a number of sites running on the same server.

The user does not know that it is virtually hosted, because they see your address as *www.mydomain.com*. Virtual hosting can be a tricky thing to purchase, as so many companies will offer you completely different prices for varying degrees of service.

When choosing a virtual hosting company, you should ask the following questions:

How much web space do I get?

In reality, websites take up very little space, a medium-sized website could be put onto a floppy disk! It depends on how much information you have and what multimedia content you have on your site. Many sites will proclaim unlimited space for all your needs. The average space you should get is 10MB — this is more than adequate for most purposes.

How many e-mail accounts do I get?

When you set up your site, you may wish to have e-mail for different departments such as sales, info, comments, etc. Your virtual hosting company should provide a minimum of 5–10 e-mail accounts. Also ensure that you can change the e-mail addresses if you wish; you should be able to do this yourself and not have to ask the hosting company to do it. Always ensure that if your domain is *www.mydomain.com* then your e-mails are in the form of *sales@mydomain.com*, etc. This looks professional; many sites have *www.mydomain.com* and then have an e-mail address of *mydomain@myisp.com*; this looks extremely unprofessional. Your e-mail addresses should always reflect your domain name.

Can I set up e-mail aliases?

E-mail aliases are an excellent feature, which hosting companies should allow. They allow you to set up your e-mail account so that if a message is sent to, say, *sales@mydomain.com*, *webmaster@mydomain.com* or *accounts@mydomain.com* they will all be handled by the one account. Whenever an e-mail comes in for any of those addresses it will automatically be sent to, say, *webmaster@mydomain.com*. It thus appears that you have different departments, but allows you to deal with all the e-mail from one account. They work very well if you're a one-person company!

Do I get autoresponders?

<u>Autoresponders</u> are a godsend to any company operating on the Internet. When someone sends an e-mail to a specific address, they will re-

ceive an automated response immediately. This response is sent out by the server; thus you have a "dedicated employee" sending out automatic responses! This is good for a number of reasons: sending an automatic, near-instantaneous response shows you are efficient. It also saves you time answering general e-mails. Many hosting companies will charge you extra for this facility.

Do I have 24/7 access?

Can you update your site whenever you want? Most hosting companies will give you this facility.

Do I get full CGI access?

If you want to create more interactive sites, with forms or discussion boards, make sure that you get a hosting service that allows you to use CGI.

How much does it cost?

Make sure you are not being ripped off. The first thing to ensure is that, if the hosting company agree to register your domain name, they do not charge you an administration fee. Some hosting companies will charge you £150 to register your name; remember, to register your name for two years should only cost $70. Registering a name is quite easy once you have done it a couple of times. It should take your hosting company about ten minutes to register the name.

When registering a domain name, you must ensure that your details, rather than the ISP's, are provided as the owner of the domain; otherwise, the ISP could, in theory, claim ownership of the domain name at a later stage.

Some companies will charge extra for some of the services outlined above. My site, *www.2hostu.com*, will provide all of the above for £199 per year for hosting!

Do I need to have a hosting service before registering a domain name?

Yes and no! In order to register a name, you must provide the naming authorities with two <u>domain name servers</u> that will resolve the IP number of your site into an alphanumeric URL.

This ensures that your site can be found on the Internet. When you buy domain hosting, your hosting company will provide you with two name servers; there are two so that if one is not working, the second one can be queried. When someone types in yournewdomain.com, their ISP will query its DNS servers to see if it can find your site, if it can't, they will query another DNS server and so on until it finds your site.

My hosting company said my site is online but I cannot see it; why is this?

The DNS system is a distributed system. Every DNS server updates itself from another DNS server, so it may take up to 72 hours for your site to be accessible worldwide!

Domain Name Parking

Many companies allow you to "park" your domain name for use at a later date. This means that when someone accesses www.mynewdomain.com, a page will appear that says the site is "parked here" while it is being developed. Most hosting companies will provide this parking service free of charge. Note that you cannot design the page that pops up; otherwise, it becomes hosting!!

Can I not just use a free service?

Why not use a service such as the ones offered by *www.geocities.com* or *www.tripod.com* or the free pages offered by your ISP? The fact is, a long URL looks unsightly and unprofessional. If you see a web design company offering their services and their address is *http://homepages.tripod.com/~webdesign*, this does not look as professional as *www.webdesign.com* — call it cyber snobbery, but it is true!

Uploading to Your Server

So you've designed your basic website, added graphics and links, registered your domain name and found a suitable host server. Now you need to be able to transfer your newly created web files to this server, or in other words to <u>upload</u> your site. A web server's function is to serve web pages to users when they request them.

How do you transfer the files from your computer to a web server? Some homepage providers allow you to transfer your files by selecting them from a web page. Some, but not many, hosting companies will provide you with the facility to use FrontPage on their server. All you do is press **Save** on your FrontPage program and it is automatically saved on the server. If you want to get a website up and running with minimum hassle, try this option! MS Office 2000 is also allowing this feature on its products.

FTP

However, it is quite likely that your hosting company will ask you to use FTP. File Transfer Protocol (FTP) is a very important protocol for web design, allowing website owners to transfer HTML files to their server.

Cast your mind back to Chapter 1; you may remember that e-mail was created by a "hack", or a modification of a program that was used to transfer files using File Transfer Protocol! Whenever you download a program or wish to transfer a program/files from one server/computer to another, you use FTP. Most browsers have built-in FTP capabilities.

If you want to experiment with FTP, e-mail *ftp@tintecsystems.com* for a free web account with full FTP capabilities. Let's assume that you have requested your free website from tintecsystems and you got your username and password back. What do you do now?

The first thing is to get an FTP client. There are two available on the website accompanying this book; one is CuteFTP and the other is WS_FTP lite. There is a tutorial on using WS_FTP lite on the website accompanying this book (*www.internetdemystified.com*).

Remember we said that some free web page providers allow you to upload your page via a web page? Is this still FTP? This is a question that confuses a lot of people. Yes, it is still FTP, because you are transferring files from your local computer to a remote server. Although you are not using an FTP client, you are using the File Transfer Protocol to send the pages over to the remote server.

Web designers must ensure that they upload the page and all the graphics associated with it. In Chapter 6, we saw that the following icon sometimes appears when a graphic cannot be displayed properly.

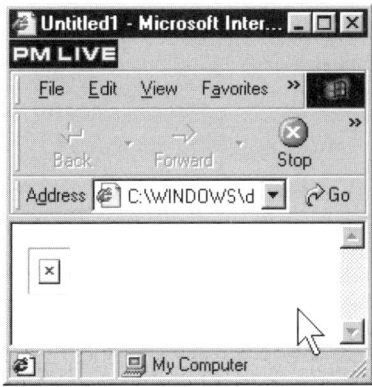

The reason is that the web designer did one of a number of things incorrectly; for example:

❖ They did not upload the correct image; therefore the browser is being instructed to display an image that does not exist.

❖ They entered the wrong name for the image. For example, if the image is called Myimage.gif and I refer to it as myimage.gif, it will not be found on the server. Many web servers are case sensitive; in this example, the web server sees the names of the images as completely different.

Marketing a Website

Once your website is up and running, your work is only beginning! Now you must concentrate on the reasons for setting it up in the first place. Whether it is selling your products or services, providing information or sharing your interests, you will, no doubt, want people to know about your site. Websites should be marketed both online and offline (i.e. in the "real" world).

Offline advertising is essential. Your web address and e-mail address should be placed on everything: business cards, letterheads and any ads you may create, such as billboards, radio ads, etc. Recently, there has been a spate of television advertisements for websites, particularly search engines such as Excite and Lycos. It gives you a quick reminder that they are there and, the next time you go online, you may remember them and use them rather than, say, Yahoo.

Whatever you do, ensure that your web/e-mail address is correct on any of these media, and also that your site is up and running. If someone visits your site and it is "under construction" or not functioning, they will not return.

Banner Advertising

Marketing a website can be expensive. Many websites sell advertising space on their pages. They may charge to display the ad, either by how many times it has been seen or how many times people have clicked on it. The higher the profile of the site, the more they will charge. However, compared to other media advertising, costs can be significantly lower.

What are <u>banner ads</u>? Banner ads are the little rectangular boxes (usually) which you will see on many websites, advertising services and offering freebies when you click on them. Their sole purpose is to entice you to click on them and visit their website!

When looking to buy advertising space, you could do one of two things:

1. Approach a website directly and see how much they charge;

2. Approach a <u>banner advertising network</u>.

The second option may be best. These networks have special programs that take your banner and rotate it around a selected number of sites which you choose. The advantage is that your banner ad may be seen on ten different websites rather than one.

You can pay for this service in two ways:

1. **Pay per impression**: Each time your ad appears on a page, you are charged. You will be told how many times per hour your ad will appear. This method is good for the website which displays your ad, as they make money even if nobody ever visits your site!

2. **Click thru**: You only pay each time someone clicks on your ad. This is good for you, as you only pay per click, but it is bad for the site displaying your ad. For this reason, it tends to be more expensive.

Most advertising is on a per impression basis.

A banner ad network should provide you with detailed statistics on how many times an ad was seen, time of day, how many times the ad was clicked (if at all), etc. If an ad achieves anything from a 1–3 per cent click-thru rate, it is doing well; i.e. for every 100 ads shown, between one and three people are clicking on it.

Believe it or not, you can get free exposure on other websites through banner advertising. Smaller sites and personal/educational sites should be aware of <u>banner exchange services</u>. In this type of service, you get one free ad placed on another site for every two ads you display on your site. These services work on a democratic basis; you get what you put in. The more people visit your site, the more ads you display; the more ads you display, the more your ads will be displayed on other sites!

For example, if 50 unique people visit my website, my ad would be shown on 25 other websites. These types of banner exchange programs can be ideal for small sites to gain some exposure. Be warned that many of these ads yield low returns — think of how many ads you have clicked on since you began to use the Internet (apart from your early surfing days, when you might have been fooled by the words "Click here"!). If you cannot afford advertising on expensive sites such as Yahoo, etc., this is an affordable and cost effective way of advertising.

There are many banner advertising networks, including:

❖ *www.linkexchange.com*

❖ *www.smartclicks.com*

❖ *www.banneradnetwork.com*

These are the better known networks. They make their money by sponsorship; they also have better deals and place your ads on better known sites if you pay a little extra. In the free services, your banner may only be put on personal homepages, which may not yield a huge amount of traffic, but it is free and worth trying!

Search engines usually search-sensitive ads; if you search for "prams", you will get ads related to prams, nappies, etc.

How do I make a banner ad?

You should think long and hard about your banner ad and seek the help of a professional in designing it. Unfortunately, on the web first impressions do count and your banner ad may be the first impression people get of your website/product.

Each network has different rules about the size of the banner, both physically and in terms of bytes; ensure that you check this carefully! Smartclicks actually has a program that will create a basic but workable banner for you. Some banner networks also include a list of people who will design a banner for free for you! Time spent making a good banner is time well spent.

What makes people click on a banner?

You should make your banner eye-catching; there are so many dull banners out there that one that catches the eye will stand out and you may get someone to click on it.

Regular surfers see so many banner ads that they soon become immune to them, but here are some tips which you should follow:

❖ People are curious by nature; when they see something that catches their attention, they will be more likely to click on it. Recently I saw ads for free international phone calls. At the time I was looking for cheap ways to make calls, so of course I clicked on it!

❖ Pose a question on your banner that makes the person curious to click to find the answer; for example: *"Find out how to save £100 on your next . . ."* People may become curious and wonder what that is about.

❖ One idea that has taken off in the US is the FUI or Fake User Interface. This is a banner ad that looks like a clickable button or a drop-down menu. It then asks you to make a selection; when you click on it, you visit the advertiser's site. FUIs were discussed in Chapter 6.

❖ Offer something free in return for clicking on the banner: *"Get free information on how to save money on web design."* Can't hurt if it is free and saves money!

❖ The most important point is to **deliver what you promise**. If I see an ad for free international phone calls, click on the ad and then arrive at a site that has nothing to do with this, I will feel fooled and will be in the wrong frame of mind to buy the product. If I feel that the free information I got on the site was useless, you have lost me as a customer. Make sure that, if your banner says you are offering something free, you hold true to that offer; otherwise people will be annoyed! Don't fool people into visiting your website, as they will feel tricked and will not use or buy your product.

Newsletters

One great way of building up a client database is to publish a newsletter that is sent out to users' e-mail addresses. When people visit your site, offer them the option of signing up for your newsletter, which contains articles or thoughts about the content of your website or on a related subject. Thus you are marketing your service but e-mailing users, with their consent, in the form of the newsletter.

Setting up and distributing a newsletter is not difficult thanks to www.listbot.com, who provide a service that allows you to automate sign-up and distribution of your newsletter. When you arrive at the site, you will be presented with two options: a free newsletter service that carries advertising or a paid-for newsletter service, with more benefits and no advertising. For most purposes, the free service is more than adequate.

Once you go through the sign-up process, you will be told how to set up links on your site to allow users to subscribe. They have a special members area that allows you to set up how the newsletter looks, provides questions that users must fill in when signing up for the newsletter, and there is also the option to send out your newsletter. When you send out your newsletter, you type in your contents on the web page and then press the Send button; this will send the newsletter to all your subscribers at once.

In my experience, the worst thing a newsletter creator can do is to proclaim their own self-worth or fill the first few screens with publicity information about their company or products. Many newsletters have been interesting when they were first launched, but as they build up readership, they begin to advertise more and more. The net effect is that the reader has to endure ad after ad, when the reason they signed up for the newsletter was *content*.

We must look to the US for exceptional newsletters. Many companies have newsletters that really grab your attention; one way of doing this is by posing teasers that lead you to their website. For example:

Great new ways to market your website!
I found this really useful guide on how to market your website
the other day, it began with the simple premise . . . <link>

You are intrigued by the catch statement and are compelled to click on the link. Some would argue that this type of newsletter does not work, as people will not click on the link, but those people are not aware of how to write good copy text. If it is compelling enough, users will click on the link. This is the equivalent of a newspaper ad: you are given some information, but only enough to catch your attention.

Tip! *Never fool your readers; don't feed them a line that raises their expectations and then trick them by bringing them to a page with a blatant advert for your product. Advertise somewhere on the page, but this should not be the main focus of the page.*

One particularly good newsletter is that of *wired.com*. They send out the main stories on their website and provide links to the site which you can visit directly from the newsletter.

Think about this for a minute. A website can usually only use what is called "pull technology" — the user must pull down the information and find it from the web. A newsletter uses push technology, where the information is "pushed" down to you, the user. It is very difficult to attract readers to your website, but this is one way.

A few tips for newsletters:

❖ Have one!

❖ Always provide clear instructions on how to unsubscribe to the newsletter — make it easy for the customer to unsubscribe, and they will actually be less likely to do so!

❖ Send it out when you promise it is to be out; never be late with a newsletter.

❖ Don't fill it with huge amounts of advertising information.

❖ Write good copy; make it interesting, make people want to read it.

Getting the most from Search Engines

If I were to ask you how people found your website, what would you say? Saw an ad? Recommended by a friend? Think again . . . How do you, as a user, find the sites to visit?

The answer, of course, is through search engines. It is a well-established fact that the vast majority of sites are found via search engines. Advertising, in many cases and for many sites, is relatively useless. When I want a plumber, I look in the Yellow Pages — a real world search directory! Because I didn't need a plumber up to that time, I had ignored all the ads I saw for plumbers.

Similarly, Internet users block out ads they see on the web. So your site must be listed on search engines; not only that, it must be ranked highly on them. It is a known fact that people only look through the first four or five pages of results. Your aim should be in the top 10 or 20 matches returned.

So how do you achieve such a ranking? As you know from Chapter 7, most search engines rely on keywords. When a user wants to look for a page, they enter keywords into the search engine, and the engine will display pages that contain the specified keywords.

Spend time thinking about what words people will use to find your product or service. List out all the keywords. Once you have made your list, you must optimise every page of your website. This means including your keywords in your pages. You should not deliberately repeat your keyword endlessly on your web pages; search engines have various techniques to ensure this does not happen!

One of the most important things to use is <u>meta tags</u>. Meta data is information about information! There are two main meta tags you will use:

❖ *<meta name="description" content="describe your website">* This tag will describe your website. When a search engine indexes it, this is the exact description that will appear in the search results. The more interesting your description, the more likely you will get "the click"!

❖ *<meta name="keywords" content="enter, your, keywords">* This tag tells the search engine which keywords it should use to index your page.

These tags go between the <head> and </head> tags.

Marketing a website is a skill you must learn and learn well. Once a person has clicked on the link to visit your website, you must make sure they stay there, perhaps make a purchase or at least return. If you want to know more about marketing your website, try reading *Managing and Marketing Your Website* by Jim Hutchinson (Oak Tree Press, 1999). Use the search engines to find out more information about web marketing. With time and patience, you can find plenty of information that will help you attract more customers to your website.

Measuring Your Website's Success

Counters

Once your site is up and running, you should see about keeping an account of how many people are visiting your site, where they are coming from, who they are and when they are coming. Imagine having all this information — surely it will cost you a fortune? Wrong!! In fact, you can get this <u>counter</u> service for free from many websites. For a comprehensive overview of many free services, try *www.counterguide.com*. Most of these services require you to be familiar with HTML and some will not work if you use a HTML editor like those described earlier.

Why do I need to use a counter service?

It is very important, once you have created a website, that you can see how popular it is. What's the point in having a website if no one is visiting it? Using a counter service can be important if you are spending money on advertising — you can see which types of ads or which websites are sending the most traffic to your site.

Without proper tracking you will never know how many people are visiting your site, which may mean you are wasting your time building and spending money on your site!

Web Tracking

Web trackers are more than just counters; they can record and present much information, including:

❖ Date, day and time the user arrived at your site

❖ Type of browser used

❖ Screen resolution, number of colours being used

❖ Country they came from

❖ Who referred them to your site.

It is essential that you can analyse how well your pages are doing and who is visiting. If people are not visiting a certain page in your website, you should ask yourself why this is. Try changing the content, see if it is out of date, if your links are working. Perhaps you need to market it better.

Without constant analysis, creating a website is futile. If no one is looking at your website, why have one at all?

A website is never finished, you should be constantly improving it and making changes to it as necessary.

The Next Step . . .

Once your site is up and marketed, the game is only beginning! You must constantly update your website. People like to see new material on websites; if the site is updated regularly, they will return.

How often should you update? This really depends on what your site is about. A news website needs to be updated at least every hour, or even every few minutes for a stock/share price site. Don't keep changing the look of the site; the user will get confused if, each time they visit your site, they see what looks like a completely different page.

The next step, once you have successfully created your website and have it up and running, is to consider selling your products over the Internet. Chapter 9 looks at the explosion in e-commerce.

Chapter 9

E-commerce

What is E-commerce?

The world of computing, and the Internet in particular, has created more new words over the last 50 years than any other area of human endeavour. While many of these "buzzwords" are just passing fads, quite a few have entered into everyday use. Over the last two or three years, the word on everybody's lips is e-commerce.

There is much confusion over exactly what e-commerce includes. As the name implies, e-commerce, or electronic commerce, concerns Internet-based business dealings. In the narrow sense, e-commerce is simply the buying and selling of goods and services over the Internet. In the broad sense of the word, however, e-commerce could be seen as *any* commercial transaction, enterprise or communication that involves or concerns the Internet. This broader definition could, for instance, encompass all of the following:

❖ Businesses that provide Internet or web services on a commercial basis (e.g. search engines, software providers, ISPs, web designers, etc.);

❖ Companies whose business is entirely Internet-based ("dotcoms");

❖ The Internet-based businesses of other companies (commercial websites or web pages), whether business-to-business or business-to-consumer;

❖ Any commercial transaction that takes place over the Internet (including, from the user's point of view, Internet shopping, auctions, etc.);

❖ Internet banking and "offline" transactions using smart cards, digital cash or similar technologies;

❖ Business-to-business marketing online;

❖ The exchange of commercially useful information, such as mailing lists or product information;

❖ Mailings through e-mail to potential customers;

❖ Security measures for online business transactions;

❖ Business contracts and other legal documentation that are "electronically signed";

❖ Etc.

The problem with this broad definition is: where do you stop? If a company allows its customers to download a piece of software for free for a trial period, would it be counted as an e-commerce transaction? What about a company which nominally advertises a product over the Internet, but can only sell the product "face-to-face"? If you buy something using a credit card in an ordinary high street shop, and your transaction is verified over a network, is it e-commerce?

Obviously, it is necessary to limit what we mean by e-commerce. For the purposes of this book, I will focus on what most people understand by the term — doing business over the Internet, particularly online shopping — whilst briefly touching on some of the other more obviously commercial aspects, such as "dotcoms", online banking and auctions.

Whatever it is, e-commerce is the lubrication that keeps the wheels of the Internet spinning. As in so many other areas of life, it is doubtful that the Internet could have expanded, or even survived, without the impetus that commercial and business interests have injected into it.

E-commerce Strategy: Doing Business on the Web

We begin by looking at e-commerce from the point of view of a company that is first venturing into the world of buying and selling their products or services over the Internet. As such, this could be seen as a follow-on from Chapter 8, "Building a Website".

Many companies should be wary of jumping on the e-commerce bandwagon. Internet consultants will insist that you have to be e-commerce enabled, but will not tell you why or how or give you any training. Before even considering e-commerce, your staff and you should be fully aware of the potential that the Internet holds and how easy it is to make a bad impression on the Internet. Learn about the Internet, take time to study different websites and build up an e-commerce strategy.

E-commerce should encompass everything that revolves around the purchase of your product, including:

* Pre-sales
* The purchase
* The delivery
* Post-sales.

E-commerce should not be seen as just the actual electronic purchase via credit card of the product. Many users will find the product they want via the Internet but decide to pay by cheque for security reasons (see later). If and when you decide to take the e-commerce route, money spent on consultation with experts will be money well spent. Also take time to do your own research on the Internet and find out as much as you can before making any decisions.

When we talked about building a website, one of the first questions I posed was: do you really need a website? Well the same has to be asked about e-commerce. Do you need it? Can your website/company survive without it? E-commerce is not going to be for everyone; there are some obvious factors here which we will discuss.

Know your Product

Exactly what is your product and is it possible to sell it over the Internet? Some products are ideally suited to the net, others are not. Products that sell well include books, CDs, videos, software and information-based products.

Why is this? Many of these products are pre-sold to you before you even touch the net. You know the book you want, you have read titles by that author before, you now want to buy it at the cheapest price you can, so you log onto the net to find it. The same goes for CDs and videos — you know what you want.

Software is also an ideal product to sell, because you can nearly always try before you buy, i.e. get a 30-day trial version to get a feel for the product. I would prefer to buy software via the Internet because of this facility and also because I can get the exact product I am looking for. Software may pose one problem: if the file is quite large, as most software will be, it may take some time to download it.

Information products are becoming big sellers on the net. These can include such items as e-books and specialist reports. I have found that buying e-books is a simple procedure and allows me to buy books on specialist topics. I can also download and read the book as soon as I have bought it; I do not have to wait for it to be delivered. Services are also a good product to sell; for example, information regarding shares, including perhaps the ability to buy and sell shares online.

Not every business is suited to using the net as an e-commerce tool. Few people would be willing to make a large purchase, such as a car or house, over the Internet. A garage would be foolish to spend a fortune creating an e-commerce website. Think about your product carefully.

Know your Customer

Who exactly is going to buy your product? Are they going to be people who have little or no knowledge of your product? Are they business people? What market are you aiming at?

A company that specialises in rare comics from the 1960s will know exactly what their customer profile is like; they may decide to dispense with a lot of information regarding the history of comics in this era, as all their customers will be looking for specifics. A more general comic site might include such information, as it will be getting visitors who are just browsing and may need more information.

How computer literate is your audience? Very technical companies, whose clients are themselves techies, may find they do not have to guide the visitor step by step through the purchasing procedure of buying one of their products. However, a site like Amazon will find it necessary to have a lot of information about privacy and security implemented on the site, how purchases are made, etc., as they will always be getting new customers, who may be inexperienced with purchasing on the net.

Pre-sales

It is essential that you have an excellent customer service department when selling over the Internet. The best way to do this is to eliminate the need for customer service! This may sound contradictory, but think about it. A product should sell itself; everything the potential buyer wants to know should be answered on your website. There is no point in briefly describing the product and then saying, "Please e-mail or phone us for more details." This will immediately lose most of your customers.

Customers will visit a site and may have made a conscious decision to visit your site; what you now have to do is convert this visitor into a purchaser. If the visitor does not find the information they require about your product, they may leave without even contacting you. If a user leaves your site in a confused state of mind about your product, they may simply not bother to return. Remember, your competition is but a mouse-click away from your website.

So how can you ensure that they stay and purchase your product/service? First, make sure that every possible question the user could ever ask about your product is covered in the site; draw up a list of Frequently Asked Questions. Take time on this. I have been to many sites assuming I would find answers to certain questions there, but to no avail.

A point I always reiterate is to make your site easy to navigate. Let's take a real world example. When you go into a shop, you want to be able to get the product you wish to purchase and get out as quickly as you can (most of the time). How many times have you visited a new supermarket or shop and spent time wandering around because the layout is different to what you are used to? You may feel frustrated and that you have wasted time. If you don't like the layout of the supermarket/shop, you may not return!

If the shop was full of bright flashing lights, dancing assistants and loud music, would you want to shop there? Now imagine you have to queue at three different checkouts in order to purchase your product! To top it all, you are asked to fill in a long questionnaire every time you wish to purchase a product. Would you shop there again? No!

So why do many websites insist on beating you over the head with these sorts of "facilities" when all you want to do is buy their product and get out? This is where many websites are falling down: they are too complex to use; they are hard to navigate; they make it difficult to actually purchase the product. Lets look at each of these points in turn:

* ❖ **Too complex to use**: Under this heading we can include the fact that many sites use too much multimedia content, requiring programs such as Flash, Director or other proprietary plug-ins. Remember never to lose sight of what the customer wants — an interesting and information-rich site without having to wait for minutes while your amazing introduction downloads.

❖ **Hard to navigate**: It cannot be stressed enough that your site has to be easy to navigate; once the user has found the product they require (always include a search facility on your website), they should be able to go straight to the "checkout" with their product. Some sites are genuinely difficult to navigate because there is so much information on them.

❖ **Hard to purchase the product**: Some sites just want to know too much about you! Before you purchase a product they ask you to fill in a questionnaire about yourself; can you imagine this happening at your local supermarket? You may initially have a registration feature, where the user enters all the information required, but on subsequent visits the user should either be remembered automatically (by the use of cookies) or have a simple log-in procedure that will bring up all the information required.

Many e-commerce sites fail and will continue to fail because they do not understand some of the basic points outlined above. Sometimes in the real world you buy from a shop and have a bad experience, but since they may be the only retailer of their sort in your area, you may stick with them simply because they are convenient. The time and effort it takes to drive to the next available retailer does not make it worthwhile.

This does not happen on the Internet. If you find a site hard to use, you can easily go to a search engine and find any number of <u>e-tailers</u> who are more than willing to take your business. The net requires little effort on the user's part; after all, the consumer is in control, they make the decision to go to your site — they can easily click onto another site if they feel you don't have what they want!

Pricing and Competition

One thing I have found is that some web-based stores are not in fact cheaper than their bricks-and-mortar counterparts. The whole idea of selling on the web is that you do not have to pay such overheads as rental premises, staff, etc. Therefore the goods you offer should be much cheaper than they would be in high street stores. If you don't sell any cheaper than high street stores, why would someone buy online, apart from the convenience factor?

Even if your price is the same, engage in non-price competition. As an online retailer, it is your job to make sure that customers are satisfied and have reason to buy from you. Never be afraid of offering something for free or giving users an incentive to buy a product. I personally will often buy a product I don't normally buy if there is some free offer attached to it; I feel I am getting a bargain.

On a basic level, a company could offer their website visitors a coupon that, when printed, allows them to buy goods at a discount in their bricks-and-mortar store. You can also entice visitors to buy from your site if you throw in a free item. I once visited a hotel that had really taken this idea on board. If you booked a room in their hotel via their website you were rewarded with a free glass of Guinness on arrival — now that was enticing! It is important to stress that if you can entice people to come to your site, it usually means they are in a frame of mind where they may be more willing to buy a product.

Offer a free piece of merchandise such as a free mouse, T-shirt, upgrade, etc. The web-based printing company, *iprint.com*, offers free post-it notes, labels or ink stamps to new customers. You pay absolutely nothing expect postage and packing, saving you around $15–$20; but if you buy any other product when you order this free product, they will immediately give you a further 25 per cent reduction on the ordered product; they know that most people cannot refuse a good offer!

Budding e-commerce retailers must be aware that it is a buyer's market. If the product is cheaper at another website, it is very easy to click away from your website and go to the competitors. You should constantly check your competitors' websites to maintain an edge. This is another beauty of the web: it is easy to check who your competitors are and what they are charging by visiting their website — much easier than driving out to the next retail park and physically examining their prices! You as an e-tailer thus have no reason not to maintain competitiveness.

Payment

The next thing to decide is how people will purchase the product! Some shareware companies may simply ask you to print out an order form and fax it to them with credit card details or mail a cheque to them. The problem with selling your product like this is that many people may simply not bother; it's just too much hassle.

Remember, once you have the user at your site, you will want to turn them into a buyer of your product. The easiest way to do this is to have an online ordering system; in other words, when the user has selected a product, one click should bring them to the virtual checkout.

Processing Credit Card Transactions

Most transactions from websites are paid for using credit cards, e-money is still not widely used, so you must ensure you have a way of accepting credit card payment.

Spend time researching on the Internet for different ways to accept credit card transactions. One company that provides a credit card transaction service is *www.ccnow.com* — they take a 9 per cent commission on every sale processed by them. Although this may seem high, they have no set-up charges and will pay you directly at the end of every month. This may be a more ideal situation for smaller companies.

Other companies include:

❖ *www.ibill.com*

❖ *www.clickpay.com*

Some stipulate that their services can only be used for certain types of goods or services.

It is important to be able to assure customers that credit card transactions on your website are secure; this issue is dealt with in detail in Chapter 12. Any company wishing to process credit card transactions online should talk to their local bank and apply for a merchant account. Many banks are wary of getting involved in small volume businesses and therefore state a minimum amount you must be generating before setting up an e-commerce facility for you. This led to many firms having to use foreign banks in order to process their credit card transactions. Recently, more banks are offering users special merchant accounts. A typical set up of one of these accounts would be:

❖ You register to set up a merchant account;

❖ You must have specific server software running on your web server, such as IIS;

❖ You must be trading for a minimum period of time;

❖ Depending on the bank, they may charge you a set-up fee — anything from £150 upwards;

❖ They may charge a monthly service fee regardless of how much you have made — this can range from £50 upwards;

❖ They then take a percentage commission of 4–8 per cent.

If you are only making £100 per month, £50 would go back to the bank, after which there would be commission, etc.

Another option is to use a company such as ccnow.com; they offer to handle all of your transactions. You provide a link from your site to their site. As soon as a user decides to purchase a product, they are redirected to a page set up for you on ccnow's site (which you can customise) where they can make their purchase. ccnow look after all the authorisation and charging of the card. You do not need to have any special server software or security installed — it is all handled by them. The only cost to you as the seller is a nine per cent commission on every sale. There are no other costs.

Many of these sites, including ccnow, also provide an order form facility, where the user can click on an item, decide on the quantity they want and proceed to purchase the product. They also provide a shopping cart facility, which allows you to fill your virtual basket as you progress through the site. When you have collected all the items you wish to purchase, you can then proceed to the checkout; all your items are remembered as you add more to the basket.

I would, as a personal preference, use one of these services, as they have been in existence for a number of years, and have huge client lists. It is, of course, up to you to decide what service is best. If you do get professional consultants in, make sure to do your homework first and find out about all the services that are available.

Order Fulfilment

How exactly will you fulfil the order? If you are selling physical goods, you must decide how they will be shipped. Will you provide different shipping options such as airmail, 48-hour delivery, next-day delivery. Will you include this in your price or will consumers have to pay extra for this?

If your product is web-based — for example, access to a members-only informational site — or software that can be distributed via the net fulfilment will be easier. Many users who buy such products expect that, once they have paid for the product, it should be available to download immediately. If they have to pay for a registration number, it should be dispatched automatically once payment is received. There are many specialist credit card processing sites that will deal with this kind of product, i.e. as soon as payment is received a registration number is sent out to the user.

Will you allow users to "track" their goods? Many companies have this facility; *www.iprint.com* again are a good example of this. They provide an area of their site that the user can log into to check what stage their order is at. There are three different stages: order received, order printing, order shipped. They also indicate how long each stage should take. Once the order is shipped, they give you a tracking number for their courier company. You can then visit the courier's site and enter your tracking number to see exactly where your goods are. I used this service and found that my products had been shipped but had not arrived; by using the tracking service, I found out that the products were stuck in customs.

Is it actually legal to ship the product you are selling to the destination country? This is one problem that many blamed Amazon for causing. It was possible get a US paperback edition of a book before it was published in Europe! Also, books that might be banned in certain countries may be available through Amazon. Then there is the whole issue of VAT and taxation to be looked into! Before considering selling an item that is to be shipped abroad, you must consider all of these issues.

Post-sales

Once a customer has purchased from you, that should not be the end of their experience with you. You should ensure that they have received the product and are happy with it. Do they have any questions that need to be answered? If a customer is 100 per cent happy with your product, you may never hear from them again; but if you do, you should be prepared to treat them well!

People often complain about the post-sales service they have received from a company or shop. The salesperson loves you while they are trying to get the sale; once they get the sale they are not too concerned. You as the seller of a product should be prepared to stand over it. You want the buyer to be happy with the product — give them reason to be. I have seen many websites, mainly for informational products such as e-books, that will give you a 100 per cent satisfaction guarantee. If you are not happy with the product (some give you a year to decide), just e-mail them and say you are not happy with the product and they will charge back the amount to your credit card, no questions asked! This is not a scam. I have bought many e-books and informational products. I decided to test out their claims and, yes, I got a full refund on the purchase price and was allowed to keep the e-book!

You must have a policy on refunds. What if the user is not happy? Do you provide free shipping back to your company? How do they arrange the shipping back to your company? If your product is worth the money the user will keep the product and will not dream of asking for a refund, but if they think they have been misled, they will want the refund. The best companies know that only a fraction of people will take them up on the offer. But they also know that by offering such a guarantee, people know that they have nothing to lose by buying.

Using Chat Rooms and Pagers for Sales and Technical Support

Many companies that provide technical support have full Internet access via leased lines. Many American companies have realised that this new medium is an ideal way to help users and to extend such departments as customer care and technical support.

Some innovative sites have chat rooms where you can talk to their representatives about a product or service they offer. This allows human interaction on a website, which can increase the likelihood of a sale. The sales rep can also help with technical questions and guide you through set-up procedures, etc.

It's as good as phoning the technical helpdesk, but cheaper and far less time-consuming! From the point of view of the company, it also means that their workers can telework from home. Since they have an Internet connection and a computer, they no longer need to be in an office.

Pagers, such as ICQ, could be very useful on internal networks as well as between regional offices. Companies that are paying a couple of thousand pounds a year for Internet access could use a pager program instead of telephoning people.

Another use of IP telephony for companies, apart from cheap calls, is the "phone me" option that many US sites are now using. By clicking a button, the surfer can connect to the company's sales department; alternatively, the company can call the user back. For companies that may not be ready for this, consider the product offered by liverperson.com; you install their product on your web server and also on your employees' PCs. You then place an icon on your website that, when clicked, will initiate a live chat with the surfer. Users are connected to a live salesperson and get a more personal shopping experience. When users can ask questions and get an immediate response they are more likely to consider buying the product. Of course, it has to be remembered that someone must be able to man this service 24 hours a day, since your website never closes down!

These days, even though web authors are being more careful about designing websites that are easy to navigate, the site can sometimes be so large that it is hard to find exactly what you are looking for. Many sites now employ the liveperson software so that the user can get assistance in quickly locating the article or area of the website that they are looking for.

Obviously, this type of business initiative has to be watched so that people actually do help sell the product/service to the customer and that the employee does not use it simply to make new friends and chat with old pals! Chat rooms can become addictive and cause people not to be as productive as they should be.

The top PC manufacturer Gateway have a chat-type facility on their US website. They realise that people need technical support but can be confused by all the information on their site. Their chat facility connects you to a Gateway employee who will help you find what you are looking for on their site. I decided to try out their service and, although I was not an American customer, they helped sort out my problem. Indeed, they will take queries from non-Gateway customers as well! This type of innovative service means that users will return to their site, gain confidence in their products and become repeat customers.

Chat rooms, pagers and IP telephony are discussed in more detail in Chapter 10.

Affiliate Programmes

How many times have you recommended a restaurant to a friend and told them they had to go there, as the food was absolutely fabulous? How many times has the restaurant known that you have sent them business? Wouldn't it be great if they paid you for this? Fat chance!

But websites will. Amazon became very popular as they thought wisely about their business model. They decided to set up partner or affiliate programmes. This meant that you would, at the most basic level, provide a link to Amazon's website; if a person clicked on your link and made a purchase on Amazon's website, you would get a percentage of the sale price!

The more you advertised their site for them, by placing eye-catching banners on your site, the more chance you had of getting a sale; the more you advertised their site the more their name became embedded in the user's mind. Amazon realised the full potential of this and teamed up with Geocities (the free website provider), allowing all Geocities members to "make money" from their websites. The amount of money that Amazon would pay out would be minimal compared to the brand name they were building up.

There is another advantage of having so many websites linking to you. Many search engines will rank sites on their popularity, and popularity is determined by how many websites are linked to yours.

Any good website that sells a product will provide an affiliate programme, as they know that it works for them. The affiliate may not make a lot of money, although some do, but the website gets a lot of free advertising and potential business.

E-mail as an Effective Business Tool

E-commerce is often looked at as a purely web-based phenomenon — how this or that company built a hugely successful business through their website. Many people forget the other major component of the Internet: e-mail. One of the first and most important things you should do if you are serious about e-commerce is to ensure that you and your staff know how to use e-mail effectively. I have had too many bad experiences with major companies, including various ISPs, that simply don't know the importance of e-mail.

E-mail should be treated very sacredly in the business world. An e-mail can be your very first contact with a customer; by replying to the e-mail, a company can show that there is a "human" at the other end. More and more people are using e-mail and many users find that it is easier and quicker to e-mail companies than to ring them. However, all too often, the company neglects to send them a prompt reply, if they send one at all. If a company can't be bothered to respond to e-mails, would you have confidence in buying from them?

Every e-mail should therefore be replied to as promptly as possible, regardless of who or what it is about. You should ensure that your e-mail is checked on a regular basis, at least every hour, and replied to as soon as it is received or at least within one working day. Make sure that whoever is answering the e-mails has a thorough knowledge of the product.

In my experiences, American companies are very aware of this; they reply almost instantaneously. They have discovered that e-mail is a cheap and effective way of communicating with customers, who appreciate a fast response. This is where the power of <u>autoresponders</u> comes in (see Chapter 8).

Don't forget to ensure that you and your employees use signature files that contain contact information such as your e-mail address, name of product/company and website address. This will help brand your product in cyberspace.

Consider keeping a list of everyone who has sent you e-mails enquiring about your product. Send them a one-time e-mail that updates them with news on your website. In order not to annoy people, tell them to reply to the e-mail with the subject "Remove" if they do not wish to receive any more e-mails from you; if they ask to be removed, ensure that you remove them or you may tarnish your reputation.

There are programs available on the net that allow you to manage your mailing lists to ensure that only people who wish to be contacted are e-mailed. You can find details of such programs on the website accompanying this book (*www.internetdemystified.com*).

Another reason why e-mail is so important is that not all your customers will be local. Overseas customers often rely on e-mail to make contact, as it may be too expensive to contact you via the telephone or fax. You should be aware of this when dealing with overseas customers.

Until businesses realise the importance of e-mail and the etiquette associated with it, they will find it hard to build customer relations in an online business model.

Dotcoms

As the twentieth century drew to a close, a new buzzword emerged to send the media into a frenzy: <u>dotcoms</u>. Everybody "in the know" would talk wisely about the dotcom industry, how the way to make money was to invest in a dotcom.

So what exactly *is* a dotcom? Obviously, the word comes from ".com". You might think it is simply a company that sells its products via the web or one that has a website, such as heinz.com. A more accurate definition of a dotcom is a company that virtually exists — that is, it exists purely on the Internet and has no bricks-and-mortar premises; a company whose operations are purely based on the Internet. Examples of dotcoms are:

❖ Yahoo

❖ Amazon

❖ Ebay

❖ Cdnow

None of these companies have walk-in premises as such; their website is their premises.

There are two main types of e-commerce models:

❖ **Business-to-Business (B2B)**: One company selling its product to another company. This type of selling usually involves low prices but large quantities.

❖ **Business-to-Consumer (B2C)**: Selling directly to an individual. More relevant to many, this is your normal retail experience.

The US market, according to a recent report from the Gartner Group, is expected to surpass $29.3 billion in expenditure. Electronic goods and banking and financial services are contributing to a large proportion of this expenditure. They conclude that the industries that will see the most growth are the entertainment and home consumable industries. When you consider that there are over 200 million users on line, there is a lot of money out there that you could capture!

The Secrets of Success?

Most "successful" dotcoms have the same thing in common — they were set up with a large amount of venture capital; huge investments were made in them. Investors hoped that at a future date these companies would be worth millions and their initial investment would pay off in huge dividends.

It has been said that if you have a good proposal for a dotcom, many companies would be willing to throw venture capital at you. However, there now seems to be a downturn in the whole dotcom industry. Investors are becoming wary of them, as they know how vulnerable these types of companies can be.

Success is measured in different ways on the Internet. Running a dotcom is no different to any other type of business. You must have the people and the money to make it work. Take the (apparently) differing fortunes of two different dotcoms: *Amazon.com* and *Boo.com*.

Amazon had a simple idea — to become the world's first virtual bookshop, cutting out the middleman of the high street bookshops, reducing

costs and helping customers find what they were looking for. When you
have found a book, you can find out what other readers thought about it
and see what other books might be of interest to you — a real personal
shopping experience. (We will look at Amazon's site from the point of
view of the customer shortly.)

Yes, Amazon is probably the earth's biggest bookstore, as they like to
say; yes, it is the best known bookseller on the net, so it is successful in
this sense. But like many other dotcoms, it is not making a profit; in fact,
it is making quite substantial losses, running into hundreds of millions.
The paradox here is that although these companies are making losses,
their share prices remain high; the reason is that investors hope that
when they start turning a profit, they will make huge gains.

Along came Boo.com with a similar idea, the difference being that
they would be a virtual clothes shop! Their site was a showcase of many
Internet technologies, from Javascript to Java, Flash and streaming audio.
This was mistake number one: in order for users to view the site properly, they would have to download a whole set of <u>plugins</u>. Also, speed of
access was a problem; over a 128K line, you might be waiting five minutes for the first page of the site to fully load! So much for making a quick
purchase!

The second mistake that Boo made was product. Is the web the ideal
medium for selling clothes? For many, the joy of shopping for clothes is
trying them on, feeling the material, etc. The look and feel of the clothes
can be a huge deciding factor in whether to make the final purchase. It is
very difficult to get the "feel" of clothes on the web! On the other hand,
books and CDs, the main goods sold by Amazon, are ideally suited to
selling over the web.

Over $134 million was invested in Boo.com, while it has been esti-
mated that they spent $1 million developing the site. Within 18 months, it
was all over. Boo.com ceased trading in the summer of 2000. Having said
that, it does not mean a clothes shop should not have a website that sells
merchandise, but they should approach it in a more strategic manner,
research the market, etc.

Many dotcoms are spending 80 per cent of their budgets on advertising and 20 per cent on working capital — a formula for disaster, which
will inevitably lead to cash flow problems. Even successful sites are finding that it may take three years or more to make a profit.

At the other extreme is the possibility that a small producer may find
larger more profitable markets by exploiting the web. Imagine a crafts-

person making wooden ornaments; the local market may be very small and reliant on a seasonal tourist trade. By setting up and promoting a website, or perhaps researching sites that sell similar products and making a deal with them, their products could be sold to a wider audience.

Branding and Customer Confidence

Brand building is of central importance on the web; people will buy brands they recognise, as most people would still be wary of security and privacy issues on the web. Building a brand online can be a problem; after all, no one has heard of you or your company. How can a business get better recognition as a website?

Companies like Amazon, Yahoo, Lycos and Excite have started advertising on terrestrial TV, on taxis, etc. They are at the point were they want the ordinary Joe Soap to begin to recognise their product, both online and offline. These names are now becoming household names; by advertising offline, people perhaps see them more as a "real" company rather than just a virtual company.

Customer testimonies are also important; many companies use quotes from satisfied customers. These could, of course, be made up, but we have to trust the companies to a certain extent!

One of the most important factors to help build customer confidence would be to use a secure way of dealing with orders; if people have never heard of the company who are dealing with your order, they may be wary of your site. The other important factor is privacy. You must make your consumers aware that you respect their privacy. Detail exactly what your privacy policy is, tell them what you do to ensure that data is kept secure. Tell them what you do with their information; give them the ability to opt out of any marketing newsletters you may wish to send them.

One recent incident happened concerning customers' private records and information. A site called Toysmart are being sued by the Federal Trade Commission in the US. Toysmart went bankrupt and sold their assets; one of their "assets" was their customer database, despite the fact that they had a privacy policy! All the information that customers had given to the company was up for sale; any bidder could buy the database and do what they wished with it. This case, as of mid-2000, was still unresolved, but may well lead to a change in US law. With the downturn in the fortunes of many dotcoms, what will happen when others fail? After all, what do they have of value? Since they have no premises, the real value is in their equipment and the information and knowledge they hold.

Your Very Own Dotcom?

Suppose you have your own ingenious idea for a dotcom — should you just get out there and launch it? Before leaving your day job, why not test the water with your idea? If you have no business experience in the real world, you will not succeed in cyberspace. With time and patience and a good idea, even those with the simplest ideas can succeed. Start off small, test the market, research well the product or service you wish to offer and then build your product or brand slowly.

Ebay is a prime example of a site that started off as nothing more than a mere hobby and then grew slowly but surely into a huge business. But as it grew, the owner of it knew to seek outside advice, to hire IT specialists, etc.

Unfortunately, some of the great ideas are already gone. Don't even think you can build a better worldwide search directory than Yahoo or a better global auction house than Ebay. Perhaps you could look for niche markets, such as providing a site that auctions telephone calling cards, or a vortal dedicated to providing great links to the best Celtic sites in the world.

Shopping on the Internet

If the Internet was set up initially as a non-profit resource for researchers, this application is being quickly surpassed by online shopping, as more and more companies realise the potential of selling goods and services to a global market online. From the user's point of view, shopping is what e-commerce is all about.

Once you have spent a couple of hours on the Internet, you will soon discover the online store. It is hard to find a website that doesn't want to sell you something, either directly or by bombarding you with advertisements for products or services from other companies. Sooner or later, you will find that you will want to buy something on the Internet, whether you thought you needed it or not! These days, you can buy anything from a car to a Beanie Baby, from last-minute holidays to music and books, right down to houses and speedboats!

There are a number of different types of online "shops":

❖ Companies who market their products directly online. Most company websites contain at least one page where you can buy their products.

❖ "Virtual storefronts" or malls.

❖ Auction sites.

Let's look at each of these in turn.

Direct Selling

This type of selling model involves you dealing directly with the company who produce the product. If you are dealing with a product that is not available through any other retail outlet, this may be the only way to buy that product. Of course, you may not get as competitive a price as you would if you could shop around.

A good example of direct selling is buying a computer directly from Dell or Gateway. If you know exactly what you want, this can be an excellent way of customising your product while also cutting out the middleman. You do not, of course, have a choice of which brand to buy! Other computers may be available either direct or through a virtual shopping mall, as discussed later on.

We saw earlier that some shoppers will buy online because of the convenience; certainly, if you were to buy a computer from either of the two aforementioned companies, this might be the case. What is important is that the company offer an incentive for buying online. Gateway have done this by offering a free upgrade on memory or a free software title if you buy online. Unless consumers feel they are getting something extra by buying online, they may not take this option.

Virtual Storefronts

These are the closest the web has to a high street shop or department store. They differ from direct selling in the sense that, generally, the goods that the company is selling are not made by themselves. In that sense, their primary function is distribution, and they make their profits by buying discounted goods in bulk from the manufacturers — just like an ordinary shop! The main advantage of Internet shopping is that you can do it all from the comfort of your own home and, once you get the hang of searching, you can compare and contrast prices. (But make sure you buy from a reputable company.)

The most famous online store is *www.amazon.com*, the world's biggest virtual bookstore (although it is no longer restricted to selling books, as it also stocks CDs, videos, etc.). It has no physical outlets, only virtual ones. It is well worth visiting the site to see why it has been successful (*www.amazon.com* or *www.amazon.co.uk*). Some of the factors that have made Amazon successful are its ease of navigation and searching; its "one-click" ordering mechanism; its interactivity (using details given at first registration to recommend reading directly to the user, etc.); and its prices, which are considerably cheaper than your local bookstore. All in all, shopping at Amazon can be more enjoyable than going to your local bookstore, although some people might miss the opportunity to read a few paragraphs from a book before making a purchase decision, or the human interaction of talking to a sales assistant. Browse through Amazon and get a taste of what shopping on the Internet is all about.

CDnow is another site that allows you to buy online; they are experts in selling CDs. This type of product is ideal to the Internet. Think about going into your local record shop: if you are interested in buying a CD, it may be because you have heard a couple of songs from it. So at most, you usually look at the list of tracks, and buy it without listening to the whole CD. CDnow knows that you are in this frame of mind, so you can go to their site and order the CD you like and also search for rare CDs. With the advent of MP3, sites such as CDnow could offer free downloads of selected tracks from chosen albums so that you could try before you buy.

Many sites have sprung up to cater for special tastes; for example, sites that sell Irish-related goods, such as www.celticlinks.com. These sites capture a niche market.

Auction Sites

Auction sites have become hugely popular recently. These sites simply auction off goods, which individuals or companies have submitted for auction. In order to buy or sell, you must sign up and register. Once you have registered, you can place a bid on an item and wait for other people to bid until the item is sold. Unlike real world auctions there is no time constraint on when you bid; you can bid 24 hours a day, 7 days a week.

There are a number of reliable auction sites such as eBay and Yahoo. The great thing about auction sites is that you can almost always find whatever you are looking for; someone is bound to be selling something that interests you. These can be wonderful sites to find rare or difficult-to-obtain items. Looking for a rare 1960s record? Check out an auction site on the web.

Sometimes bargains can be had on these sites; you may be lucky and find that no one else is bidding for an item and you end up getting it for pennies; indeed this happened to a woman on a UK auction site. She was browsing and saw an auction for a week's holiday in Europe, starting at 50 pence, she placed her bid and thought nothing of it, until she got an e-mail to say she had won the auction! A nice holiday at a nice price!

Ebay is the best-known and most established auction site. You have to be careful of selling items on other sites, as if they are not getting many visitors to their site, then you will end up paying to have your item advertised but will not sell it. If you decide to try other auction sites (there are ones that specialise in particular products), take time to see exactly what they sell, how many people have advertised and how many people are bidding. I have seen auction sites that have plenty to sell but no one bothers to bid for the items. At many of these auction sites, your sale items have to be priced attractively. People go to an auction site to look for bargains!

Ebay, along with other sites, have a number of useful facilities such as auto-bid, sometimes referred to as proxy bidding. You can enter the maximum amount you will pay for an item; when someone places a bid, the server will automatically place your bid, up to your maximum amount. Another great feature is the item watch feature. Many people only bid at auctions at the last minute. If you bid too early for a product, you will increase the price of it and others may outbid you. If you wait until the end of the auction, you may stand a better chance of not being outbid! The item watch allows you to keep an eye on the progress of any auction without having to bid. Ebay will give information such as the highest bid, how much time is left, etc.

As a buyer, you pay no fees to Ebay; you only pay the winning auction amount plus any postage and packaging that may be stipulated by the seller. As a seller, you pay an insertion fee or a fee for advertising your product. Once the auction is finished, Ebay then charge a final value fee. This is a percentage of the final selling price. In total, you may pay a total of about 7 or 8 per cent of the cost of the item. Where many people recoup this percentage fee is in the shipping costs. It may only cost $1.50 to ship the product, but you could charge $2.50 in order to recoup some of the percentage fee.

One last word on auction sites: always be aware that the item you are selling or buying may be available more cheaply from shops, either on-line or offline. I have seen books or trading cards advertised that can be bought from websites for less than their price at Ebay. Always check to see if the item really is limited edition or if it is possible to buy it from a specialist website. And be careful, as some people have been stung by unscrupulous sellers. Like everything on the web, before engaging in an activity or using a service, be sure to read all the Terms of Service (TOS).

Money-saving Sites

Many sites have sprung up that try to cut out the middleman. One such site is *www.deckchair.com*, which aims to find the cheapest flights possible. You simply enter where you want to fly from, where you want to go and when, and they will try to locate the cheapest flight available to you. By accessing the same information as the travel agents, this site aims to cut out their commission and offer you the best deal. To compete with these sites, many airlines/travel companies, such as Virgin Airlines, have special offers that are only available from their website.

The one problem with any of these sites is that they must be operated in real time. That is to say, if you book a flight, the availability of the seat that you booked must be registered as no longer available. If the information is only updated every 20 minutes, it may happen that three or four people book the same seat, which would cause major problems! One example is the Ticketmaster site. They say that they will hold your tickets for a certain number of minutes, after which the tickets return to the general pool of tickets. Obviously, if tickets were double-booked, this would be a disaster and people would lose faith in the site.

Another site worth a visit is *www.lastminute.com*, who specialise in last-minute deals that may save you money and time — be it plane tickets or concert tickets, they are an excellent one-stop-shop.

It is possible to find huge savings on the Internet. Indeed, a recent magazine article found that people could save a substantial amount by buying via the web rather than through high street stores.

Safe Shopping on the Internet

The first question everyone asks is: How safe is it to buy over the Internet? The huge fear is that someone will run off with your credit card number and end up charging a huge amount to it. To be honest, if certain precautions are taken, it is as safe to buy over the Internet as it is to buy over the telephone. You face as much danger buying via the web as you do using your credit card over the counter of a shop or paying for a meal in a restaurant. Think about it: when you want to order concert tickets, you give all the information to someone over the phone and you do not know who they are. Anyone could overhear you and take down your details.

The first rule of thumb is to buy from a reputable supplier. If you decide to buy music from Sony's website, you can be assured that such a big name will not unlawfully use your credit card. If you buy off Dodgy Dave's shabby-looking website, you are asking for trouble.

But hold on — on the World Wide Web, looks matter, right? This is a problem, as someone may have an excellent, professional-looking website, but it is all a front for a fraudulent company just waiting for your credit card details. Fraud and scamming are easier on the Internet because if a site "looks" reputable and business-like, people may feel confident about buying from them. Search engines and ISPs cannot check whether their clients' sites are genuine or not. So what can you do?

The answer is, if you are at all unsure about the owner of a site or about the company, do not buy from them. At the very least, any site selling something should contain the following information:

* Name of company

* Mailing address

* Contact e-mail address

* Telephone number.

If they do not supply this information, perhaps they have something to hide, so beware of them. If you are still in doubt, why not give them a call. One interesting development is that many sites that sell computer software will actually offer a full 100 per cent money-back guarantee if you are not happy with their product. This really does inspire consumer confidence.

So, when buying over the Internet, take the following steps:

* Research the company you are buying from.

* Ensure you know their contact details.

* Try contacting them via e-mail or telephone before purchasing.

❖ Check if reputable sites link to them; if a major company wants to uphold their reputation, they will probably make sure that all their links are to other genuine, reputable companies.

❖ Never give credit details unless the page is sent encrypted (see below).

❖ Check to see if you can get a money-back guarantee if you are unsatisfied with the service. Many sites do this.

One thing to be aware of is that many sites will automatically re-bill you when your subscription is up. They often have rather complex rules about how to stop automatic billing. Always read the small print regarding automatic billing.

If you are buying online for the first time, always buy from companies that you already know about and are familiar with in the "real" world, or brands you have heard about that people trust, such as Amazon, Sony or Adidas, etc. Again, make sure that the website *does* belong to the real company; it is all too easy for fraudsters to buy a domain name that seems like it belongs to a well-known company, and even to have their site looking similar to the genuine site.

Whatever website you decide to buy from, you must always ensure that you have the facility to <u>encrypt</u> all your details, and that the company has the facility to accept such encrypted information. This means that all your information is scrambled in transit so that if it is intercepted and someone tries to read it, it will all be gibberish.

Fraudulent use of credit cards is probably the main concern for many people when using the Internet. People are afraid to give their credit card information to a website in case it is then used illegally to purchase goods. Credit card fraud, security measures and encryption are dealt with in Chapter 12.

Chapter 10

Interactivity and the Internet

The Social Web

Although initially the web was seen as the domain of academics, geeks and general unsociable types, it can actually be one of the most social and stimulating places.

You may wonder how the Internet can be considered social. Surely it is just a collection of computers? Well, so far we have talked about how it works, how you connect to it, the hardware, cabling and software that is required, the basic tools for finding your way around, and so on . . . but we have left out one important factor: YOU!

Without you and me, the Internet is nothing. If nobody produced websites or e-mailed people or visited chat rooms, the Internet would cease to be interesting. It is only through people that the Internet is made interesting. Think of all those websites that you have visited. They were all created by people for other people.

The most used application on the Internet is e-mail; e-mail is used to communicate and communicating is social. Remember that by the mid-1970s, e-mail accounted for well over half the traffic that passed along the ARPAnet! Of course, people found it interesting to share research information, but just communicating with others in remote locations was even better!

It has been said that the Internet has helped change history in many ways. One example was the destruction of the Berlin Wall. Before you think this is completely barmy, let's look at some interesting facts:

❖ The Internet allowed academics to connect and share information with other academics;

❖ Many books, articles and other information that were banned were available over the Internet;

❖ Information could be spread quickly and easily via electronic mail.

Although the governments of many Eastern European countries were suppressing and controlling the press and media, Eastern Europeans, albeit academics and possibly students, could receive and send information out of the country easily via electronic means. As more people found out what was really going on, they began to form political groups to lobby governments, and this helped the groundswell of popular protest that eventually brought an end to communism in Eastern Europe.

During the Gulf War, Internet enthusiasts used a chat software program called Internet Relay Chat (IRC) to get information about what was going on sooner than it was aired on television or radio. The Internet is an anarchic structure in its truest and purest sense.

When something happens in the world, it is much easier for us to read what the perspective of other countries is by looking at their local newspapers. For example, I can read about a case that is happening in America in my local newspaper, but then connect to the Internet and find out what the American national newspapers are saying, even perhaps what local state and town papers are saying.

No longer do we need to take what one person/paper/government says; we can decide for ourselves. Censorship may have been easy for dictatorial governments in times gone by, but now with the spread of the Internet, somehow people in these countries can connect up and find the information they wish.

As you can imagine, this speedy dissemination of information can often work for the good, but it can also have its bad side: misinformation can be spread quickly. As we saw in Chapter 7, it is necessary to question and check all sources on the Internet to ensure that information is reliable.

Both Sides Now

It could be argued that there have been three main strands of users that have helped to make the Internet what it is. At one extreme are the researchers, academics and scientists who provided the initial impetus for its creation. At the other end of the scale are the business and commercial interests who, with their customers, have created the explosion in e-commerce.

In between these two extremes are those millions of people who have seen in the Internet the potential to create global communities, those Internet enthusiasts who use the Internet as a basic tool of communication and social interaction. It is these users who have allowed the web to develop its own life, its own interactive culture. In this chapter, we look at the interactive nature of the web and the various Internet applications that increase social interaction.

One of the main reasons why the Internet has been hailed as such a revolutionary medium is that it allows people to communicate in both directions. Traditional media such as newspapers, radio and television only allow us to consume the information; it is very difficult to produce a newspaper or radio show. The traditional telephone system may allow two-way communication, but it is obviously limited in the sort of information it can exchange.

On the Internet, not only can you be a receiver of information, by viewing a website; you can also become a provider of information. Simply by e-mailing a site owner, you become an information provider. You could even go a step further and set up your own website. Of course, as Chapter 8 showed, this can just as difficult as producing a newspaper!

But it isn't necessary to set up a website to become an information provider on the web. You can take part in this two-way information exchange through making use of the many interactive tools on the web. Interactivity means that the web surfer can do more than view information. In the early days of web design, users just wanted to find out information; now they want more and web designers can offer them more. We will see in this chapter some technologies that introduce interactivity to websites, and also other technologies that use standalone applications to communicate via the Internet.

Nearly all sites will allow you to interact in some way, from the very basic level (sending an e-mail) to more advanced level (having a chat room). Before continuing, we need to make a distinction about Internet communication. Some of the technologies described here are based on and accessed through web pages; some are programs that only use the Internet as the transport medium. As you will see, all that is great is not necessarily web-based!

Web-based Interaction

OK, things are getting confusing, right? You must remember that the World Wide Web is only an application that is used on the Internet. So any interaction that is accessed through a web page or initiated through a web page is termed as being <u>web-based</u>. This list includes:

* ❖ Guest books

* ❖ E-mail links

* ❖ Feedback forms

* ❖ Discussion boards

* ❖ Chat rooms

* ❖ Online communities

* ❖ Newsgroups.

Non-web-based interaction

Any interaction that is not initiated from a web page is known, strangely enough, as <u>non-web-based</u>. The list would include:

* ❖ Internet Relay Chat (IRC)

* ❖ Internet pagers

* ❖ Internet telephone programs

* ❖ Newsgroups.

All of the above are standalone applications that can function without a separate web browser, but remember that all of them, web-based or non-web-based, use the Internet as the means of transport. Having said that, notice that one particular form of interaction is mentioned in both groups: <u>newsgroups</u>. Why this is so will be explained later!

Guestbooks

The first interactive form of communication is a <u>guestbook</u> on a website. This type of interaction is much the same as guestbooks you see when you visit tourist attractions. A lot of small personal websites provide such guestbooks, where you can leave a message for the site author about their site. The web page is created so as to allow you to enter information via a series of questions. When you have answered all the questions, you click on a button, usually entitled **Submit**. As soon as you press the Submit button, your comments are added to the website immediately.

This type of interaction is usually one-way; other than an automatic reply, you do not get any other response.

Guestbooks are used only on smaller websites; it is way of showing off the compliments and endorsements the website has received from others! One problem is that some people may leave offensive or abusive entries just for the fun of it; because of this, you will see few companies with guestbooks on their sites. Guestbooks were a must-have item on websites many years ago but have declined in popularity.

Web-based E-mail Links

The next form of interaction in a web-based form is a simple e-mail link. By clicking on a link with the person's e-mail from the web page, your computer will open up a new e-mail message with the person's e-mail address filled in automatically. This allows the web surfer to e-mail the site owner directly, either requesting information or to comment on the site. If you have comments about the site, you can e-mail them back to the proper department.

The problem with this form of communication is that you must wait for the person to receive your e-mail, hope they will read it and then that they will reply to it.

Discussion Boards

The best way of making a site interesting is to have some sort of content that is updated on a regular basis; this can be achieved by using a <u>discussion board</u>. Many discussion boards can be maintenance-free, meaning that the site developer or owner can let it work by itself and does not need to tend to it much.

A discussion board is a part of a website reserved for discussing certain topics with like-minded individuals, whether it is about a company's products, about ideas put forward by the website or on other matters of mutual interest. For example, a website that sells gardening products may find that a discussion board about gardening topics will enhance their website no end. Many sites have discussion boards because:

❖ They attract visitors of like minds to discuss topics

❖ They attract people to come back and read replies to comments.

Discussion boards should not be confused with discussion groups or newsgroups, which are discussed later in this chapter.

How does a discussion board work?

A discussion board is very simple to use. The owner of the site will set up general topics to discuss. Discussion boards can have a number of pre-set topics but can also be configured to allow users to set up sub-topics within the main topics.

A user will then post (type and send) a comment about the topic. When the person has submitted their post, it will appear on the discussion board. They then come back in an hour or a day or two to see what other comments have been posted in reply to their comments. How quickly replies appear depends on how frequently the discussion board is used.

Over time, if the discussion board is used a lot and the topic is interesting, people will post comments to the original topic, while others will post replies to other people's comments. When someone posts a reply to a topic and then others reply to it, this builds up a thread of conversation.

> A **thread** is a list of replies to a certain topic. If you have a comment about a certain topic, you will post it under the last comment made. If you post a new topic or question, then you are creating a new thread.

This is what makes discussion groups interesting — you can read other people's replies and follow the thread.

Discussion boards are good for both the site owner and web surfers. For the site owner, people keep visiting, which can help sell advertising. Surfers get to express their views and gain useful information. A good example of a discussion board can be found at *www.motorweb.ie*; their discussion board is of benefit to anyone with an interest in cars or any aspect of the motor industry. Valuable tips can be posted and read by all.

Moderated and Unmoderated

Discussion boards can become very interesting, but it is important to note that some are <u>moderated</u> and some are <u>unmoderated</u>.

 *A **moderated** discussion board means that someone is in charge of either the whole discussion board or there are a number of different people in charge of each topic. It is their job to check all posts before they are posted or to delete any unwanted or offensive posts.*

The advantage of a moderated board is that silly comments or blatant advertising do not appear on the discussion board. There are some individuals who gain pleasure in writing offensive or irrelevant messages on discussion boards!

Moderated discussion boards may also ask you to register with them before you can post any messages. This ensures that only people interested in the topic will take the time to register and should lead to more interesting discussions.

One obvious worry that a lot of people have about moderated discussion boards is: Who is censoring the information and why? Moderated discussion boards can also slow down the discussion, as you are depending on the moderator to read and post comments. If they go on holiday, nothing might happen for two weeks!

*An **unmoderated** discussion board is one where anyone can post a message and no one checks the messages before they are posted.*

An unmoderated discussion board may cause undue work for the owner of the site, as they may need to be constantly checking every single message as it is posted.

Technical Support Discussion Boards

Many companies use discussion boards very effectively, especially as a means of technical support. A customer with a query can visit the discussion board and see if there are messages concerning his or her problems.

For example, many software companies will run a discussion board dedicated to solving technical support issues. This is often referred to as a Knowledge Base, with categories such as:

❖ Installation problems

❖ Common errors

❖ Upgrading from Version X to Version Y.

More often than not, other customers who experienced similar problems may be able to help the customer with the query. This leads to a good sense of community. Discussion boards like these are usually moderated, so that the moderator can ensure that all questions/answers are relevant.

This type of discussion board can ease the strain for technical support staff, as the board can be run with little or no intervention, and it is the customers themselves who answer each other's problems. Since the tech support people may not have encountered every single problem, they may also gain invaluable information from problems that others have had, which can then be fixed in newer versions of the software.

Chat Rooms

The most popular form of web-based interactivity comes from chat rooms. Chat rooms are areas of a website that people can visit to "talk" to each other. (Note for the uninitiated: while they are called "chat rooms", you type out your messages; you don't physically speak to the person as you would on the phone.) The chat room screen is usually spilt into three areas, as illustrated below:

Area where conversation takes place	*List of users*
Area where you enter what you wish to say	

You must keep an eye on the screen to see when someone responds to you. All responses are seen by everyone else, unless they are specially directed to you.

Chat rooms evolved because people wanted to interact in <u>real time</u>. This is the essential difference between a discussion board and a chat room.

 ***Real Time*** *refers to the fact that messages are sent to individuals as soon as you have typed them and hit the return key. E-mail is not a real time medium, as the e-mail is sent out and you must wait for a reply.*

Most popular websites have chat rooms in some shape or form. They are usually free to use. Website owners know that people like to be social and interact and if they can get a good chat room going, people will return to their site. This doesn't mean that the website owners aren't making any money. There may be an area of the window that displays a banner or advertisement, which the website owners hope you will click on! Although the chat software can be expensive for the company to buy, they realise that if the chat room is successful they can sell advertising space to other companies.

Types of Chat Rooms

There are two types of chat rooms that you will see on websites; the former is now becoming less popular:

❖ **HTML-based**: These chat rooms tend to be rather slow and need to be updated manually, i.e. every time you wish to see if someone has spoken, you must click on a Reload button. They tend to have few features and are cumbersome to use.

❖ **Java-based**: These chat rooms take a while to start up on your computer, but can offer anything from basic chat (much faster than HTML) to full multimedia chat — allowing you to send sounds/files to other users. They update automatically. Most chat rooms are programmed in Java.

What is Java?

Java is a fully functioning programming language, similar to C or C++, and was developed by Sun Microsystems. The key difference between Java and other programming languages is that it is platform-independent. Java programs can be used on any machine and do not have to be reprogrammed to work with different machines/platforms.

In order to run Java, you must have a program installed called the Java Virtual Machine. When you install any of the modern browsers, this is installed automatically. Once you have this installed, you can run <u>Java applets</u>.

 *A **Java Applet** is a small program that you run in your web browser. It can be anything from a program that displays an attractive, interactive menu on screen, to a fully functioning chat room.*

Depending on your installation of IE, you should automatically have Java Virtual machine installed.

There have been hostile applets written in order to show what Java could potentially do to your computer. Java applets are run in a <u>sandbox</u>, a special area on your computer reserved for Java. The applet cannot access files from your computer or write to your disk.

Where to Find Chat Rooms

There are many websites that provide chat rooms for users. Most are free, but some will ask you to register your name and e-mail address with them. When you enter a chat room you will see how many users are in the room. Depending on the site the layout of the chat room may vary.

Many chat sites will have a list of available rooms that you can chat in. For example, Yahoo Chat has about 100 categories to choose from, ranging from Adult to Zoology. Under each category is a sub-category of topics. In the Romance category, there may be sub-categories for different age groups.

By looking at the title of the chat room, you should get a fair idea about the topics of conversation that will take place in them.

Chat Room Features

There are a number of features that nearly every chat room will have, including the following:

Nicknames

A <u>nickname</u> is a name you use in a chat room that identifies you. Most users do not reveal their real name and therefore their nicknames usually represent who or what they are. For example, if you saw the names "fluffybunny" or "hardman", you would get some idea of what the person thinks of themselves!

It is wise not to use your real name when in a chat room, as you do not know who you might be chatting too. This is particularly relevant to children and young people, as we shall see in Chapter 13.

Some chat rooms will insist that you register a nickname with them, also known as a <u>chat handle</u>. This nickname becomes your own unique identifying name that no one else can use. It is protected by a password. The advantage of having a unique registered chat handle is that no one can impersonate you and you can be sure that you are always talking to the same person in the chat room. With a registered handle you can therefore build up relationships with other chatters.

When you log into the chat room, you will be asked to enter your nickname and your password. If you do not enter the correct password, you will not be allowed to enter the chat room using that handle.

Some chat rooms do not have the facility to register nicknames. Once you leave, anyone can use that handle and therefore impersonate you. This is obviously not a good thing.

Private Messaging

Sometimes you will want to send a private message to someone; this is a message that only they can see. Remember that when chatting in a chat room, everyone can read your message unless it is sent privately. Imagine a room where everybody is talking out loud, so that everybody can hear what everybody else says. If you want to have a private conversation with somebody, you will have to go to a quiet corner of the room, or into a different room altogether.

Nearly every chat room should have this ability in some shape or form. Some chat rooms, such as Yahoo Chat, implement this quite well, since private messages are conducted in a separate chat window that make it easier to follow the conversation. Other chat rooms are quite awkward, as the private messages are displayed in the same window as normal messages, but appear in different colours from general messages. This makes it quite easy to miss messages directed to you.

Ignore Button

This is an essential feature of a chat room. Nearly every modern chat room will have this facility. An Ignore button allows you to ignore users who may be annoying you or flooding the chat room (see later).

Some chat rooms will remember all the people that you have ignored so that the next time you use the chat software, those persons will automatically be ignored.

Buddy List

When you begin to chat to a person, you may want to remember their nickname. Instead of having to write it down you can add it to your buddy list. This works much like Internet Explorer's Favourites; when you log onto the chat site, your buddy list will tell you if any of your buddies are online and then you can instantly start to chat with them.

These are the basic functions you must have in order to experience an enjoyable chatting session. More advanced chat rooms will have some or all of the following:

Voice Messaging

Voice messaging will allow you to talk to one or more people via a microphone attached to your computer. This is quite a new technology for chat rooms, but is implemented on Yahoo Chat in special chat areas. At the moment, it only allows one user at a time to use the voice facility; therefore one person can monopolise the conversation. We will be looking at more sophisticated packages for voice chat later on.

Ability to create and maintain your own chat room on the main chat site

Some chat services actually allow users to set up and maintain their own chat room on the chat server. In essence, this means that you can have your very own chat room that people can visit. You can then be an administrator of that chat room, which means that you can allow or disallow certain users; if they cause problems, you can kick them out.

Video Chat

Some chat rooms now have video chat. If you have a <u>web camera</u>, often referred to as a cam, using appropriate software you can chat with people who can see live video feed of you, or the camera can take a snapshot of you every 15 seconds and send those snaps to the chat room. The latter software would not provide true video chat. One example is mplayer.com, who provide free software that will allow you to connect to their server and video chat with other users.

One important thing to note is that some of these programs allow users to save the pictures that you transmit by clicking on the picture. As you can imagine, some of the images that are transmitted are far from tasteful — parents and educators should be aware of this.

Netmeeting

One true video conferencing package is Netmeeting from Microsoft. Available either with Internet Explorer or as a free download from the Microsoft site, it allows two users to have a real video conference; that is, you can talk and see the other person in real time. This package, like others, will usually transmit up to 12 frames per second, which will give reasonable quality video but will still look a bit choppy.

If you wish to talk to a random user, Netmeeting allows you to connect to servers that will help you to find people from a directory of users. Alternatively, you can connect with a user directly by entering in their IP number directly into the program.

Chat Room Problems

Chat rooms are a great form of interaction but can be problematic, just as, in the real world, when a group of people get together, there could be problems. The dangers are heightened on the Internet, since it is very easy to remain anonymous.

We will first look at general problems that you will encounter in chat rooms:

Flooding

Some people like to bombard the chat room with messages so that no one can read anything else on the screen. They may either copy a huge passage of text repeatedly (these people have some brain power!) or others (the less intelligent) will simply press a key repeatedly. Whichever method they use, the effect is the same: no one can see any other messages except those sent by this individual. This is known as <u>flooding</u> or <u>scrolling the screen</u>.

Other users will go in to the chat room and try to advertise a new website that is of no interest to anyone. Most chat rooms do not allow you to advertise. A variation of these types of messages is when someone posts offensive messages simply to irritate other users.

More serious problems include:

Sexually charged conversations

Be warned: a lot of chat rooms, no matter what they are supposed to be about, become sexual in nature. This is a major problem that parents and educators should be aware of. For this reason, no matter what the supposed subject matter, it can be dangerous to allow children into chat rooms unsupervised.

Like discussion boards, there are moderated and unmoderated chat rooms. In the former, there will be a <u>chat monitor</u> who oversees the conversation and <u>boots</u> (remove) any user that is causing offence or hassle.

Unmoderated chat rooms do not have chat monitors, so "anything goes", although many still employ a <u>word filter</u> that will not display swear words or sexual words. If one does enter such a word it will either be replaced with another word or with ****.

"No one knows you are a dog" syndrome

One phrase that sprung up on the Internet a number of years ago was: *"On the Internet, no one knows you are a dog"*. Think about it: a lot of the time, you do not know anything about the person you are e-mailing or chatting to. They may tell you what you want to hear or whatever fantasies they have dreamed up, but you have no way of proving it. This can be one of the drawing points of the chat scene — you can be who you want to be. In this way, it is something like an old-fashioned "masked ball"! This can, however, lead to dangerous situations, particularly for children. We will look at ways of checking up on children and protecting them and others from the dangers of the Internet in Chapter 13.

"Love at first byte!" syndrome

Another real danger of chat rooms is cyber affairs. For the past number of years, there have been many reports about people who "meet" over the Internet — either via e-mail, chat rooms, discussion boards or classified ads — and begin "cyber relationships". They communicate with each other, get to know each other, fall in love and eventually may marry! This has in fact happened on a few occasions. A lovely romantic story? Wrong!

The Internet is now becoming a major reason why marriages and relationships are breaking up. Men and women have found a new way of meeting someone in secret without really meeting them. They do this through the chat room.

Many people are now addicted to chat rooms and live completely different lives in "cyberspace". There are many recorded instances of husbands or wives spending hours and hours on the Internet chatting to "cyber lovers"; they spend more time in their cyber relationships than they do with their real-life relationships, which causes an obvious strain. Similarly, even for unattached people who are genuinely looking for romance on the Internet, the reality, when it hits, can be deeply disappointing. The key point to be made is, whether you are a girlfriend, boyfriend, father, mother, husband or wife, know what your partner or child is doing on the computer, who they are chatting to and for how long. This point cannot be stressed enough and is again dealt with in Chapter 13.

Security Measures

In practice, it is nearly impossible to trace a user who has caused problems in a chat room. One reason is that even though someone has registered with a chat room and given all their details, they may have falsified those details. Some methods that chat sites use are as follows:

IP Number

The chat room software records the IP number of every person who enters the chat room; therefore, if someone reports that person for whatever reason, the chat room owners can trace the IP number back to the ISP and then possibly back to the user.

In reality, this can be very difficult. If you remember from an earlier chapter, we said that all ISPs rent out IP numbers to users for the duration of their surfing time. When the user logs off, the IP number goes back into a pool of IP numbers. It is highly unlikely that the same user would get the same IP number twice in a row. The best a chat site could do would be to trace the IP number back to the ISP. Depending on the ISP, they may have the ability to trace back every IP number to every single user. For an ISP to do this would take a lot of time and money; therefore, they may only do it under exceptional circumstances. We will see in Chapter 13 how people can disguise their IP numbers.

If a problem is reported, it may take a day or two for the site operators to deal with it, by which time the user will be well and truly logged off; if the user has a fixed line or a fixed IP number, then it would be possible for the site owners to trace and locate the offender.

Transcripts

Chat sites may record transcripts of all conversations. This means that every conversation that goes on is recorded as a text file, so that the owners of the chat service can view the file and it will show them who said what to whom and when! This allows the service to ban any users that may be offensive or flooding the chat room. In effect, the site can ban the user called fluffybunny, but all the user has to do is re-register under a new name!

As you can see, chat rooms, although fun, can also be dangerous if kids are left unsupervised in them.

Redeeming Features of Chat Rooms

Although we have focused on the bad elements of chat rooms up to now, they do have some redeeming features:

❖ Many schools are now setting up links with other schools for the purpose of chatting. One example I heard about was in the North of Ireland, where a Protestant and Catholic school were communicating like this. There were no hang-ups, no physical barriers about religion, politics, etc. Everyone was equal in the chat room. This sort of usage of chat rooms is fantastic, as people come face-to-face with each other's personalities and forget about any hang-ups or prejudices they may have.

❖ Some people find it easier to talk to strangers and therefore can share their problems with others in a chat room. Someone may be feeling down or need to talk about a problem; they may find it easier to go into a chat room, strike up a conversation with someone and discuss their problem. Of course, there is no knowing if the person listening may be psychotic, or just plain stupid and offer bad advice or taunt the person — so just be careful out there!

❖ The best thing about chat rooms is the easygoing, informal nature of them. The usual way a conversation is struck up in a chat room is by private messaging someone with the following: *a/s/l*, meaning Age, Sex, Location. Imagine going into a bar and using that as your chat-up line; somehow, I don't think you would get very far!

Non-web-based Interaction

Any form of communications over the Internet that are not initiated from or do not utilise a web page/website can be categorised as <u>non-web-based interaction</u>. Always remember that the web is only an application that uses the Internet as its transport medium. E-mail is the most obvious example of non-web-based interaction. When composing, sending and receiving e-mail, you use a separate program. You do not need to have web access or a browser to send e-mail, but you must have Internet access. Obviously, we have dealt with e-mail in a previous chapter. Here we look at some less-well-known forms of non-web-based interaction.

Internet Relay Chat

Most people have never heard of Internet Relay Chat (IRC) or, if they have, they have steered away from it, having been told it is difficult to use.

Internet Relay Chat is over 12 years old, having been created in 1988 by Jarkko Oikarinen in Finland. IRC has been called the CB radio of the Internet — the difference is, you can chat to people all over the world! IRC conversations are all text-based, much like the average chat room.

IRC was one of the first commercial chat programs available. Like the modern chat interfaces, the screen is divided into an area that gives a list of all the users of the chat room, an area where you see the conversations and an area where you can type in your text.

Since IRC is not web-based, you need to use an <u>IRC client</u>.

 *A **client** is a program or computer that requests services from another computer known as a server.*

One of the most popular IRC clients is mIRC, available on the website accompanying this book (*www.internetdemystified.com*).

One of the first disadvantages of IRC presents itself at this point — you need to use a separate piece of software in order to take part. This may put many people off, as they may prefer to use a single piece of software (such as Internet Explorer or Netscape Navigator) for all their needs (e-mail, newsgroups, chat, etc.).

IRC use the Internet to pass its information from the client to the server. Like the web, IRC is only an application that uses the Internet as its transportation medium!

Where can I find a list of servers to connect to?

When starting out with mIRC, you may try the servers located at *www.mirc.com/servers.html.* For a full list, go to Yahoo and type "IRC servers" into the Search area. mIRC will also list quite a number of servers you can connect to.

What is a channel?

A channel is an area where people chat, like a virtual room. It is the IRC equivalent of a chat room. Every IRC server will have a number of permanent channels on different topics. These channels will always be available to chatters. People with like-minded interests will chat in a particular channel. Some channels are permanent; some disappear when the last person leaves them. Every channel will have a # in front of its name; for example, #Ireland is the Ireland channel.

Every channel will also have a channel operator, who has the power to kick people out if they are being abusive. You can always tell who the channel operator is, since they will have an @ beside their name; therefore if you see @richard, this means I am the channel operator for that particular channel. If you create a new channel, you automatically become a channel operator for that channel.

Many IRC servers allow users to set up and administer their own channels or create their own chat rooms/areas. These user-created channels are temporary channels. The server is set up so that once there are no users left in the channel, the channel will cease to exist.

Chat Room versus IRC

So is there any difference between a chat room and an IRC channel? Yes and no! Apart from the fact that chat rooms are web-based while IRC is not, IRC is the same as a chat room in the sense that you enter a room (channel) where you can chat with other people; however, chat rooms are usually fairly user-friendly. When using IRC, you will need to learn some basic commands, but first you must connect to an IRC server. You need to enter some information, such as your e-mail address, a nickname and the name of a server you wish to connect to. The website accompanying this book has a step-by-step guide on connecting to an IRC server.

With mIRC, a list of channels will automatically pop up; this is a small list and not a complete list of channels on the server.

Tip! *Any time you enter text, it is sent to the chat area, but when you put a forward slash (/) before text, the server will think it is a command. So if you type "help" the word help will be displayed on the screen; if you type "/help", you will get information to help you with IRC!*

You can try saying "hello" and see if anyone answers. You may end up talking to yourself for a while, but eventually someone will answer you!

You should take time to read the help instructions that come with the program in order to fully understand IRC. But as you can see from our quick overview, it is quite difficult to jump in and start using it. With a bit of time and some effort, you will find that IRC can be more enjoyable than standard chat rooms!

Pager Software

An application that was developed some years ago was <u>pager</u> software, sometimes referred to as <u>instant messaging</u> software. This software allows you to chat and share files with other people across the Internet. All paging services have a buddy list that will immediately tell you when any of your friends have logged onto the Internet.

Using pager software, you can instantly contact your friends without having to visit a chat room. Pager software will stay as an icon minimised on your taskbar/system tray. As soon as a new message is received, the pager software will pop up and display the message. Pager software is like SMS on GSM phones (see below); you can send short messages to people easily and quickly.

like SMS on GSM phones (see below); you can send short messages to people easily and quickly.

Privacy is a big advantage of this type of interaction, as you do not have to be in a crowded room where everyone can see whom you are talking to. You also do not have other people bothering you. Many of the software products have extra facilities such as collaborative white boards, facilities to transfer files, etc.

The one problem with pager software is that it is not designed for meeting people. When you enter a chat room, you can see a list of people that you can chat to; with pager software, you see no list until you add people to your buddy list! People usually use such software when they have found "friends" in chat rooms. They then arrange so that both parties download the particular brand of pager software. Once this is done, they can chat via the pager software in a more relaxed and private atmosphere.

There are a number of well-used paging software systems including:

❖ ICQ — *www.icq.com*

❖ Powwow — *www.tribalvoice.com*

❖ Yahoo Pager — *www.yahoo.com*

Powwow

Powwow is an instant messaging and chat system. It is a program that uses the Internet as its medium of transport; you simply install their special program and then connect up with other chatters.

Powwow is good if you wish to chat with a person one-on-one; all you need is their Powwow address, you do not have to go into a crowded chat room and see other people's messages. Powwow also has other features, such as being able to use a collaborative whiteboard, as well as being able to share files and exchange them. Powwow can also inform you when your friends log on by using a buddy list.

For a beginner looking at interactivity on the Internet, Powwow may not be ideal, as you may find it hard to talk to people you do not know without first entering a chat room. But once you get to know a few people, it is ideal for private chatting. As you become familiar with Powwow, you can also take part in communities and group chats.

ICQ and Yahoo Pager

ICQ (pronounced *I Seek You*) is an instant messaging program similar to Powwow; it will also alert you when your friends are online. ICQ allows you to send instant messages — like instantaneous e-mails — or to chat with friends in real time. You can also share files and play games, all on-line! Both ICQ and Powwow allow you to hold conferences, where you can chat to a number of people at the same time.

ICQ is very popular. When you first load up ICQ, you will be assigned a unique number that identities you on the ICQ network. You can give people your ICQ number (similar in some respects to an IP number)and they can then contact you.

One major advantage of ICQ is that you can set the program up so that if people wish to add you to their list of contacts, they must get your permission first. This helps you identify whose buddy list you want to be on. This is very important because if you are on someone's buddy list they will know immediately when you log onto the Internet. People could use this maliciously to send you abusive e-mails, annoy you, etc.

Yahoo Pager is a similar program but is not as advanced as ICQ.

All of the above programs have a built-in facility that allows you to signal to other users whether you are at your computer, busy or do not want to be disturbed. This facility is very handy, because then you don't waste your time trying to send messages if the person is not at their computer. One facility they also have is the ability to appear invisible — this means that, although you are online, it will not register on anyone's buddy lists. They will not be able to find you. This is useful if you are being harassed; you can contact your buddies to initiate a conversation, while still ensuring you are not visible to other users.

You will find many other such pieces of software, and it is only by trial and error that you can sort the good from the bad and enjoy them. Many take time to learn, like IRC; others, such as Powwow and ICQ, are easier to use because of their clearer user interfaces.

GSM and Pager Services

Digital mobile phones allow users to send simple text message or <u>SMSs</u> (Short Message Service) to each other. It was only a matter of time before a <u>gateway</u> was set up to allow people to send SMSs from the Internet to phones.

> *A **Gateway** is a way of transferring information from one type of network to another. In this case, data from the Internet is being sent to a GSM phone. The gateway ensures that the information is translated correctly.*

Many sites now offer this service. You usually first subscribe; you are then sent a password that you use with your mobile number in order to access the site. After you log in, you can then simply type your message and press **Send**.

The following websites are two of the most reliable I have seen on the Internet for sending SMS:

❖ *www.hooya.com*: limit of five messages a day to any one mobile phone.

❖ *www.mtn.co.za*: only works on the 086 network.

Some providers also allow for a paging service to mobile phones via the Internet.

Businesses could really benefit from these services. Since many businesses have dedicated access to the Internet, it would be cheaper and more effective to send pages to employees via the Internet rather than incur the cost of a phone call and wait for the operator to send the message. Most companies do not realise they can do this with their existing dedicated lines!

Internet Telephone/Voice Chat

As companies saw opportunities with the Internet and chat software, they decided to take it one step further and create actual "chat" software — that is, software that enabled users with microphones and headsets to talk to each other via the web.

All the user needs is a special piece of software, which is usually free, and then a sound card, microphone and headset so that they can communicate. When you register with the software company, you are given a special phone number that people can call you at; you then can decide whether to accept the call or not.

Over time, this type of facility has improved in quality; if you have a decent specification machine, you can have quite a good conversation via the Internet in real time. This in turn means that you can now make long distance calls for very little!

The one disadvantage of this facility was that both parties have to have the same software available on their computer.

IP Telephony

Taking things a step further was the experiment of IP Telephony. This allows people to use their computers to communicate with other users via the telephone network, without the user at the other end needing to have a computer — you can ring their home phone or mobile directly!

Two different companies — Voltec and net2phone — using different technologies began experimenting some time ago with the idea of sending voice data over the Internet between PCs. Their idea was both simple and fantastic. They saw that many people were using the Internet to communicate via chat rooms; this was usually text-based, but also through voice pagers such as Powwow. Powwow, as discussed, is a piece of Internet communication software that allows for voice communication. Both parties must be running the powwow software.

Using such software, people who had a sound card, a microphone and speakers/headphones and the powwow software could communicate with each other through voice communication. Powwow was incredible — you could now *talk* to people, in the real sense of the word, on the other side of the globe for the price of a local call. This was the start of Internet phones — software that allowed you to have voice conversations with people over the Internet.

But what if it was possible to convert the voice packet and connect it up to the main telephone system? Remember we said that modems modulated and demodulated signals? Well, how about demodulating the signal so it could be passed as a voice signal, rather than a data signal, over the telephone network?

Net2phone saw this as a brilliant idea and developed their software. As with Voltec, you can now use their software on your computer to dial real telephones. This is the key to their service — the other user does not need to have a computer. The person at the other end receives the call on their telephone and not their computer. For all intents and purposes, they would not realise that the person at the other end of the phone is actually placing the call over the Internet.

All calls originate from the call centre in the US; therefore, rather than paying for a call from Europe to the US, the call is actually originating in the US, therefore you are charged only local call or trunk call rates! If one uses the software to call Europe it is like calling Europe from the US! Suddenly, cheap calls are a reality: now you could ring anybody anywhere in the world and all they would cost you is the price of your local call to your ISP.

Think how a company could save money. If they already had a leased line, they could download this software and start saving money on international calls. With the introduction of flat rate pricing for Internet access by telephone companies, people can make cheaper international calls, and not even have to worry about the price of their local calls, since they are paying a flat fee regardless of how long they access the Internet.

OK, so what is the drawback? First and foremost, since the calls are routed over the Internet, two problems arise:

❖ Since the Internet is a packet-based network, packets may get dropped, leading to lower quality calls and breaks in transmissions;

❖ You still need to have a computer to initiate the phone call, as well as a sound card, microphone and speakers.

Since these initial experiments, computer technology has expanded, communication speeds have increased and new updated software has been released. Many service providers have now taken things a step further with trials of Voice Over Internet Protocol (aka Voice Over IP or VOIP). Essentially, this uses the same concept — voice signals are transmitted using the Internet protocols. There is one fundamental difference: instead of using public Internet connections to transport calls; calls are routed over private dedicated lines that only take voice data. This leads to a better sound quality and more reliable service.

Newsgroups

Newsgroups have been in existence for over 20 years, but very few "modern" surfers know a lot about them and many people do not really understand them.

Let's delve back into Internet history to understand a little bit more about newsgroups. ARPAnet, as we know, was invented to allow military and scientific researchers exchange information. As it became more popular, some universities joined the network to share and communicate information.

But there were many who were not connected to this network, as to do so cost universities a large amount of money, so many universities could not afford to connect. Also, many universities may not have been entitled to join for non-research reasons.

Propagation

A new protocol was introduced into the Unix operating system called Unix-to-Unix Copy Protocol (UUCP). This protocol allowed files to be copied from one Unix-based computer to another. Using dial-up modems, it was possible for one computer to call up another one and check to see what files had been updated on a machine. All updates could then be downloaded.

In 1979, two students from Duke University, Tom Truscott and Jim Ellis, with the help of Steve Bellovin of the University of North Carolina, began experimenting with UUCP. They soon developed a program called Net News. This program would call up another UNIX machine and using UUCP it would check for files that had been updated — in this case news — and then copy any new news from one computer to another.

The year 1980 saw a new revision of this program called **Usenet News**. Usenet News allowed any user with a UNIX-based machine to write a message, dial up another local computer and transfer this news to the other computer. The computer they dialled up would then dial another computer and pass on any new messages. This procedure continued until, bit by bit, your message would **propagate** over this new network.

Usenet was often called the poor man's ARPAnet; it cost very little and was an efficient way of passing information from one host to another. ARPAnet already had what were called mailing discussion lists, where users could send messages to all others on the discussion list. One problem persisted — some of the lists were moderated. Usenet was not moderated and was therefore a truly democratic and system of free speech.

Newsgroups became a distributed bulletin board system. They are distributed because they do not reside on one computer server, but are available on many servers. Each server updates itself with the latest additions to the newsgroup.

problem persisted — some of the lists were moderated. Usenet was not moderated and was therefore a truly democratic and system of free speech.

Newsgroups became a distributed bulletin board system. They are distributed because they do not reside on one computer server, but are available on many servers. Each server updates itself with the latest additions to the newsgroup.

Newsgroups are like the discussion boards we mentioned earlier, in the sense that they have topics of conversation that people can reply to and create new messages. They differ from discussion boards since they are not web-based. They also cover every conceivable topic.

In 1981, there was a new and interesting development. A new version of the news software was brought out that enabled newsgroups to be either moderated or unmoderated. People began to scream about censorship, authority being imposed on newsgroups, etc.

Seven categories or hierarchies of newsgroups were created:

* ❖ Comp — dealt with computer related information
* ❖ Misc — anything of a miscellaneous nature
* ❖ News — anything to do with news
* ❖ Rec — dealing with all recreational topics
* ❖ Sci — dealt with science issues
* ❖ Soc — dealt with social and society-related issues
* ❖ Talk — anything controversial that needed to be discussed.

Every newsgroup is structured in a hierarchical fashion. For example, if I am looking for information about Windows 98, I may look in the following newsgroup: *comp.os.win98.** — notice the star, which means that this newsgroup has many sub-topics. These could be about video card problems (*comp.os.win98.video*) or Internet information could be contained in *comp.os.win98.Internet*.

A new category, the ALT or alternative newsgroup, was created in 1988. What a can of worms this opened! Anything alternative could be discussed in this category. This has led to some problems. There are newsgroups that deal with every type of perversion imaginable. Others deal with trading passwords for computer systems, hacking information and software piracy.

argument for not carrying some groups. Groups that are very popular can generate hundreds of posts (messages) a day. Since they must update their servers with the latest posts, if they carry 20 newsgroups which each have 1,000 posts a day — a very moderate number of posts! — this would mean they would be getting 20,000 items going through their server a day. This may create more network traffic then they really want, and therefore slow down their network. So most ISPs will not carry all newsgroups.

Newsgroup Readers

To use newsgroups, you need a <u>newsgroup reader</u>. Back in the dark ages of the Internet (aka a few years ago), you needed a special program to read newsgroups called a newsreader. Many browsers or e-mail programs now come with newsreaders built in. There are many of these available and most are free. In fact, you probably have at least one already in the form of Outlook Express. You should contact your Internet Service Provider to see if they carry newsgroups; some free services may not give users access to newsgroups.

Newsgroups can be tricky to use and as such most surfers have heard about them but never used them before. The website accompanying this book describes how to set up Outlook Express as a news reader.

Newsgroups Terms

❖ **FAQ**: An FAQ is a list of Frequently Asked Questions. Most newsgroups should have one that will deal with information regarding the newsgroup, such as what to post and what not to post, etc. Many websites also contain FAQs; they are an easy way of finding information such as technical support, company information, etc.

❖ **Lurking**: Lurking has unsavoury connotations in the real world, but in the online world, it refers to the act of watching posts on a discussion board or newsgroup and reading them before replying to them. It is always a good idea to do this to ensure you fully understand what the newsgroup is about.

❖ **Posting**: Posting means sending a message to a newsgroup. Remember that everyone subscribed to or viewing that newsgroup will see your message!

❖ **Follow-up**: A follow-up is a post in reply to another post. For example, if I post a message about needing help in researching a new book, if someone replies to that they have posted a follow-up message.

> **What is the difference between a thread and a follow-up?** *A follow-up is a reply to a message; a thread is a list of messages and follow-ups on one topic.*

❖ **Flaming**: Flaming means sending abusive messages to someone, often containing personal attacks. This can lead to a flame war, where such messages are sent back and forth between people.

One problem with newsgroups is that there are so many of them that finding the right information can take some time; also, since there is little structure to them, you cannot be assured of finding correct information as you require.

Can newsgroups be web-based?

Remember at the start of this chapter we said that newsgroups could also be web-based? We will now see how this is and why it is easier to view newsgroups through a web page.

There is a site dedicated to helping you locate information from newsgroups via a simple web interface. There are so many newsgroups and so many sub-categories that it can often be an impossible task to try to find the relevant newsgroup you are looking for.

Dejanews (*www.dejanews.com* or *www.deja.com*) was set up to help people search newsgroups using a web-based interface. It is also useful for those who, for some reason, may not have access to newsgroups in their workplace, college or through their ISP. You can set up a free account with Dejanews that will allow you to create an identity for posting to newsgroups. Many people do not like people knowing who they are when posting to newsgroups for fear of being <u>flamed</u>.

Within Dejanews you will find a section that will allow you to search many of the popular newsgroups available. This makes life much easier for people to participate in newsgroups, as they may not know exactly what they are looking for but can search a range of newsgroups by using keywords, much like in the search engines. Indeed, it is worthwhile checking to see if your favourite search engine also allows you to search through newsgroups. Experiment with Dejanews and see how you get on with newsgroups!

Before posting to a newsgroup, you should follow some simple guidelines (if only to ensure you are not flamed!):

❖ Read about the newsgroup or lurk before you post. This means that you should ensure you understand what the newsgroup is about. For example, do not post to a technical newsgroup if you want advice on how to install a program — this is bad netiquette! You should always read the FAQ that should be available.

❖ Following on from the above, do not advertise in a newsgroup. This can lead to flaming. Newsgroups are primarily for discussion, although there are some that welcome promotion. People do not like to read advertisements. Remember, they have to download the messages, which can cost them money and time. If the feel that they have been fooled by your subject line and have wasted time downloading a message, they may flame you.

❖ Don't post purely for the sake of posting. You may often see "me too" posts. For example, someone may post a message and ask if people want to join a new website; one person may reply "I do", and others will then reply "me too"; this is just a waste.

❖ Always keep to the point of a threaded discussion. If you have a personal opinion that may deviate from the chosen topic, you should consider e-mailing the author of the post rather than typing in your thoughts and posting them to the newsgroup, which means they will be read by everyone, most of whom may find your comments irrelevant.

❖ **Never**, ever, post the contents of an e-mail to a newsgroup, unless you have permission from the author. Remember that the author of the e-mail is the copyrighted owner of that e-mail; therefore you are in breach of copyright. This also applies to general e-mail.

❖ When an opinion is expressed in a newsgroup, it is the opinion of the poster and not of the organisation they work for. Therefore, if someone posts a message and they work for a company that you know, they are expressing their personal opinion and not the opinion of the company.

❖ Provide a small <u>signature</u> at the end of your post so that people may contact you, but do not overdo it. As in e-mail, a signature should be no more than three lines long.

❖ It should go without saying that information regarding illegal activities should not be posted. Do not post messages on how to break into your corporate network or where to find passwords for software, etc.

Online Communities

Many people share the same interests but find it hard to find like-minded people, since cyberspace is so big. People want a place where they can meet and discuss their ideas. Companies and organisations realised this and began to set up websites that allowed people with like-minded ideas and mutual interests to build websites together.

Again, we see the social aspect of the Internet; people from all around the world can come together and build virtual communities together.

In the early days of the Internet, two such companies set up:

❖ www.geocities.com

❖ www.tripod.com

Their idea was to allow people to build their websites on their servers; they would provide all the tools needed.

Remember, a server is a computer that other computers (clients) connect to. In the case of Geocities and Tripod, they allowed users to create websites on their servers. As you can imagine, unless you have very good security in place, it can be dangerous to allow people to access and store information on your server. These companies have special programs and security features to ensure that people cannot access any other information stored on their servers (mainly other people's files).

Geocities began by dividing up its server into different topics of interest. If you wanted to build a website with them, you moved into one of their virtual communities that catered for your interests. Thus, communities such as "Hollywood" existed for any site that dealt with TV, movies, actors, etc. If you were interested in poetry or academia, you set up your website in the Athens community. Other sites allow users to share photos, set up community notice boards. As you will discover as you travel around the net people want to communicate and share their information and thoughts with countless others.

"Community leaders" were appointed to ensure that the spirit of the community was kept in place; i.e. ensuring that no undesirable sites would appear. This idea was fantastic from a business perspective: provide the space for people to build websites and let them build the content of your overall website. Geocities proved to be very popular; their one stipulation was that an ad was placed on your web page. Thus, the service itself was free but paid for by advertisers.

Geocities was bought over by Yahoo in 1999; it still provides the same basic functions. The other website, tripod.com, was a little less organised but eventually came up with the idea of grouping web pages into pods, a similar idea to communities. At about the same time as Geocities was bought, Tripod was bought by the Lycos network.

These sites are popular because they provide a place for like-minded individuals to build websites and express themselves. One problem that did occur was that it was impossible to ensure that every single site hosted by these companies actually related to the community it was in. There were many sites that were hacking or porn-based that operated from these free servers.

Community leaders did their best to ensure all pages were kept in the spirit of the community but found this difficult as many people created sites that were, on first impression, "normal sites". These users then created other pages not linked from any page within the "pseudo" site. To access these pages, you had to know their exact URL. The legitimate site may have an address like *www.geocities.com/hollywood/1906*, but the secret site might be *www.geocities.com/hollywood/1906/secrets.htm*. The web page secrets.htm would not be linked to any page on their site, thus making it hard for the community leader to find such pages.

On a general note, it is impossible to know what lurks on the Internet, because if the page is not linked, only those in the know will find out about the site. This is a worry for businesses and schools who run websites; if an employee/student sets up a page containing illegal or indecent material, you may be none the wiser but it could damage your site/reputation.

Portal Sites

Many sites understand the importance and need for a sense of community on the Internet. They know that people now want more from a website. In the old days (four or five years ago), a website provided information on maybe one or two topics and people were happy with that. Once they gave you the information you were searching for, it was time to leave the site. Nowadays websites are providing more and more content.

Yahoo used to be just a search directory. You visited Yahoo, looked for something in the search directory and then visited the other website. As time progressed, they discovered that it was important to build a brand name on the web and to try to get people to visit your site and stay on it. Along came the idea of a portal site.

This was a site that people would use as a starting point on all their Internet travels. It would provide more than just a directory or information about a company. It would provide everything. Now Yahoo is much more. You can find everything you want in Yahoo without having to visit any other site. Currently you can:

❖ Chat

❖ Build a website

❖ Buy or sell at an auction

❖ Read classified ads

❖ View maps of towns and states

❖ Play online games

❖ Read the latest headlines.

It seems likely that these uses will expand in the future. Basically, it is a one-stop shop for all your needs.

What companies now want to do is to make you spend more and more time at their site. The reason for this is that, as you visit pages on their website, they can track your every move using cookies. They can then target advertising at your particular needs. Advertisers will buy more ads if they think their ads are more targeted to each consumer group.

 *A **cookie** is a small text file sent by a web server to your hard drive when you connect. Its purpose is to help customise and enhance your surfing experience and to help the website to target their marketing.*

A very good example of a portal site in Ireland is *www.ireland.com*, *The Irish Times* website. Originally, they only provided *The Irish Times* newspaper on their site, but they recognised the need to develop a range of services. They therefore now provide free e-mail, restaurant guides, special news reports, an archive, a whole section about Dublin and what's on.

They knew that people would visit the *Irish Times* site, but they wanted to make sure that the public stayed on the site. Providing free e-mail accounts was an inspired idea. Now people could read the paper and then check their e-mail without having to type in a new website address or open a separate program.

More and more niche portal sites will develop over the coming months and years that will cater for specific needs of local communities or industries. These niche portals are now known as <u>Vortals</u> or Vertical Portals! They provide specialised information for particular groups; for example, if you wanted to find accommodation in County Limerick, instead of having a site all about accommodation in Ireland, this one site would just provide information about the Limerick area.

Online Gaming

Ever played a computer game but wanted more than just playing against the computer? Well, now you can challenge the world! For the past number of years, games like Doom have been "<u>network aware</u>"; they can be played at the same time by different users against each other on a network.

Doom, probably one of the best known computer games, sounds on paper like hundreds of similar games: it involves the user "walking" through a number of levels, killing aliens and mutants — great fun! But add in the next dimension — the ability to network the game and see other users in the network playing the game — and the excitement can be increased tenfold! Many games now allow for this facility, which enhances and extends the game's boundaries. Quake, a similar game to Doom, allows this feature.

A quick search in any search engine for "online gaming" or "Quake servers" will give you a list of sites to discover. It must be noted that you must have the full retail copy of the game in order to play. Sega's latest Dreamcast console also has this feature built in.

For those who like tradition, many sites, including Yahoo, offer classic games such as card games, chess and backgammon, all of which can be played remotely over the Internet!

Chapter 11

Downloading

Get Down

If you had never explored the Internet before reading this book, you might at this stage feel a bit overwhelmed with the range of things you can do in cyberspace. This chapter will help you get even more out of the Internet!

One of the chief benefits that the Internet brought to the world was the ability to transfer files and programs from one computer to another. This use of the Internet has expanded greatly in recent years, particularly as <u>bandwidth</u> has increased, to the extent that it is now possible to <u>download</u> everything from small text files to large documents, images, streaming video, games and even whole albums of music!

We will look at some of the types of material that can be downloaded shortly. The first thing we must understand is what downloading means and how to download from the Internet. Downloading refers to information or files, usually pictures, programs, audio or video, being transferred from one computer "down" to another, the opposite being uploading from one computer to another (which is what happens when you are sending a web page to a server). The ability to transfer files has been around since the early 1970s. E-mail was invented from a program that was used to transfer files from one computer to another.

So what happens when you download something? You copy the file from a server to your computer; the key word is *copy*. The original file always stays on the server, much like the copy and paste function in word processors. How difficult is it to download a file? The simple answer is, if you can click on a web page, you can download!

When you download a file, you use a protocol called FTP or File Transfer Protocol, which has already been discussed in Chapter 8. Most modern browsers have basic FTP capabilities built into them; at the very least, they can download files. Instead of having to use a separate program to download, everything can be done from within your browser.

Downloading is an essential skill to be familiar with on the Internet. To download means to copy a file/program from the Internet to your hard disk. The original file stays on their server. The bigger the file, the longer it will take to download. As with everything on the Internet, it is cheaper to download during off-peak hours rather than during the day.

An FTP server is a server that is used for downloading or uploading files. Some companies will set up FTP servers so that clients can download updates to their programs. If you see the following in your browser you will know for sure you are at an FTP site and not a web page:

Free for All!

One of the most attractive things about the Internet is the sense of sharing that is prevalent among many individuals. Remember, one of the original reasons for creating the network was the sharing of resources.

When companies developed an interest in the web, it was feared that the web would become too commercial. In fact, it seems to have helped people share resources even more, at the same time as totally altering the way many companies think about their business. When they are trying to do business on the web, companies have to look at how they can create a successful and profit-making website. When people visit a company's website, they do so for a number of reasons:

1. Find out more about the company

2. Find out more about a certain product

3. Find reviews of a product

4. See if they can try out the product before they buy it

5. Purchase the product

6. Get support or help for a product

The fourth point is very interesting: try out a product before you buy it. What a great idea! Let people see your product and use if for 30 days, after which time the user can choose to buy it or not. Here we are, of course, assuming the product is downloadable such products include:

❖ Sample chapters of a book

❖ Sample tracks from a CD

❖ Software (most common)

Companies simply could not afford to do this using traditional distribution channels. The company would have to produce a CD or set of disks for the product, include some sort of instructions, package and distribute the product; it would not be worth it if the customer was then going to return it 30 days later.

But being able to try a product before you buy it is essential for a consumer. Along comes the Internet and changes all of that. Many companies are now offering free trials of their products that users can download and use for a certain length of time.

Distribution Methods

The Internet provides an ideal distribution method, mainly because companies do not have to produce a CD/set of disks, package and present the product. The user simply downloads it and manuals can be downloaded as well.

It is possible to download trial versions of many different types of products. Smaller companies that could not even afford to advertise in foreign countries gain another great advantage. They can now offer their products for sale over the Internet and reach a far wider audience.

For example, if I were to produce a product for creating crossword puzzles, it would cost me a fortune to market and distribute the product internationally — so much so that either I would have to charge a ridiculous amount for the product or not sell it at all.

With the Internet, I can submit my product to certain websites that keep information about software than can be downloaded.

Much of the software you find on the net is either:

❖ **Trial Version**: This type of software is usually the full product with certain limitations or key functions disabled, which are only enabled once payment has been made.

❖ **Shareware**: This is where you may get the full product (sometimes like the above, where key functions are disabled) and must pay for the product after using if for 30 days. Usually after 30 days, the product will stop working.

❖ **Freeware**: This is where the product is completely free of charge —
you pay nothing for using it! Authors create utilities that are freeware
simply to get their name known around the Internet.

❖ **Beta software**: This refers to software that is nearly complete but not
quite ready for commercial release. It is released free of charge so
that "real users" can use it and then comment on how it can be improved and report problems that they may have had with it.

The great thing about distributing software this way is that the whole
product can be shipped but will only be completely usable when the
user pays the licence fee. The author then sends a registration or serial
key to unlock the limited product and make it a full version

Shareware

Let's look at shareware in more detail. From the beginning of computing,
many enthusiasts wanted to share great programs they had developed.
These were often programs that filled a gap in the market, i.e. specialist
programs, such as a utility to help organise your favourites in Internet
Explorer, or a program that allows you to quickly create and manipulate
images. This type of program is useful, but large software companies
may not see it as a revenue-generating product; thus they would not
bother developing it.

Some shareware companies started out small but have become well
known for their products. One such company is JASC, who to compete
with more expensive graphic imaging products created a program
called Paint Shop Pro. Many such companies would not have the money
to advertise their products worldwide; they also would not be a recognised brand name, so they could not charge high prices for their software. Such companies want to keep the price of software down so it is
accessible by all.

Along came the idea of sharing your software — allowing people to,
in fact encouraging them to share it with their friends. They company en-
sured that the people would distribute the trial version to all and sundry,
thus penetrating a large market of users. Thus shareware was born.
Shareware has boomed because it is now more accessible via the Internet but it was around before the average person had access to the Internet. Some users, albeit those who were "computer nerds", shared files
using something called bulletin boards.

In the olden days, shareware software was not very good, in fact a lot of it was pretty awful, but the quality and list of applications has now risen, to the extent that some shareware even rivals commercial software. Whatever you do, don't think that good shareware is in any way of a lesser quality than commercially produced software!

Shareware is always protected in one of a number of ways:

❖ **Crippled**: Some shareware programs have certain vital functions such as printing or saving disabled. This is known as crippling the application.

❖ **Time restrictions**: Many authors will program the shareware version so that it expires after 30 days or after it has been run a certain number of times.

❖ The shareware usually also has a **nag screen** — this is a screen that appears every time you either start or exit the program. The nag screen will appear for maybe 10 seconds or more reminding you to purchase the full product.

An obvious question to be asked is, how much does shareware cost when it comes to registering or purchasing the full version? It depends, but it can be from as little as $5 to $100. So why should you register? There are a number of very valid reasons to register if you wish to continue to use the software:

❖ Software may not work after allocated time limit!

❖ Supporting the author: this encourages the author to produce more updates to the software, which in turn will lead to better software.

❖ Manuals: more often than not, when you register you will get the manuals e-mailed to you or available via a password-protected web page. Operating instructions that come with shareware are usually sparse or not included at all.

❖ Updates: many, but not necessarily all, authors will provide free updates on software during the lifetime of the current version you have bought. As small fixes come out for version 1, you will get updates until version 2 is released. Some will even give you a free upgrade from the current version to the next version.

By and large, if you are looking for a utility or a specialised piece of software, you will find it as shareware.

Freeware on the other hand is free! Many companies provide old versions of their programs for free download, much like programs on the free CDs accompanying computer magazines. Others provide cut-down versions of their commercial programs, that will be fully functional but may not contain all the features of the full product. An example of this is FrontPage Express (a cut down version of FrontPage).

The aim of both freeware and shareware is to allow you to try out the software and then get you hooked! Look around, explore the Internet, you will find much *legal* software and utilities for free.

Software

A lot of very good software is actually shareware-based. More authors are getting their software recognised since they find it cheaper to distribute via the Internet and can now reach a wider market.

There are a number of sites that can help you located the software you are looking for, the best known being:

❖ *www.shareware.com*

❖ *www.download.com*

You can simply browse through different categories or search by a keyword or title. When you find the title you want, simply click on the link. You will see that information is given about the product, author, company and how many people have downloaded the product. You should see the usual screen asking you to save the program to disk or run it from its current location.

Save the program to disk, remembering which directory you saved it in. Depending on the size of the program and the speed of your modem and connection, this could take anything from ten minutes to ten hours! You have been warned! This is where a service that provides flat rate pricing for Internet access is really beneficial. No matter how long you are online for, you don't get charged any more.

Some software asks you to select "Install and run the program from this location"; if you are asked to do this, do it; otherwise you should save the file to disk.

At this stage, chances are you will have to install the program. What you have downloaded is a setup program. Much of the time when you download the software, you may get very few instructions on how to install it or use the function contained in it. You usually get a manual when you pay for the product. Installing the software should be a simple matter of finding where you saved it on your hard drive and running the setup program (simply by double-clicking on it).

If you have never set up a program before, don't worry — try it now! When you double-click on the set-up file, the computer will take you through the installation step by step. Just read all instructions carefully! Some programs will request you to restart your computer before proceeding; this is normal.

The Internet is thus great for individuals, businesses and educators, as they can find much of the software that they need. This is how Netscape's browser became so popular — it was given away for free using the Internet as the distribution channel. Microsoft also use this facility; they give out the updates to Internet Explorer via the Internet.

Distribution Problems

Since the Internet is a great way of distributing software, software piracy has become a major problem for many companies. It is possible to locate any piece of commercial software for free on the Internet. Remember, no single group controls the Internet; therefore it is very hard to police. Sites appear for a couple of hours or days, specifically to trade pirated software. This is known as **Warez**.

Warez is the act of providing illegal copies of commercial software on a website for public or private download.

Companies are losing millions of dollars to these sites. You may think that it is great to be able to download free commercial software, but it is illegal! Warez sites are discussed further in the next chapter.

Viruses

When downloading from the Internet, viruses are a real threat. Often you may find a great piece of software and download it. The software will run and do what it is supposed to do, but suddenly you computer may "hang" or crash.

The issues of software piracy, copyright and viruses are very contentious; Chapter 12 looks at these issues more closely. The important thing to note for now is that you should always save any downloaded files/programs to disk, as you would with an e-mail attachment, and then run your virus checker on them.

Patches and Add-ons

Many companies also release <u>patches</u> for their programs, which you can download free of charge. Patches are small "fixes" for bugs in software that might not have been detected when the software was first released. Thus, if a software company discover a problem with the software they have released — for example, it crashes every time you do X, Y or Z — they will supply a small program that, when run, fixes or patches the problem. Similar to patches, many companies also provide free add-on software (like <u>plug-ins</u> — see below) that can enhance the software you bought from them. These add-ons might improve the functionality of a program, or provide some extra options for the application. Like the word "hack", the word patches has another, more sinister meaning — a way to "patch" a trial program and make it into a full version.

The Internet is an ideal way to supply patches and add-ons, as the user can download the patch when they want, rather than the company having to spend a fortune posting it out to users. In recent times, Microsoft has made patches available when problems are found in their software, particularly security problems such as those experienced in Internet Explorer.

Drivers

Every time you buy a new piece of hardware for your computer, you must always install the proper <u>device driver</u>.

 *A **device driver** is a piece of software that drives or makes your new hardware work correctly with your particular computer.*

Unfortunately, what can sometimes happen is that you lose the device driver disks, or you are given a present of a printer but no driver disks come with it. This is no longer a problem, as all you have to do is access the company's website, find the appropriate device driver, download it and install it.

Nearly all computer manufacturers will have a "downloads" section on their website that will provide drivers, patches and other files. Always go to the company's website to see if they can help you first; a good example is the Gateway website, who provide up-to-date drivers for all their products.

Be careful — if you download and install an incorrect driver, your systems may not function correctly.

Plug-ins

From your understanding of the history of the Internet and the World Wide Web, you will remember that the whole system was developed for military and then academic use. When the standards were written for HTML (the language that web pages are encoded with) what could not have been foreseen were the sophisticated purposes to which the Internet would be put. All the academics wanted was a way to make a page that had plain text. This is why web pages are sometimes boring!

As more and more people used the Internet, their needs and wants for what they could see and do on the web developed. Programmers and companies started designing new and improved software that could run from a web page. Nowadays, web pages have a lot more to them. You can have video, you can have sound, you can even walk through virtual landscapes and have conversations in virtual worlds!

How is all this possible, you may wonder? Enter the plug-in, also known as the helper application. A plug-in is a small program that you can download that will "plug" itself into your browser. When you visit a page with content that the plug-in uses, the plug-in or helper application takes over and displays the content. For example, let's say you visit a page with a virtual reality landscape. If you have the plug-in for that type of material, the virtual landscape will appear and you will be able to explore it.

Sometimes a program will install a plug-in so that when its content is encountered on a web page, a separate program will not run; the content will appear in the web browser. (In my experience, Internet Explorer handles such instances best — another plus for IE!)

The next question is: What happens if you do not have the plug-in? Simple: the computer will tell you that you do not have it and ask you whether you want to download it and install it!

Now comes the difficult part — you must get the plug-in, download it, install it, maybe restart your browser or, even worse still, restart your computer, and then visit the web page again! (Remember if you are doing this to first save all your work in other applications!) Luckily, this only needs to be done once per plug-in, but it can be a daunting and annoying task.

Many of the modern browsers come with a number of popular plug-ins already installed, but listed below are some plug-ins that you will need if you are to get the most from the Internet's multimedia content.

Real Audio/Real Video

Real Player is the first plug-in we will look at, available from www.real.com. This plug-in allows you to watch streaming video and audio via the Internet. <u>Streaming</u> refers to a way in which video and sound can be delivered in one continuous "stream". Instead of having to wait while the video/audio is downloaded completely, the computer downloads a few seconds of video/audio and then begins to play it. While it is playing these seconds of video/audio, it is downloading more, which it begins to play. This constant playing and downloading gives the effect of one continuous stream of video without the need to wait for whole video to download.

So is real audio/video any good? At the moment, video over the Internet can be quite slow or appear choppy. Many sites use it for informational guides, perhaps explaining how their product works. One example I have seen is a computer manufacturer which uses real video to show how to install components on a computer.

News stations can show video of their newscasts. One popular application is for radio stations to broadcast over the net! Some broadcast live; others have pre-recorded shows. Many bands and artists are using the web to do <u>webcasts</u> of their concerts; indeed, Sky Broadcasting did a live web cast of a Robbie Williams concert where surfers could visit the site and watch the concert from different cams!

Tip! Go to the **View** menu in IE5, chose **Toolbars**, then **Radio** — a new radio toolbar appears! Now you can listen to radio broadcasts! You may be prompted to download Real Player or Windows Media Player.

If you click on a link to listen to a radio broadcast but don't have Real Player installed, you will be asked to save a file with a .ram extension – this is a Real Player file! Once Real Player is installed, it will know to automatically play the file rather than try to download it.

Director/Flash

This plug-in allows users to view highly interactive websites. Flash (produced by Macromedia) is a program that allows a site developer to build custom interfaces, with elaborate animation and graphics, for a website. Flash allows a high level of interactivity with low file size. This means that the user does not have to wait forever for the site to download. Using Flash, a site designer can develop a site that would normally take hours to download. Budding web designers note: always ensure you have a "non-Flash" site for users who do not have Flash or other proprietary technology — don't assume everyone has it.

Macromedia's Director allows for richer content than allowed by Flash, including games, training products, etc.

Acrobat Reader

Acrobat Reader from Adobe allows a user to view a document formatted exactly as the author intended. It is one of the most essential plug-ins to have. The user can view and print the document but cannot make changes to it. Acrobat provides document authors with an ideal way of distributing manuals and other documents.

As you know, the key reason that the web was successful was because everyone could access web pages and view them regardless of what computer they were using. If files are saved in Word format, users without Word will not be able to view the document. If documents are saved in Acrobat format, all the user has to do is download a piece of software to view the document. The author is assured that the document will look the same on all platforms.

Another useful feature is that the user cannot alter the document's contents. The danger with distributing any type of text is that another user may copy and paste the text and distribute it as their own work. Acrobat does not allow this. The reason for this is that all Acrobat documents are encoded using Acrobat software. The full version of the Acrobat encoder allows the author to lock the files so that no editing, copying or printing of the file is allowed. Even if you have the encoder program, you will not be able to change the contents of the files.

Acrobat is often used to create e-books, or electronic books, since they are so secure. No matter what type of computer the user has, if they have Acrobat Reader they will see the files as they were created, fonts, graphics and layout included.

Once you download Acrobat Reader, you will be able to view PDF files (Portable Document Format). If you come across such a file on a website, Acrobat Reader will display the file in your browser. If you do not have Acrobat Reader you will be asked to save the file to disk; you must then download the Reader.

A number of plug-ins are supplied on the website accompanying this book (*www.internetdemystified.com*) in order to save you the time and hassle of trying to find them.

If you come across a site that needs to be used with a plug-in, a message will appear telling you that you should download the appropriate plug-in. If you run a website, ensure that you tell your visitors what plug-ins may be required before they click on a file. I recently came across a university's website, which allowed you to view their prospectus online — but they did not inform the user they had to have Acrobat installed!

MP3 and the Music Revolution

No book on Internet technologies would be complete without discussing MP3. MP3 is a new way of distributing audio tracks via the Internet. MP3 files are digitally encoded, highly compressed, CD quality music tracks. Users can download MP3 tracks and play them on their computer using such software as Winamp or by downloading the MP3 tracks onto an MP3 player.

An MP3 player is a device that looks like a small personal stereo that allows you to download music from your computer into its memory. One major advantage of MP3 is that there are no moving parts; therefore if you are running or exercising, you will find that the music does not "jump" as it may do with a conventional personal CD player. MP3 players have memory cards, usually 32MB, though some come with only 16MB. The more memory the player has, the more music they can store. Depending on your Internet connection, MP3 files may take some time to download; an average track might be 3.2MB or larger. Also, quality can vary; the higher the quality of the track, the larger the file will be.

It is easy to find MP3-playing software on the net — the best known being Winamp — which allow you to listen to your MP3s. Some will also contain <u>MP3 rippers</u>. To rip a track means to copy it from a CD onto your computer and compress it into MP3 format. This has caused a number of problems, as users are infringing copyright by ripping tracks!

Do you have a legal right to copy a CD track and convert it to MP3 format for your own use? Probably not! However, this problem is a relatively insignificant problem for records companies — it is like making a tape of your favourite CD. During the 1970s and 1980s, the record industry had problems with home copying of tapes; while they lost money, it was generally on a very small scale. Anyone who wanted to distribute on a mass scale would have had to invest in expensive equipment. Now the problem of "home recording" has exploded globally.

Where record companies have major concerns is when users are trading MP3 files via the Internet. Recently there has been a lot of controversy surrounding MP3, because record companies have suddenly discovered a number of sites that contain entire albums of many well-known musicians available for free download from the site. These are essentially pirated albums. Since MP3 is CD-quality audio, many people are downloading complete albums from the Internet and thus musicians and record companies are losing huge amounts of money from such activities.

Another problem is that musicians are now beginning to realise that the Internet is a more efficient way of distributing CD music "officially", and CDs should and could be bought from the Internet and downloaded to your computer for a lot less than the current price of a CD in the shops. Obviously this would save the consumer money but could reduce profits of record companies.

It has also been claimed that new bands and musicians will become famous on the Internet. It is easier and cheaper for a new musician to reach a wider audience, and they do not need to have a record company deal. They will also find it cheaper and easier to encode and sell their music.

MP3s are now one of the most downloaded items on the net; go to any search engine, type in MP3 and the name of the band and you are sure to find something of interest!

MP3.com and Napster

MP3.com is a huge database of music that is stored on the company's servers in MP3 format. The site allows you to download MP3s that have been placed on its servers either by new bands or by bands that allow you to purchase their music. Part of the MP3.com site is called my.MP3.com, which allows users to store their music collection on the web on their servers; you can listen to any of the stored tracks by logging onto their website. MP3.com has a huge database of albums, but you can only listen to albums that you have bought. If you want to add an album to your collection, you must first physically insert it into the CD drive of your computer; using special technology, MP3.com can read the CD, ensure it is the correct CD and then transfer the MP3 songs from its database into your personal storage space — this happens in less than three minutes!

One of the advantages of this is that any CD you have could be stored on MP3.com's site. No matter what computer you are working on, all you have to do is log onto MP3.com and you have access to all your music. The key here is that you never need to download the MP3s onto your computer; everything is done through streaming technology.

MP3.com ran into problems when they allowed people to buy CDs from their site. As soon as you had bought a CD, you could listen to it via the website; you did not have to wait until the CD was delivered. Not only did you get the real CD, but it was automatically added to your MP3.com selection. This is where legal problems occurred.

Some would argue this is like buying a CD and then recording it onto tape in order to listen to it on a Walkman! The record companies thought differently! They felt that MP3.com were breaching copyright. You had a CD but an illegal copy of it was also stored on the servers of MP3.com; as of mid-2000, the legal battle continues, but it looks as if MP3.com will end up paying rights to continue to provide this service.

Napster.com is a completely different story! Napster is a piece of software that a user downloads. Once the software is downloaded, users can share their MP3s with other users. Your computer in essence becomes a server that allows others to download MP3 files that you have made available. Only MP3s are available in a special directory on your computer — according to Napster, no other access to your hard drive is allowed. Once you have downloaded and installed the Napster program, you can search for and download songs by thousands of recording artists for free; most of these downloads are, unfortunately, pirated copies.

As you can imagine, record companies and many bands are not happy with this. Napster is currently in the middle of a huge legal battle. One key issue is the fact that Napster itself does not store any of the MP3s on its server; unlike MP3.com, its program is purely a search engine and a connection program that allows you to search the computers of millions of users. Thus, it is very difficult to say who has committed the crime — Napster or you, the user!

Napster claim they only allow users to connect to each other and search for files and they specifically ask people not to trade illegal MP3s. There are many sites appearing on the net that allow users to store files on a remote server, acting as an i-drive or Internet drive. These companies give you up to 100MB of storage space to save files. What happens if someone decides to save illegal copies of programs on these drives and allow people to have access to them?

Napster and MP3.com have both argued that their respective services actually encourage users to buy the real CDs. Why? Simply because many people will listen to a song (like one does in a record store) and then decide to buy the album. Both of these sites say that the big record companies want to put them out of business so they can produce their own variation of MP3 and capitalise on this music revolution.

At the time of going to press, a US judge has ordered Napster to cease providing a mechanism for people to exchange copyrighted music over the Internet. Napster have since ceased allowing access to their services. It is now up to Napster to implement a policy that will eliminate the facility that allows all copyrighted music to be distributed. Presumably, if unsigned bands wish to trade their MP3s, there is no problem. (Having visited Napster's site, I noted that the graphic link to download files was gone, but — whether intentionally or by accident — the actual download link was still available! A small defiant stance?)

To say that there has been uproar following the judgement is an understatement; as soon as the judgement was heard, hundreds of sites sprung up in Napster's defence. People like to share on the Internet; they don't want law and order imposed on the web!

What will happen next? Big record companies' sites being hacked, perhaps? E-mail bombing of their sites? Who knows; the Internet can be a formidable force.

Another problem is that the record companies have not succeed in stopping the illegal distribution of MP3s; in fact, they have helped to publicise what is out there.

This ruling will in no way eradicate the problem. People will still trade illegal MP3s, but now they will do it via FTP sites (which people have also been doing up to this point), while programs similar to Napster have sprung up.

Ultimately, we are back to the same dilemma. Building a completely decentralised network was a great idea, but the drawback was that it is now too difficult, if not impossible, to control; the original pioneers could not have seen all the problems that would be caused.

The Future of MP3?

A company called Digital Payloads thinks it has the answer. Their idea is simple: embed a digital ad into every MP3. This will allow users to listen to the MP3s but not remove the ads, thereby giving the users what they want (the MP3) but also encouraging them to get the full CD. This would seem to be a good option, but if a user buys a legitimate copy of a CD, they can still rip the track and upload it onto the net. Even if Napster and MP3.com were to be closed down, there are plenty of other sites that would spring up.

Another idea is to devise an encryption method so that if a user buys a piece of music via the net, it will be "tied down" to their hardware and, using special identification methods, it would only be playable on their computer. This option would certainly stop piracy.

Perhaps the solution will be the use of digital cash. Many companies do not want to accept credit cards for small transactions (under $5 or $10). With digital cash, people would be able to make micro payments (under $1); most people would probably be willing to pay a small amount to listen to sample tracks from albums. Up to this point, digital cash has been available, but most people have been more inclined to use credit cards.

Part Four

BURNING ISSUES

Chapter 12

Dangers of the Internet I: Security Issues

Although the Internet is a wonderful resource, it is not without its problems. Just as in "real life", there are many unscrupulous, even dangerous, individuals willing to prey on the naivety, innocence, vulnerability or carelessness of many Internet users. There are also dangerous or unhealthy situations which the user can allow themselves to slip into through nobody else's fault. There are a host of issues that have arisen as the Internet has grown, some relatively harmless, such as e-mail spamming, many not so harmless, ranging from pornography and paedophilia to viruses and credit card fraud. Many of these issues are well-known, while there are a number of less easily identifiable issues that you should be aware of.

Some of these issues have been dealt with briefly in other chapters, but in this chapter and the next, I will look in detail at some of the problems you may encounter, and suggest some possible solutions. In this chapter, I will look at issues that mostly affect businesses, such as:

❖ Viruses

❖ Hacking

❖ E-mail abuse and spam

❖ Copyright

❖ Security measures

❖ Internet rules for business.

In Chapter 13, I will look at problems that you are more likely to encounter in your personal use of the Internet, though there is obviously some crossover. These issues include pornography, censorship and freedom of speech, personal privacy, Internet addiction and the resultant costs, and so on.

Viruses

A danger that is common to both business and home users is that of viruses transmitted over the Internet. Viruses pose a great danger on the Internet. The reason is that the virus can spread and replicate itself with great ease.

Before we see how viruses are spread, let's first define what a virus is:

> *A **virus** is any program that maliciously interferes with and causes problems on your computer system. The damage a virus can cause can be very insignificant, such as putting an insulting message on your desktop, or it can be potentially deadly, such as corrupting data or damaging your hard drive.*

Computer viruses are not a new thing. In the olden days, floppy disks were the only way of transferring files from computer to computer. If the user was not wary enough, a virus on one computer could attach itself either to the files on the disk or to the disk's boot record. The boot record, in its simplest form, is like the index of the disk; it contains a lot of important information. If the boot record is infected, this disk becomes unusable. Nine times out of ten, the boot record can be cleaned (depending on the payload of the virus). While many viruses still circulate in this way, their potential for damage is limited by the way they are distributed. Since the floppy disk is only going from one computer to another, there is only the immediate threat of one computer being newly infected. Even if this second computer user fails to detect the virus, sooner or later, if they try to transfer a file to a more careful user, the virus will be detected and, hopefully, cleaned from the system.

However, the Internet has opened up a can of worms (sometimes literally — certain types of viruses are known as "worms"!). It is now much easier to distribute viruses via the Internet, and they are often more difficult to detect. The two main sources of viruses are e-mail attachments and downloaded programs and files. Both work in much the same way, as we shall see shortly.

Many viruses are more of a nuisance than anything else. On average, there are probably about 1,000 viruses created every year. Out of that number, how many actually cause widespread damage is unknown.

How Viruses Spread

Viruses can come in many shapes and forms. For our purposes, the following two are the most relevant:

❖ **Trojan Viruses**: These types of viruses appear to be doing one thing (for example, they pretend to be a new game), but in reality they are deleting your hard drive or altering the contents of it. You could download a new "utility" for drawing 3D pictures, but while you are using the software, without your knowledge another program may be launched and begin deleting important files on your computer or worse!

❖ **Macro Viruses**: Trojan viruses are hidden in malicious programs, but unfortunately viruses can also be spread through word-processing documents or spreadsheets. Since most modern word-processing programs have the ability to program macros (a special programming language that allows you to customise the program to your needs) many people are now creating macro viruses that only infect when the word-processing document is opened.

Notice from the above that viruses attack under two conditions:

❖ You run the attached program; or

❖ You open the document.

Only by actively running/opening the program/word-processing document can you infect your system.

Many viruses are sent via e-mail, but they are attached to the message. Only when you open or run the attachment can the virus infect. Whenever you receive an attachment, you should *always* take the following precautions:

1. When you click on the attachment, you should always get a warning asking if you wish to save the attachment or open it. **Under no cir-**

cumstances should you ever open an attachment — always save it first! See Chapter 5 for more on e-mail attachments.

2. Save the attachment to a floppy disk if possible.

3. Run your virus-checking software on the A-drive or on your hard disk if you saved it in a directory on your hard disk, to ensure that there are no viruses on the disk after you have saved the attachment.

4. If the attachment is "clean", it should be safe to open it now.

5. If the attachment is in any way suspect, particularly if it is a program supposedly sent through as a "joke", and if you were not expecting it, the safest thing to do is just to delete the e-mail completely.

Suppose a trusted friend sends you an e-mail with an attachment; surely there is no reason to virus-check the attachment? Wrong! Trust no one, not even friends! The reason is simple: virus programmers are getting smarter with their viruses. They have now written them in such a way that if you run the virus, it will look in your e-mail program's address book and send a copy of itself to everyone in your address book. Thus, the virus appears to be coming from you, a legitimate source, so if your contacts open the attachment, then *their* PCs become infected and the virus sends itself out to everyone in their address book, and so on and so forth. . . . It spreads — literally — like a virus.

During 1999, the first of these viruses hit the headlines. Known simply as Melissa, it was a Word macro virus. You would receive an e-mail from someone you know with a message that said something like:

"Here is the list you wanted ;-)"

Since it was from someone you knew, you might open it. What the document contained was a list of pornographic sites. When opened, the virus would infect your system by sending itself out to the first 50 people in your address book. It sent a copy of the list of pornographic websites, and since it sent itself out from your e-mail program, people assumed the e-mail came from you! Of course, if your contacts opened the e-mail attachment, it would trigger off the same process.

The main <u>payload</u> (or damage) this virus did was to overload e-mail servers, since so many messages were being sent out. Think of the domino effect it would cause: you may have 20 contacts in your e-mail address book, each contact might have another 20 contacts in their address book . . . that leads to a lot of e-mail travelling through the Internet. Beyond this, it did nothing malicious to your computer.

A deadlier virus came out in mid-2000, known as the "love bug". This virus was highly sophisticated and again arrived as an attachment. The e-mail and attachment would always arrive from someone you knew (like the Melissa virus) but it contained a subject line saying "I love you" and had a "love letter" text document attached to it. Once the document was opened, the virus spread itself. Melissa only sent itself out to the first 50 names in your address book; the love bug did not stop until it reached the last address in your address book! Not only this, but it also changed files and their extensions. The damage this virus caused to businesses worldwide was enormous.

The bottom line is, if in doubt, delete the e-mail.

Remote Access Programs

Suppose you downloaded a game and, ever since, your computer has been acting strangely; files are being deleted, strange messages are appearing; what could be the problem? Unbeknown to you, a "remote access" program may have been installed on your computer. These programs, when used legally, allow support technicians to take control of your computer to help diagnose problems and sort them out. These programs give the remote user full access to your computer; it is as if they were sitting at your keyboard — they can open programs, change settings, close the computer down, etc. One such program is PC Anywhere.

Many of these programs have two different operating modes: one allows the remote user to take control of the computer; the second allows the remote user to observe what the user is doing. Some companies may consider buying such a program so that they can randomly keep an eye on what employees are doing. As with e-mail, companies maintain they have a right to do this as their property is being used.

Of course, devious individuals have created identical programs but with the intention of taking control of your PC without your knowledge. These rogue programs are so clever that you would have no physical evidence that they are running. Many virus detection programs will not detect these programs because, as such, they are not viruses! Uninstalling such programs may be difficult; in the worst case scenario, you may have to re-format your hard drive!

So how are these programs installed on your computer? They could be hidden in other programs, like a Trojan virus. Let's say you are chatting to someone and they e-mail you a game as an attachment. You download the game and play it, but unbeknown to you, the game set up the remote access program.

The user at the other end can now do one of two things. On most programs, they will need to find out your IP number, which they can find from the headers on your e-mail. Some more advanced programs will actually search out and find computers that have this remote access program installed. Once they have located you, they have full control of your computer! Again, the bottom line is do not accept programs from anyone you don't really "know" and also be wary of programs from those you do know!

How can I protect myself from viruses?

The safest thing to do is to buy good virus detection software that will detect and protect you from attachments and the Internet. There are many anti-virus software packages available that offer virus protection for Internet usage, including e-mail virus protection. The most popular virus protection programs are Norton Anti-Virus and Dr Solomon's. Both are available for different platforms There are many other good virus checkers available, some for eradicating or protecting against specific viruses.

Many companies are now producing special box sets that contain not only the virus checker but also other software to help protect you while online. Check your local computer store for the different types. No matter what virus checker you have, it is essential that you always update the software; new viruses are created daily, most never succeed in mass infection but others, like Melissa or the Love Bug virus, can spread so easily via e-mail.

On the upside, once a virus is detected the anti-virus software companies can post details of it on their website and offer solutions. So although the Internet has increased the spread of infection of viruses, it has also speeded up the distribution of the cure!

Hacking and Cyber Warfare

Apart from porn sites, which are dealt with in Chapter 13, there are many other dangerous websites or users who participate in or condone criminal activities. These include cyber-terrorist activities, criminal activities, pirated software and pirated music and hacking. There is plenty of information on the Internet about illegal activities; most of them are categorised under the general term of hacking.

> *The old definition of "**hacking**" meant using clever tricks to make programs run faster, altering programs to do certain things, etc. Nowadays, hacking means gaining illegal entry into computer systems.*

One generally does not hear much about hacking, mainly because no company would ever admit that their electronic security measures were breached! At any given point, there may be any number of hackers either attempting to break into a computer system or actually in a computer system, snooping around.

There are hundreds of sites on the Internet dealing with hacking; many of them are just rehashes of other sites, but there are some interesting sites. Hacking sites can contain information on gaining unauthorised access to computer systems without the knowledge of the company or organisation. Many top profile sites have been hacked, such as the CIA, FBI and the White House.

Cyber-terrorists

Cyber warfare has been created by a new breed of cyber-terrorists. It is impossible to describe the "typical" cyber-terrorist; it could be a disgruntled employee, a high school kid, a housewife . . . But one group of "cyber-terrorists" you might not immediately think of are governments. Surely not?!

The Washington Post wrote an article about this topic. The powers that be in the Pentagon had debated whether to engage in cyber warfare against Serbia. They decided, after much thought, not to go ahead with it. One wonders if this was a result of the knowledge factor or the lack of it! One of the official reasons was that they could have been charged with war crimes.

Cyber warfare may be more effective than sending in killing machines. Since our lives are "run" by computers — all the information about us, management systems, electricity plants, etc. — breaking into a country's computer systems and making changes or shutting them down could cripple that country economically; this would be better than a lot of bloodshed.

Why do hackers do what they do?

Many hackers will only break into a computer system to prove they can, or to demonstrate to the company or site that their system is vulnerable to attack. They do not get any financial reward out of it. However, some hackers have been so successful at this that the company has hired them to "fix" their security problems! Most hackers will not destroy or interfere with a system. Other hackers (sometimes called crackers) will alter, delete of sell information that they find.

Look again at the two alternative definitions of "hacking". In the early days of computing, a hack was simply when you altered a program, making things work smoother and better. If a modern-day hacker is aiming to show up the vulnerabilities of a computer system, surely this could be seen in the same positive light? Nowadays people see hackers as bad people; most hackers would feel they are the freedom fighters of the new cyberspace frontier, gaining knowledge of computer systems purely for the thrill.

What is a Cracker?

There are two definitions of a <u>cracker</u>. One is a hacker who alters a computer system or makes money from their hacking. The other definition we will see shortly.

Crackers will often break into a system for a specific purpose, such as deleting records, altering system settings, etc. Remember, a hacker, in the true spirit of the word, will only do it because they can.

Most hacking occurs because of lax security on the part of the company or individual. If you are on a network and share resources (directories on any of the network's computers) with other users on that network, those directories are available and accessible to everyone on the Internet as soon as one of your computers connects up to the Internet. This is a reality that few businesses realise.

The problem here is that many users who are on a network at home, college or work never think of password-protecting files or directories, mainly because it is too much bother to have to type in a password every time you wish to access the resource. By downloading a simple program off the Internet, it is possible for hackers to scan a range of IP numbers and find any of these shared directories on any remote computer! The dangers posed by this are threefold:

1. Hackers can get access to your files;

2. A hacker could install a program on your system that may be used to attack other computers;

3. A hacker may install a program that allows them to fully control your system remotely without your knowledge.

The hackers can gain more information about the computer system simply by finding out the range of IP numbers which a company has. The range simply means the starting IP number and ending IP number. On a network that uses TCP/IP for communication, whether it consists of two or 200 computers, all computers must be identifiable to every other computer on the network, therefore they all use an IP number from a certain range. For example, all the computers that form part of an ISP's network would share a range of IPs such as 195.124.1.1 to 195.124.1.255. If a user on this network changes their IP number to 196.204.2.1, they will not be able to connect to the network, as they will not be seen to be on the network.

What many hackers try to do is either target computers on your network or, using software called IP spoofing software, they attempt to fool your network into thinking they are part of your network by spoofing their IP number. This is a very simplistic overview, but for our purposes, it serves to illustrate the issue.

If a hacker finds out which computer is connected with which IP number, they can begin to attack your network. They do this by using what is known as a Denial Of Service (DOS) attack. This type of attack sends endless amounts of data to your computer — the memory becomes overloaded until the computer is forced to reset or just stops working.

The problem is finding the culprits; some of the attacks come from legitimate users. By using remote access software, which we talked about earlier, the rogue program could be installed on a user's computer and triggered at a certain time!

This type of attack happened to some of the major international websites during February 2000. Amazon, Yahoo, eBay and other sites were "down" for up to three hours. It emerged that hackers had sent a stream of data (1 gigabyte a second!) to their main computers. The computers were getting so much data they could not cope. This type of attack is on the increase and is very worrying for website owners. If you consider that a company like Yahoo rely on advertising, three hours is a very long and expensive time to be "down".

For companies with permanent connections to the Internet, this can also be a problem. If a hacker finds out the range of IP numbers you are using for your company network, they could bombard each computer on your network with endless data, which would force all of your computers to grind to a halt.

These are very real dangers that could cost companies millions. By taking a few simple steps, companies and individuals could prevent this from happening. These steps are outlined under "Security Measures" later in the chapter.

Why are hacking sites not closed down?

The main reason why hacking sites are allowed to operate is freedom of expression (enshrined in the US Constitution in the First Amendment). It is not illegal to talk about hacking; it is illegal when it is discussed in relation to committing a crime. Therefore I can talk about an imaginary situation and the security vulnerabilities, but if I were to encourage or detail exact ways of breaking into a system, then it would be illegal. Most of these sites get around this by stating that the information they provide is purely for educational purposes or as personal information and should not be used to commit crimes!

I remember being in a shop that sold scanning devices for listening in on transmissions from CB radios. The shop assistant told a customer that to sell them was not illegal, but to use them was!

As well as freedom of expression, the other argument is that these sites can help system administrators protect their system, since they can see the loopholes.

Antionline.com is a very good website that provides information about security issues, how to deal with them, sites that have been hacked, etc. Again, this site could be regarded as telling other users how to hack systems. It is a case of whether the glass is half empty or half full!

It is important to understand that the information contained in these sites is illegal to use and could be used maliciously either by students or employees. We will see later how to stop people accessing these sites.

Hacking Culture

Hacking has been around since the dawn of computers. Hackers were seen as the stereotypical "computer geeks" — spending hours in front of the computer screen, papers, pizzas and empty coffee cups everywhere! These people were learning, experimenting and intentionally defeating computer systems.

At this point in time (mid- to late 1970s), in order to hack remote computers, users connected to other computers via a protocol called <u>Telnet</u>, this protocol and its accompanying program allowed users to connect to remote computers and operate them as if they were sitting in front of them. Any commands you issue are executed on the remote computer system, not locally.

The trick hackers use is to Telnet from computer A to computer B, right down to computer F. They then hack from computer F; therefore if the hack was discovered, it would be seen to originate from computer F! By the time it was discovered that computer A was responsible, the hacker was long gone. Combined with this method was the idea of accessing computers from another state or country. So FBI computers could be hacked by the boy next door, via Russia!

The dream of the hacker was to get root access — the highest level of access to a system. They would then be in control of the system or have full access to account creation, deletion of information, etc. If a user got root access, they could then create an account for themselves where they could hack away undetected.

So how did they get into a system in the first place? The answer was usually careless use of passwords by an individual. Each Telnet session begins by asking you for a username and password. Hackers read all the documentation they could find about a system and then found out how to discover which users were currently logged on. They would then use programs that would go through either a predefined list of passwords or would make up passwords using random characters. This program would attempt to log into the user's account using every conceivable password. The less obvious the password, the better and the harder it is for such a program to find out your password. Once the hacker got a valid username and password they could explore the system.

These hackers could be caught because many systems keep records of what time users logged in. Therefore if I saw that the last time "I" logged in at was 4.00 a.m., I would know that something was up and would contact the system administrator. But if the hacker could set up their own account, they could work away!

One problem emerged for these hackers: if they were connecting to remote computers in different states or countries, their phone bills would become quite high! Once they saw the phone bills, they would freak out — or should I say, they decided to phreak! Phreaking is the term given to a branch of hackers who find ways of circumventing the phone company's systems.

The first well-known phreaker was Captain Crunch, named after a breakfast cereal! You may think that this name was not good for his street cred, but in fact he is a hero in the hacking culture. He found that by blowing a free plastic whistle that came with the cereal, the tone emitted could bypass the telephone company's system of charging! Suddenly, sales of the breakfast cereal went up and phreaking was born.

Crackers and Copyright Protection

Another definition of a cracker is a person who writes software to defeat the copy protection on a program. They write small programs that generate serial numbers, which turn trial version software into fully operational software. These are known as keymaking programs.

If someone uses pirated software using someone else's username and serial number (serial numbers are usually unique to the username), it would be easy to find out where the software was pirated from. So crackers have created these keymaking programs that will allow people to enter their details and receive a valid serial number. What the crackers have done is to reverse engineer the software and have found out the algorithm used to create the serial numbers for the programs.

The possession of such programs on your computer is of course illegal; companies, schools and colleges should be aware of this and ensure that no users are saving such files onto their computers and that they are not installing software illegally using such generated serial numbers.

Other programs, called cracks or patches, patch the program so that it becomes a full version. It is not registered to you but the nag screen will be removed and the program will not terminate after a certain number of days/uses.

Companies are therefore faced with a dilemma: distribute using traditional distribution channels, but incur high costs for distribution, packaging, etc.; or use the Internet and face the risk of the software being hacked.

Of course, if you ever come across a site that has "cracks", they claim that they are all for "educational purposes". Some crackers say that using trial software often does not allow you to see the full potential of the software as a result of some functions being disabled. Therefore, by using their crack, you can see how the software really works. They then insist that you delete the software and buy it so that you support the programmers; this is their "legal disclaimer", as it demonstrates that they are not encouraging the use of pirate software! Whether that disclaimer would hold up in court is another question!

Many crackers create the cracks because they want to highlight how little interest they believe that software companies have in protecting their software. Again, it could be seen that the crackers are doing the software companies a favour in helping them see the flaws in their software protection.

Warez it @?

Another problem for educators, employers and parents is that many of these sites contain, or link to, Warez sites. As described in Chapter 11, Warez sites are sites that allow you to download pirated software free of charge. Many also contain "patches" that will allow a user to turn a trial version of software into a fully working piece of software

Many Warez sites only stay around for a number of weeks, days or even hours. So if you find a site, it may not exist next week. These sites pose a number of problems:

1. It is illegal to use pirated software.

2. The software could contain viruses.

3. Since all websites register your IP number when you visit them, if you download illegal software, you could be traced. I have heard stories of great sites for downloading that are in fact sites set up by law enforcement officials! You have been warned!

4. Individuals may download and set up the software on company computers, thereby endangering the company, since illegal software is being used on a company computer.

5. Since most programs are rather large, employees may try to download them on company time; this will lead to network congestion, which will affect all users of the network.

Be aware that, as an employer or educator, you must ensure that illegal software is not:

❖ Downloaded onto your computers;

❖ Used on your computers.

Remember also that with very simple web server software, a user could set up a server and distribute illegal software from your network. There are a number of simple rules which every business should follow; these are outlined at the end of the chapter.

Credit Card Fraud

About five per cent of all transactions conducted over the Internet are with stolen credit card numbers.

Let's look at an infamous example. A couple of years ago, an Irish teenager "made up" a credit card number and used it to buy $2,000 of chocolate, which was delivered to his house. It was not discovered until a man in Argentina looked at his credit card bill and saw a charge for chocolate he never ordered! An investigation was started; the offender was traced to a location in south County Dublin. When his house was raided, he and a friend were caught chomping away on the chocolate, which had been hidden in his bedroom — much to the surprise of his parents, who knew nothing about it!

You might think that the kids were very lucky to make up a real credit card. In fact, it is more likely that the kids knew the credit card number was authentic. There are underground sites that specialise in trading credit card numbers with other like-minded individuals. These sites also deal in passwords to gain access to sites illegally; while these are sometimes for ordinary company websites, they are more likely to be for pornographic sites where membership fees must be paid in order to access material.

Another way they could have made up a number was to use a "carding" program. The first four numbers of a credit card identify the bank or organisation that issues the card; the rest are a random set of numbers, which are generated using special algorithms. The "carding" programs have cracked the algorithm and can generate numbers that are valid credit card numbers. When verified, the numbers will appear to be valid. One problem for many sites is that they just verify that the number is valid without checking to ensure that the card actually exists or is in service. This is because if the transaction is for a small amount of money, a quick authorisation is done.

So, a clever hacker can make use of your credit card number through no fault of your own. However, it is sometimes down to the fault of the consumer if fraudulent use of their credit card takes place. For example, many people are careless when out shopping and just throw away their credit card slips without thinking twice. This can be the biggest means to finding out your credit card details. If someone were to pick up the slip, they would be able to find out your credit card number and expiry date — often, that is all you need on the Internet to purchase some goods. You can make up any name you wish.

In fact, when dealing with credit cards you always have to be careful. A reputable company based in the real world may have a disgruntled employee who will steal the customer database before they resign. We can never be assured of security; human error can cause problems.

When your card has to be physically swiped, as in the "real" world the credit card company can detail where and when the transaction took place, and since the card was swiped they would have specimen signatures. But since the Internet does not have this facility, fraud tends to be a lot more widespread. Since no signature is present, how does a company know you are the authorised user of the card?

You as a user must always check statements, query any charges which you do not recognise and seek assistance from your bank if you feel something has been charged without your permission.

Personally, I have bought a lot of software over the Internet and have never had any major problems. There was one company that were selling Internet hosting services; they set up an account for me without my consent (set-up fee was $58) and then billed me for my first month's service, when I specifically told them I did not want their services! Eventually, after many irate e-mails, they apologised and charged the money back to my credit card.

The bottom line is to be aware of who you are buying from, ensure you check out their website and contact them if necessary. If you think you will be using your credit card to buy over the Internet on a regular basis, however, it might be worth looking at some of the security options described at the end of this chapter.

Dangers of E-mail

Junk E-mail and Spam

As well as the danger posed by viruses spread by e-mail attachments, e-mail users face other problems. Junk e-mail and <u>spam</u>, discussed in Chapter 5, may be less of a threat to a company's computer systems, but they can be a major nuisance.

Another form of junk e-mail is targeted e-mail. This is e-mail that is sent to you because you asked for it — even if you think you've never done so! You may be wondering how this could be so. Think about real-life situations: when you are filling up application forms or forms requesting information, there is usually a box at the bottom of the form asking you if you will allow related companies to send you special promotional information. It usually asks you to tick if you *don't* want this information sent to you. How many people actually remember to tick the box?

On the web, the same thing happens. When you are signing up for a free service on a site or downloading software, a box is often already ticked for you that says something along the lines of "sign me up for a free newsletter". You probably never even notice this! You are therefore signed up for a newsletter that will be sent out daily or weekly to your e-mail address.

Most sites now offer a privacy statement, detailing exactly what they do with the information they gain from you and who, if anyone, they share it with. Always look for this privacy statement to ensure you know what is happening to all your information.

Scams

Another problem with junk e-mail is the amount of scams you may be sent, all designed to part you from your money. The Federal Trade Commission has listed some of the scams as follows:[1]

❖ Business Opportunities: "Earn up to £1,000 per day!"

❖ Bulk e-mail: "Buy lists of addresses to promote your business"

❖ Chain letters: "Mary's last wish was to have this e-mail sent on to all your friends!"

❖ Work-at-home schemes: "Make loads of money"

---

[1] http://www.safekids.com/articles/scamftc.htm

* Health and diet scams: "Lose pounds effortlessly"

* Free offers: get free goods through the post

* Investment opportunities: stocks, bonds and shares

* Cable descrambler kits: "Get all those channels for free!"

* "Viagra — get this amazing drug without prescription"

As you can see, most of them offer monetary happiness without any effort; if you read the e-mail, you will find how easy the scheme is and the rewards it offers. Some tricksters will even include links to web pages, showing monthly statements of "their accounts". All of these schemes are scams, usually pyramid selling. At all costs, they should be avoided; after all, if they were true, I would be driving a Porsche and living in the Bahamas now!

E-mail Abuse

Another problem that may occur, although less common, is somebody sending you abusive e-mail or even sending you pornographic pictures or signing you up to a mailing list that sends you such pictures everyday. If that person has your business or home e-mail address, you may incur a cost to change your e-mail address.

As a parent or educator, you may find it necessary to keep an eye on e-mail received by young children. Since you do not know who they are communicating with, they may have found an e-mail "pal" who will be passing illegal information or pornographic pictures to them. Guidelines for parents are given in Chapter 13.

What can you do?

Recall, from Chapter 5, the use of filters. If you are always getting abusive e-mail or spam from a certain e-mail address, set up a filter so that any e-mail from that person is automatically deleted.

If you are on a mailing list or a newsletter, check to see if there are instructions at the bottom that tell you how to unsubscribe to the mailing list. All good mailing lists should provide this information.

One piece of advice I give to users is to set up a free e-mail account, such as those provided by Hotmail. Whenever you are signing up for a free service or registering with a site, enter your free e-mail service account, then if you do get a lot of junk e-mail it will go to that account and not your personal or business e-mail address!

Spyware

Using a simple program called a scanner, it is possible to scan a range of IP numbers to look for any shared directories on computers connected to the net. The program will then display the IP number and directories available on the remote computer; by selecting a directory and clicking on a button, you can then map (or connect to) the drive! You now have full access to that person's hard drive/directory.

I have experimented with this program and have found it truly horrifying, as it shows how easy it could be for anyone to access information on any computer connected to the Internet.

Remember we talked about freeware and shareware? Well, authors have come to realise that they could run banner ads in their programs while users are using the software. Programs such as Real Player do this. It turns out that a little program, which could be called a Trojan, is installed in some shareware titles. It downloads ads to display when the program is running.

The worry is that free programs may contain Trojans that will gather information about you. In a recent article (July 2000), *Time* magazine called these programs ET programs; like ET, they want to "phone home". In other words, their prime purpose is to connect up to the server that sent them and send back information!

These programs will do a number of things. For example, one program, which allowed you to view "cute" cursors while on a web page, was accused of installing an ET program that recorded a list of all the sites you visited and then sent that information back to the company so they could target advertising more. The makers of Real Player were also accused of this. If you used their software to play music CDs on your computer, it recorded what CDs you listened to and sent details back to the parent company.

All these companies maintain that they cannot match a user to their web activities. All they know is that user123 is visiting such and such a site, but cannot establish that user123 is called Richard Butler. With so much information stored on your computer, this claim would seem to be contradictory.

Another danger is so called "paid to surf" programs. Certain companies have sprung up claiming that they will pay you while you surf or use your computer while connected to the Internet. All you do is download their ad bar (a program that allows the company to display ads on your computer). You are asked to click on the ads that interest you occasionally. Some of these programs will pay you up to 60 cents per hour, so the more you use it the more you make. They also allow you to earn money by signing people up, and you get a percentage of what they earn — pyramid selling if I ever saw it!

Of course, the problem here is that these companies are building a huge profile of you and your surfing habits and they can match statistics to people. Some would argue that this is OK, since they are actually paying you for doing this. I suppose they are being more honest than others! Before signing up for any of these services, read their privacy policy first. Check out the website for a full list of these companies.

This software is now commonly referred to as spyware. It is obviously highly illegal to engage in this type of market research *without your permission*, but unfortunately, you may have given them the right to do this. How many times to you read the licence agreement that asks you, before installing the software, to accept all the conditions of use of the software? According to the article in *Time*, one company in question had a clause in their agreement saying that they could change their privacy policy at any time in the future!

So is this a new way of spying on users? Not really — the first piece of known spyware was contained in early releases of Windows 95! After installing Windows 95, you would be asked to register the product; one option was to register via the web. What was apparently happening was that information about your system was sent back to Microsoft. They could then find out how many users were not using Microsoft products and perhaps contact them with special offers.

The problem is that any piece of software that you install, either shareware or commercial, could contain such Trojans that can track your progress as you move around the web.

Copyright

Copyright is a huge issue on the web at the present. Let's look at some important aspects of copyright and where problems may occur:

Website Contents

Anything that is written on a website is copyright protected; if you have produced the material, it would seem that it is covered by intellectual copyright law. If in doubt, you should check with a lawyer. By and large, you should never copy passages of text from a website and use them as your own material. For example, don't set up a site about current affairs in England and get all your information by copying and pasting from *The Times* website.

If you have a website, be sure to include a disclaimer on it, stating that all information is presented on your website "as is" and that users should realise that you cannot be held legally responsible for any information contained on your site that is acted on if the information proves inaccurate. This is standard a legal disclaimer in the "real world". Add such copyright notices to your e-mails; it is too easy to leave out a word on your e-mail or web page and convey the incorrect meaning!

There was a case in England were a well known retailer priced its TVs at .99p instead of £99; let's just say that orders went through the roof! The company in question did not fulfil the orders, as they said it was an obvious mistake! But be careful of such mistakes, as they may prove costly.

Programs/Music/Text

Remember that programs, music and text are covered by copyright law. Web servers cannot allow users of their network or website to create their own pages unless the server has a feature to ensure the users are not putting up any offensive or illegal material. The owner of a web server is responsible for its contents. Always ensure proper security is in place so this does not happen.

As a rule of thumb, laws that are explicit in the real world should be considered laws in the online world. Perhaps a few years ago people could get away with a lot more and give the excuse of not knowing that what they did was wrong. As time has progressed and lawyers have discovered a new avenue of revenue, they are more than willing to take on cases of copyright infringement via the Internet! If you are in any doubt about any legal aspect of the net, your best line of defence is to contact a lawyer and discuss your uncertainties with them.

Images

Copyright infringement of pictures, graphics and images is probably the most common form of "piracy" on the Internet, largely because it is so easy to download images and also because many people do not realise that they are breaking the law. You might come across a site that says "free images", little knowing that the website owners themselves may have pirated these images from their copyright owners.

Graphics companies put in hours of works to produce the right images for you. If you are a web designer, it is up to you to ensure that you make it clear in your copyright notice that these graphics are yours and should not be copied. The web is so big that people could copy your graphics and use them as their own. One possible way of protecting your graphics is to implement a Javascript solution. Using a simple script, you can disable the facility for a user to right-click on an image; when they do so, a dialog box can appear to tell them not to steal your graphics! Unfortunately, if the user disables Javascript in their browser's options, they can overcome this. One company that seems to have produced a solution is *http://www.gamacles.com*, who have created a program that will actually encrypt your HTML and ensure that if a user does right-click on an image, they cannot save it; not only this but if they try to view the HTML, they will not see the source code.

The ability to allow people to copy images is a headache for web designers and site owners. If a website owner has paid a graphic designer to create custom images for his or her website, any Joe Soap can copy those images. Since the web is so vast, I could then re-use those images on my website or use them to create a site for a client. It may well happen that the original website owner would be none the wiser. Obviously you should never copy and use images that do not belong to you.

If you copy an image, the owners of the website have little or no way of finding out that you did so. What you must not do is use that image on your own web pages or pages you create for others. Most websites will have a copyright notice that you should read. If you don't see this notice, be wary of downloading images. If there is a copyright notice, you may need to seek their permission to reproduce the images, unless they specifically say you can download them for free. Some websites do allow you to copy their images for use on personal homepages or for non-profit organisations.

Before you even think of copying an image and using it as your own, be warned that there are now image chaser lawyers! You've heard of lawyers that chase ambulances? Well, this is a new breed of lawyers in the US that are trawling websites looking for infringement of copyrighted information and/or images.

Some image creation programs allow you to embed a watermark that cannot be deleted, this helps them protect their investment — you have been warned!

Security Measures

What can you do?

When you visit pages on the web, any information you may send from those pages, such as passwords or e-mail addresses, are sent as plain text. This means that anyone can read the information contained in the packets as they are sent over the Internet.

Giving credit card details over the net is secure as long as the user uses a <u>secure server</u> to send the details. It is very important that when you are making a purchase via the net that you ensure that your credit card details are sent via a secure server.

> **Secure Server** is a server that will encrypt any information that is sent from your computer to the retailer's server. If someone does get hold of your information it will be all gibberish and make no sense at all.

There are two ways of knowing whether you are viewing a page over a secure connection

1. If you look at the status bar at the bottom of your browser, Internet Explorer will show a locked padlock, as follows:

The lock indicates that the site is using a secure server, in other words, that any information sent from here will be encrypted. Only certain parts of websites will be located on secure servers.

2. Another way of knowing is if the web address begins **https://**. HTTPS is Secure HyperText Transfer Protocol. Any information passed from your computer to the server is encrypted. This ensures that if your information is intercepted, the interceptor will not be able to read it!

There are some sites that still do not use secure servers to conduct credit card transactions; they are not only putting their clients at risk, but also their own business, as more savvy users will not buy from them. If a ompany cannot afford or be bothered to use a secure server, perhaps you are better off not dealing with them.

It is the retailer's responsibility to ensure that all credit card details are held safely and securely. Unfortunately, at the moment, no Internet security is completely hack-proof. Where there is money, there will be criminals, in this case cyber-criminals, who will attempt to undermine the security of the website in order to gain access to credit card details. This happened recently to an online CD store. Hackers, or crackers, penetrated their security and stole thousands of credit card details, which they then proceeded to sell via the Internet!

The future of shopping on the web lies in ways of creating extremely secure transactions and providing a way of verifying user's credentials. One way of verifying your identity to another party is via digital signatures. Your information is encrypted using your <u>private key</u> and then the user at the other end decrypts it with your <u>public key</u>. This allows them to verify your identity.

 *A **private key** is a way of generating a scrambled or encrypted message. You then allow people to decrypt your message by use of your **public key**.*

The private key and the public key work in tandem. You cannot use person X's public key to decrypt person Y's message; therefore, you can authenticate that the sender of the information is who they say they are.

At present, this type of model has not been successfully integrated into an e-commerce payment system.

Privacy Policy

Of course, sending information securely through a secure server is only half the battle; suppose a small site is set up in such a way that when orders are received, the hosting company e-mails a list of customers with what they have ordered, along with all their details, via un-encrypted e-mail. This causes a security problem. If the computer(s) that hold the customer information database is hacked, then all the information can be stolen. Unfortunately, you will never know how secure the company's computer systems are; you have to trust them.

In late July 2000, a major English bank suffered a security problem with its online banking service. A number of customers found that when they logged into the service, they were able to see other users' accounts! It transpired that the fault resulted from the upgrading of software. Perhaps the service should have been taken offline for a number of hours during the night, and then the software upgraded and tested to ensure that it was working properly.

One incident like this could spread fear amongst other consumers, not only of the bank where the problem occurred but also amongst other banks. If customers, who are still only getting used to online banking or shopping, get frightened of using the service, even if this was an isolated incident it could spell disaster.

One vital part of a website is its privacy policy. Web authors should do everything to reassure and tell their customers exactly what they do, if anything, with the information they submit to you. More and more reports are making their way into the newspapers regarding privacy and the Internet, and more and more customers are now going to be looking out for your privacy policy, if you run a website. If you do not display a privacy policy, many users may decide not to purchase from you. If you can't be bothered assuring them of what you do with their information, why should they be bothered giving you their money? Remember, web consumers are in control here; they can go from one site to another and will hold few loyalties to websites.

How do you go about writing a privacy policy? Well, use the web to see what other sites do; get ideas from the web itself. Educate yourself with the medium you are using. After you have written your privacy policy, you may then want to have it passed by a lawyer to ensure that it is legally sound.

Proxy Servers

One of the main ways that hackers gain access to computers is through tracing the IP number of the user while they are online. To prevent people finding out your IP number, many companies use what is known as a <u>proxy server</u>.

In everyday life, a proxy is usually a person who acts on behalf of another. If someone is sent to a meeting as a proxy, they act on behalf of the person who should be at the meeting.

A proxy server works on behalf of all the computers on the network. Its two functions are:

❖ Providing one IP number to all computers on a network that connect to the Internet. Instead of allowing each individual computer and their corresponding IP to access the Internet, the proxy server handles all the requests from computers on the company network.

❖ When a document is requested, the proxy will fetch it. The website sees only the IP number of the proxy server and not of the computer that requested the information.

Think of a proxy server as being similar to a switchboard. Each person may have a direct line but when they phone someone, they go through the switchboard. The person who receives the call (if they have caller ID) will see the number of the switchboard appear on their phone and not the direct line number. This means that people do not get your direct line number. All calls go through the switchboard or proxy server.

Remember, since your internal IP numbers are not sent out over the Internet (only the proxy server IP is sent out), your employees would also find it difficult to run server software if they wished to distribute illegal software or pornography from your network.

When you have a proxy server in place, it means that if a Denial of Service attack is directed at your company, only the proxy server will go down, which will mean that your company will not have Internet access, but the internal computers will not be affected.

Other Functions of Proxy Servers

Many companies use proxy servers, but they can hinder the user's experience of the Internet. Many new Internet technologies do not work if you try to access them from a proxy server. Technologies such as Real Player, net2phone, Powwow, etc., will not work if you are using a proxy server. Many of these technologies rely on using your IP number to identify you uniquely. This is obviously a disappointment to the user, but companies realise that such technologies can waste valuable bandwidth and denying employees access to these technologies is advantageous to them.

The proxy server can also work in such a way that it denies access to certain content, such as chat programs. The system administrator can deny access to certain websites as well. Employers should also make sure that employees do not have access to web-based e-mail, such as Hotmail, Yahoo mail etc. As it is web-based, employers cannot keep an eye on it as closely as they can with their own company e-mail. Company e-mail goes out through the company servers; therefore a system can be put in place to monitor the contents of all e-mail.

A proxy server has a second important function — it acts as a <u>cache</u>. In other words, a proxy server can hold a set number of frequently visited web pages on its hard disk. These pages are said to be cached (stored) on the proxy server. When a person requests the site, the proxy server will display the page from cache, thus the page loads more quickly, as it is only coming from your local network.

If five people in one company wish to view *Yahoo.com*, a lot of network traffic is taken up by the five individual machines accessing the same information. With a proxy server, the first person accesses the information and then it becomes cached on the proxy server. When the next four people open the site, they simply access it from the proxy server. This means that the information arrives at their browser more quickly and network bandwidth is preserved.

Of course, there is one problem with having a proxy server that caches documents. When people wish to access a site, it will be taken from the local cache. If the cache is not updated on a regular basis, the document stored in the cache may not be the most up-to-date. The cache must be purged every couple of days to ensure that up-to-date information is available to the user.

Depending on what software you have to run the proxy server, there may be options to automatically update the cache every couple of hours or days.

Proxy Servers and Home Users

For individuals, a proxy server gives you privacy and anonymity on the net. No one can see your IP number, only the number of the proxy server. You can thus remain in some ways anonymous.

There are some websites that will allow you to use their proxy server to serve the Internet. These sites will thus help you remain anonymous (the website contains a complete list of such sites). Some are free, others will charge you a small subscription charge per year.

Although you may be surfing using a dialup account, you can still use a proxy server. There are many free services that allow you to use a proxy server to protect your identity. One such service was ProxyMate from Lucent Technologies (*www.proxymate.com*). This was a free service, paid for by advertising that appeared at the top of every page.

One word of caution: although the proxy server hides your IP number when surfing the web — be it using chat rooms, posting to discussion boards or using web-based e-mail — if you send an e-mail from your e-mail package such as Outlook Express, your "real" IP number will appear.

Another service that recently appeared came from freedom.net, who realised that people want to remain anonymous on the net. Freedom.net allow you to download a piece of software that will create <u>nyms</u>. These are pseudonyms that you use to connect up to the Internet. You enter any information you wish as your pseudonym. When information is requested about you, the website will only find out your nym and nothing more. When a website wishes to set a cookie it can and will, using your nym for identification, but since you are using a nym, no private information is revealed.

This idea of a nym works not only for web browsing but also for other applications such as e-mail and Telnet. The beauty of the service is that not even freedom.net know who you are. You set up your nym (you can buy multiple nyms for multiple identities) and include or make up any information you want. No one will be able to trace your nym back to you. Every time you request a website using this software, your request is routed through a number of freedom.net servers, which completely hide your identity. The information is encrypted and every trace of your IP number, etc. is deleted.

While users can now feel safe and anonymous while online, this does create problems. When ordering goods over the Internet, many sites rely on IP numbers to identify individuals who purchase goods with a stolen credit card. Now we have a situation where the Freedom Network will hide this information, so if someone did use a credit card number for fraud, the authorities cannot trace them.

Of course the other danger is in regard to paedophiles who may be able to disguise their tracks completely and no one will be able to trace them. The same goes for hackers.

Firewalls

Would you leave the door of your house unlocked? Ever thought about getting rid of the security guard at the entrance to your building? Of course not; these are the first lines of defence against attackers. But as illustrated above, many users and companies have decided to leave their computer and the whole network wide open to anyone who wishes to come in and have a good look around!

Companies who have a network of any sort, and individuals who work from home, should consider getting a <u>firewall</u>. A firewall is a system (usually made up of hardware and software) that can be set up to:

❖ Protect the company's network from hackers;

❖ Disallow connection to certain websites/Internet applications;

❖ Audit all network traffic.

A computer firewall is like its real-life counterpart: it protects your system from attack. Granted, if a user is determined enough, all the security in the world will not stop them from eventually gaining entry, but it will deter the casual attacker.

A firewall may simply be a piece of software running on a particular computer or it may be specialised hardware and software running on the network. The essential thing is to ensure that all traffic from your network goes through the same firewall; many firewalls are used in conjunction with proxy servers so that all traffic enters and leaves the company network at the same point.

The danger is that if a user has a modem connected to their computer and this connection is not routed out through the firewall, the network again becomes vulnerable.

Companies will use a firewall for many reasons:

❖ Once a company connects up to the Internet, their company-wide network may be exposed to untold dangers from computer hackers, viruses and Internet abuse by employees. If one computer connects up to the Internet and that computer is connected to the network, in essence every single computer is now available to the Internet.

❖ A company may wish to make sure that users do not use free e-mail services like Hotmail, so they can ban these sites. They may also wish to ban sites that contain chat rooms, etc.

❖ Another feature built into most company security would be the ability to track and audit everything that everyone does while on the Internet. This allows companies to see how long each employee is spending online and exactly what he or she is doing. Companies must realise that the Internet can be a necessity in today's business world, but also that it can open the floodgates to many different problems.

So what is the difference between a firewall and a proxy server? A proxy server works on behalf of the network users and can deny access to some sites, but it can be circumvented. They may also act as a local store for frequently requested pages, thus speeding up network access.

A firewall is more advanced — it can be set up to deny or allow access to the Internet by application. Therefore you can set up the firewall so that any access by the Telnet program is denied. Some firewalls will analyse every packet of information flowing through the firewall. Every word in an e-mail can be scanned. Every access by every program on the Internet can be monitored as it accesses the Internet. Firewalls are also more than just a software solution. It can also involve buying specialist hardware.

How Vulnerable is your Computer?

So you think your network is safe or that your home computer is safe? Surely no one is going to be interested in your computer?

If you want to see how vulnerable your computer is and also find solutions to the vulnerabilities, visit *grc.com*; this website will, with your permission, examine your computer system and report back on its findings. This site deals with security issues associated with the net and is a great source to read about these security problems. When you visit the site, click on the "Shields UP" icon; you will be asked to click an icon to initiate the procedure of checking your computer — you may be startled by what you see!

One of the pages contains information about a product called Zone Alarm. This is a personal firewall which is free to individuals. When run it will protect your computer from being "probed" or checked by other Internet users. Every time a program tries to access the Internet, a message will appear on screen asking you if that program is allowed to access the Internet. You can then either allow it or disallow it, depending on what the program is. This is an excellent way of defeating the spyware programs discussed earlier.

Zone Alarm will help in that if any rogue program tries to access the web, it will allow you to deny access to it. It will also detect people trying to use scanner programs against your computer. I logged on one night and in the space of 10 minutes had over 75 alerts to scanners probing my computer!

If you are a small company, you might decide to have one computer designated for Internet access rather than having a computer connected to the network which is in turn connected to the web. If you must have all computers accessing the Internet, at the very lease consider having Zone Alarm installed on all computers. This will offer you some protection. Obviously, for highly sensitive networks the best bet is a professional firewall and proxy server solution.

Take time to read the pages contained on the *grc.com* website, as you will learn many valuable tips and have your eyes opened to website security.

Internet Rules for Business

In summary, management must under all circumstances have some sort of auditing software in place that can track what employees are doing on the Internet. Certainly from a business point of view, censorship by the company is essential for a number of reasons. For example:

❖ A worker visits a porn site and another worker takes offence. The company could face problems with sexual harassment cases. You would not allow your employees to hang up girlie calendars; equally they should not be viewing such pictures on their monitors.

❖ Your network may slow down due to large amounts of traffic coming in from the Internet. You would not let your employee hog the photocopying machine or telephone for personal use; why should they be allowed to hog the network resources of your company?

❖ Third and most important is the danger of an employee downloading a virus through software or as an e-mail attachment. This could cause thousands of pounds worth of damage, or at the very least down time for the computers and the network.

Allowing employees to use e-mail can cause untold problems for companies. It is essential that companies (as well as schools and colleges) not only have software and hardware to protect and audit Internet usage; they should also have a written AUP or Acceptable Usage Policy. An Acceptable Usage Policy defines how and for what purpose the Internet and e-mail may be used and sanctions that will be taken if it is abused. It should address issues such as e-mail attachments, use of e-mail purely for business reasons, use of Internet for research purposes only, etc. If your company does not have an AUP, you should consider getting one together to avoid confrontations at a later stage.

A major problem for employers is that employees may spend a lot of time e-mailing friends and colleagues for non-business purposes. Instead of increasing productivity, it may decrease the overall productivity of the office.

Some employees may decide to send out CVs to other companies via e-mail, as it is easier and "free" (they are not being charged for it). All employees should be aware that many companies employ automatic filters that check every e-mail before it is sent out for certain keywords, such as CV, Curriculum Vitae, Résumé, etc. If such a word is found in an e-mail, it may be quarantined and a message sent to the system administrator.

Employees must remember that an e-mail originating from the company is the equivalent of sending out a letter from the company. Therefore if an employee sends out an abusive e-mail from their company e-mail address, many might take this as the view of the company, which will tarnish the company's image.

Another major risk is that confidential documents could be sent out to others, either deliberately or mistakenly. If an employee wanted to send out confidential information, it may be easier to do so by using the attachment function on the e-mail package than trying to smuggle out physical documents. This could cause major problems for employers, because those documents could be forwarded to another party.

What a lot of companies now do is:

1. Scan all documents before they leave the company's network to ensure that nothing that should not be sent is sent out;

2. Automatically add a disclaimer to the end of each message that says something like the following:

    This e-mail and its contents are for the intended recipients only. Contents of this e-mail may not be reproduced or forwarded.

It is very important, in this age of litigation, for companies to put legal disclaimers at the end of of each outgoing e-mail. Those of you who have been paying attention will know that the above could be achieved by use of a signature! But in the case of a universal signature, it would take too much time to manually configure each user's e-mail account to add the appropriate signature. Instead, many e-mail server programs will have a way of adding the signature automatically to every outgoing e-mail.

Always assume that your website and network are vulnerable; investigate security-related products that can ensure you have a secure network. Be prepared as company to spend at least £5,000 on a decent firewall package that will take care of most of your security needs. If in doubt, spend the money to get a security consultant in to secure your website and network.

Even more important than this is having a strict IT policy in place. Is there any point in having a security guard in place if you don't give him/her instructions or allow users to discuss confidential documents or take them home? Web security should mirror real-life security. The key rule is that time and money spent on security is time and money well spent. Hackers may at this very moment be attacking your company network. It is very hard to know when someone has been snooping around on your network. In the physical world, you can tell, but in cyberspace, nobody sees your footprints . . .

Chapter 13

Dangers of the Internet II: Privacy, Pornography and Censorship

In Chapter 12, I looked at some of the problems that businesses might encounter on the Internet. In this chapter, I focus in on some of the issues that concern you as an individual and a family, including:

- ❖ Pornography, censorship and freedom of speech

- ❖ The dangers of chat rooms and newsgroups, particularly the threat of paedophiles

- ❖ Internet addiction and cybersex

- ❖ Cyberchondria

- ❖ Personal privacy

- ❖ Self-protection and protecting your children.

Pornography, Censorship and Freedom of Speech

The Internet provides a wealth of knowledge, a place to learn about other countries, cultures and customs. But it also has a dark murky side. It is estimated that about 65–75 per cent of websites deal with pornography; this is a difficult figure to confirm, but there are a lot of websites whose sole purpose is the selling or dissemination of pornographic material.

The problem with the Internet — or some would say the beauty of it — is that it is so accessible. This means that anybody, teenagers and younger children included, are in effect now able to access porn without leaving the house. I have heard so many stories of how quiet Johnny is and how he stays in his room playing on the Internet — "Ah sure it's harmless" — little do Johnny's parents know the type of stuff that he could be looking at!

 ***Tip!*** *If you have a computer with access to the Internet, keep it in a family room. This means that you can keep an eye on what your kids are doing.*

Same name, different spelling

Getting into a porn site can be as easy as adding the wrong extension to a web address. Many "clever" and "enterprising" individuals try to register domain names that are similar to existing popular sites. They do this for two reasons: they hope people will enter their website address by accident and they will receive the hits and possibly get return visits to their site. They also set it up so that they can sell advertising. Sometimes they may do it as a joke; look at *www.whitehouse.gov* and *www.whitehouse.net*. The first site is the official White House site; the second is a skit but looks exactly like the official site! Spelling mistakes can also be a problem. What about the free e-mail service hotmail and hotmale?

Why is porn so big on the net?

The main reason pornography is so successful on the Internet is because there is a market for it. Pornographers of all shapes and forms have realised that they can make money, and a lot of it, from their sites. Most offer a subscription-based service, which can range from $1.95 per week to $50 per month.

The sort of people who visit these sites like the services they offer, because they can "enjoy" them from the comfort of their own homes. Everyone is happy except the general public!

Who controls the Internet?

You may ask why these sites cannot be banned. Remember that no one controls the Internet; it was built as a decentralised, distributed network, with no central core and no central body in charge of it. The US wanted a network system that was fault-resistant. They achieved their aim but perhaps opened up a can of worms in the process.

In the US, where many sites would originate, they cannot ban many of the sites because of the First Amendment, which guarantees freedom of speech.

One of the main problems lies with definitions of pornography. The First Amendment protects indecent material, but does not protect obscene material. What is the difference? Certainly, there is plenty of "obscene" material available on the Internet. However, what one person may define as obscene another may see as merely indecent. Different people or communities will see obscenity as being different things.

But where do you draw the line? How can you define where art ends and pornography begins? What one person considers artistic and harmless, another person may find offensive and vulgar.

The debate rages, although the American government did try to curtail pornography under the Exxon Amendment attached to the Communications Act of 1994. Section 223 of that Act prohibits obscene materials from being carried over the telephone network, but does permit indecent materials, as long as the operator of the service takes steps to ensure that the material is kept from minors. The Exxon Amendment would extend section 223 to include all online service providers, whether the material they transmit was voice or digital.

This seemed reasonable enough, but the Exxon Amendment went a step further. . . . Any system owner who made obscene materials available to users, whether the system owner was aware of it or not, would be liable. This meant that an ISP would be liable if a user looked at pornography through its dial-up service.

Effectively, ISPs would have to ensure that every user was over the age of 18 before they could use the Internet. Regardless of what sites they were looking at, there could be a danger that they would view pornography, which would make the ISP responsible. As you know from earlier chapters, ISPs allow you to access the Internet through their network, and while they *could* monitor each and every website you visit, it would be a very laborious task.

To say that this proposed amendment angered people would be an understatement. Eventually, the Communications Decency Act of 1996 was passed with the Exxon amendment, but one year later it was found to be unconstitutional. Since the Internet was so accessible, there was little or no barrier to people under the age of 18 viewing such material.

The Internet was to be protected as an area of free speech; after all, if something was permitted in the real world, such as pornographic magazines, the same rules should apply to the cyber world.

The US has been one of the first countries to enact laws regarding the Internet, but of course on the Internet nothing is quite clear-cut. It is very hard to judge whose law is violated if a crime is committed. Who is at fault: a server located in a foreign country or the user who viewed the site?

Take, for example, a book that is banned in a foreign country, perhaps on religious grounds. If a person from that country accesses and downloads an e-copy of that book, can there be any action taken against the server it was downloaded from? What is freedom of speech in one country may not be freedom of speech in another country.

This will cause many problems in the future, some of which may be relevant to Ireland. Ireland recently signed into law a privacy bill that allows people to encrypt data and to send it via the web. People are not under obligation to give out the key to decrypt the message if requested by the police.

In the UK, the opposite has happened. The British government, like all governments, has realised that much criminal activity, including paedophilia, is being conducted via e-mail. They have tried to bring through a law that will:

❖ Allow them to ask all people who use encryption software to give the police a key with which they can decrypt messages. If a person fails to comply with this, they can be charged with withholding information.

❖ Initiate a procedure that would scan all e-mails leaving and entering British service providers. This system would operate in real time and would scan e-mails for particular keywords that may be of interest to the security forces.

What happens if a message is sent from Ireland, which has privacy laws, into a country where keys must be given up, if requested, to the police? Suppose an Irish-based company is sending encrypted e-mail from their office in Dublin to their office in London; whose law applies?

No one government can control the net, unless they control all access points and ISPs. Even if the government did control all ISPs, they could not control people dialling up service providers in other countries.

Sex Sells

The other major problem is the amount of money involved. "Good" porn sites can make millions every year from subscriptions. On a recent TV programme discussing the issue of porn on the net, there was a young American "entrepreneur" who said that good sites could easily make $10,000 a month in revenue. This money would come from subscriptions, advertising, etc. A new generation of pornographers have emerged who realised that they can make a large amount of money and provide their service to a global audience. Therefore, on the net you will find every "niche market" covered on every conceivable topic.

Since it is very inexpensive to set up websites, if a site is shut down, it can be up and running again on a different server within days, or even hours!

How easy it is to find porn on the net

Unfortunately, it is all too easy to find porn on the Internet. There are many ways of doing this; one way is simply to guess the name of a site. Anything with "sex" in the URL is almost certain to be a porn site.

The other way is simply to go to any search engine and either type in the word "porn" or any other sexual word. You will see huge lists of sites are returned as matches.

Why do search engines do nothing about this? Once again, the reason is freedom of speech and the notion that there should be no censorship or policing on the Internet. Some search engines now have family guards on them that warn you when you may be using a keyword that could lead to adult-related material. We will discuss these, and also a number of child safe search engines, at the end of the chapter.

Paedophiles

Even those who argue that porn sites should not be banned because of the right to freedom of expression fall silent when it comes to discussing the most dangerous of all Internet-based threats: paedophiles. We shall see later how paedophiles use chat rooms to prey on children.

It is very hard to catalogue what is on the Internet; therefore, there could be hundreds of thousands of child porn sites out there that may never be found, simply because no one knows they are there, except the paedophile rings.

For companies, this poses a huge problem; if they have lax security, it is very easy to set up your own server on your desktop computer and allow others to access information you decide to publish. Many companies, will, if they find downloaded porn on their computers, dismiss employees responsible but will not press charges for fear of bad publicity and tarnishing of the company image. Indeed, a Department of Defence computer in England was recently found to contain a huge amount of pornography that employees had downloaded. Another high profile case was that of former 1970s pop star Gary Glitter, who was arrested for possession of child pornography on his computer. It was only discovered when his computer was sent in for repair, and a technician accessed the hard drive. Colleges and businesses have to be on the lookout for this type of abuse by their students/workers, as discussed at the end of Chapter 12.

The Internet, certainly in the US, is helping win the fight against paedophiles. There are many government-run sites that allow the user to enter in the state and area where they live and receive a list of paedophiles living in their area. The Internet is thus keeping people informed. The important thing here is that the service is government-backed. The danger is that someone could set up a web page about another person and accuse them of some such crime. Or if the information is not kept up to date, someone who may have lived in a particular house may have moved on.

Through the anonymous nature of the Internet, it may be easier for law officials to infiltrate paedophile rings, as they can pretend to be paedophiles. Police forces across the world are setting up cyber crime units. In fact, in the US some police forces have officers in chat rooms seeking out paedophiles soliciting children.

The contribution the porn industry has made to the Internet!

Believe it or not, we owe some thanks to the porn industry for many of the technologies we use today — a discomforting thought.

The first is e-commerce! A porn site is no good unless it can charge for its content; after all, it was not set up purely for the "good" of the consumer. Although people are willing to pay for access to the site, they had to make sure that they had nearly instantaneous access. People did not want to have to send off a cheque and wait a month before the application was processed, etc. Along came real-time processing of credit cards; such sites were amongst the first to use this, allowing users to gain instant access to the site.

 ***Real time processing*** *means your credit card can be authorised and charged straight away, in much the same way as when your card is swiped in a shop.*

With real time credit card processing, you can have a shop that is open for business 24 hours a day, 7 days a week, 365 days a year — a capitalist's dream business model! This has led to companies of all kinds making huge amounts of money on the Internet.

Video conferencing is very big business with porn sites; again, they helped pioneer the software, test it and get it accepted for use on the net. Everyday, people use video conferencing software to conduct meetings, hold conferences, etc.

Indeed, historically, many of the luxuries we use in everyday society — such as video, CDs (and now DVD) and premium call numbers — were originally used and exploited extensively by the porn industry. It is very common for competition lines to use premium call numbers.

Other programs have been developed to stop password sharing. Password sharing is where one consumer buys a password for a website and then shares it with a number of users, thus denying the company of revenue. This activity is commonly used to access porn sites. Programs have been developed to stop this and terminate accounts that engage in this. Such software would be invaluable to any company that needs to protect its site again this activity.

All of this is only to illustrate that, although bad, the industry has helped develop some of the technology used on the Internet and in mainstream society.

At the end of the chapter, we will look at some ways to protect yourself and your family from the dangers of the Internet, particularly pornography.

Dangers of Newsgroups

Newsgroups are often overlooked on the Internet. Most Internet users — i.e. those who have only gone online in the last five or six years — have probably heard about them but never use them. Newsgroups are like modern-day bulletin boards that are distributed from one news server to another. They contain a number of top-level categories that deal with everything under the sun! These include:

❖ Bus   dealing with business matters

❖ Soc   dealing with social matters

❖ Rec   dealing with recreational activities

❖ Alt   dealing with everything alternative!

Many of the ALT newsgroups contain newsgroups that deal with sexual fantasies and perversions. There are also alt.binary newsgroups. Binaries are usually pictures, but can also be programs or games. Some of the binary newsgroups are used either for swapping and posting pornographic pictures or for advertising pornographic websites.

There are numerous hacking newsgroups as well. Some (mainly binary) groups use the net to exchange information regarding pirated software, stolen credit card numbers, etc.

Not all Internet Service Providers carry the full list of newsgroups. Many ISPs don't carry the more sexual newsgroups or those that deal with hacking. But that does not mean that others cannot access them. There are many sites that offer access to any newsgroup under the sun, for a subscription.

You may ask why this service is on offer. The answer again is freedom of speech. In certain countries (or closer to home), a particular newsgroup may be banned. These servers offer their services to maintain freedom of speech. Although they can also be used to gain access to pornographic newsgroups, it is important to bear in mind those who live in countries where censorship is taking place, for whom newsgroups can be a sign of hope.

Dangers of Chat Rooms

Chat rooms are dangerous in the sense that they are a place where people interact; in any social interaction, there is potential for danger where a vulnerable or naïve individual meets someone who is not averse to exploiting their vulnerabilities. In chat rooms, this is exacerbated by the nature of the interaction.

As you may remember from our discussion of chat rooms, visitors register a chat nickname or handle in order to chat with others. Since "no one knows you are a dog on the Internet", you do not know what or who you or your child is talking to. Although the person may say they are a 15-year-old girl, they could in fact be a 50-year-old man! Again, you must be aware of what your child/student/employee is doing.

There was a story of a paedophile who was chatting in a kids' chat room (how could anyone have known who or how old he was?) and arranged to meet a child at a certain place. When he arrived for his meeting, he was arrested! Little did he suspect that while he was pretending to be a child, the "child" on the other end was a law enforcement official! In this case, it worked both ways — he thought he was fooling the child, never suspecting that someone might do it to him! But not all such dangerous people are caught.

The introduction and use of video chat has increased these problems tenfold. Some of those who use video chat do it for purely voyeuristic reasons. If text-based chat rooms have conversations that often degenerate into lewd conversations . . . well let's just say you can imagine what could go on in such a chat room.

If you do use video chat (perfectly innocently), you are essentially letting people into your home, allowing them to see you and your personal space. Text-based chat rooms at least allow for some anonymity. The bottom line is that educators and parents have to aware all the time of what their children are doing. No matter what filtering software you may have on your computer (see later), you can be sure that your child will find a way around it, or find a patch or crack on the Internet to circumvent it. Education is one of the key solutions. Your children are probably a lot smarter when it come to the Internet than you might think!

Most companies will not allow access to chat rooms for a number of reasons. The main reason is that they waste valuable company time. Also, the employee in the chat room may spread slanderous or confidential information to others in the chat room.

One of the major problems of chat rooms is that they are fertile ground for Internet addiction.

Internet Addiction

Everybody knows about alcohol addiction or drug addiction; the latest addiction we are now hearing about is Internet addiction.

Much study has been done in the US about this new problem. Dr Ivan Goldberg, a psychiatrist from New York, proposed a new term called Internet Addiction Disorder. In studies, it was found that people were spending more and more time on the Internet, neglecting their loved ones, their jobs, forgetting to eat and sleep. Relationships and marriages are breaking up due to the Internet.

Internet addiction was seen to be evident in offices, schools, colleges, anywhere with access or exposure to the Internet. Many people are finding that everything they "need" can be found in cyberspace. Food, books, clothes, etc., can be ordered, "friends" can be made and communication can take place via any of the interactive mediums of the net — e-mail, chat rooms, pagers and video conferencing.

The Internet is indeed a very social place; friends and relationships can be made in cyberspace. It is possible to find new people to talk to on the net with very little effort. You don't have to get dressed up; you can just go to a chat room and begin a conversation with someone. No one judges you on how you look, what you wear . . . everyone is equal in a chat room.

The problem is that this social contact is offered in an easy and "unrealistic" way. Things happen more quickly on the Internet. When you enter a chat room, one of the first things you are asked is "a/s/l" or age, sex, location. You can then begin to chat about anything and everything; there are no boundaries, no guidelines that you must adhere to as you would in real life. People begin to act without inhibitions, as they would not normally do in real life.

Before you know it, you "know" a person. You can dispense with the formalities of a real-world relationship. You may find you have no need for "real" social interaction and as a result, your behaviour changes, you begin to lose the "social graces" that help you interact with people in the real world. You feel in many ways detached from reality. You are a new person, no one knows you. You have disposed of any social responsibilities you may have. Inevitably, any close relationship you do have in the outside world will suffer.

Another overriding factor that lures people to the Internet is anonymity. You can be who you want to be, you have no responsibilities. Just because you are a 40-year-old business executive, you do not have to act like one. You can be a male or a female, you can pretend you are younger/older, richer/poorer than you really are. You can, in fact, create a fantasy world and an entire persona for yourself. The more time you spend on the Internet, the more you live in this world, the greater the chance that you will begin to believe in this false persona.

People are not afraid of the consequences of their actions on the Internet; if they say something that offends a person or are rude to a person, they know that the person can simply ignore them. After all, there are so many other people to talk to. You can always find someone else. It is possible to form a "one-to-many" type of relationship on the net. In real life, one person would usually engage your attention at any one time. On the net, you can chat to five different people without any of them being any the wiser.

When the above factors are combined, you have a potentially lethal cocktail.

Cybersex

Flirting or talking suggestively in chat rooms is commonplace and sometimes harmless. The problem is, since there are no "rules" on the net, people don't know when to stop. In real life, flirting is often a normal and acceptable thing to do in social situations, but people know where to draw the line; in cyberspace, where is the line?

This, coupled with the anonymous and fast-paced nature of the net, can lead people to engage in <u>cybersex</u>.

 *Cybersex* occurs when people talk in highly sexually charged language in order to gain gratification.

The net is often used instead of expensive dating/sex lines; log on to a chat room, see if you can have an erotic conversation with someone, save money.

The big problem occurs when people begin to spend more time on the net with their "cyber-partner" and less with their real partner. Many users find that the net is more exciting, more erotic than real life. They do not realise that the Internet is a land of unreality. You may be pretending you are rich, handsome, etc., but so might the wonderful person you are talking to!

Dr David N. Greenfield, from virtual-addiction.com, has said that about 22 per cent of online users cyber-flirt. He puts this down to two things: accelerated intimacy (things happen faster on the net) and disinhibition (people saying things online they would not say or do in real life).

Another thinker on this topic, Dr John Suler, did a study of an online chat room called The Palace. This chat room is quite different, as people take on avatars or physical personas that others can see. He found that many people were on the chat channels, day in day out. When he questioned why they spent so much time, most found it hard to give an answer.

So what is the draw of chat rooms? Mostly, it is a sense of belonging. People go into a chat room and are all equals to some extent; there are no prejudices; everyone has the same standing in the chat room. In today's world, things are rushed, people don't have time for each other, no one knows your name; but in a chat room people are there to take time out, to chat, to meet people. People feel they belong to a community.

The problem lies in realising that this is artificial space; the relationships and bonds that are tied may be real, but should not take precedence over real world relationships.

Dr Suler has related chat rooms to Maslow's hierarchy of needs. Maslow proposed that people had certain needs that had to be fulfilled, from the most basic to more advanced. People would strive to fulfil each need at each level before trying to achieve the next need. The following is a list of human needs; you don't find the urge for the higher need until you have successfully achieved the next available need:

❖ *Physiological*: our most basic needs are for food, water and oxygen.

❖ *Safety*: our next need is the need to feel safe.

❖ *Love, Affection and Belongingness:* when we feel safe, we need to feel loved and have a sense of belonging.

❖ *Esteem*: it is nice to feel that people regard you well and that you are confident in what you do.

❖ *Self-actualisation*: this is the need for self-fulfilment, to do what you were born to do, perhaps to lead or help others.

One need that we have early on, according to Maslow, is the need for interaction and acceptance, which fits in with the third-level need for belonging.

This is what chat rooms can offer people. In today's busy world, no one knows your name but you can become recognised in chat rooms due the use of consistent nicknames or chat handles. As you become known, people will listen to you, accept your points of view (fulfilling a higher-level need). This leads to a greater feeling of belonging and acceptance; people respect you. Your opinion is listened to.

For many, a great honour would be to become a chat master, or moderator in a chat room. They are now in control; they come from being an ordinary chatter, who was unknown, to someone who is recognised. They have reached self-actualisation. They have become a leader of the chat room and can help others when they need help.

As I am sure you can begin to see, this is what attracts many people to the chat rooms and to the Internet in general. They can rebuild their personalities. They can be accepted and respected, something they may not get in real life. How long does it take to become respected and accepted in real life? For some, it never happens!

Unfortunately for some, the distinction between reality and unreality becomes blurred.

Other Types of Internet Addiction

Internet addiction is not just taking place in chat rooms. The Centre for Net Addiction (*www.netaddiction.com*), have looked at other net compulsions, including:

- ❖ Online gambling
- ❖ Online auction addiction
- ❖ Online trading.

It is so easy to visit a gambling website, sign up for an account with them and begin gambling. No need to leave your house or be seen outside a bookmakers! The same applies to pornography; the stigma of feeding your habit is diminished, as no one knows you are doing it.

There are so many sites that offer gambling, either by clicking a picture until you find money or actual online casinos. The worry is that you are detached from reality; you don't notice the money you are losing, since it would be charged to your credit card. There is the same buzz of gambling, apparently without the problems.

It's a cutthroat business on the web, and many gambling sites offer incentives to gamble with them. Some sites will offer free $20 bets; of course, that's credited to your account once you have signed up with them.

In real world casinos, there are real life "card sharks"; at least you may feel better losing to a human, but online, you can never tell how rigged the games are!

Many bookmakers are now setting up online betting shops. Users can now log onto their website, open an account and place bets. Again, the stigma of being seen going to a betting office is gone. For people who may never have betted before but would like to try it, this makes it easier for them to do so. Many people would have no idea how to place a bet in a betting office and would feel silly going in and asking — if this was your barrier to placing a bet, that barrier is now gone with online betting.

Online auctions are another problem. Like an ordinary auction, online auctions allow you to view a description of a product and then place a bid on it. Some people find that they get a huge buzz from this and are buying goods for the sake of it, or to see if they can outbid other people. They then end up with goods they did not want in the first place.

Online trading is another problem area. Many people are now buying and selling shares via the net. They can find all the information that they wish about companies and feel that they are getting up-to-the-minute, accurate information that they may not get through a broker. They often take more risks than they would in "real life".

So what do all of the above have in common? *netaddiction.com* calls it the ACE model:

❖ **Accessibility**: All these activities are accessible, no matter where you are — at home, at work or on a plane! You can get information immediately and also receive gratification immediately. Also, where flat-rate pricing or extremely cheap connection allows it, many people feel that it isn't costing them anything to stay online, day in, day out. Auctions via WAP phones could increase this problem.

❖ **Control**: netaddiction.com see this factor as important for such things as online trading. You are in control of where, when and how you get information about companies. Online auctions, they go on to say, allow people the ability to control what they buy and when.

❖ **Excitement**: With all activities we crave the excitement or buzz we receive. On the net, the buzz can be instantaneous, this reinforces the need to try again and again. This is where the danger occurs.

So how can you tell if you are addicted to the Internet or if a loved one is addicted? Sites such as *netaddiction.com* and *virtual-addiction.com* refer to the following list:

❖ Are you feeling preoccupied with the Internet, thinking about it while you are offline, thinking about when you will be online again?

❖ Is your net usage time increasing to gain the same amount of satisfaction?

❖ Are you finding you have spent more time on the net than originally intended?

❖ Have your efforts to cut down or eliminate net usage failed?

❖ If and when you cut down on the Internet do you feel moody?

❖ Have you risked or put in jeopardy a real relationship, job, etc.?

❖ Have you lied to friends and family about Internet usage?

❖ Is the Internet a way of escaping life's problems for you?

Of course, there is a danger here, as Suler has pointed out. The majority of net "addicts" may not actually exist. Many people go through periods of time where they use the net constantly and then leave it alone once they have seen the hype and enjoyed it.

Is this perhaps another problem that needs a psychologist to solve? There are some who will just be using the net excessively, but in many of these cases, the user has had other addictions. They simply have the type of personality that makes them addicted to different things.

The rule of thumb is to make sure that the Internet is not taking precedence over your work or your social life. If you feel your social skills are suffering or that you cannot pull yourself away from the computer, then you may have a problem.

Look out for your colleagues, partners and children too; are they acting differently, are they spending less time at social events, ignoring tea breaks, lunch breaks, etc.? Does your colleague's or your child's work seem to be suffering rather than improving due to the amount of time they spend online? It is very easy to think that these people must be more productive since they are spending so much time "researching". Always take an active interest in what others around you are doing.

Costs

Apart from the potential social and psychological damage of Internet addiction, there is also the obvious issue of costs. Internet costs, as described in Chapter 3, are often hidden in the sense that they are not immediately obvious. You can spend hours on the Internet without thinking about how much it is costing you, and only find out how serious the situation is when you receive a whopping telephone bill. For those who are truly addicted to the Internet, even this may not be a deterrent. As with other addictions, by the time you really begin to feel the costs hitting your wallet, it may be too late; you may be so hooked that the costs seem irrelevant. Any delayed impact like this will mean that, psychologically, the connection between your phone bill and your Internet usage can seem remote.

This can then be exacerbated if your particular addiction involves spending money online. For example, suppose your obsession is with online auctions, trading or shopping; as well as spending hours online, you may also be clocking up hundreds or even thousands of pounds on your credit card. Again, because credit cards delay the impact, it may be a month or more before you realise how much you have spent, by which time you may be in over your head.

Costs are a big problem for spouses or parents. If your husband or wife is addicted to the Internet, not only is the time they are spending online putting a strain on your relationship, it is also putting a strain on your finances. For parents, the problem of costs can be huge, because if your children have no responsibility for paying the phone bill, they may not realise or even care how much their Internet usage is costing you. We will look at some things that parents can do about their children's Internet usage shortly.

So what if you are fortunate enough to live somewhere that allows flat-rate Internet connection? Surely this will solve all your problems? Well, while it may keep your costs down, it may actually encourage the addiction. After all, if it doesn't cost any more to be online 24 hours a day, who are you hurting?

Business and Internet Addiction

Internet addiction can also be a serious problem for companies. The cost issues discussed above are just as relevant in the workplace. Also, workers may in fact reduce productivity because they are spending a lot of time online "researching" information. Social interaction may be hampered — why walk down the hall when you can e-mail your colleague — which can lead to a drop in morale.

Largely because of the Internet, many companies are now introducing teleworking or working from home. Teleworking has many advantages. If enough people work from home, office space can be reduced. Also, in theory, punctuality shouldn't be a problem; there should be reduced traffic congestion; and parents can stay at home and mind the kids while they work. There are also disadvantages; for example, people may become less social as they see their colleagues less and less. There is no more after-work drink in the pub. And as teleworkers come to rely more on e-mail and the net for research, they may find themselves "addicted" to e-mail and the Internet.

(Has the technology made people less communicative? I know for a fact that I now type things more often than I would write them out by hand. With the advent of voice recognition software, we may not even need to type anymore! In years to come, we may have forgotten how to write!)

Other dangers include confidential documents being leaked, viruses spreading, or even false press statements being sent out by a disgruntled colleague, or messages posted on a newsgroup concerning company information.

All of these could adversely affect your business. Statistics seem to indicate that much of the hacking of business computers is done from within; so many people are concerned with outsiders getting in that they forget to secure the internal network from insiders (employees) causing problems. The best policy for businesses is to ensure that they have tight security in their internal network and to ensure that they can audit everything that each user does.

You will probably find that at some stage of your Internet travels, you too will become "temporarily addicted". I myself find this — I go through phases of using the Internet every night to check e-mail, research for information, etc.; I could spend five hours online and not notice the time go by. The key thing to note is that this is only *every so often*. When people feel that they cannot live without the Internet or need to log on first thing every morning, last thing every night and countless times during the day, then they may have a problem.

If you want to find out if you are addicted to the Internet, try the test provided at: *http://www.netaddiction.com/resources/test.htm*

Cyberchondria

Another worrying phenomenon has appeared on the Internet; it is known as **cyberchondria**. A hypochondriac is a person who has an abnormal anxiety, often to the point of obsession, about their health. A cyberchondriac is a person who becomes obsessed with visiting medical websites to diagnose themselves of supposed illnesses. They then go to their GP armed with all the information about what they think is wrong with them!

The Internet has made information, like medical information, more accessible to people. Instead of spending money on huge medical encyclopaedias, all the information is available and searchable at the click of a mouse. Many of these sites serve a useful purpose, helping doctors and medical researchers to find information quickly. Also, if a person has a rare illness or needs information about drugs they may be taking, it is more accessible than ever for them to get this information. They may well find relevant support groups via the web. Often when you ask your doctor about something, you sometimes get a vague answer; now you can be more informed.

These medical sites are often set up by experts in a particular field, by a support group for a particular illness, or by a pharmaceutical company as a "valued added" part of their website. However, one has to be careful to authenticate the authors of the site. Anybody may set up a site about asthma and give advice and information, but if they are not qualified in that area, it would be dangerous if people were to follow their advice. What works for one individual with asthma may not work for another patient. Therefore if I say that I felt fine giving up my medication and then running for two miles every day, this might be OK for me but could lead another sufferer to get worse. Review the chapter on searching and authenticating sources of information to refresh your memory on how you can do your best to ensure that the information given is correct.

What many GPs are finding is that, even with genuine sites, some people are accessing the information improperly, i.e. they are not trained to read the information, assess its value and make an informed judgement. Users are finding out how they think they should be treated, what drugs should be prescribed — all of which causes more headaches for doctors. Worse still are those who don't even visit their doctors when there *is* something seriously wrong with them, because they have been "reassured" by a medical website.

Cyberstalking

A new breed of Internet danger has emerged in the form of the cyberstalker. Like real-life stalkers, these people meet others and then bombard them with obscene e-mails, follow them into chat rooms, etc.

This is another reason to set up a free web-based e-mail account. If you give out your real e-mail address or your business e-mail address, the cyberstalker will know a little bit more about you (either the name of the company you work for or the ISP you are with); using this information they could track you down.

One of the many worrying aspects of the Internet is the facility, mainly provided by US sites, to search for people online. There are many websites, legitimate ones, which allow you to search for long lost friends and family. One such site is www.whowhere.com, who have a huge database containing all the names and addresses of people in the telephone book. You can search for people by last name and area they live in and find full details of their address. Of course, you can do this anyway in the real world if you can get your hands on the local phone book for the region you are looking for. But that takes time and effort. On the net, the same information is available but it is also more easily accessible.

Herein lies the problem. A cyberstalker or other like-minded individual starts talking to, say, an American in a chat room. The conversation progresses and names are exchanged. The cyberstalker then asks what part of the US the other individual is in; they find out the state, then possibly the county. From there it is a matter of going to one of these people-search sites and entering in the information. Bingo! Within a few minutes, the cyberstalker has their full address and phone number.

Very few people realise that their personal information is online for all to see. However, this is also a great resource to find people you may have lost contact with; most people will use these facilities for their intended purposes, but there will always be those who will abuse it.

Personal Privacy

When you begin to use the Internet, and particularly when you start shopping on the net, you supply a lot of information to websites. Sometimes when you return to a site you have visited or shopped at, it will remember you and welcome you and possibly even suggest items that have changed or special offers that might interest you! Sounds like a great idea? Read on to find out what information websites know about you . . .

You may have heard the following being said about the Internet:

❖ It's anonymous

❖ No one knows what sites you have been to

❖ No site keeps a record of your visit.

If you believe these to be true, you have been misled! Although you may think no one knows who you are, you may be mistaken. Before you panic, this does not mean that every other web user will know all about you; but more and more websites collect information about you and what you do at their site!

Before explaining how and why this happens, let's review some concepts learned from earlier chapters. When connecting to a website (web server), the information you request is sent to you and then the connection between the web server and your computer is terminated. The website has so many other visitors that it does not want to keep every connection "alive". This system allows many users to connect and receive information from a website without causing a bottleneck on the network. The Hyper Text Transfer Protocol (http), which allows you to receive web pages, is known as a stateless protocol, i.e. it does not remember anything about any user.

As the web developed and surfers became more sophisticated, website developers wanted to personalise the web experience. Wouldn't it be great to be welcomed to a website by name? Or how about personalising what appears on the homepage according to your preferences? Suppose you just wanted to see local weather information or local headlines; wouldn't it be great to be able to customise the homepage for every user?

If only there was a way of remembering a user. This would be advantageous to both the user, who would get customised information each time they visited the page, and the website because people would return to the site on a regular basis and targeted marketing would be possible.

The solution came in something called <u>cookies</u>. Cookies are small text files that are sent by the web server to the user's hard disk. They contain information that cannot be read by an individual; they only make sense to the web server that sent the cookie. The next time you access a site, the web server will see if you have been sent a cookie; if you have, it will request it to be sent from your hard drive to the server.

Now already you can see the problem. The web server seems to be writing data to your hard drive and then is looking at your hard drive to see if there is any information that it may have placed there. How do you know that confidential information is not being sent back to the server? What information is being recorded on your hard drive?

Let's dispel some myths at this point:

❖ Cookies can cause viruses: *Not true* — a cookie is merely a text file that cannot access anything on your hard drive.

❖ Cookies can take up huge amounts of space on your computer: *Not true* — both Internet Explorer and Netscape Navigator will only allow a certain number of cookies to be stored on your computer's hard disk.

❖ Cookies can be read by any website: *Not true* — cookies can only be read by the site that sent them.

❖ Cookies can read information on your computer's hard drive and then send it back to a server: *Not true* — cookies can only save information about a website onto your server into a particular directory.

But there is still a problem. In Chapter 6, we described how some web addresses don't begin with *www*, but instead take the form *sales.howsitgoing.com* or *subscriptions.howsitgoing.com*. You are just accessing a different part of the same site. The part before the domain (*howsitgoing*) is known as a sub-domain; it is a sub-section of the main site or domain.

One company has been using sub-domains like this in order to track users from one website to another. Doubleclick.com are the largest online advertising firm. They place ads on all the major websites. As you travel from one website to another, it is possible for them to track you via cookies.

Let's assume you visit Yahoo. If you click on an ad at Yahoo, you will be sent a cookie from *yahoo.doubleclick.com*. If you then visit Infoseek, the cookie there will be from *infoseek.doubleclick.com* and so on and so forth. Since all the cookies originate from *doubleclick.com*, the Doubleclick server can read each and every cookie from the various sites you have visited. They could then build up a complete profile of you and your activities across various sites. Doubleclick got a lot of bad press over this, as it was seen as a major invasion of privacy that few users were aware of.

Remaining Anonymous

As discussed above, when you visit a site you may be sent cookies. Not only this, but your IP number is recorded.

This worries many people, as it is seen as an invasion into their private life. You would not let people write down information about what products you saw in the supermarket, what products you bought, how long you shopped for. You would complain about this and you would be justified in doing so. Yet this information is being tracked every day by companies on the web.

As we have seen, personal privacy is becoming more important and users are becoming more aware of what companies can do and how they can track you. We already discussed the problem of "spyware" that can send back information to a server on the Internet. Even if people unwillingly agree to this, because they need a particular piece of software, what concerns many users is what happens to the information. When a dotcom company goes bust, the only tangible assets, apart from its computer hardware, may be its customer database. Unfortunately, as we have seen, it is a difficult and murky legal area. Suppose an Irish company is set up and registered in a foreign country and its servers reside in a foreign country but it has offices in Dublin. Under whose law is the information gathered by this company governed? Some countries may have quiet relaxed laws about data protection!

If in doubt, always read the privacy statement that accompanies a website. Take time to read any agreements before you click on the "I Accept" button! Once you have agreed to the terms and conditions, it may be too late to change your mind.

As an individual, there are a number of things you can do to prevent this tracking, but the most important is to disable cookies, which may reduce the functionality of some websites.

Protecting Yourself and Your Children

There are a number of ways of protecting yourself and your children while online. Some of these are relevant to businesses also, and have therefore already been discussed in Chapter 12, while others are more specifically aimed at the home user.

Filtering Software

There are a number of companies that provide <u>filtering</u> software for the Internet. This software is set up on your computer and automatically filters out sites that are deemed unsuitable. You can also add sites that you consider unsuitable to their list of banned sites. The software can be configured not only to ban sites, but also to filter out words. Therefore if the word "hacking" is entered into the browser, a warning will be issued and you will be notified when you access the computer next.

These software packages also have the ability to stop pictures being displayed on the screen, which is obviously of major importance in preventing your computer being used for downloading pornography. They can also protect the files on your computer from prying eyes!

This type of software is good for individuals or schools, where one cannot be watching children all the time. However, many people have reservations about this type of software. Much of the software has automatic updating facilities, which means that every time you log on to the Internet, the software will update its list of banned websites automatically from the manufacturer's website. The problem here is that you are letting someone else censor websites for you. You cannot be sure whether they have any hidden political, religious or any other type of agenda.

Another problem is that they may be too restrictive. I know of someone who installed the software, found it too restrictive and had to take it off their computer as it made surfing more laborious.

The most popular software packages include:

❖ Cyperpatrol   *www.cyberpatrol.com*

❖ Net Nanny   *www.netnanny.com*

❖ Surfwatch   *www.surfwatch.com*

Most of the packages outlined, and there are many more, usually allow
you to download the software and try it free for 30 days. Remember to
check that the software not only safeguards your children while on the
web but also filters e-mail and newsgroups.

Some other packages will prevent user's personal details from being
transmitted via the net. For example, if a person tries to send an e-mail
with their real name or address on it, the software will automatically
block it. This type of software can be essential, as children may tend to
trust and believe people they meet in chat rooms.

 ***Warning!*** *Before installing any such protection software
— in fact before installing any software from the net —
make sure you have back-ups of important files, just in
case the system crashes or does something unexpected.*

If you want to allow children just to surf the net from child-safe websites
— without being able to enter in web addresses — run the program
called Childbrowser in the browser section of the website
(*www.internetdemystified.com*). This is a cut-down browser that lists a
number of child safe search engines where children can begin their web
exploration safely.

Parental Guardians

Mainstream search engines and directories do not censor much of the
information included on them. This causes many problems for teachers
and parents especially; simply by typing in the word "sex", or any other
sexual word, you will get a list of all the sites it has categorised. Many
people believe that it is up to the individual to censor and not up to the
search engine.

However, a number of search engines such as Altavista, Infoseek, Excite and Lycos, among others, have a special feature that allows you to
put a "guard" on the search engine. This means that when your child,
partner, girlfriend or boyfriend use that search engine, they will be denied access to certain sites that are linked from the search engine. Very
useful indeed!

If you can switch this guard on, surely you have to do it every time you log on to the Internet? The answer is no; sites such as Altavista and Infoseek place a cookie on your hard drive and remember that you visited the site and turned the parental guard on.

These guards cannot just be turned off. The sites have an optional password that you can add. This means that if someone wants to disable the parental guard, they must enter the password you set. In effect, this stops anyone from finding undesirable sites from the search engine and visiting them. Remember: this will only work on the computer you are currently using.

Infoseek GoGuardian

Infoseek's parental control is called GoGuardian. You can set it up on any browser you have on your computer. A cookie will be placed on your hard drive that will remember you the next time you visit the site. You can enter an optional password, which is advisable, that will ensure that no one can turn off the GoGuardian without the password. This service also turns off access to newsgroups, which is useful, as some of the ALT category newsgroups contain undesirable information.

Altavista Family Filter

Altavista has a similar tool called Family Filter. It will reduce the amount of unsuitable information that will be displayed, including any pages relating to gambling, racism, drugs, violence, etc. It can also filter out any pages that refer to or have chat rooms on them, which is great for parents!

Since you can use Altavista to search for images, it also has a way of screening any offensive images from appearing on your screen. This is important, as many sites will try to fool search engines so that when you search for an image of a house, it may show a pornographic image.

Altavista has different settings for you to choose from:

❖ **Multimedia Only**: This option will filter everything that is searched for except web pages; therefore it will not show images, video and audio.

❖ **All**: Filters all types of content — the safest option.

❖ **None**: Turns off all filtering.

As with GoGuardian, you can set up a password that will make sure no one else can turn off the filtering.

One of the drawbacks of Family Filter is that it will not filter out newsgroups, which can be a source of a lot of objectionable material. Also it only works for the English language. Since Altavista can be searched in multiple languages, this can be a problem.

Child-safe Search Engines

As well as these filters, there are certain search engines that are specifically designed to be child safe. These search engines ensure that all content that is listed by them is aimed at kids.

The most famous search directory is Yahoo — now meet Yahooligans, a search directory especially for kids. This search engine resembles Yahoo, as illustrated below:

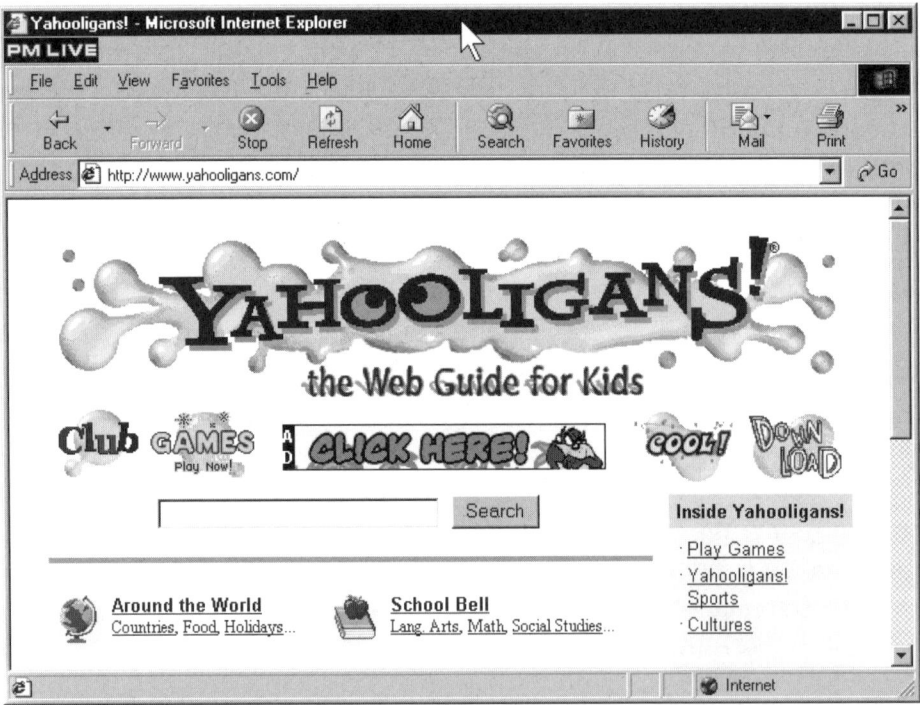

Listed below are some other child-friendly websites that either provide ways of searching specially selected sites or contain a list of interesting sites for kids:

❖ **Searchopolis** (*www.searchopolis.com*): This is a very good search engine for educators and students alike, offering many utilities once you register with them. These include safe e-mail for students, ideal for a school environment, and "virtual lockers" where you can store files, favourite web addresses, etc.

❖ **Awesome Library** (*www.awesomelibrary.org*): This site is a search directory of over 14,000 sites that have all been checked and classified for students, teachers and parents. Like any search directory, you either browse or search for the information:

❖ **CyberSleuth Kids** (*cybersleuth-kids.com*): This site lists educational sites that can help with homework assignments.

❖ **EdView Smart Zone** (*school.edview.com/search*): This site has links to over seven million sites that are safe for children. The sites have been reviewed by teachers. Each site is categorised by subject and there is an indication of what age group it is appropriate for.

❖ **Family Web Files** (*www.familywebfiles.com*): Unusually, a site presented both in Spanish and English, which provides a directory of child-safe websites.

❖ **Infoplease Kid's Almanac** (*kids.infoplease.com*): This site provides interesting facts and information that is oriented around the needs of children.

❖ **Linkopedia Kidzone** (*www.linkopedia.com/kids.html*): A directory that rates and reviews sites that are suitable for kids from the ages of two (a bit young to be on the web perhaps!) to ten.

❖ **Saluki Search** (*www.salukisearch.com*): Another search directory that is completely child safe. Using the same structure as any other search directory, kids can search for information or browse through categories for the information they want.

❖ **StudyWeb** (*www.studyweb.com*): Study Web is an ideal site for children who may be researching a project or report. It contains over 100,000 fully reviewed and categorised websites. It indicates what levels each site is aimed at and also will tell you if any visual aids are available.

On a related topic, for many years there have been "term paper" sites on the Internet. "Enterprising" high school or college students realised that since many students follow the same curriculum, they may also get the same or similar essay topics to write about. Why not share past essays with others?! Up sprang searchable sites, which allowed you to download different essays for different courses, for a price. For example, for $5 you could download a complete essay on the "Metaphors uses in early Shakespearean poetry"; the essay would also tell you what grade was given. I have even heard of sites where you can buy full Masters and PhD theses!

Most college lecturers and teachers are now aware of such sites, but how do they prove it is not the students' work if they can't find the original website. Given the global nature of the net, it may be impossible to find the original author of the work.

Child Safe Meta Search Engines

Meta search engines — which base their listings on searching a number of other engines — were discussed in Chapter 7. The popular AskJeeves has a special meta search engine for kids (*www.ajkids.com*). Family Friendly Search (*www.familyfriendlysearch.com*) is another child-friendly meta search engine, which provides a meta search service that will only query major child-safe search engines.

Now your kids have the power to search in a safe environment. It is great to have all these engines, but the main problem is that all the children need to do is type in the address of any other search engine or any other website and they can access inappropriate information.

To overcome this, you can run the program in the kids' directory of the website (*www.internetdemystified.com*) that will open a web browser and web page that will link to all of the sites mentioned above. Your children will only be able to use this browser to access the sites set up!

General Surfing Rules

While it is a good idea to install some of the software detailed above, the most important way of protecting yourself online is just to be careful! Try following some simple guidelines:

* ❖ **Identity**: Never reveal your true identity to someone on the Internet whilst in chat rooms or in discussion groups. It is very important to stress again that "no one knows you are a dog on the Internet". You have no way of knowing who you are dealing with when you chat to someone, take part in a discussion, etc.

❖ **Personal Information**: You should not reveal information regarding where you live, your telephone number, etc. I would also recommend that you do not give anyone your "real" e-mail address. Set up a new web-based e-mail address that you give out to people you meet online.

❖ **Shopping**: When shopping try to find out as much information about the company you are dealing with before you buy their product. Most companies will have a page about themselves and should provide substantial contact details, including postal addresses and telephone and fax numbers; if they do not, perhaps you should e-mail them and see why they don't. If in doubt, call them to see what their customer service is like.

Internet Rules for Kids

The websites *www.safekids.com*[1] and *www.ctw.org*[2] offer some good tips for parents about safety on the Internet:

❖ Never give out identifying information of any sort, including full name, address, telephone number, date of birth, etc.

❖ Get to know the services your child uses; don't assume they know what they are doing; involve yourself in their Internet activities as much as possible.

❖ Instil in your children the danger of arranging to meet face-to-face with someone they have met on the Internet.

❖ Ensure that your children know they should talk to you if they feel uncomfortable about any aspect of the Internet.

❖ Tell your children that people online may not be who they say they are.

❖ Children should be taught not to trust everything they read on a website or in a chat room.

❖ Children should be responsible and courteous online and not be abusive to people in chat rooms/discussion boards.

---

[1] http://www.safekids.com/parent_guidelines.htm
[2] http://www.ctw.org/parents/safecruising/aftab02/0,1217,,00.html

❖ Ensure your children balance online time with offline activities. The Internet may be a great learning tool but time needs to be spent engaging in group activities and other social skills.

Education is the key. Parents should keep a watchful eye on children and educate them on the dangers of the web. You tell them not to talk to strangers on the street; this should be reinforced on the Internet. *Everyone* on the Internet should be treated as a stranger.

Try to take an active interest in what your child is doing on the computer and the Internet. This way the Internet can become a family event. Keeping the computer in a room where you can see it is always advisable. Children are far less likely to be up to no good when they know they may be caught at any second. The same applies to employees. Make sure your employees know that viewing offensive material is not tolerated.

Managers and teachers should make sure they are aware of the dangers involved in allowing Internet access in the workplace or school. The best security system begins with *you* being educated to the dangers and realising what is out there.

I am constantly asked during lectures and seminars about my personal opinion on censorship on the Internet. I always give the same answer — "I don't believe in censorship" — and always receive the same reaction (gasps, looks of dismay, etc.). However, let me qualify this: I believe it is up to the individual to censor what is seen by them and their family on the Internet.

Think about everyday life. How many videos or TV programmes do your children see with violence in them? Do you allow your child to watch any video they wish? You cannot ask the video shop not to stock a video. You cannot go into a bookshop and ask them not to carry a sexually explicit book, because your kids may see them. It is up to you to ensure that your kids do not buy or see such books, videos or programmes. You as a parent or educator must keep an eye on what your child is doing or watching. The same applies to the Internet. Too many parents and educators I deal with are unaware of the dangers of the Internet. Then, suddenly, at the end of a seminar, they begin to wonder and think about what their children are doing, and they panic.

Chapter 14

The Future

It is very difficult to say what the future may hold in any field. When we come to talk about future technologies, particularly with regard to the Internet, the future becomes telescoped. Remember that in Internet terms, one year of Internet time is roughly equivalent to 2.6 months of "real" time. To look twenty, ten, even five years in advance is to invite ridicule from future readers and historians. So the best thing to do is to examine a selection of "probable" and "almost definite" predictions. I'm cheating a bit; many of the technologies that are discussed in the following pages are already reality in the US and will very soon become mainstream in Europe.

Future Computers and Computing Powers

The last 30 years have seen the size and price of computers drop, while the specifications and performance have improved and accelerated. Indeed, the average home computer now has more computing power than the computers that guided the first moon landing!

What we will see in the months and years to come are more intelligent devices; partly because of something called Bluetooth technology (discussed below) and also because each device will have a miniature "computer" in it. Computers will get smaller and smaller and more powerful. Already MIT have been conducting and building prototypes for wearable computers, which will have hard disk space, run windows, be voice-activated and be able to recognise objects visually. The monitor will be located in little screens in your visor! It may sound like science fiction, but it is already happening!

Another likely development is the possibility of having every application you may need available over the web. In this day and age, software packages are very expensive and many users, both business and home, do not fully utilise the products they buy. How many people have an occasional need for a product, or need just one component of a large "package", but cannot justify buying the whole product so do without? This is certainly the case in the SME sector The solution to this and other problems is to provide the software on a temporary basis via the web. This development has led to the creation of yet another new tla (three letter acronym!) called ASP or Application Service Provider. ASPs will allow users to rent or lease applications via the web!

Such ideas are not new; many websites have already done this with small-scale products. One prime example is at www.listbot.com, the site that allows you to create and manage your own mailing list. This application, running on a remote server, takes care of many of the day-to-day tasks such as signing up or unsubscribing users. If you wanted to run a mailing list without using listbot or a similar service, you would need to buy special list management software, install it on your server, ensure it is running all the time and have the technical expertise to rectify any problems — too much hassle for many companies!

This idea of leasing applications causes fewer headaches, as the "experts" are looking after everything for you. Also the applications, since they are web-based, will be available to you whenever you need them, from any location!

Other free applications I have seen include:

❖ **Contact management programs** that will keep a list of your contacts and provide a calendar and appointment service, which you can access via the web. The service is paid for by advertisers.

❖ **Image manipulation programs** that give you the functionality, to a point, of programs such as Photoshop, but for free — ideal for a web designer on the move who needs to tweak a graphic. One of the very first applications I saw was called gifwizard, which could compress the size of your graphics and then save the compressed image to your hard drive. This was a free service until it was found that some companies were abusing it to compress the size of images on their sites so that their site would download quicker. It seems that the problem got so bad that these companies were hogging the service!

So what other applications could be provided in this manner? Well anything really; since many could and will be Java-based, they are accessible by anyone with a Java-enabled browser. Since Java is a full programming language, anything from spreadsheets to web marketing programs could be designed and used. Imagine the time and effort saved by not having to install the program on every computer!

WBT or web-based training is a similar application. Users could sign up for a course and get, say, two months to complete it; there would thus be no need to install software on the client computer.

In many senses, virtual hosting, where another company hosts your website on their server, is an example of the advantages of ASP. If you were to host your own site yourself, you would need to have the technical resources and the dedicated line, etc. With virtual hosting, this is all taken care of for you!

So what are the disadvantages of ASP?

❖ **Speed**: Some of these applications will be incredibly bandwidth hungry, demanding extremely fast connections to the net. They may not be usable on ordinary dial-up connections, so this may push certain sectors, such as the consumer sector, out of this market. Until we get full broadband, high-speed access, such applications may not be accessible or functional.

❖ **Reliability**: You must have 100 per cent guarantees that the application server will not go down, or if it does that there is another (redundant) server that can take over. Imagine a situation where you have an online marketing database program and you need to get an ad campaign out. If that server goes down, the application goes down, leaving you in a sticky situation. The worry is always that if you give control of something over to a third party, you are at their mercy. If you have the application in-house, you are fully aware of its status, and can remedy problems as soon as possible.

❖ **Security**: This is another obvious concern. If you are storing confidential information, such as names and addresses of clients, on the ASP server, what type of security do they have in place to ensure that no one can gain illegal access to the information?

ASPs will certainly develop more and more, but where many people may find that success lies is in the ability to use a free business model. This involves giving some or all of the application away for free on the Internet, but providing a value-added section that will give more functionality to the user. The fear of many companies is that giving away something for free does not work. We must learn from companies such as Netscape to see how this can work in your favour. People want and expect something for free when they are on the net. Others are more than willing to pay an annual subscription for a service they think is good. Use the free service to beta test the wants of users. Most of all, don't be afraid of the four-letter f-word . . . free!

Speed of Access

One of the most obvious things that will change in the future is the speed of access to the Internet. Already in the US, broadband Internet access is common; this involves high-speed connections to the Internet; it is always connected, so there is no need to dial up each time. It also allows for the use of many channels. You may remember from Chapter 3 that ISDN allows for two channels — one that could be used for data while the other could be used for voice technology. Broadband offers more channels, much like the way a television signal can carry many channels, so you could be surfing and talking on the phone using broadband.

Europe is still waking up to the possibilities of broadband. As we discussed earlier, the main broadband transmission methods include:

❖ **Cable**: Cable operators are now beginning to install Internet access via the same cable that brings in your TV channels.

❖ **DSL**: The main problem with this is that signal quality can be quite poor on some of the lines if it has to travel long distances from the exchange.

❖ **Satellites**: Currently, this is another way to get broadband transmission; it is more common in Australia. But there is a problem as, in its current state, many users will get broadband download but if they wish to upload information, they will still have to use a dial-up ISP account, so they are not getting full duplex broadband.

Bluetooth

No, this is not the result of too much sugar! Bluetooth is actually the next generation of technology that will allow users to connect devices without wires. Wireless technology is certainly not new; for years, laptops, mobile phones and printers have either had infrared ports built in or can have them added. The advantage, the manufacturers claimed, was a cable-free office, helping make it safer for the end user.

What they didn't mention were the problems such technology would bring. In order to transfer information, the devices had to be pointed directly at each other — much the way traditional remote controls have to be pointed directly at the television.

Another problem was that the devices could only be up to five metres away from each other and if for any reason the signal was interrupted — for example, by someone standing in the way — the device moving the connection would be dropped after 20 or 30 seconds and the transfer would have to be started again. In a modern office, this type of set-up would be far from ideal.

Along came Bluetooth; instead of using infrared, it uses radio waves to transmit, the obvious advantage being that direct line of vision between the two devices does not need to kept constant. As long as the two devices are within about 10 metres of each other, they can communicate.

Bluetooth will allow you to have intelligent devices that will be able to communicate effortlessly with each other via radio signals. Imagine, as you meet a new client your wearable computer and his could exchange all your documentation without the need to copy disks, etc.

One of the first such intelligent devices will be mobile phones. Ericsson were among the first to produce a Bluetooth device in their t28 mobile phone. They have introduced the first true hands- and wire-free kit for their phone. By use of a headset within 10 metres of the phone, you can make (by voice recognition dialling) and answer calls. As you can imagine, this should lead to safer phone use, as fewer wires, especially when driving, will lead to fewer problems.

Zdnet UK ran an article about Bluetooth[1] and mobile phones. It seems that if manufacturers have their way, the mobile phone will be at the centre of the communications revolution. Your mobile will soon be able to talk to other devices in your house. You will be able to program the video recorder, open the garage door and control all devices from that little phone! They further go on to say that you may be able to use your phone to purchase goods. You simply point your phone, which would have your credit card details stored on it, at the cash register, press a button and, bang, the product has been paid for.

---

[1] http://www.zdnet.co.uk/news/2000/24/ns-16046.html

Smart Houses

More and more houses will come networked and wired for the Internet. I heard of an apartment block in Texas that was sold on the merit it that it had T1 connections into each apartment, which gave superb Internet access. The whole apartment was wired for networking!

Houses will begin to have this facility, and once wired up the owner will be able to control the house from their desktop. This will become standard, again due to Bluetooth technology.

Bluetooth technology will be inserted, via a chip, into many household devices. It is estimated that by 2005 there will 670 million Bluetooth-enabled devices. This means that many of the objects we have in our house are going to become "intelligent". When I point my Personal Digital Assistant at the phone, it will automatically synchronise my address book on the phone and on the PDA. As I walk through the door, my computer will be able to synchronise files that I have stored on my laptop.

IBM ran a very good advertising campaign in which a repairman knocks on the door of a house; when the door opens, the owner of the house is surprised to see the repairman there. The repairman says he is there to fix the refrigerator; she is puzzled, as she never called them. What has happened is that the refrigerator sent out the call to be repaired *before* it broke! There is already talk of a refrigerator that will scan all produce as it is placed in it and then the refrigerator will be able to tell you what is out of date, what recipes you could prepare with the food it has stored, suggest reordering products, etc.

Of course, the obvious problem here is that if your house is networked and can be controlled via the Internet or your mobile phone, what if a virus gets into the system? If your household applications can be controllable via the Internet, the danger is that someone will find out your password, "hack" their way into your house and destroy it! No system is completely secure. Imagine being told your house had performed an illegal operation and would be shut down! Perhaps the old style bricks and mortar are better for now . . .

Digital TV

Sky TV in the UK have been promoting digital TV heavily for the last year. One of the advantages of delivering data in a digital format is that more channels can be received than ever before, while clarity and sound also improve. Another advantage, perhaps more relevant to our look at the Internet, is that programs can become more interactive, allowing you, for example, to change the camera angle for sports events; when watching replays, you can see the action from different angles. Video on demand will also be available; you can order videos and receive them through your digital box. There are also many value-added services. You can purchase products, do your banking, etc.

One problem with digital TV is that it is too region-specific. For example, if Irish users are to get access to Sky Digital, will the cable provider localise the services offered, such as online banking and online shopping, to cater for the Irish market? The advantage of the web is the global nature of it. This may not be the case with digital TV.

In the future, there may be no need to access the web through a computer; it may all be done via your television. At the moment, you see an ad for a website, but you must physically go to your computer, boot it up, log onto the Internet, remember the website address, type it in — a rather laborious process to say the least. Now imagine seeing an ad on TV for a product; at the press of a button, you could access the website of the company. This may increase the likelihood of the user purchasing the product.

Digital TV will also appeal to technophobes. If users who were afraid of computers, or even those who felt they had no need to use a computer, knew they could access the Internet through their television, they may be more inclined to use it.

Unfortunately, some types of Internet usage, such as pagers, some chat programs, flash-enabled sites or any other content that may need to be downloaded, may not work with these access devices. The same applies to WebTV (discussed in Chapter 3). Most of these programs must be installed and run on a computer before they can be used. Web designers will need to take this into account, or developers of access devices will need to plan on how such technologies will be displayed when encountered.

Web Design

One thing that will certainly happen is that the web will become even more interactive, with more multimedia-rich websites. Sites will talk to you, have live video of cinematic quality and other mind-blowing effects.

There are two problems here. Firstly, as we get faster access to the net, designers will be tempted to create more and more complex sites; eventually we will get to a situation like we have now — the net will become slow again. Secondly, and more importantly, many sites may actually deteriorate in quality. Web authors will be too concerned about how the site looks and may lose track of the actual content.

Remember that for a website to succeed, one of the most important qualities it must have is content. At the end of the day, that is why your visitor is there. A clever designer will combine both aesthetics with excellent content.

Electronic Payments, Digital Cash and Smart Cards

So what will be the future of e-commerce? Certainly, the volume of commercial transactions over the Internet will continue to increase. But the outstanding problem, which will block further growth, is the issue of finding an efficient, secure payment system. Such a system will depend on improvements in security. But in the meantime, there are a number of innovative solutions being proposed so that users will not have to risk having their credit card information stolen every time they try to buy something on the web.

For example, small retailers who wish to sell cheap information-based goods — say, a search engine selling reports or short documents — often find that charging less than a couple of dollars for a report is not worth it. However, their users find reports costing more than a few dollars too expensive. The solution has to be to find a way to let people pay small amounts (say 50 cents) for items. There are two options available:

❖ The search engine/company could ask users to register and buy credit in blocks of $25 or more;

❖ Digital cash could be used.

Digital cash is a way of storing money electronically on your computer. Amounts can be deducted automatically from your hard drive by the merchant when necessary. Digital cash in some form will revolutionise websites and purchasing online. Using digital cash, you gain a number of advantages:

❖ Anonymity

❖ Micro Payments.

When you use your credit card, the merchant finds information out about you; this is true either online or in the real world. When you use cash, a merchant knows nothing about you at all.

At the moment, large sites are able to keep a record of what you buy on the Internet and then use that to send junk e-mail to you. Digital cash should be like real cash — completely anonymous. The funds are transferred from one system to the other without the merchant or anyone else finding out any details about you.

Micro payments are another important aspect of e-commerce. When you go into a shop, you pay for small items, such as newspapers, sweets, etc., with cash. You would not use your credit card to pay for these items, while the shop would not accept a credit card for payment of an item costing less than a couple of pounds.

Digital cash would have this feature built in; users could purchase small items over the Internet without problems. This would be useful for websites offering information-rich goods such as reports, short documents, etc. Another use would be for downloading music from the Internet; an artist could charge 90 cents or less per track from their album.

Smart cards are another current development. These are the same size as a credit card, but they contain a chip which can store far more information than a credit card. A smart card is like a mini-wallet in the sense that it would, like digital cash, be used for micro-payments. You would load, say, £50 onto your card from your bank account, use it to pay for newspapers, books, etc., and top it up as needed. It is not, as such, an Internet technology in the sense that smart cards will initially only be usable "offline" — i.e. in ordinary shops — but it has been proposed to make them compatible with computers, so that the user would swipe the card through a device attached to or built into their computer; it would then become like digital cash.

It has been proposed that smart cards could be used not just as cash alternatives, but also to store all sorts of information, such as social security numbers, loyalty points, medical information, etc. However, there have been a number of trials of smart cards in various places in Europe, so far without much success. It seems that many people just don't feel the need for change, at least not yet!

One Irish company has come up with an alternative solution. Orbiscom (www.orbiscom.com) have introduced virtual throwaway credit cards! The key to this service is that your credit card information never travels across the Internet. The only institution that has a record of your credit card is your bank.

When you wish to buy a product, you log onto your bank's online banking service; the Orbiscom software will then generate a virtual credit card number, which is a 16-digit alternative to your real number. This number will then be passed to the merchant. From this point on, the transaction proceeds as normal, the merchant gets paid as per normal, and you get your goods safe in the knowledge that your credit card details are secure. Using this system, you can declare that the virtual number can only be used a certain number of times or only for a certain amount.

The key benefit is that no merchant will ever know your real credit card number; if they try to use your virtual card number, it will be detected immediately, as the number will no longer be valid, or was only valid for a certain amount. The current problem with credit card purchasing via the net is that if you visit and purchase goods from 15 different websites, each merchant will hold a record of your name, address and credit card number. Thus it is 15 times more possible that your credit card could be used for a fraudulent transaction. With the Orbiscom software, only your bank will have your details.

Orbiscom assure the public that this is the most secure way of using your credit card online. Other technologies such as cyber cash or cyber cheques have not really been very successful or widespread. One of the reasons may very well be that you must have a credit card in order to buy the cyber cash — defeating the purpose. If you are not willing to use your credit card on the Internet, how do you buy your cyber cash?

M-commerce and W-commerce

Companies will find every way possible to get money out of you; thus, m-commerce (mobile commerce) or w-commerce (WAP-commerce) is being introduced. By using your WAP-enabled phone, you will be able to visit sites and purchase goods. Whether this will really take off is another story. So far, any application using WAP takes so long either to appear on screen or to type out that it would seem easier to wait until you get back to the office or simply to phone your order in to the particular company. Yes, it is wonderful to be able to check your bank balance online, check your auction biddings, etc., but until the phones can access the information faster and the phones become easier to type on, this type of application is very ambitious.

The idea of "Internet in your pocket" will really only come about when more telephones are produced with bigger screens and possibly keyboards. Samsung and Motorola are already producing such phones for other markets. The phone will be bigger but will function as a Personal Digital Assistant as well as a phone. When this becomes more mainstream, the ideal of Internet in your pocket will become a reality.

Online Banking

Although very much a present-day product, more and more people, as they get connected, will begin to realise the ease with which they can conduct their banking business online. Will this mean an end to traditional banks? Well, we have seen recent closures, both in the UK and Ireland, of many smaller branches countrywide.

A few e-banks have been set up with no physical locations; all their business is conducted via the web. This is fine, but leads to two obvious problems:

❖ Lodging your money;

❖ Withdrawing your money.

In order to lodge money, you will need to be able to use the lodgement services of another bank. In order to withdraw money, you will have to use the ATM of a competing bank. As you can imagine, this is where charges will be incurred, since you have to use a third party bank for such essential services. I can't really see such banks becoming very popular; rather, we will see the main banks offering more and more services via the web, such as loan applications, mortgage applications, etc.

Before online banking becomes a dominant force, however, there is one thing that will need a major upgrade: security. We have already seen how a leading bank in England had problems with users being able to view other users' accounts online. Any small incident like this will undermine months or years of work that has been done to reassure customers on how safe the service is.

So how could security be improved? Biometrics could well be the answer — using parts of the body to identify the person. Using a biometric solution, which already has been implemented in some buildings, people can be identified in a number of ways:

* ❖ **Retina identification**: An image of your eye is scanned by a harmless ray of light, and if the pattern matches the pattern stored on disk, you are allowed entry.

* ❖ **Fingerprint identification**: The same procedure applies, except that you place either your hand of one finger on a touch pad, that will verify you are how you say you are.

* ❖ **Voice recognition**: By repeating a certain phrase, your voice will be analysed to see if it matches the sample on computer.

Another possibility is genetic identification, but this will rely on developments in a different area of science! All of these methods of identification seem to work, since they are unique to everyone. But how could they be applied to the online world? By developing and attaching small devices to a user's computer and then using encrypted transmission procedures, there is no reason why such verification could not be sent over the Internet. Thus, instead of logging in with a password and username, which anyone could find out, it will all be done, for example, by placing your finger on a small touch pad. Many companies are already looking at this technology as ways to protect both themselves and consumers.

Smart Applications

In the future, applications will become smarter. I include search engines as an "application" here in the sense that you are accessing their database software. As the web has developed, search engines have become more intelligent in that they are now able to bring up related search words or suggestions that may be of interest to you. A search engine can trawl through thousands of sites and find what you want in seconds.

What would be of interest is search engines that are personalised for your searching tastes; as you search, they would record a list of things you have looked for. As soon as you revisit their website, results would be displayed for new websites that may be of interest of you.

This technology should not be far away; Amazon, although not a search engine, already uses this technology. As you browse and buy books, it makes recommendations based on previous purchases and displays them for you. It makes great use of its database. When it sees that you have requested or bought a book by Stephen King, it will recommend books that others who bought that book also bought.

A similar application, mytv, is hosted by ireland.com. This application allows you to set up your viewing tastes and make a record of what you like and don't like. The more you use the service, the more the service learns about you and will then make recommendations on what it thinks you might like to see. The service works by using basic artificial intelligence that allows it to make decisions based on your past choices.

Publishing: E-books and Print on Demand

The idea of publishing a book electronically is not new; in fact they have been available and talked about for about two years. So why is it only now that people seem to have heard of e-books? Two words: Stephen King. Yes, that famous author has made the leap from traditional book author to e-book author with the Internet-only release of his book *Riding the Bullet*, over 400,000 copies of which have been downloaded. He charged $2.50 per copy; even at this price, many pirated copies were placed on the net! It seems some people will never be happy to pay, no matter how cheap they are. At the time of going to press, his new novel, *The Plant*, is being made available for download by instalments — about 5,000 words per instalment for a price of $1.

For many, reading a book off a computer screen is less than appealing, so they have to print it out; of course, the cost and hassle of printing out the book may be as much as buying the fully bound book! In my experience, e-books are good low-cost alternatives for authors who cannot get published or perhaps wish to market, sell and keep the profits from their endeavours. Certainly, more kudos has been given by this one publication by Stephen King than all the advertising and lobbying e-book authors have done to try to get e-books accepted.

E-books can come in a number of formats. Firstly, they can be created in HTML and packed in a special browser. This allows the author to take full control of the book and make it fully interactive and multimedia-based — anything you can do in a normal website can be done in this type of e-book. The second and probably more popular way is to create it in Adobe Acrobat and distribute this way. Indeed, Adobe have introduced ways of providing e-book publishers with increased security and means of selling these books via the net. Check Adobe's website for more information on this; alternatively, check the website accompanying this book, www.internetdemystified.com, for links to e-book publishing software. Microsoft, not to be left out, have introduced Microsoft Reader, a software program you can download for free that can be installed on your computer and using special technology will give you very clear text on the screen.

For the most part, e-books are read from your computer, either in standard browser format or by downloading Acrobat Reader. But what about bookworms who must read while on the move? But for the ultimate bookworm, there is the Rocket eBook, a hand held device that can store around 20–30 books that can be read while on the move. The device is pocket-sized and allows you to connect to your PC and download e-books from the net. Unfortunately, you can only download books de-signed for the Rocket eBook hardware. At around $269, it is quite expensive considering how many "real" books you could get for that price! Also, many people still prefer to have the feel of the book; not only this, but as we know many people read more slowly off a screen and would find it annoying to use such a device! Such devices have had little impact in Europe but seem to be gaining more popularity in the US.

The latest innovation being used in the publishing and printing industries is Print on Demand. Bookshops often find that they buy large quantities of books that don't sell, which therefore take up valuable shelf space. These books are then returned to publishers and take up valuable storage space in their warehouse!

The solution? For books that may not sell in large quantities, only print them when needed. When a user orders a copy of a book, that book can be downloaded from a computer system, printed out and bound in a matter of minutes. Usually, the difference in quality between a print-on-demand book and an ordinary book is very small. Currently in the US, it is possible to buy the necessary equipment for around $40,000 — quite an investment for a small printer, but in the long term it could save money.

Other industries that would benefit are companies that produce training manuals. Instead of having to print a large number of manuals, they can print enough to keep them going until more are needed.

The Music Industry

The future of the music industry? Well, at this stage, it's anyone's guess! As we go to press, the Napster case (see Chapter 11) is still unresolved; they are allowed to continue their service pending their court case in September.

Using special hardware and software, musicians can now connect with each other and have a virtual music session, each one playing an instrument and the results being broadcast through their speakers! As connections improve and speed increases, we will see more sites, such as www.rocketnetwork.com, that allow users to "jam" over the Internet.

Digital compression and distribution of music will still be possible, but it is likely that methods of encryption will be found so that only music bought by an individual can be used on a single computer. Tracks with adverts will become the norm, although at the moment it is still possible to "rip" CDs and save them in MP3 format.

It would seem that, no matter what industry we look at, the need for increased security is paramount. If people are to distribute their goods and services electronically, they must be able to ensure that it is not possible to crack or pirate their goods. Otherwise, the software industry will suffer, the music industry will suffer and the e-book industry will suffer. Why would I create an e-book and distribute it online if I know that it will be pirated and I will make no money on it? I have to be sure that it is secure and safe and that I will make money from it. Artists of all forms need to be reassured that their copyright will be protected.

As more and more people and companies are taking legal action for various incidents happening on the net, we will see more laws being implemented that provide for global acceptance of Internet activities and the consequences when they are not adhered to. The biggest stumbling block is jurisdiction and implementation of laws.

Future Society

The 1980s and 1990s brought us couch potatoes; are we now seeing a new generation of mouse potatoes? As we saw in Chapter 13, Internet addiction is now a problem and certainly could become a bigger problem as everything becomes wired and available on the net. As we get faster, cheaper, permanent connections, more people may spend more and more time online.

Employees will become more reliant on e-mail to communicate. Companies who don't have or can't use email may find business markets closing up. Will we become a society of information haves and have nots? This is certainly one aspect of the future that worries me.

I remember a movie that I saw years ago called *Sneakers*, which told the story of hackers who were hired to test security of business networks; one line in particular stuck in my mind and that was that, in this day and age, **Information is Power**. Information empowers businesses; those that can get the latest fund information, the latest stock market news, the latest anything relating to business, will have the advantage over smaller businesses.

What about education? In my own experience with the students whom I teach, those with access to computers at home do better, in most cases, than those without. In secondary and primary education, students who have access to CD-ROM encyclopaedias may be able to get more information for projects than those who do not. Research on the Internet will help students find out more information than those who do not have access to it. But there is also a downside to this. Students may lose the ability to write and think for themselves; they can simply copy and paste information straight from websites into a Word document! Creative thinking may suffer; less work will be put into assignments. Work is sometimes handed in that the teacher is certain was copied off the Internet, but how can they prove it? The Internet being so vast, it is very difficult to find each and every extract of information.

As for society in general, the Internet is here to stay and will become more integrated into our lives and into the devices that we use. More intelligent devices will hopefully mean a better world where people will be more informed and safer. The distinction between computers and television and Internet access will blur even further.

Faster electronic communication will mean that everyone can have a part to play in the future. People in power are now becoming more accessible via e-mail and websites. Being informed is the key. Everyone needs to know what is going on around them regarding the technology and its uses. Like all technologies, there will be those who use it wisely and those who use it for profit and personal gain.

Future society is being moulded as we speak; we as citizens of the present can make the changes that will make the future a better, more harmonious place.

Glossary

3-click rule
A "rule" in web design stating that people should be able to find the information they want from your website within three clicks of the mouse.

active content
Any content that updates after a web page has downloaded onto your screen. Animations, Flash movies, Java applets are all examples of active content.

add-on
A small program that adds extra functionality to a program; similar in ways to a plug-in.

address
(i) The unique location (URL) of any file or web page; (ii) in terms of e-mail, a unique way of contacting a user.

address book
A folder for storing e-mail addresses and contact details of people that you contact on a regular basis.

applet
See Java applet.

application
Any program that is used on a computer; common Internet applications are browsers, e-mail clients, etc.

ARPA
Advanced Research Project Agency. The agency that was set up in response to the launch of the Sputnik satellite. ARPAnet became the first working network that would lead to the eventual development of the Internet.

ASCII
American Standard Code for Information Interchange. Documents saved in ASCII are often referred to as text files, as they contain no formatting and should be readable by any word processing or other such application on any OS.

attachment
Any document or file attached to an e-mail..

AUP
Acceptable Usage Policy. A policy documenting what is acceptable use of company equipment; especially important for companies that allow users access to the Internet, World Wide Web and e-mail.

autocomplete
A facility in both Internet Explorer and Outlook Express that will automatically attempt to complete web and e-mail addresses as you type them.

autoresponder
A server-based utility that will automatically send a pre-prepared automated e-mail as a reply to a user's request.

B2B
Business to Business. The term used to describe the selling of services and products by one business to another, characterised by high quantity and low price.

B2C
Business to Consumer. The term used to describe the selling of services and products to consumers, characterised by low quantity and higher price.

backbone
The main cable that carries Internet traffic. The user connects into the backbone of your ISP, who along with other ISPs connect into a larger backbone.

bandwidth
The amount of data that can be transferred within a fixed amount of time. Bandwidth speed is affected by the number of users using the same network at any one time.

banner ads
Ads placed on web pages to advertise a service or product. When clicked, they will take the user to the website of the advertiser.

beta
An "unfinished" or trial version of a program, sent out to testers, often actual consumers, who do a final test to ensure the product is working correctly. Beta testers will record problems and suggest improvements to the manufacturer.

binary file
A name used for any file such as a program or image.

bit
A binary digit that represents either a 0 or 1. Eight bits make up one byte, which is equal to one letter or character. See BPS.

Bluetooth

The latest technology that allows small personal wireless radio networks to exist to enable small devices to communicate with each other.

bookmarks

A way of recording Internet addresses so that the user can access the sites at a later date. See favorites.

Boolean

In relation to search engines, the user can use such words as AND (or plus sign) and AND NOT (or minus sign) to include or exclude words in their search.

boot

(i) In the context of chat rooms, to boot means to remove a person from the chat room; (ii) to start your computer.

BPS

Bits Per Second. The unit of measurement for modem speeds. A standard modem can transfer 56,000 bits (56KB) per second.

browse

The act of using the web and moving from one page to another.

browser

A piece of software that allows the user to view HTML pages. The best known browsers are Netscape Navigator and Internet Explorer.

bus

A type of network topology. In a bus network, each computer is connected to the next. If one computer gets disconnected from the network all computers go down.

byte

A collection of eight bits. One byte equals one character.

cache

An area on your hard disk where frequently visited pages are stored.

centralised network

A network design where one central computer controls everything, including all processing, often used for mainframes.

CGI

Common Gateway Interface. Any program or script that accepts input from a web page and then processes the information on the web server and returns the results as a web page – mainly programmed in a language called PERL.

chat handle

A nickname that a user uses to identify themselves in a chat room.

chat monitor
A person who monitors the conversations taking place in a chat room and has the power to boot users who are flooding or causing problems.

circuit switching
A way of communicating in which a person gets a dedicated line or circuit for the duration of their communication; similar to the telephone system. The opposite of packet switching.

click-through
The number of times a banner ad is clicked on by website visitors.

client
A computer that requests information from another computer or server.

Client-side scripting
Scripting, such as Javascript, that is executed on the client's computer, after the page has downloaded.

client/server model
The network model that the Internet is based on, as are many networks. Every computer that provides services, such as printing or serving up of web pages, is called a server. Those computers that connect to the server are called clients.

contacts
A list of e-mail addresses that you use frequently.

cookie
A small text file that a server places on your hard drive in order to help personalise your visit to their site the next time you visit.

crippled
Software that has certain key functions, such as printing and saving, disabled.

CUE
Commercial Unsolicited E-mail. E-mail sent out in bulk advertising a product or service, which the recipient did not request.

cyberspace
The term, coined by William Gibson, to describe the virtual space or area that is created by computers. Much communication and interaction happens in this non-physical world.

cyber-terrorists
People who use the Internet to launch attacks on websites or networks to cause disruption and possible damage to businesses or governments.

decentralised network

A network design where a number of smaller sub-networks link in at various points to a server.

decryption

The process of unscrambling a message that has been encrypted. In order to decrypt a message you need to have a key that allows you to unscramble the message.

dedicated line

Another name for a leased line.

deleted items

A folder where items you have deleted are stored until you empty the folder.

device drivers

Programs that set up and allow devices such as printers and scanners to connect and work with your computer.

DHCP

Dynamic Host Configuration Protocol. The protocol that automatically assigns an IP address to a user when they connect to the network.

dial-up

The process of ringing up and connecting to the network, usually through an ISP. Compare with dedicated line.

directory

An area on a computer's hard drive where related files are stored; also called a folder.

discussion board

A facility on a website that allows users to read and post messages to each other. Discussion boards can be moderated or unmoderated.

distributed network

A network, like the Internet, where all tasks are distributed among many computers. No one computer has full control.

distribution list

A list of e-mail addresses, particularly used in marketing, which is used to send an e-mail to a number of different users.

document management system

A system that allows the user to scan in documents and have them automatically indexed and categorised.

domain name
An alphanumeric name that represents a server on the Internet; for example, in the URL *www.internetdemystified.com*, internetdemystified is the domain name.

domain name server
A server that finds the IP numbers that corresponds with a domain name.

domain name system
The system that matches IP numbers and domain names.

domain speculation
The process whereby a person buys a domain name and hopes that the name can be sold in the future for huge profits.

dotcom
The buzzword given to describe "virtual" companies that exist only in cyber-space.

download
Transferring files from one computer to another; specifically, copying files from a server to a local computer.

draft
An e-mail message that is not completely finished.

dragging and dropping
The method of clicking and holding the mouse button on an icon or filename and then moving the icon to another location, by dragging.

DSL
Digital Subscriber Line. A very fast connection method to the Internet.

dumb terminal
A computer monitor and keyboard attached to a larger computer, particularly a mainframe. All processing is done on the server and none is done on the local computer.

e-commerce
The act of buying and selling over the Internet.

e-mail
Electronic mail. The process of sending messages from one computer to another via a network, usually the Internet, or one such message.

encryption
The process of scrambling a message or electronic transmission so that if intercepted it cannot be read. In order to read the message, the receiver of the message must decrypt it.

external modem

A modem that is connected to a computer via the serial or parallel port.

fake user interface

A method used in banner advertising to simulate a dialog box so that the user is tricked into clicking on it.

FAQ

Frequently Asked Questions. A file or web page that details questions and answers that visitors to a website commonly ask either about the site or product.

favorites

A way of recording websites that interest you. Netscape calls favorites book marks.

favourware

A variation of freeware whereby the author will ask the user to do them a favour if they use the software.

file

Any document, program or image on a computer.

filter

A method of restricting certain content from being downloaded to your computer.

firewall

A way of protecting your computer system from unauthorised access, usually through software or a combination of hardware, software and user policy.

flame

An insulting message, often a personal attack, posted on a newsgroup or a discussion board. Can lead to a flame war, where users insult each other back and forth.

flooding

Sending endless streams of text to a chat room repeatedly so that the screen scrolls very quickly, thus disrupting the flow of conversation.

folder

An area on your hard drive where related files are kept, also referred to as a directory.

follow-up

A reply to a message on a particular topic posted on a discussion board.

freeware

Software that is free to download and use. The author does not request any payment for its use.

FTP

File Transfer Protocol. The protocol used to transfer files from one computer to another.

gateway

A way of connecting two different networks together, usually through a combination of hardware and software.

GIF

Graphics Interchange Format. A way of saving images so that they are highly compressed for use on the web.

GUI

Graphical User Interface. A way of interacting with a computer operating system by using a mouse, icons and pointers. Instead of typing in commands to execute programs a user can click on an icon. Windows is an example of a GUI.

guestbook

A page on a website that allows a user to leave comments, which are then automatically posted to the website.

hack

A clever trick that alters or improves a program so that it does something other than what it was originally programmed to do.

hacker

A person who hacks. In modern times, hackers are seen as people who try to circumvent the security of a company's website/network.

harvesting software

Software that is used to find and record e-mail addresses from web pages, usually to spam users.

header

With regard to e-mail, the header details where the e-mail was sent from, including the ISP's server name, IP address, etc.

helper applications

Similar to plug-ins.

history

A list of all websites and web pages within those sites which you have visited over a certain period.

hits

In search engine terminology, the number of results that are returned from a search query.

homepage

(i) The very first page that appears in your browser when you start it up; (ii) the page that appears when you click on the Home button; (iii) the first page of any website.

host

(i) Sometimes used interchangeably with the word "server"; (ii) in relation to web addresses, the host is the part before the domain name, usually www.

hosting

When a website is located on a web server; dedicated hosting is where the website owner purchases all the equipment and server software; virtual hosting is where they lease space on someone else's server.

HTML

HyperText Mark-up Language. The language used to create web pages.

HTTP

Hyper Text Transfer Protocol. The protocol used to transfer web pages over the Internet.

HTTPS

Secure HTTP; if a website begins with https: it means that any information sent from that website is encrypted.

hub

A central point that all computers on a star network connect into. If the hub goes down, the whole network goes down.

hyperlink

Links web pages to other pages, documents or files.

hypermedia

Different forms of media, including video and sound files, which are linked together through web pages containing hyperlinks.

hypertext

Text that is linked together by means of hyperlinks.

IMPs

Interface Message Processors. The original computers that were set up to help route traffic and do mundane tasks on the network.

inbox

A folder in an e-mail program that stores all new and read messages.

install

To put a program onto your computer so that it will work.

instant messages
In chat rooms and on pagers, these are messages that are directed specifically to one user.

interactive form
A form on a web page that allows the user to send feedback, comments or requests back to the website authors or to a certain department.

internal modem
A modem that is installed inside a computer.

Internet
The network that allows worldwide communication between computers. The Internet is the infrastructure while e-mail and the World Wide Web are applications that use the Internet to communicate.

Internet Explorer
Microsoft's program for browsing the web.

interpreted language
A computer programming language that is executed line by line when the program is run. Most commonly seen in scripting languages such as JavaScript.

IP
Internet Protocol, used in conjunction with TCP.

IP numbers
A unique number given to every computer that connects to a network running TCP/IP. In order to connect to the Internet, the user must have an IP number, which is usually assigned automatically by an ISP.

IRC
Internet Relay Chat. The original chat program that took the Internet by storm in the late 1980s.

IRC client
A program used to connect up to IRC servers; the most common one is mIRC.

ISDN
Integrated Services Data Network. A digital phone line that provides faster access to the Internet and allows the user to surf and use a phone at the same time.

ISP
Internet Service Provider. A company that allows the user to become part of their network so that they can surf the net.

Java

A fully featured programming language, Java is unique in that it is platform independent. Anything coded in Java can be run on any type of computer, as long as they have the Java Virtual Machine installed.

Java applet

A small program written in Java that is run from within a web browser.

JavaScript

A scripting language that extends the functionality of HTML. JavaScript and Java are completely different, the former being a scripting language and the latter being a full-blown programming language.

JPEG/JPG

Joint Photographic Experts Group. A method of saving and compressing photographic images that have millions of colours.

keymaker

An illegal program used to register software.

keyword

A word entered into a search engine to find a particular topic.

killer application

A revolutionary application that changes the course of computing. Mosaic was heralded as the killer app of the 1990s.

LAN

Local Area Network. A network used to connect computers within a certain radius. For example, all computers connected to the same network in an office or in a whole building would make up a local area network.

leased line

A fast, permanent connection to the Internet that is leased on a yearly basis (usually) from an ISP.

links

Also called hyperlinks, these are words (often underlined), icons or images, usually on a web page, that when clicked on bring the user to another page.

lurking

Reading messages on a discussion board without making a contribution or saying nothing in a chat room.

macro virus

A virus that usually attaches itself to Word or Excel documents and can cause various problems.

mainframe
A central computer that has dumb terminals connected to it. All processing is done on the mainframe and not on the local machine.

mark-up language
A language that uses tags to tell a browser or application how to display content on a page. The most common mark-up language is HTML.

m-commerce
Mobile commerce. Allowing commercial transactions to take place on mobile devices such as WAP-enabled telephones.

meta search engines
Search engines that pass a query to numerous search engines and collate the results.

meta tags
Special HTML code that when used correctly can achieve a higher rating on search engines.

Milnet
The network that carries military traffic.

MIME
Multipurpose Internet Mail Extensions. Allows users to send video, sound and images in their e-mails. With MIME-compatible e-mail clients, the sound/video or image will automatically appear in the message.

mirror
An exact copy of a website hosted on another server. If a website is very popular it may be mirrored to other servers to try to spread the load of traffic.

modem
A device that converts digital signals from a computer into analogue signals that are passed down telephone lines and reconverted into digital signals at the receiving computer.

moderated
Used when talking about discussion boards (implies that postings are checked and edited) and chat rooms (implies that the chat room is supervised).

Mosaic
One of the first graphic browsers used to surf the web.

MP3
A way of compressing music digitally yet still retaining CD quality output.

MP3 player

A device like a personal stereo that allows a user to download MP3 files onto them and listen to them.

MP3 rippers

Illegal programs that allow a user to copy CD tracks onto their hard drive and convert them into MP3 format.

MPEG

Moving Picture Experts Group. A method of digitally encoding video that produces high quality video sequences.

nag screen

A screen that appears until you purchase and register a piece of software.

netiquette

The "rules" one should follow when using the Internet. Many of the rules pertain to e-mail and newsgroup postings.

Netscape Navigator

Netscape's web browser; for many years the dominant and most widely used web browser, now has been superseded by Microsoft's Internet Explorer.

network

Any number of computers connected together that share resources.

network-aware

Programs or devices that can use the network for updates, etc.

network card

A card inserted into a computer that allows it to join a network.

newbie

A new user of the Internet or a newsgroup.

newsgroups

The original discussion boards, but located on servers worldwide. They are a distributed system, every server updates its newsgroups from another server.

newsgroup reader

A program whose sole function is to allow a user to read and post to newsgroups. Some programs like Outlook Express have built-in readers.

nickname

A name used to represent a user. E-mail packages allow you to set up contacts and assign a nickname which makes it easier to address emails. Nicknames are also used in chat rooms to allow people to conceal their real identity.

NNTP
Network News Transfer Protocol. The protocol used to receive newsgroups on a computer.

node
A point on a network.

non-web-based
Any activity that is not initiated from a web page, such as pager programs.

NSFnet
National Science Foundation Network. Allowed ordinary academic users to access the ARPAnet but also became the backbone to the Internet.

offline
When a computer is not connected to the Internet it is said to be offline.

online
When a computer is connected to the Internet it is said to be online.

online communities
Websites or servers where people with the same ideas meet to discuss topics.

Open Source Movement
A movement that promotes the distribution of the source code (programming code) of software. Users are free to download the source code and make alterations, provided others can download the altered source code and make changes to it too. Linux, a free OS, is part of this open source movement.

operating system
The core program that makes a computer run. Common operating systems include Windows, Mac OS, UNIX.

opt-in subscribers
A method of conducting e-mail marketing in a professional manner; people who have indicated they wish to receive e-mails from a particular company.

outbox
A folder in an e-mail program where e-mails are stored before being sent out.

Outlook Express
An e-mail package that comes bundled with Internet Explorer.

packet
A piece of data that when combined with other packets make up a message or file.

packet switching

A system whereby data can be broken up into packets and sent over the network via different routes; the packets go from one computer to the next until they reach their destination. Once at their destination, they are re-assembled.

pager

An application that allows the user to chat and send messages to other users of the same software.

password

A secret string of text or numbers that allows the user to access services.

patches

(i) Small programs that fix problems with commercially released programs. Patches can usually be downloaded from the manufacturer's website. (ii) Illegal programs that convert trial version copies of software into full version software.

pay-per-click

When advertising on a website, many advertisers will pay the website only when a user has clicked on their ad. Contrast with pay-per-impression.

pay-per-impression

Every time an ad is displayed, the advertiser is charged.

payload

The effect a virus has on a computer system.

PERL

Practical Extraction and Report Language. A server-side scripting language used to create interactive content on the web. Many programs such as discussion boards are programmed in PERL.

Phreaking

An illegal method of circumventing the security measures of telephone companies in order to gain free calls for Internet connection.

ping

A way of testing a network connection. A ping program sends out a packet to a server and records the response and how long it took the packet to arrive and get sent back.

plug-in

A small program that literally plugs itself into a browser and is launched when certain content is accessed.

POP

Points of presence. Local numbers used by ISPs to allow users to dial in at a local rate from any part of the country.

POP3
Post Office Protocol 3. The protocol used to receive e-mails.

portal
A site that offers the user a collection of resources and facilities based on the one site, such as news, free e-mail, chat, discussion boards, etc.

ports
A logical connection to a server. Each service running on a web server receives connections via different ports.

post
The action of writing a message and leaving in on a discussion board or newsgroup.

piracy
The illegal copying and use of copyrighted material, particularly software.

private key
In encryption, a user decrypts a message using their private key that no one else knows. See public key.

protocol
A set of rules by which computers can communicate.

proxy server
A server that acts on behalf of all other users on the network.

public domain
The status of any piece of software, text or clipart image that is free to copy or distribute without charge.

public key
In encryption, a user encrypts a message using their public key. See private key.

PUE
Personal Unsolicited Mail. E-mail that is sent to a user asking for a personal favour or request. Similar to chain letters.

real time
Anything, be it a chat room conversation or credit card transaction, that takes place immediately is said to be done in real time.

redundancy
Where equipment, usually a server, is available but is never used unless an emergency arises. Essential for the smooth operation of the Internet.

related searches

The ability that many search engines have to suggest other searches that may be relevant to what you are looking for.

RFC

Request For Comments. A document format, still in existence, used to propose new standards or changes in the Internet and its protocols, ensuring a democratic "open source" spirit as was intended from the early days of the ARPAnet.

robot

An automated program sent out by search engines to index and categorise websites and pages. Similar to a spider.

root directory

The main directory in the directory structure of a hard disk. If you have root directory access, it is possible to have complete access to the hard disk of a computer.

routers

Hardware devices that decide the best way to send a packet from one computer or network to another.

routing table

A list of the best and shortest possible ways to send packets between two networks.

sandbox

A segregated space on a computer's hard drive where Java applets are stored, to prevent them from interacting with your hard disk.

scripting language

A language that allows a programmer to add functionality to a program. A scripting language can only be run from within a program such as a browser. An example of a scripting language is JavaScript.

scrolling the screen

The act of flooding a chat room.

search

A facility on a website that allows the user to find information either on the website or on the World Wide Web.

search directory

A website that contains a database of websites that have been categorised by different topic headings and have been manually assessed by human editors.

search engine
A website that allows the user to search for topics solely by keywords. Web designers can submit their websites, which are automatically categorised and recorded by an automated program called a spider.

sent items
A folder in Outlook Express that contains all the e-mails you have sent out.

server
A computer that offers services to other computers (clients). On the Internet there are web servers, FTP servers and e-mail servers, to name but a few.

shareware
A method of distributing software that is free to use for a limited period, after which payment should be made to the author.

shortcuts
A method, used under Windows, that allows the user to click on an icon on their desktop or anywhere else on their computer that will run a program or open a file that is located somewhere else on the hard disk.

signature
A small piece of text added to the end of an e-mail or posting to a discussion board/newsgroup that usually contains contact details about the sender.

site map
A web page that gives a full list of every page on the website, which makes navigation easier for the user.

SMTP
Simple Mail Transfer Protocol. The protocol used to send mail from one computer to another.

spamming
The process of sending out unsolicited e-mails to a large list of users.

spider
An automated program used by search engines to automatically categorise and index websites and web pages.

spyware
Software installed on a computer whose sole purpose is to keep track of websites visited or products used. The information is then sent back to the parent company, who can build up information about the user's surfing habits.

star
A type of network topology where all computers are connected to a central device called a hub. If one computer goes down, the network does not fail as in the bus topology, but if the hub goes down the whole network goes down.

store and forward
The technique used by e-mail where information is stored on a server and then forwarded on to the next stop. In essence, this happens very quickly but all e-mail will eventually stored on the ISP's server until the user decides to collect it.

storyboarding
A method of mapping out each web page and illustrating what it will look like before it is created; helps authors and programmers visualise their website.

streaming
A way of delivering audio and video content in one continuous flow without the need to wait until the whole file has downloaded.

sub-directory
A directory that is created within another directory.

submit
A button or icon at the end of a form that sends the form or comments made to the server.

tags
HTML instructions that tell the browser how to display items on a page, if they are to be displayed at all!

taskbar
On Windows 95 and later, the taskbar is the bar that contains the Start menu and shows all programs or tasks that are currently running.

TCP/IP
Transfer Control Protocol/Internet Protocol. The fundamental protocol that is needed to connect to the Internet. TCP ensures that packets are delivered correctly over the Internet, IP ensures that they are correctly addressed.

telephone lines
Many connections over the Internet are made by telephone lines, which can be either analogue connections are digital in the form of ISDN.

Telnet
Terminal Emulation. A program that allows the user to connect to a remote server and access services on that server as if you were sitting in front of it.

terminator
A device attached to the end of bus network that ensures that the data being sent knows where the network stops, otherwise the information will "fall off" the end of the network and will render network communications impossible.

thread
When a topic on a discussion board has a number of replies to the original topic, this is said to be a thread of conversation.

time restricted

In relation to software, time restriction means that you can only use the software for a certain length of time before it ceases to work.

time-shared

A system used in early computer models that allowed many users to share the computing power of a larger server. Each user would be allocated a time in which they could carry out their processing task.

timeout

After a certain length of time, if an e-mail client or browser cannot connect to a remote server it will timeout or basically give up!

TLA

Three Letter Acronyms. Used to save time when typing e-mails or chatting.

topology

The way in which a network is physically laid out.

transclusion

The ability to place a virtual copy of one document, or part of it, in another document, without the location of the original document changing.

transcript

A record of conversations that have taken place in a chat room or chat program. Transcripts may be kept so that offensive users can be banned.

trial version

A program, with certain functions restricted, that users can download and use for a particular length of time or a set number of times.

Trojan

A program that pretends to do one thing but in fact is doing something else. Many viruses come in Trojan form.

UNIX

An operating system used by a large number of web servers.

unmoderated

A chat room or discussion board that is not censored or edited.

upload

The process of transferring a file from a local computer to a remote server usually located on the Internet.

URL

Universal Resource Locator. Another name for a web address, a unique address for a resource, such as a web page, website, image, video, etc. on the Internet.

Usenet news
Another name for the newsgroup network.

username
A unique name that allows the user gain access to different resources on the Internet when used in conjunction with a password. On e-mail addresses, it is the part before the @ symbol.

UUCP
UNIX to UNIX Copy Protocol. The original protocol used to transfer news postings from one UNIX computer to another.

virtual hosting
For those who cannot afford to have their own dedicated server for their website, many companies will virtually host it on their servers.

virus
A malicious program whose only purpose is to cause destruction or disruption to your computer system. Viruses are very easily spread through e-mail.

VOIP
Voice Over IP. The facility enabling the transmission of voice over the Internet. The remote user does not need to have a computer, as their call is placed to their telephone handset.

vortals
Niche market portals that concentrate on one very specific aspect of a market or topic.

WAN
Wide Area Network. A network that is not contained in only one building. Companies may have a WAN that connects all regional offices. The best known WAN is the Internet itself.

WAP
Wireless Application Protocol. The protocol used to allow mobile devices, such as mobile phones, to connect to the web.

w-commerce
WAP commerce. As in m-commerce, the ability to use a mobile phone to engage in electronic commerce transactions.

web authoring
The process of creating a web page.

web-based
Any program or activity that is initiated from a web page.

web camera
A device connected to a computer that allows video images to be sent over the Internet.

webcast
A facility some radio stations and entertainment companies use to "broadcast" concerts over the web.

web pages
Individual pages within a website created using HTML.

website
A collection of web pages.

web tracker
A program that keeps track of the number of visitors to a website, where they came from, how they found the site, etc.

web bot
An automated piece of code in FrontPage that creates scrolling text, counters, etc., without the need to program them; require a server enabled with Front-Page extensions.

Windows
A GUI operating system introduced on PCs by Microsoft.

Winzip
An essential program to download; used to compress files.

word filter
In chat rooms, a word filter will removes objectionable words automatically and replaces them either with other words or simply with *****.

www
A TLA for World Wide Web, or sometimes World Wide Wait!

WYSIWYG
What You See Is What You Get. A type of web design package (the term originally comes from word processing/DTP packages) that allows a web author to work in such a way that what they see on screen is exactly how the page will look on the web.

Xanadu
Ted Nelson's revolutionary, but proprietary, idea for a system that would record and contain all information that could be accessed instantly. All information would be cross-linked.

Index

(Note: Page numbers in bold indicate illustrations)

Acrobat Reader 287–8, 369–70
address books 102–8
    distribution lists 104–8
addresses
    e-mail 70, 85–7
    web 123–47, 144–6
Adobe Acrobat *see* Acrobat Reader
Advanced Research Projects
    Agency *see* ARPA
Altavista 168
Amazon 230–1, 233–4, 238, 368–9
Andreessen, Marc 27–9
AOL 56–7, 66
ARPA 11–14
ARPAnet 7, 14, 19–23, 39, 69, 266–7
As We May Think 8
Atlantic Monthly 8
attachments 74, 76, 98–102
    viruses 98, 100–2, 297–9
auction sites 238–40, 339–40
autocomplete function 137–8
Autodesk 10

backbone 19, 23
bandwidth 52–3, 277
banking 367–8
banner advertising 139, 210–13
Baran, Paul 14–17, 37
Bellovin, Steve 267
Berners-Lee, Tim 25–7, 28, 30, 31
bits 49

Bluetooth 360–2
BNN 19–20
Boo 233–4
Boolean searches 166–7
browsers 27–30, 58–61, 278
    basics 123–47
    Internet Explorer 128–36
Bush, Vannevar 8–9, 25
business users 62–3
    equipment needed 63
    and Internet addiction 342–4
    leased lines 63
    multi-users 62
    rules 324–6
    security 64
    on the web 220–32
bytes 49

censorship 327–56
centralised systems 33–5
Centre for Net Addiction 339–40
Cerf, Vinton 21–2
CERN 25–7
chat rooms 250–9
    in e-commerce 229
    features 253–4
    Java 252
    Netmeeting 255
    problems and dangers 255–7,
      334–5
    real time 251

chat rooms (cont'd)
  redeeming features 258–9
  security 257–8
  types of 251–2
  versus Internet Relay Chat 260–1
  video chat 255
  where to find 252
child-safe search engines 352–4
childbrowser 350
Citrix Meta Frame 33–4
Clark, Jim 28–9
Clark, Welden 13
Communication Nets 17
CompuServe 56–7, 66
Computer Science Network 23
computers
  future of 357–60
  and Internet 47–8
  laptop 37
cookies 274–5, 347–8
copyright 306–7, 313–16, 371
crackers 302–7
credit card fraud 308–9
CSNET 23
cyber cafés 61, 65–6
cyber warfare 300–2
cyberchondria 344–5
cybersex 337–9
cyerstalking 345
CYPNET 20–1

Davies, Donald 14, 16, 37
decentralised systems 33–5
Dial-Up Connection 83
digital cash 364–6
Digital Payloads 292
digital TV 362–3
Direct Hit 170
directories 43, 157–60
discussion boards 247–50
  moderated and unmoderated 249
  technical support 249–50
  threads 248
distributed systems 33–5
distribution lists 104–8

document management systems 8
domain names 24, 40, 64, 125–6
  choosing 200–2
  registering 207–8
dotcoms 232–3
  branding and customer confi-
    dence 235–6
  secrets of success 233–5
downloading 277–91
  device drivers 284–5
  distribution 279–83
  free trials 278–9
  music 288–92
  patches and add-ons 284
  plug-ins 285–6
  shareware 279–82
  software 279–84
  viruses 283–4
DSL 51–2
Duke University 267
dumb terminals 12, 33

e-commerce 219–42
  affiliate programmes 230–1
  chat rooms 229
  credit card transactions 226–7
  customers 222
  dotcoms 232–3
  and e-mail 231–2
  Frequently Asked Questions 223
  future of 364
  order fulfilment 227–8
  pagers 229–30
  payment 225
  post-sales 228–9
  pre-sales 222–3
  pricing and competition 224–5
  products 221–2
  real-time processing 332–3
  strategy 220–32
  technical support 229–30
e-mail
  abbreviations 76
  abuse 311
  address books 102–8

addresses 70, 85–7
advanced techniques 97–122
attachments 74, 76, 98–102, 297–9
basic functions 77–89
business users 62–4, 231–2
checking for new 79–80
cost 70–1
creating new message 80–3
cyberstalking 96
dangers of 310–12
deleting messages 92–3
and e-commerce 231–2
early 12, 20–1
emoticons 76
faking 121–2
filters 108–10, 311–12
first message 20
formatting 115–16
forwarding 89
guidelines 75–7
how it works 71–3
identities 119–20
introduction to 69–96
junk and spam 310
mailing lists 120–1
maintenance 118
message management 90–3
in Netscape Navigator 30
Outbox 71, 82
priority settings 111
and privacy 73–5, 96
replying 76, 87–9
saving 85
scams 310–11
signatures 116–17
spamming 104–5
user name and password 77
viruses 98, 100–2, 297–9
web-based 93–6, 247, 311–12
see also Outlook Express
Ebay 236, 238–9
Eisenhower, President Dwight 11
electronic mail *see* e-mail
electronic payments 364–6
elibrary.com 176–7

Ellis, Jim 267
Ericsson 361
Excite 168–9

Fake User Interfaces 139
Fast Search 170
Favorites 144–6
Federal Trade Commission 235–6
File Transfer Protocol 21, 28, 277–8
filters 108–10, 311–12, 349–50
firewall 204
folders 79, 82, 83, 90–3, 145–6
Freeserve 54–5

gambling 339–40
games 275–6
Gates, Bill 29
gateways 22, 263–4
Geocities 231, 272–3
glossary 373–94
Goldberg, Dr Ivan 336
Google 171
GoTo 170–1
Graphical User Interface 139
Greenfield, Dr David N. 338

hacking 95, 300–7, 372
Harris, Robert 151, 156
history of Internet 7–30
    the 1950s 11–12
    the 1960s 12–19
    the 1970s 19–22
    the 1980s 22–4
    the 1990s 24–30
HotBot 171–2
Hotmail 95–6, 311–12
HTML 26, 29, 40–2, 189–93, 192–3
HTTP 27, 137
HyperCard 10–11
hyperlinks 8, 40–1
hypermedia 9, 41
Hypertalk 10–11
hypertext 9, 40–1
HyperText Markup Language *see* HTML

HyperText Transfer Protocol *see*
  HTTP

IBM 12, 362
IMPs 18–19, 22
Information Processing Techniques
  Office 17
Integrated Services Digital Network
  see ISDN
interactivity 243–76
  chat rooms 250–9
  cookies 274–5
  discussion boards 247–50
  GSM and pager services 263–4
  guestbooks 246–7
  internet relay chat 259–61
  Internet telephone/voice chat
    264–6
  IP telephony 265–6
  newsgroups 266–7
  non-web-based 259–70
  online communities 272–3
  online games 275–6
  pager software 261–4
  portal sites 274–5
  powwow 262
  social 243–4
  two-way communication 244–5
  web-based 246–59
Internet
  and Apple Mac 48
  cable access 51
  and computers 47–8
  connecting to 36–7, 47–67
  dangers 295–356
  e-mail 62
  the future 357–72
  history 7–30
  infrastructure 32–40
  modems 36–7, 49
  rules for business 324–6
  security 295–326
  shopping 236–42
  speed of access 360
  structure 31–43

Internet addiction 336–44
  auctions 339–40
  and business users 342–4
  Centre for Net Addiction 339–40
  costs 342
  cybersex 337–9
  gambling 339–40
  trading 339–40
Internet Explorer 26, 29–30, 48, 59–
  60, 78, 128–36
  screen **129, 131, 140, 143–7, 175**
  status bar **316**
  toolbar **130, 136, 138, 174**
  see also Microsoft; Outlook Ex-
    press
Internet Ireland 65
Internet kiosks 61, 65–6
Internet Relay Chat 259–61
  versus chat rooms 260–1
Internet Service Provider *see* ISP
Internet telephone/voice chat 264–6
Internet-in-a-box 205
Intranet 29, 56, 66
introduction 1–4
IP numbers 24, 38–9, 57–8
IP telephony 265–6
IPV6 39
Irish Times, The 125–6, 275
ISDN 36–7, 50–1
ISP 36–7, 53–8
  and Apple Mac 48
  and domain names 40
  e-mail 70–3, 77, 78, 87, 105
  flat-rate pricing 55, 70
  free or paid access 54
  local call prices 54

Java 252

Kahn, Bob 21–2
King, Stephen 369
Kleinrock, Leonard 12, 14, 17

LANs 73–4, 204
Licklider, J.R. 13–14

links 8, 60, 76, 132, 138
Local Area Networks *see* LANs
LookSmart 172
Lycos 169, 273

m-commerce 366–7
Macromedia's Flash 26
mainframes 33–5
Man–Computer Symbiosis 13
Maslow 338–9
MCI 23
Memex 8–9
message blocks 16
meta search engines 173–4
    child-safe 354
    see also search engines
Microsoft 29–30, 95–6
    see also Internet Explorer; Out-
        look Express
Microsoft Word 29, 101
military research 14–15
MILNET 23
MIME 115–16
mobile phones 37, 66–7, 361
modems 36–7, 49
Mosaic 27–9
Motorola 66
MP3 288–92, 371
MSG 21
Multipurpose Internet Mail Exten-
    sion *see* MIME
music 288–92, 371

Napster 290–2, 371
NASA 12
National Centre for Supercomputing
    Applications *see* NCSA
National Science Foundation 23
NCSA 27–9
Nelson, Ted 9–10
netiquette 75–7
Netscape Communications 28–30
Netscape Navigator 29–30, 59–60,
    129
network building 15

network cards 35–6
Network Control Protocol 19–21
newsgroups 27, 30, 112, 266–7
    dangers 334
    and ISPs 268–9
    propagation 267–8
    readers 269
    terms 269
    web-based 270–2
newsletters 213–15
Nokia 66, 153
non-linear thought 9
Northern Lights 172–3, 176
NSFnet 23, 37

offline, working 70–1, 83–5, 135–6,
    144
Oikarinen, Jarkko 259
On Distributed Communications
    Networks 14
online, working 78
online communities 43, 272–3
Online Man–Computer Communica-
    tion 13
Outlook Express 60, 70, 75, 78–81
    customising 111–19
    message management 90–3
    screen **78, 80–1, 83–5, 88–9, 90–3,**
        99–100, 102–4, 106–7, 109, 111–
        13, 115–18, 120, 122
    taskbar **80**
    see also e-mail; Internet Explorer;
        Microsoft

packet switching 16–17, 37–8, 72–3
pager software 261–4
Personal Digital Assistant 362
plug-ins
    Acrobat Reader 287–8
    Director/Flash 287
    real audio/real video 286–7
POP3 72–3, 75
pornography 327–56
    paedophiles 331–2
    protection against 349–56

portals 43
Post Office Protocol 3 *see* POP3
prehistory of Web 7–11
printing web pages 142–4
privacy 73–5, 96, 327–56, 346–9
protecting yourself and your children 349–56
*Protocol for Packet Network Inter-
   connection, A* 22
protocols 19–22, 58, 72–3
   FTP 21, 28, 277–8
   HTTP 27, 137
   and IP numbers 38–9
   Network Control Protocol 19–21
   POP3 72–3, 75
   TCP/IP 22–3, 27, 38–9
publishing 369–70

RAND 14–15
remote access programs 299–300
Roberts, Lawrence G. 14

satellite technology 11
saving individual images 141–2
search buttons 174–5
search engines 43, 157, 160–3
   Altavista 168
   child-safe 352–4
   Direct Hit 170
   Excite 168–9
   Fast Search 170
   getting the most from 215–16
   Google 171
   GoTo 170–1
   help pages 162
   HotBot 171–2
   list 177–8
   LookSmart 172
   Lycos 169
   Northern Lights 172–3
   Snap 173
   specialised 175–6
   Webcrawler 169–70
   what to look for 167–8
   see also meta search engines

searching 149–78
   accuracy and timelessness 153–4
   by category 159
   by keyword 159–60
   CAFE method 156–7
   CARS test 151–6
   credibility 151–3
   future of 176–8
   keywords 157, 163–6
   reasonableness 154–5
   sources 155–6
   techniques 163–7
security 64, 73–5, 316–24
   firewalls 322–3
   privacy 73–5, 317–18
   proxy servers 319–22
   Secure Server 316–17
   vulnerability 323–4
shareware 279–82
shopping on Internet 236–42
   auction sites 238–40, 339–40
   direct selling 237
   money-saving sites 240
   safety 240–2
   virtual storefronts 237–8
shortcuts 10
signals, analogue vs. digital 15–16
Silicon Graphics 28–9
Simple Mail Transfer Protocol 72, 77
smart applications 368–9
smart cards 364–6
smart houses 362
Snap 173
Sneakers 372
software, filtering 349–50
spamming 104–5, 162–3
spelling 82, 117
Spyglass 29
spyware 312–13
Stanford Research Institute 19
Stanford University 158
Suler, Dr John 338
surfing rules 354–6

Taylor, Bob 17

TCP/IP 22–3, 27, 38–9
telephone connections 15–17, 36–7, 49–52, 50
teleworking 343
terminator 35–6
Time magazine 312
time-shared computers 12
Tomlinson, Ray 20–1, 69
Toysmart 235–6
trading 339–40
trails 8–9
Transmission Control Protocol/Internet Protocol *see* TCP/IP
Tripod 272–3
Truscott, Tom 267

Unison 65
Universal Resource Locator *see* URL
University of California, Los Angeles 19, 20
University of California, Santa Barbara 19
University of Utah 19
Unix 267
upgrading 60–1
URL 27, 40, 123–8, 152
Usenet News 267
user interface 25–6

Vanguard University of Southern California 151
video conferencing 333
viruses 74, 296–300
   and downloading 283–4
   and e-mail attachments 98, 100–2, 297–9
   how they spread 297–9
   macro viruses 101
   protection from 300
   remote access programs 299–300
Vittal, John 21
vortals 43

w-commerce 366–7
WAP mobile phones 66–7, 366–7

Warez 307–8
web pages 41–3, 128
   cache 136
   content 42, 133–4
   saving and printing 140–4
   screen **133**
   see also website building; websites; World Wide Web
web TV 64–5
Webcrawler 169–70
website building 181–218
   3-click rule 188
   audience definition 183
   banner advertising 210–13
   choosing domain name 200
   client-side versus server-side scripting 198
   content 186
   creating site 189
   creative thought 200
   discussion boards 195–6
   example 183–5
   FTP 209–10
   graphics 193–5
   hosting website 202–8
   HTML 189–93
   interaction 195–9
   JavaScript 197–8
   marketing 210–16
   measuring success 216–17
   newsletters 213–15
   PERL and CGI 196–7
   planning layout 187–9
   preliminaries 185–7
   presentation 185–6
   scripting and security 198–9
   security 204
   site map 188
   size of web page 191–2
   statement of objectives 182–3
   statement of purpose 181–2
   updating 217–18
   uploading 208–9
   see also web pages; websites; World Wide Web

websites 41–3, 123–47
  opening 136–7
  subdirectories 127
  types of 43
  see also web pages; website
    building; World Wide Web
Windows 26, 29–30, 33–4, 38, 60
working offline 70–1, 83–5, 135–6,
  144
working online 78
World Wide Web
  addresses 123–47, 136–7
  CARS test 151
  chat rooms 229, 250–9, 260–1,
    334–5
  connecting 131
  design 363–4
  development 30
  Favorites 144–6
  finding information on 157
  History function 146–7

  history of 7–30
  homepages 132, 150
  introducing 123–78
  invention 24–7
  links 132, 138
  navigating 128–36
  searching 149–78
  web-based e-mail 93–6, 247, 311–
    12
  see also web pages; website
    building; websites
World Wide Web Consortium 27

Xanadu 9

Yahoo 156–60, 199, 236, 238–9, 260,
  263, 273, 274
  screens **158, 352**

Zdnet UK 361